For the Good of the Country

FOR THE GOOD OF THE COUNTRY

World War II Baseball in the Major and Minor Leagues

by David Finoli

McFarland & Company, Inc., Publishers
Jefferson, North Carolina, and London

Library of Congress Cataloguing-in-Publication Data

Finoli, David, 1961–
    For the good of the country : World War II baseball in the major and
minor leagues / by David Finoli.
       p.   cm.
    Includes bibliographical references and index.

    ISBN 0-7864-1370-0 (softcover : 50# alkaline paper)

    1. Baseball — United States— History — 20th century. 2. Baseball
players— United States— 20th century — Statistics. 3. World War,
1939–1945 — United States— Influence. I. Title.
GV863.A1F56   2002
796.357'0973'0944 — dc21   2002006094

British Library cataloguing data are available

Cover photographs (foreground): Hugh Mulcahy during World War II
(*Transcendental Graphics*)
Background image ©2002 PhotoSpin

Manufactured in the United States of America

McFarland & Company, Inc., Publishers
  Box 611, Jefferson, North Carolina 28640
    www.mcfarlandpub.com

To my wife Viv and my three children Tony, Matt and Cara, whose love and support were pivotal in the completion of this work and essential in the magnificent life we all share together.

Also, to my father Domenic and my Uncle Vince, along with my uncles John (Duffy), Tom and Bob, who thought nothing of sacrificing everything they had to serve their country bravely during World War II. It was an effort such as theirs that led to this wonderful free country we all enjoy today. For that along with everything else I am eternally grateful.

Acknowledgments

I'd like to thank the following people for their help during this project:

- My Mother, brother James and sister Mary for supporting me in this endeavor and all others.
- My partner in baseball analysis (among other things), Bill Ranier, who was always there to bounce ideas off of.
- Tom Aikens, writer extraordinaire, who helped me outline exactly what I wanted to include in the book and gave me tips on how to put it all together.
- Chris Fletcher, editor and publisher of *Pittsburgh Magazine* and fellow Duquesne University journalism alumnus, who helped guide me with some suggestions on getting the book published as well as other areas I needed help on.
- The Cincinnati Reds, the St. Louis Cardinals and the Pittsburgh Pirates. All three generously donated photographs to the project.
- Bryan Reilly of Photo File, Inc., Mark Rucker of Transcendental Graphics and Bill Burdick of the Baseball Hall of Fame. All were very helpful with their time and provided this book with wonderful photographs.
- The entire SABR (Society for American Baseball Research) online community, especially Dennis Van Langen, Dave Anderson, John Holway, Russell Gagnon, Rex Hamann, Bob Lanphere, Bruce Ferris, Charlie Bevis, Royse Parr, Dorothy Mills, James G. Robinson (The Baseball Online Library), Bill Deane and Steve Gietschier (*The Sporting News*), who were there to provide much needed suggestions when I was at a standstill with certain subjects.

- Dan Price, the son of war hero Fred Price, who not only generously gave me his time, but also provided me several pieces of important research on his father's career.
- Players such as Virgil Trucks, Benny McCoy and Hugh Mulcahy — the latter of whom unfortunately passed away during the writing of this book — who were all very helpful and kind with their insights on the game during that time period and their careers in general.
- Viv and Salvatore Pansino for their support.
- The Monroeville, Pennsylvania, Library staff, who patiently helped me conquer the microfilm machine.

Books, magazines and papers that were most helpful in the research of the time period:

- *The Pittsburgh Press*—1942–1945
- *The Sporting News*—1942–1945
- Gary Bedingfield's Baseball in Wartime Bibliography website: http://baseballinwartime.freeservers.com/bibliography.htm
- The Baseball Online Library: http://cbs.sportsline.com/u/baseball/bol
- Baseball and the Armed Services by Harrington E. Crissey: http://enelpunto.net/beisbol/history/leagues/military/armedintro.html
- The Navy's Greatest Team: Baseball in Norfolk website: http://www.hrnm.navy.mil/baseball.htm
- *The Sports Encyclopedia: Baseball* by David S. Neft, Roland T. Johnson, Richard M. Cohen and Jordan A. Deutsch (1974).
- *Total Baseball*, edited by John Thorn, Pete Palmer and Michael Gershman, 7th edition (2001).
- *The Baseball Encyclopedia*, 10th edition, published by Macmillan (1996).
- *The Baseball Timeline* by Burt Solomon (2001).
- *Spartan Seasons* by Richard Goldstein (1980).
- 1944 through 1947 *Major League Baseball Guides*, published by Whitman.
- *The World Series* by David S. Neft and Richard M. Cohen (1990).
- *The Biographical Encyclopedia of Baseball* by the editors of *Total Baseball* (2000).
- *The Biographical History of Baseball* by Donald Dewey and Nicholas Acocella (1995).

- *The Bill James Historical Abstract* (1986) and *Whatever Happened to the Hall of Fame?* (1995) by Bill James.
- *Koppett's Concise History of Major League Baseball* by Leonard Koppett (1998).
- *Baseball Dynasties* by Rob Neyer and Eddie Epstein (2000).
- *The Biographical Encyclopedia of the Negro Baseball Leagues* by James Riley (1994).
- *The Complete Book of Baseball's Negro Leagues* by John Holway (2001).
- *Pennant Races: Baseball at Its Best* by Dave Anderson (1994).
- *Ace* by Phil Marchildon (1993).
- *The Encyclopedia of Minor League Baseball*, edited by Lloyd Johnson and Miles Wolff, second edition (1997).
- A website on the Norfolk Naval Station Team from the Hampton Roads Naval Museum's Daybook web site at: http://www.hrnm.navy.mil/baseball.htm.
- *The 2001 National Baseball Hall of Fame and Museum Yearbook.*

Contents

Introduction

Imagine going to spring training with the New York Yankees when one day Derek Jeter leaves and Erick Almonte replaces him. The next day Bernie Williams leaves and in comes Luis Polonia. After that Roger Clemens goes and Allen Watson takes his spot. Pretty soon what was the three time world champions becomes a team that is hard to recognize. The level of play, which was arguably one of the greatest of all time, basically becomes a shell of itself. As illogical as the above scenario sounds, this is the situation major league teams and fans found themselves in during the war seasons between 1942 and 1945.

While most baseball historians attach an asterisk to these seasons and discount the performances and results achieved during this time period, it would certainly be shortsighted to forget the fine players who either entertained the nation when it needed a morale boost or sacrificed the better part of their careers in order to serve their country proudly. Wartime also brought some lasting changes to the game, such as night baseball.

It is undeniable that the game was being played at a substandard level. Bill James in his *Historical Baseball Abstract* estimated that only 40 percent of the players that played during that time period actually had the talent to play in the majors. He furthered his point with an interesting stat, that out of 64 regulars that played in the National League in 1945, only 22 played 100 or more games the following year.

Nonetheless, some fine performances and careers were launched during the war years. Players such as Phil Cavarretta and Vern Stephens would not only become superstars during war ball but also go on to have wonderful careers. Others such as Nick Etten and Ray Sanders would serve the sport well, making the most of their opportunities before fading away with the return of the soldiers in '45 and '46. From a playing standpoint, these were the best players the country had to offer during a most difficult time period, and for no other reason their stories and achievements should not be just cast aside. To do so would be no better than to discount Lefty Grove's career because he never faced Josh Gibson, Mule Suttles or Turkey Stearnes of the great Negro Leagues, or Babe Ruth because three of the greatest pitchers of all time — Satchel Paige, Smokey Joe Williams and Bullet Bill Rogan — would be restricted from playing white baseball and would not be able to challenge the Bambino.

From a pure baseball research and historical sense the war years are one of the most fascinating times in the history of the sport. Teams such as the Detroit Tigers would be completely devastated, going from an AL championship in 1940 to the second division in '42 and '43 only to recapture the title again in '45 when some of their great players, including Hank Greenberg and Virgil Trucks, came home. The American League's perennial doormats, the St. Louis Browns, with most of the best talent gone, would find their way to the top of he heap, winning their only AL pennant in 1944. The cream of the crop in each league, the St. Louis Cardinals and the New York Yankees, would take the philosophies that made them great — the Cardinals with their incredibly deep farm system and the Yankees with their incredibly deep wallets — to stay at the top of the sport and win world championships.

On a player level, the war years not only took average players such as Nels Potter, Etten and Sanders and give them above average career numbers, it also forced historians to go into deeper analysis when rating some of the time periods players in the context of who was the greatest of all time. On the surface a Hank Greenberg, who hit only 326 career homers, had a nice career but certainly not Hall of Fame numbers and shouldn't be talked about among the elite sluggers in history, but taking into consideration the better than four years he missed, at the pace he was going he would certainly have reached 500 homers. In retrospect he had one of the great peak values of all time and certainly does deserve to be mentioned along with great sluggers such as Jimmie Foxx.

Ted Williams rarely gets mentioned in the same light as Ruth and Hank Aaron when it comes to homers, yet had he not gone to war in World War II and Korea, he would have had a great shot at becoming the third player ever to eclipse 700 homers, therefore potentially ending the argument as to who was the greatest hitter of all time. Bob Feller, had he not spent time in the service, would have likely cracked the top five all time in both wins and strikeouts.

On the other side of the coin, Hall of Famers such as Lou Boudreau and Hal Newhouser, who both had their peak years during war ball, may have seen their career stats inflated to the point that their Hall of Fame elections might have been misguided.

Perhaps one of the best things that war ball gave us was the increased importance of night baseball. The owners declared let there be light, but it was not without a lot of kicking and screaming. The visionary owner on the subject was Washington Senators chief Clark Griffith, who saw it as an opportunity to open up a new fan base, while others such as Ed Barrow saw it as a potential hazard that would lead the Nazis right to the brightly lighted stadiums by air. What it gave us in the short term was an opportunity for people to have a diversion after a hard workday with the pressure of the world's events firmly in their heads, which is the intention FDR had when he tried to influence Commissioner Landis and the owners to increase the night contests. In the long term from a business standpoint it would eventually give us what Griffith thought, a new fan base. Rather than wait for the occasional day off or the weekend, a person now would have the opportunity to go to a game anytime he wanted.

On a grander scale, without night baseball's increased importance the televised game would not have been able to become the cash cow that it eventually would become, and the game, even though people argue about its lessening importance on the American sports skyline, would certainly not continually break attendance records with numbers that its forefathers of the first half of the 20th century never would have imagined. To go to the next level, perhaps imagine life without Monday Night Football or night contests in other sports that would eventually be influenced by night games during World War II.

If night baseball was one of the best things to happen to the game financially, then perhaps the signing of Jackie Robinson at the tail end of 1945 was the single most spectacular gift that the time period not only gave baseball, but American society as a whole.

While we talk about statistics and the eventual financial boom of night baseball, perhaps the true meaning of wartime baseball was not what happened to the players who played or came back to have successful careers, but the players such as Benny McCoy, Cecil Travis or Hugh Mulcahy, men who left their careers to serve their country but through battle injury, illness or just the erosion of their skills during the long period of time between playing games, would never play again or would not achieve the level of success they did before the war. Let us also not forget the efforts of players such as Elmer Gedeon or Harry O'Neill, men who not only gave up their careers, but their lives defending their country.

The intent of this book is to give not only a glimpse and an analysis of what went on during the war, but to look at each player who went off to serve. It does so in the following manner:

- Year by year recap for each season between 1942 and 1945.
- A team by team yearly recap with the following:
  - (1) The highlights of the particular season for the teams.
  - (2) The yearly starting lineup for each squad with a comparison to the starting lineup of 1941, the last year of peacetime baseball. This will show just how dramatically the war changed the game.
  - (3) A list of which players went off to war by team on a year by year basis with a list of who replaced them on the roster if they were a starter or one of the four starting pitchers. The players are listed by the year in which they missed their first full season.
  - (4) A thumbnail statistical sketch on each player that left for war, how they were before the war, how they were after, pertinent war stories and how they were replaced if they were a starter or one of the starting four pitchers, and a short recap of their careers.
  - (5) A list of wartime players who lost their starting jobs in 1946, minor league players who perished in the war and a list of Negro League players drafted.
- Reports on the following
  - (1) Great military teams, such as Great Lakes Naval. Teams that arguably were better than their major league counterparts.
  - (2) Hall of Fame careers that were affected by the war (Lou Boudreau and Hal Newhouser particularly, whose numbers may have been inflated by playing in the war ball seasons)
  - (3) Sabermetrics report on the players who stayed during the war. The report looks at whose careers were most affected by playing during war ball. This is the work that inspired the book.

We begin in 1942 and the game that, during a very troubled time, needed to be continued for the good of the country.

Notes and Introduction of the War Years Section

- The starting lineups each year are taken from *The Sports Encyclopedia: Baseball* by David S. Neft, Roland T. Johnson, Richard M. Cohen and Jordan A. Deutsch (1974). The starting four in the rotation are also taken from this book (in order of games started during the season) as well as any injury listed unless otherwise noted.
- All trades are taken from *The Baseball Encyclopedia*, 10th edition, published by Macmillan (1996).

Elbie Fletcher (left) of the Pirates and Johnny Mize (right) of the Giants discuss batting techniques while playing in the service. Courtesy of Transcendental Graphics.

- All stats and statistical analysis for each thumbnail sketch as well as all nicknames are taken from *Total Baseball* edited by John Thorn, Pete Palmer and Michael Gershman, 7th edition (2001) as well as the MVP votes.
- The list of who went to war was taken from *The Sports Encyclopedia: Baseball* by David S. Neft, Roland T. Johnson, Richard M. Cohen and Jordan A. Deutsch (1974). They are separated by year when the player missed his first full season. There are obviously many others who served bravely such as Hall of Famer Yogi Berra, but since the book is an analysis of the time period between 1942 and 1945, I include only players who missed seasons during those years.
- All Negro League stats are taken from the book *The Complete Book of Baseball's Negro Leagues* by John Holway.
- OBA=Opponents' Batting Average. When measured against the league batting average of all hitters against all pitchers, the OBA indicates who, in the matchup of particular hitters and a pitcher, enjoys the edge. Pitchers who seize the head-to-head advantage are said to "hold" batters to low averages.

- TPI=Total Pitcher Ranking. It is a sabermetric term that as stated in *Total Baseball* is the sum of a pitcher's pitching runs, relief ranking runs, batting runs and fielding runs all divided by runs per win factor for that year.[1] If you take all the pitchers' stats and put them into the above formulas, you theoretically should get who are the best pitchers of a particular season. To understand what is a successful TPI, the best single season of all time was 11.0 by Charlie Radbourn in 1884, the 100th best was Randy Johnson in 1997 at 5.8. For a career, Walter Johnson is number one at 91.4. Rip Sewell is in a four-way tie at 296 at 9.1 (considering how many pitchers have appeared in a major league game, 296 is pretty impressive).

- TPR=Total Player Ranking. It is an offensive sabermetric term that as stated in *Total Baseball* is the sum of a players' adjusted batting runs, fielding runs and base stealing runs, minus his positional adjustment all divided by the runs per win factor for that year (usually in the 9–11 range).[2] Basically, it takes into account every stat an everyday player accumulates, puts it through the above formulas and should indicate who had the best overall season. Babe Ruth has the best figure for a single season of all time with a 10.8 in 1923; Hank Aaron in 1959 is tied with Ty Cobb, 1910 and 1911, Joe Jackson, 1912, Rogers Hornsby, 1927, and Joe Cronin, 1930, for 92nd place at 6.8. The TPR leader for a lifetime is the Babe at 108.9; number 300 is Bob Allison at 14.0.

- Fielding Runs. Fielding runs is a calculation that basically takes into account a fielder's assists, putouts and double plays versus the league averages. Second baseman, shortstop and third baseman's stats are weighted heavier than a pitcher or first baseman. There are also different calculations for outfielders.[3] The technical formula is much more advanced that what is given here, but basically fielding runs is a good statistical measure of a fielder's effectiveness on the entire game.

Fielding percentage does not always take into account the total picture, as a player might not boot many balls, but he might also not have good range and therefore can't get to as many plays.

As interesting a figure as it is, it does have some detractors as some fans question how Hank Sauer, a player known for his poor defensive play, had 22 career fielding runs while Johnny Bench, considered one of the best defensive catchers in history, winner of 10 straight Gold Gloves, had -80. As with any formula, there will be some players that come out with very strange results, as nothing takes the place of actually seeing the player perform. For the most part, though, the formula seems to give a fairly accurate picture.

Top Fielding runs for a season is Glenn Hubbard in 1985 at 61.8 while Herman Franks had the 99th best with 32.2. Considering there are negative fielding runs, anything in the positive range is a decent season. The lifetime leader in fielding runs is Nap Lajoie at 366, slightly ahead of Bill Mazeroski with 362. Third baseman Matt Williams is tied with 3 others for 95th place at 108. The best of all time by position are:

> 1st base: Keith Hernandez, 150
> 2nd base: Nap Lajoie, 368
> Shortstop: Bill Dahlen, 304
> 3rd base: Mike Schmidt, 265
> Outfield: Tris Speaker, 248
> Catcher: Pop Snyder, 151
> Pitcher: Ed Walsh, 84

- IP/H=Innings pitched to hits ratio. Although it varies by year, depending on hitting years versus pitching years, usually if you've given up fewer hits than innings pitched, you've had a nice season.

- K/BB=Strikeouts compared to walks ratio. It is one way to measure a pitcher's control. The more that strikeouts tower over walks the better the season a pitcher has had.

- ERA=Earned Run Average. Simply how many earned runs a pitcher gives up per 9 innings of work.

- When the production of the different players is compared, i.e., the player drafted into the military is compared to those who took over for them, it should be noted that the replacement player is performing during a war year and the same stats during a war season obviously may not be as impressive as during a non-war year due to the lower quality of play.

- The thumbnail sketches of the drafted players are basically meant to cover four things:

    (1) A short statistical analysis of the drafted player.
    (2) Pertinent stories of their war record or other short interesting anecdotes of their careers.
    (3) A comparison of their season before they went into the service with that of who replaced them in the lineup (only for starting positional players and the top four starting pitchers).
    (4) What statistical levels a player missed out on due to their participation in the military. This is only used if it is determined that the player missed out on significant statistical marks.

- A hitter's stats, listed as 17–85–.285, include homers, RBIs, and batting average. A pitcher's stats, listed as 18–5–2.32, are wins, losses, and ERA.

1

1942

Coming off a season of endless optimism about the sport referred to as our national pastime, baseball owners had no inkling that the matter soon to occupy their days and nights would be the game's very continuance in the wake of Pearl Harbor. They were probably engaged by the sort of fiscal prefiguring that experience had led them to: What promotions to arrange, what demographic needed courting, how the successes of the season just past might be leveraged as advertisers came knocking. They wondered if Williams would top .400 again or whether DiMaggio might make it 57 games this time. But before long, owners—and indeed all of baseball—would think only of whether or not the Splendid Splinter would get his draft deferment.

It truly was a different time for baseball and 1942 would surely prove to be one of the most unusual seasons in the history of the sport. The year 1942, of course, would be the season that would usher in the war ball era, a time that would last through the end of the war in 1945. It was also a year in which most of the game's stars would go off to war and those who stayed behind would help raise the morale of a country that had lost itself.

The first decision that would be made was if in fact the game would continue. The possibility of suspending the season was a real one in the weeks following the Japanese attack. On February 16, 1942, Franklin Roosevelt put an end to any discussion of not to play in his "Green Light" letter to Commissioner Landis. Roosevelt said that while the final decision rested with Landis and the owners, he thought, "if 300 teams use 5,000–6,000 players, those players are a definite recreational asset to at least 20,000,000 of their fellow citizens—and that in my judgment is thoroughly worthwhile.... It would be best for the country if baseball continued."[1] Bottom line, the game would go on.

While the game went on, it would be without two of its foremost stars, Hank Greenberg and Bob Feller. Greenberg, who was drafted on

May 6, 1941, left baseball with a monster game hitting two home runs against the Yankees.[2] Feller left exactly eight months later on January 6, 1942, reporting to the Navy in Norfolk, Virginia.[3]

A third star, Ted Williams, almost left in '42, but ended up embroiled in a controversy that would stick with him for most of the season. On January 24th, the induction of Williams was placed on appeal. As Minnesota's Hennepin County draft board member William Price put it, "The Draft board appeal agent has appealed the Williams case to determine whether or not Williams' mother would be left without support in the event of his induction." He also stated that Williams did not ask for the appeal himself, which turned out to be an incorrect point.[4]

FDR ordered on February 5th that the Splinter's draft status would be changed from 1-A to 3-A in order for him to support his mother. The decision claimed that his immediate induction into the army would "cause his mother undue hardship." The ruling would allow Williams to report to the Red Sox for the 1942 season.[5]

The nation did not take the decision very well as controversy would follow him afterwards. Some Boston fans protested by promising not to go to any ballgames while Williams "was in the uniform of the Red Sox instead of Uncle Sam." While the Splinter continued to deny he asked for the appeal that eventually led to his deferment, it came out according to Minnesota state selective service director Col. J.E. Nelson that Williams did in fact make the appeal himself.[6]

Eventually, on March 5th, Ted recanted and announced that he would play the 1942 season, and then enlist. Williams stated that "My conscience is clear and I think I'm doing the right thing for my mother, my country and myself. If the true facts were known I don't think anyone would try and crucify me."[7]

He went on further to explain that he made enough money in 1941 to invest $6,000 in annuities and if he went into the service the money would be lost. His thought was he would make enough in 1942 to pay all the annuities off, and then he could enlist. The explanation did not seem to go over well.[8]

On May 23rd, Ted Williams would end all controversies by surprisingly enlisting and being sworn in as a Naval Aviation Cadet. He would go in at the end of the season allowing him to continue his Triple Crown assault. Williams would go on to be one of the greatest military veterans in baseball history, fighting not only in World War II, but also in Korea.[9]

While the Red Sox happily welcomed Williams into the fold, teams such as the Cincinnati Reds would openly encourage their players to go into the service. In a letter that was reportedly sent out in January, Reds

GM Warren Giles asked all Reds to seek opportunities to serve. He said that he would "urge every player on the Cincinnati club to take stock of his personal situation, analyze it carefully and ask himself the question can I stand at the bar of public opinion in war time and conscientiously justify good and significant reasons for not being in government service."[10]

Public sentiment on whether or not to have the players serve in the military aside, the owners still needed to meet and decide on what steps needed to be taken in order to have a successful transition from peacetime baseball into war ball.

The owners would meet on February 3rd to outline just how best to keep the game going. On January 25th, they had a meeting to discuss what topics would be decided on the 3rd. The following subjects that needed to be answered were:

- Do they follow what FDR asked for and have more night games and how many would each team be permitted to have?
- Should they fix the salaries of the players to combat the expected lower attendance?
- Should they admit servicemen free?
- Do they play a normal All-Star game or alter it to meet wartime decisions?
- How best to contribute to the war relief fund.[11]

Out of all these points, the one that would be most hotly contested would be how many night games to play if any. The main opponents of the measure were the Dodgers' Larry MacPhail, the Yankees' Ed Barrow, Cleveland's Alva Bradley and Red Sox owner Tom Yawkey. MacPhail, who ironically was the one who originally brought night games to baseball at Cincinnati in 1935, was probably the biggest opponent of increasing night contests fearing that there would be "no stopping the radicals (people who wanted more night games) if we open it up." They thought if it happened, there would be more night than day games.[12]

Barrow's opposition to playing night games was a little more paranoid, yet more understandable with the times. He said, "If I were a club president, I would not want the responsibility of luring the enemy planes with a brightly lighted park too many nights a week."[13]

The question of what would happen at night games if there were an air raid was raised. The decision was made to shut off the lights and have the fans go underneath the grandstand. If they did not have time to go, they would be asked to stay very quietly in their seats. They even made a call on how to handle games that were postponed due to air raids. They would treat it like a rain delay. If it happened after 4½ innings, it was a complete game, otherwise it would be replayed, provided the park was still there. It sounds bizarre, but they wanted to be prepared in any situation that would come up.[14]

Clark Griffith, owner of the Senators, was completely on the other side of the issue. He wanted to play an unlimited amount of night games. He was a visionary in this matter and saw the opportunity to maximize his attendance by playing his games after the workday was done. He felt it would open up to a whole new fan base. How ironic that the vision was taking place in a city that would lose its baseball team twice.[15]

There was also a suggestion to make the All-Star game a contest between major league stars and military stars such as Greenberg and Feller in Ebbets Field, the stadium that was supposed to host the game originally. There was also talk of moving it to Yankee Stadium to take advantage of the increased potential attendance and donate the proceeds to the war relief effort.[16]

MacPhail, who was the biggest opponent of night games, was the biggest proponent of contributing to the war effort, demanding that baseball raise at least $500,000 to the war relief fund. On the lighter side, he also suggested baseball buy a bomber and staff it with baseball people.[17] Though his views were sometimes outside the mainstream, his passion to raise money for the war was genuine and led to an aggressive stance by baseball to do just that.

The owners did gather on February 3rd in the Roosevelt Hotel in New York City to answer those questions and more.

They decided that each team would be allowed to play a maximum of 14 night home games apiece, double the number allowed in 1941. Washington, to honor Griffith's request, was given permission to increase their allotment by 7 to 21 games. It was also put into policy that no inning of a night game could begin after 12:50 A.M.[18]

As not to disrupt the integrity of the All-Star game, the owners approved the sanctioning of two games. The first game on July 6th was to be a normal All-Star game, league vs. league, that was to be played in the Polo Grounds instead of Brooklyn for increased attendance. The second, the next day, would be a contest of the All-Star game winner vs. an All-Star team from the armed forces in Cleveland's cavernous Municipal Stadium. The owners had considered dropping the military All-Star game out of fear there might not be enough players to put together a formidable team, but they decided to go ahead with it anyway.

In order to make sure the All-Star manager would not burn out a pitcher's arm in the two games played, a rule was adopted that no pitcher would be able to throw more than 5 innings unless he was the last pitcher and the game was in extra innings. Any pitcher that played in the first game would not be permitted in the second.[19]

Each team would be given the opportunity, on their own, to decide whether or not to admit servicemen free. The Pirates and the Yankees had beaten the owners to the punch by announcing they would let them in at no charge 5 days earlier.[20]

Landis came out strong on the subject of military donations, by first donating 10 percent of his salary and baseball income and that of his secretary Leslie O'Connor to be invested in war bonds. He also "highly suggested" that major league teams play exhibitions against military teams, teams that would eventually be stronger than their traditional counterparts, and donate the proceeds to the relief effort. Designated regular season games would also be slated to donate receipts to the armed forces.

The bat and ball fund, a fund that would provide baseball equipment to camps all around the world, would be the primary beneficiary of the MacPhail led goal of $500,000 that Landis wanted to raise in '42 and '43. One unique way the fans were asked to contribute to the fund was by throwing back any foul ball or home run that was hit. Those balls would be sent straight to the military.[21]

Other issues that were settled included pulling back all restrictions on Sunday doubleheaders in respect to when they could be played. There would be no limit to the amount of twilight games that could be played as an alternative to night games. Cleveland's Bradley at one point wanted to start all his games at 4:00, which he eventually did not.[22]

Once that the major issues were settled, it was time to go to spring training. One interesting thing to look at with all the players being drafted was how the rookie class of 1942 would fill in the holes. Unlike previous seasons when a rookie could come up slowly and ease his way into the lineup, the players would be expected to come in right away and contribute. Since Brooklyn's Pete Reiser would come in for the 1941 season and lead the league in hitting, the pressure on these guys would be turned up dramatically.

In a January article the *Pittsburgh Press* presented a list of players that they felt would be the new stars of war ball. Names such as Stan Musial, Howard Pollet, Hank Sauer, Babe Barna, Emil Kush, Johnny Schmitz, 35-year-old Ray Starr, Dave Koslo, Vince Smith, Culley Rickard, Whitey Kurowski, Emil Lochbaum and Russell Meers were mentioned. Later in the article they mentioned Johnny Wolaj, who hit .296 for Kansas City in 1941, and was mentioned as a replacement for Ted Williams if he left and Wilkes-Barre's Red Embree, who was 21–5 with a

1.69 ERA, was thought to be a replacement for Feller. Musial, Kurowski and Sauer had nice years and careers in total, but Wolaj and Embree would be nowhere near what Williams and Feller were. All in all rookies would occupy 79 of the 400 roster positions that were open by the end of spring training and played a pivotal part in the season.[23]

As spring training began, the other problem that the owners spent a lot of time on was whether or not to cut the players' salaries in order to control costs in the face of the expected dwindling attendance. This controversy was really beginning to rear its ugly head, especially when it came to the world champion New York Yankees. When the Bronx Bombers went to camp on February 24th, only 12 players showed up for conditioning. Red Ruffing, Johnny Murphy, Marius Russo, Spud Chandler, Bill Dickey, Joe Gordon, Red Rolfe, Charlie Keller and Joltin' Joe DiMaggio would all refuse to sign their new contracts.[24]

Eventually they all recanted, most not quite as successfully as DiMaggio did. On March 12th, he finally came back in the fold. Instead of the pay cut they were asking him to take, he received a $6,250 raise for his 1941 MVP performance, to $43,750.28. Detroit cut their payroll by $200,000 including the $20,000 cut pitcher Bobo Newsom took taking his salary from $32,500 to $12,500. The idea was that the Tigers, who drew 1.11 million in their American League championship run in 1940, would only have to draw 600,000 in 1942 to make money (they would eventually only draw 580,000).

Most of the spring training talk, which normally centers on who will make the team and who will be traded, this year had a different flavor. The majority of the discussions as the Grapefruit league wound down was about who would be classified 1-A and who would be allowed to support their families.

In Brooklyn, the joy of acquiring future Hall of Famer Arky Vaughan was replaced by the announcement that outfielder Don Padgett was a 1-A and superstar sophomore outfielder Pete Reiser was about to get the same classification.[25] In Boston rookie shortstop Johnny Pesky was given a 1-A and player manager Joe Cronin was going to have to give up his plans to retire.[26]

Other than the threat of the impending battle hanging over everyone's head, the season that was 1942 began like any other. The big difference was that teams from the military were also beginning the season such as the Norfolk Naval Base team with Feller and Pirate Vince Smith who combined to defeat the University of Richmond 13–1.[27]

On April 15th, the regular major league season began as an impressive 193,000 customers showed up, only 5,000 less than the year before.[28]

Most teams were scheduling designated regular season games, as they vowed to do at the February 3rd meeting, to benefit the war effort. On May 8th the Dodgers and Giants generated almost $58,000 to the cause.[29] These games would be more than just having fans come in to watch a baseball game; they were mini festivals with several events scheduled throughout the day. On July 9th, the Bucs and Phils put on such a show for the war relief effort. They would schedule bands to play; Tommy Dorsey was there, several events for the players such as a 100-yard dash, accuracy in throwing to second, accuracy in throwing from the outfield to home plate and a fungo-hitting contest.

A total of 29,488 showed up at Forbes Field to see the Pirates crush their cross state rivals 9–0 and raised $36,908 for the cause (Stan Benjamin, for those who care, won the 100 in 10.2 seconds).[30]

With the success of those games, similar ones were scheduled in just about every other city.

On the field there were several thrills throughout the season. The pennant race in the senior circuit was one for the ages as the defending champion Dodgers raced out to a 70–30 record and a 10½ game lead by August. After sweeping a doubleheader from Brooklyn, the Cardinals would go on a 43–8 streak to end the season, catching the Dodgers and winning by 2 games. The American League was much less dramatic as the Yankees won by 9 games over Boston.

In one of the biggest and most controversial deals of the off season, the Giants acquired Johnny Mize from the Cardinals for Ken O'Shea, Bill Lohrman, Johnny McCarthy and $50,000. The controversy arose in spring trading when it was discovered that Mize had hurt his shoulder. He went through a miserable slump and there was talk of voiding the trade.[31] New York decided to keep Mize, which turned out to be a very wise choice as he hit 26 homers and hit .305 while leading the league in RBIs with 110 and slugging percentage at .521.

Babe Ruth made the headlines a couple of times, the first for his severe battle with pneumonia at the beginning of the season[32] and then being compared to, of all people, Boston Brave pitcher Jim Tobin. It was a curious comparison between one of the game's all time greats and Tobin, but on May 14th, Tobin became the first pitcher since 1886 (Guy Hecker) to hit three homers in a game. He would just miss an all time record tying 4th by inches, thus becoming the greatest hitting pitcher since the Bambino himself.[33]

Tobin, who was a decent knuckleballer with a career 105–112 record, was on top of the world this day as he improved his record to 5–3 while hitting homers 3, 4 and 5 of the young season. The bubble would soon burst for the Brave hurler as he went 7–18 the rest of the way to finish with a league leading 21 losses.

The greatest milestone that was to be attained in '42 would not be Tobin's three homers, but Hall of Famer Paul Waner's 3,000th hit. Waner came into the season needing 44 hits to become the 7th man in history to reach the ultimate hitter's goal. Ironically the hit would come against the team he spent 15 years with, Rip Sewell and the Pittsburgh Pirates.[34] While it was true Big Poison probably received more playing time due to the war, he would have gotten there eventually.

If Waner's hit was the greatest milestone of the year, than the second All-Star game between the Military and the American League in Cleveland was the greatest event.

The junior circuit won the right to play the service stars the night before in the Polo Grounds by defeating the NL 3–1.

The game itself would not be particularly memorable as the American League easily defeated the all military team 5–0 before 62,094 at Municipal Stadium, knocking out Bob Feller in the second inning by scoring three runs, but what was unforgettable was the fact it was the first war time All-Star game vs. the military in any sport and according to columnist Joe Williams would be a sign of things to come.[35]

Williams, who proved to be very prophetic, correctly predicted that service teams would grow in importance and that most players would be in uniform by next season. He further pointed out that events such as this needed to be included in all sports and all should be geared in a military flavor, such as they did in Cleveland this day. Williams said that "two objectives must be kept foremost in the promotional mind (in putting on these events) (1) to get funds, (2) to stress war psychology."[36]

After a season of many emotional twists and turns, the World Series, which was in jeopardy at one point and time, finally began between the Cardinals and the favored Bronx Bombers. Earlier in the year there had been talk of postponing the World Series for the first time since 1904 if the season had to be shortened as it was in World War I. Luckily the 1942 campaign played out into its completion and the Series went off without a hitch, while parts of the gate receipts were donated to the cause.

New York won the first game before St. Louis, led by Johnny Beazley's two complete game victories, won four consecutive games, the last 4–2 on Whitey Kurowski's two run homer in the 9th, to win the world championship in 5 games.

For Yankee skipper Joe McCarthy, it would be his only World Series loss while wearing the pinstripes. The Yankees, after winning eight consecutive series they had played in, would have to wait until '43 to get revenge.

Perhaps a more intriguing World Series matchup was that of the

Negro Leagues, when Satchel Paige's Kansas City Monarchs took on Josh Gibson's Washington-Homestead Grays.

After Satchel pasted the Grays 8–0 in the opener, the second game provided the stuff legends are made from. Paige with a 2–0 lead loaded the bases purposely to face Gibson. Paige would tell Gibson what was coming. The first pitch was a fastball when the disbelieving Josh expected a curve, for strike one. Another fastball came in for strike two. The third pitch was a sidearm curveball, which went past Gibson for the strikeout. The Monarchs would go on to win Game 2, 8–4, and the series in five. Satchel Paige, the hero of the classic became the only player in World Series history, white or black, to pitch in every game.[37]

The Negro leagues were, by most accounts, just about the equal of the major leagues if not better. The armed forces, which became integrated in the war, would help ease the integration between the two leagues. Unfortunately in 1942 that time was not upon us yet as Jackie Robinson and pitcher Nate Moreland were not offered contracts by the White Sox after they worked out for them, despite the fact they highly impressed manager Jimmy Dykes.[38]

Now that the season was over it became time to take a look back at how the league fared financially and what to do for the next season.

Attendance, which on May 12th provided the owners with much optimism by topping 1941 by over 150,000, eventually fell off by over 1 million fans drawing 8.55 million versus a 1941 figure of 9.69 million. Brooklyn led the way, becoming the only team to reach the 1 million plateau. The Phillies, who were the National League low at 230,183, were headed for severe financial trouble and the St. Louis Browns, who only one season ago were about to be approved for a transfer to Los Angeles only to be put on hold by Pearl Harbor, were the low in the AL with 255,617. Ironically the attack not only temporarily kept the Browns in St. Louis, but also had the transfer taken place, perhaps the Dodgers would still be part of the New York landscape.

The establishment that was most vulnerable in all this was the minor leagues. Major League baseball decided to have an isolationist outlook over the minors and chose to look out for themselves only. In 1941 there were 304 minor league teams in existence, by the end of '42, 98 teams would fold bringing the number down to 206. It was a situation that would continue to downtrend as the years went on. Eventually major league baseball would feel the effects. The majors and minors would sign a contract on December 3rd agreeing to freeze minor league contracts until after the war in an effort to save the game.[39]

As the year was about to end the owners got together to agree on the one question that seemed to be foremost in their minds throughout the year, how many night games to play. Griffith wanted each team to decide on the subject themselves but was voted down. The National League wanted to go back to 7 games, but eventually the only change was that Griffith was now permitted to have his Senators play 28 games after dark; everybody else would get 14 once again.[40]

One of the GMs who had played a pivotal part in the original transition of war ball, Larry MacPhail, backed up his passion to support the war by resigning to become a lieutenant colonel in the Army. As fate would have it, the move allowed St. Louis GM Branch Rickey to move into the top slot with the Dodgers, a move that would create history 4 years later when he signed Jackie Robinson.[41]All in all it was a very trying year for everyone inside baseball and out. As 1943 approached, things would get worse instead of better. The game would fall down into a two year low.

Starting Lineups and Who Went to War

AMERICAN LEAGUE

1942 New York Yankees
106–42–0 GB

1941	1942
1B-Johnny Sturm	Buddy Hassett
2B-Joe Gordon	Gordon
SS-Phil Rizzuto	Rizzuto
3B-Red Rolfe	Frank Crosetti
OF-Tommy Henrich	Henrich
OF-Joe DiMaggio	DiMaggio
OF-Charlie Keller	Keller
CA-Bill Dickey	Dickey
PI-Marius Russo	Tiny Bonham
PI-Red Ruffing	Chandler
PI-Lefty Gomez	Ruffing
PI-Spud Chandler	Hank Borowy

If you were going to bet on the defending world champions to repeat as AL champions, you weren't going to win a lot of money as they went off as 2–5 favorites. Of course there was the spring training hold out by DiMaggio, but he would eventually come back. They had a celebrated All-Star lineup and the war losses were minimal. Bottom line, unless an earthquake swallowed up Yankee Stadium and the team, there was not much chance they weren't going back to the World Series, which in fact, they did.

In winning the pennant by 9 games over Boston, before their disappointing loss to the Cardinals in the Series, the Yanks put up several big numbers. Second baseman Joe Gordon, who won a disputed MVP award, would post an 18 homer, 103 RBI, .322 average performance. DiMaggio and Charlie Keller would back him up with 21–114–.305 and 26–108–.292 seasons respectively.

As impressive as the hitting was, the pitching was even more spectacular, leading the league with a 2.91 ERA. The staff was led by 6'2" 225 lb. Tiny Bonham. Bonham, who had a nasty forkball, came through with a breakout season in '42, leading the league in complete games with 22, shutouts with 6, and OBA at .259. He finished with a 21–5 record and a 2.27 ERA. Had there been a Cy Young Award then, he certainly would have won it. Rookie Hank Borowy, 15–4–2.52 and Spud Chandler, who began his impressive 2-year war ball run at 16–5–2.38, also led the way for the Bombers.

Who Left for the War	*Who Replaced Them*
CA-Ken Silvestri	
1B-Johnny Sturm	Buddy Hassett
PI-Steve Peek	
PI-Charlie Stanceu	

Ken Silvestri— Silvestri was a reserve catcher for New York in 1941, hitting .250 in only 40 at-bats. He came back in 1946 and played 5 more years for the Yankees and Phillies although only getting 64 more career at-bats and finishing with a .217 career average.

Johnny Sturm— Sturm started for the Yanks in his rookie season of 1941 when he hit 3 homers, with 36 RBIs and a .239 average. Unfortunately those would be Sturm's career stats, as he would never play again. Buddy Hassett was picked up with Gene Moore from the Braves for Tommy Holmes to replace Sturm. He was a slight improvement going 5–48–.284 in '42. War legend Nick Etten would replace Hassett in '43.

Charlie Stanceu— He had an unimpressive 3–3 record in 1941 for the champs, with a 5.63 ERA. He did get one last shot in 1946 playing the majority of the season with the Philadelphia Phillies going 2–4–4.22.

Steve Peek— Peek threw 80 innings for the Yankees in 1941 going 4–2 with an unimpressive 5.06 ERA. Unlike Stanceu, he would get no more chances.

1942 Boston Red Sox
93–59–9 GB

1941	*1942*
1B-Jimmie Foxx	Tony Lupien
2B-Bobby Doerr	Doerr
SS-Joe Cronin	Johnny Pesky
3B-Jim Tabor	Tabor
OF-Lou Finney	Finney
OF-Dom DiMaggio	DiMaggio
OF-Ted Williams	Williams
CA-Frankie Pytlak	Bill Conroy
PI-Dick Newsome	Tex Hughson
PI-Charlie Wagner	Wagner
PI-Mickey Harris	Joe Dobson
PI-Lefty Grove	Newsome

Ted Williams' shoulders must have really gotten sore. He held up the Red Sox in almost every way imaginable. He led the league in almost every major category, runs with 141, homers with 36, RBIs 137, batting average .356, walks 145, OBP .499 and slugging at .648. His Triple Crown effort led Boston to another second place finish to the Yankees. If that's not an MVP performance, I guess the Devil Rays are the smartest organization in baseball. According to the sportswriters who voted on the MVP in '42 (I guess they would all be Tampa Bay fans if they were around today) they elected Joe Gordon, who had a fine season, but who arguably was not even the MVP on his own team, the award winner.

Although Williams was the major reason for the Red Sox' banner year, he did get some help from the gallery. Rookie shortstop Johnny Pesky led the league in hits with 205 and was second in batting at .331. Twenty-four-year-old second baseman Bobby Doerr completed his second of seven consecutive All-Star seasons with a 15–109–.290 performance.

Ted Hughson was the leader of an improved pitching staff. His sophomore season was a true breakout one with a 22–6 record and a 2.59 ERA. He tied for the league lead with 22 complete games and led the circuit with 281 innings pitched and 113 strikeouts as well as wins.

Who Left for the War	*Who Replaced Them*
CA-Frankie Pytlak	Bill Conroy
1B-Al Flair	
PI-Mickey Harris	Joe Dobson
PI-Earl Johnson	
PI-Emerson Dickman	

Frankie Pytlak— Pytlak was probably the most important Red Sox to leave for the military in '42. He hit .271 in 1941 with 39 RBIs. Frankie did return in 1945 and 1946 for Boston, but could muster up only 31 at-bats and batting averages of .118 and .143 respectively, far under his career .282 average. Bill Conroy replaced Pytlak after a 4-year hiatus from the majors. He came nowhere near Pytlak's output by hitting .200 in 250 at-bats. Conroy would play only 58 more games in two years for the Red Sox.

Al Flair— Little used first baseman hit .200 in 30 at-bats with Boston in 1941, his only season in the majors.

Mickey Harris— Mickey finished 1941 as Boston's number three starter, although he only had an 8–14 record for the second place Red Sox. Upon his return in 1946, Harris pitched like he never did before going 17–9 with a career high 131 strikeouts in his only All-Star season. He hung on for 6 more seasons with Boston, Washington and Cleveland, never again reaching the level he did in '46, finishing with a 59–71 record.

Joe Dobson more than successfully picked up the slack with the departure of Harris by going 11–9 with a 3.30 ERA. Dobson, who would leave for the military himself in 1944, ended up with a fine 14-year career.

Earl Johnson— Johnson finished the 1941 season at 4–5 in 12 starts. He came back in 1946 for Boston before winning 12 and 10 games respectively in 1947 and 1948. He stayed until 1951, but consecutive ERAs of 7.48, 7.24 and 6.35 his last three seasons pretty much ended things for Earl.

Emerson Dickman— Dickman pitched in parts of 5 seasons for the Red Sox from 1936 to 1941. In 1938–40 he started 21 games, threw 317⅔ innings with a 21–14 record. On the bad side he had ERAs of 5.28, 4.43 and 6.03. In 1941 he finished with a 1–1 record and a 6.39 ERA in 31 innings. After entering the military in '41, his major league baseball career was over.

There were two sure things in the American League in the first half of the 20th century: one was the Yankees would almost assuredly be in the thick of the pennant race, and the other was that the St. Louis Browns would not. Whereas the war years would not be kind to most, in what was a strange twist of fate, they would be very kind to the Browns. St. Louis enjoyed a success, between 1942 and 1945, that would elude them for most of the tenure, beginning with an 82–69 record in 1942, which was 12 games better than the previous year. One of the biggest reasons for the turnaround was the emergence of rookie shortstop Vern Stephens. He compiled a 14 HR, 92 RBI, .294 average season while replacing future soap opera star John Berardino who left early in the season for the military.

St. Louis Browns
82–69–19.5 GB

1941	*1942*
1B-George McQuinn	McQuinn
2B-Don Heffner	Don Gutteridge
SS-Johnny Berardino	Vern Stephens
3B-Harland Clift	Clift
OF-Chet Laabs	Laabs
OF-Walt Judnich	Judnich
OF-Roy Cullenbine	Glenn McQuillen
CA-Rick Ferrell	Ferrell
PI-Elden Auker	Auker
PI-Bob Muncrief	Johnny Niggeling
PI-Bob Harris	Galehouse
PI-Denny Galehouse	Al Hollingsworth

The pitching staff, which lowered its team ERA from 4.72 in 1941 to 3.60 the next season, was led by a 38-year-old 4th year pro by the name of Johnny Niggeling. Niggeling, who broke in at 34 with the Reds, provided St. Louis with a 15–11 record and a 2.66 ERA, which was by far and away the best record he had in the majors to that point. After toiling in the big leagues for six largely unsuccessful seasons, veteran lefty Al Hollingsworth also came up big chipping in with a 10–6 record and a 2.96 ERA.

Who Left for the War	*Who Replaced Them*
1B-George Archie	
INF-Johnny Lucadello	
OF-Joe Grace	
PI-Maury Newlin	

George Archie— Archie was a late season pick up from Washington in 1941 for Bobby Estalella. In his only full season in the majors, he would hit .277 with 3 homers and 53 RBIs. He came back for a very brief time in 1946 playing in only 4 games, hitting .182 in 11 at-bats.

Maury Newlin— After tossing one game in 1940, Maury would play in one more abbreviated season in '41 as Newlin gave up 55 base runners in only 27 innings.

Johnny Lucadello— In his first full season in the big leagues, Lucadello hit .279 in 351 at-bats in 1941. In '46, when he came back, he hit .248, splitting time between second and third, before falling off to .083 in 12 at-bats with the Yanks in 1947. Lucadello would play in the second All-Star game in 1942 as a member of the all-military team.

Joe Grace— Grace had his best season in 1941 hitting .309 in 362 at-bats with 6 homers and 60 RBIs. He played in the Cleveland All-Star game in '42 with Lucadello for the all-military team before coming back in 1946 when Grace's star did not shine so bright, hitting only .230 with the Browns. St. Louis sent him to Washington with Al La Macchia for Jeff Heath in midseason where he woke up with the Senators, hitting .302 the rest of the way. He leveled off to .248 for the 1947 campaign and was out of the majors the next season.

1942 Cleveland Indians
75–79–28 GB

1941	1942
1B-Hal Trosky	Les Fleming
2B-Ray Mack	Mack
SS-Lou Boudreau	Boudreau
3B-Ken Keltner	Keltner
OF-Jeff Heath	Oris Hockert
OF-Roy Weatherly	Weatherly
OF-Gee Walker	Heath
CA-Rollie Hemsley	Otto Denning
PI-Bob Feller	Bagby
PI-Al Milner	Mel Harder
PI-Al Smith	Smith
PI-Jim Bagby	Chubby Dean

Their record was exactly the same as it was in 1941, but it was anything but the same as the Tribe lost superstar pitcher Bob Feller to the Navy and star first baseman Hal Trosky, who temporarily retired due to severe migraines.

The Tribe started hot, reeling off 13 consecutive victories early in the season before eventually falling off big.

Rookie Les Fleming, who had a big freshman season hitting .292 with 14 homers and 82 RBIs, replaced Trosky. Fleming also had a nice .412 on base percentage and led the American League in fielding for first baseman with a .993 mark. Feller, as you will see a little further down, was not so easily replaced. Left fielder Gee Walker was sold to Cincinnati in spring training after a lengthy contract holdout.

Who Left for the War	Who Replaced Them
INF-Jack Conway	
OF-Soup Campbell	
PI-Bob Feller	Jim Bagby
PI-Cal Dorsett	

Jack Conway— After getting only 2 at-bats in 1941, Conway would come back a little stronger after the war. He hit .225 in 258 at-bats in 1946 before slumping to .180 and .245 in only 99 combined at-bats for the Tribe and Giants in '47 and '48, his last two major league seasons.

Soup Campbell— Campbell played mostly center field for the Indians in 1941 hitting .250 in 328 at-bats his second year in the show. Unlike his three other Cleveland colleagues who went off to battle in 1941, he would not return again.

Bob Feller— Feller, who enlisted in the Navy two days after Pearl Harbor, joined his new company in the Norfolk, Virginia, on January 6th. Feller claimed upon reporting, "I always wanted to be on the winning side and this time I know that I'm with a winner."[42]

The Indians were not feeling as positive as Feller who was coming off a spectacular season in which he led the league with 25 wins, 40 games started, 343 innings pitched, 260 strikeouts and 6 shutouts in 1941. It was Feller's third consecutive 20-win season, leading the AL in wins each year.

Bob went into the Navy after the year, where he not only successfully pitched for two of the greatest naval squads, the Norfolk Naval Station and later for the Great Lakes Naval Station, but he won five campaign ribbons and eight battle stars.[43]

Feller came back at the end of 1945, returning August 24th striking out 12 Tigers in a 4–2 win in Cleveland before 46,477. He would not give up a hit in the game for the first 6⅔ innings. The Indian flamethrower finished his first season back at 5–3 in nine starts. He would lead the league in wins in 1946 and 1947 with 26 and 20 respectively, doing it again in 1951 with 22. Feller ended his career in 1956 with a Hall of Fame 266–162 record.

By leaving the majors for the better part of 4 years in his prime for the war, Feller cost himself 85–90 wins and between 900–1,000 strikeouts which would have placed him 8th in wins and 5th in strikeouts all time, numbers of which Feller certainly had no regrets of giving up to serve his country.

The capable Jim Bagby, who had admirable numbers with a 17–9 record and a 2.96 ERA, replaced him as the number 1 starter. The less than admirable Chubby Dean, who went 8–11 with a 3.81 ERA, replaced Bagby as the number 4 starter. The 8 wins marked the high water mark in wins for Dean's career. As you can plainly see, it took a combined effort of Dean and Bagby just to reach Feller's win total in 1941. It was thought that rookie Red Embree, who lit up the minor leagues with a 21–5 record, would replace Feller, but he threw only 63 innings in '42 and finished 3–4.

Cal Dorsett— As significant as Feller's career was when he came back, Cal Dorsett's was just the opposite. Dorsett allowed a mind boggling 31 runners in 11 innings in 1941. He came back to pitch one more bad inning in '47, giving up a homer, 4 runs and 3 hits in his last frame.

1942 Detroit Tigers
73–81–30 GB

1941	*1942*
1B-Rudy York	York
2B-Charlie Gehringer	Jimmy Bloodworth
SS-Frank Croucher	Billy Hitchcock
3B-Pinky Higgins	Higgins
CA-Birdie Tebbetts	Tebbetts
OF-Bruce Campbell	Ned Harris
OF-Barney McCosky	Doc Cramer
OF-Rip Radcliff	McCoskey
PI-Bobo Newsome	Al Benton
PI-Hal Newhouser	Dizzy Trout
PI-Tommy Bridges	Hal White
PI-Johnny Gorsica	Newhouser

If Bob Feller was the most important loss of 1942, then the loss of Hank Greenberg the year prior had to be the greatest loss of '41. After winning the American League pennant in 1940, Greenberg became the first major league everyday player to be drafted on May 6th, 1941. The Tigers immediately began to fall, dropping to 75–79 that year. In '42 they fell a little further off the pace at 73–81.

The offense, which led the league in '40 with a .286 average and runs scored with 888, had fallen off significantly to .246 and 300 runs less at 589. Hall of Famer Charlie Gehringer, who was coming off a very subpar .220 season in 1941, was called up to military service, in midseason. Johnny Bloodworth, who was picked up by Detroit with Doc Cramer from Washington for Frank Croucher and Bruce Campbell in the off season, took over with a slight improvement, hitting .242 with 13 homers and 57 RBIs.

There was a light at the end of the tunnel for the Tigers as the pitching staff, led by rookies Virgil Trucks, 14–8–2.74, and Hal White, 12–12–2.91, took off over a full run from their team ERA of 1941, 4.18 down to 3.14.

Who Left for the War	*Who Replaced Them*
OF-Hank Greenberg	Rip Radcliff
OF-Pat Mullin	
OF-Hub Walker	
PI-Fred Hutchinson	
PI-Les Mueller	

Hank Greenberg— Even though he left early in the 1941 season, his loss could still be felt 2 years later. Hank's last full season in the majors was a banner one, leading the league in homers with 41, RBIs with 150, doubles with 50 and slugging with a .670 percentage. Greenberg also chipped in with a .433 on base percentage and a .340 average.

After he was drafted in May of 1941, the Tiger slugger, who at 30 was discharged a sergeant due to the military limit of drafting no one over the age of 28 seven months later. He would then immediately enlist in the Army Air Corps and become a captain.

During the war he did not get much of a chance to play as he spent most of his term in India and China. In fact Hank did not think he would ever play again in the event of a long war, which it became. In an interview he gave to columnist Joe Williams in spring training of 1942, Greenberg said "...I'm not kidding myself about this war. I'm going to be in a long time.... What I'm going to do when I come out I don't know. But I do know that I'm through as Greenberg the ball player."[44]

In a statement that showed what a truly class individual he was and that the fact being in the Army would cost him his shot at reaching the ultimate career achievement of a slugger by hitting 500 homers (which he more than had a chance to do being that he hit 172 the 4 years prior to the war — more than the 169 he needed to achieve the mark) Greenberg went on further to say, "One thing I do know: I'm going to be a better citizen than I ever was.... It's so much more important than driving in runs and winning pennants. It's the real big league — the big league of living. There aren't many things about war that are nice: but there is one thing about war that is nice — it starts you to thinking, and thinking seriously about the only things that matter. Your country, your home life and all the people you are close to."[45] That last thought put things into perspective, especially the fact that saving the country was more important to Greenberg and many other baseball players who went to war than achieving the stats and extending baseball careers. The happy ending to all this was that Greenberg would come back, and come back in a big way.

On July 1st, 1945, he returned to a large throng at Detroit and hit a homer to lead the Tigers to a victory.

In 78 games in 1945, Hank hit .311 with 13 homers and 60 RBIs. More importantly, Greenberg would hit a grand slam on the final day of the season against the Browns to give the Tigers a 6–3 win and clinching the pennant for Detroit, who went on to defeat the Cubs in seven games to win the world championship. This would be a prime argument that he was perhaps biggest loss to a team during the war years. The Tigers were 314–302 without him, while winning the AL pennant in 1940 and the world championship in 1945, his last season before the war and his first one back.

Greenberg would go on to have a banner 1946 with 44 homers and 127 RBIs before being sold to the Pirates in 1947 for $75,000. The Bucs made him the National League's first $100,000 man and brought in the fences 35 feet in cavernous Forbes Field to make the park more appealing to the slugger. They called it Greenberg Gardens. A back ailment limited him to a .249 average and only 25 homers in his last major league season.

After Pat Mullin also went off to the military, Rip Radcliff was chosen to replace Greenberg in left. Although he hit .317 in 96 games for the Tigers, his power numbers were nowhere near Greenberg's as he hit 3 homers and 14 doubles for a .404 slugging percentage. Barney McCoskey replaced him the next season in 1942 hitting 7 homers with a .293 average.

Pat Mullin— Slated to become Greenberg's replacement after batting .345 in 220 at-bats in his rookie season he 1941, Mullin joined him in going to the military.

He came back for 8 more seasons after the war, making the All-Star game in back to back seasons in 1947–48, with a career best season in '48 of 23 homers, 80 RBIs a .288 average and a .504 slugging percentage. He ended up with a .271 career average after retiring in 1953.

Hub Walker— Walker, who had not played in the majors since 1937 with the Reds, went off to war and returned for one abbreviated season with the Tigers in 1945 hitting .130 in 23 at-bats.

Fred Hutchinson— Hutchinson, who was more known as the great manager for the Tigers, Cards and Reds before tragically dying of lung cancer in'64, left for the Coast Guard early in 1941 after compiling a 6–13 record in 1939 and '40. He came back in 1946, with an impressive 14–11 record with a 3.09 ERA.

Hutchinson pitched for seven seasons after the war, going 89–58, including a selection to the AL squad for the All-Star game in 1951, although '49 and '50 were his better seasons. In 1952 he became player-manager for the Tigers. He went on to St. Louis where he won the manager of the year in 1957 before winning the National League pennant with the Reds in 1961 and another UPI award as manager of the year. He finished his managerial career with an 830–827 record.[46]

Les Mueller— Mueller threw only 13 innings for the Tigers in 1941 before he left for the military. He came back for one season going 6–8 with a 3.68 ERA.

1942 Chicago White Sox
66–82–34 GB

1941	1942
1B-Joe Kuhel	Kuhel
2B-Bill Knickerbocker	Don Kolloway
SS-Luke Appling	Appling
3B-Dario Lodigiani	Bob Kennedy
OF-Taffy Wright	Wally Moses
OF-Mike Kreevich	Hoag
OF-Myril Hoag	Wright
CA-Mike Tresh	Tresh
PI-Thornton Lee	John Humphries
PI-Eddie Smith	Smith
PI-Johnny Rigney	Bill Dietrich
PI-Ted Lyons	Lyons

What was the difference between Ted Williams and the Chicago White Sox in 1942? How about 11 home runs in Williams' favor? Williams who cranked 36 home runs for the season had 11 more than the entire Chicago club, led by Wally Moses with 7 out of the total output of 25.

You could call this club the "hitless wonders" as they did in their world championship season of 1906, except there was no wonder on how they finished 66–82 — they couldn't hit. There were some bright spots — second baseman Don Kolloway led the AL in doubles with 40, Taffy Wright hit .333 and the team stole a league high 114 bases. The problem was, they only hit .246 as a team with an American League low 538 runs scored.

The pitching staff was led by 41-year-old Ted Lyons who went 14–6 with a league leading 2.10 ERA. On the flip side, Eddie Smith lost a league high 20 games, going 7–20.

Although we will get into their records in the 1943 chapter, the White Sox did lose 4 players to the military in the middle of 1942. Starting third baseman Bob Kennedy, catcher George Dickey, outfielder Val Heim and first baseman Jake Jones all left at various times throughout the year.

Who Left for the War	Who Replaced Them
OF-Dave Short	
PH-Stan Goletz	

Dave Short— His name was very appropriate for his career — short. The 24-year-old Short was 1 for 11 in his 2-year career in 1940 and 1941.

Stan Goletz— Goletz was an impressive 3 for 5 pinch-hitting for the 1941 Sox. He would end his career with an impressive .600 batting average, as he would never play again.

1942 Washington Senators
62–89–39.5 GB

1941	*1942*
1B-Mickey Vernon	Vernon
2B-Jimmy Bloodworth	Ellis Clary
SS-Cecil Travis	John Sullivan
3B-George Archie	Bobby Estalella
OF-Buddy Lewis	Bruce Campbell
OF-Doc Cramer	Stan Spence
OF-George Case	Case
CA-Jake Early	Early
PI-Dutch Leonard	Bobo Newsom
PI-Sid Hudson	Hudson
PI-Ken Chase	Early Wynn
PI-Steve Sundra	Alex Carrasquel

It's tough enough improving your lot in life in Major League Baseball when you're the Washington Senators, but when you lose nine players off your roster in 1941 and another three after the 1942 season began, then it becomes very clear how they lost 8 more games than the year before.

The outfield was the lone beacon of light to an otherwise dreary season for Washington as they were led by Stan Spence, who hit .323, leading the league in triples with 15, and George Case, who pitched in with a .320 average and stole an AL high 44 bases. The third member of the Senator outfield was Bruce Campbell. Campbell hit a respectable .278, before joining the military before the end of the season.

What Washington did possess in 1942 was a rookie future Hall of Famer Early Wynn. What the Senators didn't possess in 1942 was a Wynn with his Hall of Fame stats as he went 10–16 with a 5.12 ERA.

Who Left for the War	*Who Replaced Them*
1B-Jack Sanford	
SS-Cecil Travis	John Sullivan
3B-Hillis Layne	
OF-Buddy Lewis	Bruce Campbell
OF-Elmer Gedeon	
OF-Jim Mallory	
PI-Rod Anderson	
PI-Ronnie Miller	
PI-Lou Thuman	
PI-Dick Mulligan	
PI-Bert Shepard	

Jack Sanford—Most of Sanford's career occurred in his freshman campaign in 1940 where he hit .197 in 122 at-bats. He would go 2 for 5 in

1941 before he was off to serve. Sanford would come back for one more hurrah in 1946, hitting .231 in 26 at-bats.

Cecil Travis — Travis was the star shortstop for the Senators between 1933 and 1941. He was a career .314 hitter and hit at least .300 in every prewar season but 1939 when he dipped to .292 after he contracted influenza. Travis was selected to three All-Star teams between 1938 and 1941.

Cecil started out in a big way his official rookie campaign, hitting .319 in 1934. He followed that up with four consecutive .300 years before battling his illness in 1939.

Cecil Travis of the Washington Senators was on his way to a Hall of Fame career hitting .300 in seven of his first eight seasons when the war broke out and Travis was drafted after the 1941 season. He suffered from severe frostbite on his feet while fighting in the Battle of the Bulge. When he returned, whether from the frostbite or just from the fact he lost his timing, Travis would not hit over .252 again and was out of the majors by 1947. Courtesy of Photo File, Inc.

Travis came back after his sub-par year with his two best seasons, first with an All-Star 2–76–.322 year in 1940 before his marquee season of 1941 where Cecil had career highs in homers, 7, RBIs, 101, runs, 106, batting average, .359, on base percentage, .410, slugging, .520 and hits, 218, which led the junior circuit.

His baseball career, for all intents, was done at that point. Travis went into the military following the 1941 season and suffered frostbitten feet while fighting in the Battle of the Bulge in 1944.[47] He came back for 15 games in 1945 and lasted only two more seasons. He hit only .241, .252 and .216 respectively those last three years and retired after the 1947 season. The injury suffered during the war presumably limited his mobility tremendously and he was never the same.

If not for his troubled

time in the military, Travis might have had a career worthy of the Hall of Fame. He had 1,426 hits in his 8½ prewar seasons and at the pace he was at, would have added 750–800 in the four years he missed. Had he not suffered the setback, which some claim was as much a problem with Travis just losing his skills in the 4 years in the military and not just the war injury, Cecil would have had an outstanding shot at breaking the 3,000 hit plateau. He could have been the one player whose career was most hurt by his time in the service.

John Sullivan, who took over for him in 1942, was nowhere near the shortstop Travis was. Although not a bad fielder, Sullivan would hang around until 1949, only mustering up a career .230 average.

Hillis Layne— Layne was a third baseman with the 1941 Washington club hitting .280 in 50 at-bats. He returned in 1944 to hit a measly .195 before having his best season in '45 at .299 in 147 at-bats while smacking his only career homer. He ended it on a high note, as it would be his last major league season.

Buddy Lewis— Lewis had a successful run with Washington between 1935 and 1941, being chosen for the All-Star game in 1938, where he had a career best 12 homers and 91 RBIs and never hitting below .296.

Buddy's best prewar season was 1939 when he led the circuit in triples with 16 while smacking 10 homers with a .319 average

He came back successfully, hitting .333 in his return season of 1945. Lewis made the All-Star team in 1947 and retired afterwards. He made a brief comeback in 1949 hitting .245 before leaving the show for good.

His war record turned out to be more spectacular than his one in baseball as he was awarded the Distinguished Flying Cross in 1944 for his flying mission in the Burmese theater.[48]

Bruce Campbell replaced him after he left in 1941 and adequately filled his position, hitting .278. Campbell, as we stated before, did leave for the military in the middle of the 1942 season.

Elmer Gedeon — Gedeon was an outfielder that played briefly with the 1939 Senators. He was 3 for 15 in his short stay.

Gedeon's baseball career was insignificant when compared to the ultimate sacrifice he would make. While flying a mission for the Army Air Corps over St. Pol, France, on April 20th, 1944, five days after his 27th birthday, Gedeon was shot down and killed, becoming the first Major Leaguer to die in battle during the war. He would be one of only two players to lose their lives in action.

Jim Mallory— Mallory's Washington career lasted only 12 at-bats in 1940 where he hit .167. His comeback season in 1945 was split between the Cards and Giants, where he hit .277 in his final 137 at-bats.

Red Anderson—Anderson pitched in parts of three seasons for Washington in 1937, 1940 and 1941 before being summoned to the military. The bulk of his career came in 1941 where he pitched 112 of his 137 career innings going 4–6 with a 4.18 ERA. He would not return to the majors.

Ronnie Miller—Miller's career lasted all of 1 game in 1941, where he gave up a run on 2 hits.

Lou Thuman—Thuman's career lasted a little longer than Miller's, 9 innings in 1939 and 1940, but it was just as unsuccessful giving up 15 hits and 12 earned runs for a 12.00 ERA before he went to war.

Dick Mulligan—Mulligan threw 9 innings for the '41 Senators giving up 11 hits for a 5.00 ERA. Unlike Miller and Thuman, he did come back after the war with the Phillies and the Braves. In 1946 he went 3–2 with a 4.24 ERA splitting time with both teams before spending his last season with Boston in 1947 tossing only 2 innings.

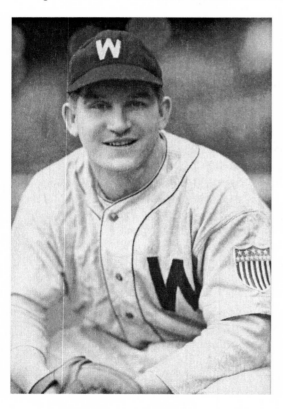

Bert Shepard lost his leg after being captured by the Germans when his plane went down. Miraculously, Shepherd not only survived, but also was signed by the Washington Senators, pitching 5⅓ innings with a prosthetic leg in 1945. Courtesy of Photo File, Inc.

Bert Shepard—Shepard was one of the great stories in World War II. He was shot down over France in May of 1944 and taken in to a German POW camp where a German doctor saved his life by amputating his leg. He was freed in October of '44 and was fitted with an artificial limb. He would fulfill his desire by first appearing in several exhibition games for the Senators, before finally playing a regular season game on August 4th, 1945. He pitched spectacularly in 5⅓ innings of relief work, coming in with the bases jammed and striking out George Metkovich. He would give up 1 run and 3 hits in his only major league game.[49]

1942 Philadelphia Athletics
55–99–48 GB

1941	1942
1B-Dick Siebert	Siebert
2B-Bennie McCoy	Bill Knickerbocker
SS-Al Brancato	Suder
3B-Pete Suder	Buddy Blair
OF-Wally Moses	Elmer Valo
OF-Sam Chapman	Mike Kreevich
OF-Bob Johnson	Johnson
CA-Frankie Hays	Hal Wagner
PI-Phil Marchildon	Marchildon
PI-Jack Knott	Roger Wolff
PI-Les McCrabb	Lum Harris
PI-Bill Beckman	Dick Fowler

What happens when you take the worst team in baseball and take away three starters into the military? Well, you get an even worse team. Sure there were some things they led the league in such as walks given up, 639 — a figure that was 41 walks worse than they next offender, but bottom line, they were a bad team.

It wasn't just on the mound that the A's were hurting; they were the other team in the AL (the first being the White Sox) that Ted Williams outhomered 36 to 33. Left fielder Bob Johnson was by far and away the offensive force on Philadelphia, hitting 13 of the 33 homers, 80 RBIs, 35 doubles and a .291 average.

Phil Marchildon, whose incredible war record we will discuss in the 1943 chapter, had a mind boggling 17 of the team's 55 wins, going 17–14. His BB/K ratio was far less impressive, leading the league by 26 walks with 140 while only striking out 110. The A's were 38–85 without him.

Who Left for the War	Who Replaced Them
CA-Harry O'Neill	
2B-Benny McCoy	Bill Knickerbocker
SS-Al Brancato	Pete Suder
3B-Don Richmond	
PH-Ray Poole	
OF-Sam Chapman	Mike Kreevich
PI-Rankin Johnson	
PI-Porter Vaughan	

Harry O'Neill— O'Neill had a Moonlight Graham career, playing in only one game as catcher for the A's in 1939, never getting to the plate. As it turned out, despite the lack of an at-bat, O'Neill would become an important figure in baseball and American history on March 6th, 1945. That was the day that the 27-year-old O'Neill would become the second and last major league player to die on the battlefield as he was killed at Iwo Jima, Marianas Islands.

Benny McCoy— McCoy was the starting second baseman for the A's in '40 and '41 smacking 7 homers, knocking in 62 and hitting .257 in 1940 before improving to 8–61–.271 the following season. When he left for the war in 1941, he unfortunately would never return to the majors. While in the service, McCoy played on the all-military team that played the AL All-Stars in the second 1942 All-Star game. He also teamed up with Yankee great Phil Rizzuto on the Norfolk Naval team that went 92–8 in '42.[50]

McCoy was unhappy he was not given a chance to resume his career after the war. "I was given my release the night before we broke camp in West Palm Beach, Florida. I didn't think it gave me a chance to play (for other teams), when all clubs are breaking camp (at the same time). I think my contract was involved also."[51]

Replacing McCoy at second in 1942 was Bill Knickerbocker, who was picked up from the White Sox on waivers. For Knickerbocker, 1942 was the last season in his 10-year career, hitting .253 for the A's with only a homer and 19 RBIs.

Al Brancato— The other member of the starting Philadelphia middle infield to go was Al Brancato. Brancato had the best year of his 2½ year prewar career in 1941, hitting 2 homers with 49 RBIs and a .234 average. He returned to the majors with the A's for 10 games in 1945, hitting .118. It would turn out to be his last 10 games.

Even more memorable than his career, which was very forgettable, was the controversy surrounding Brancato during his military stint. According to the classic baseball book *Spartan Seasons* by Richard Goldstein, Brancato was rumored to be receiving an easy assignment in Philly at a navy supply store, taking advantage of his experience running a sporting goods store before the war, in a deal for enlisting in the military shortly after Pearl Harbor. The deal supposedly would allow Brancato to continue playing for the A's. The Navy was indignant, claiming that after a short stint in a navy supply office he would be sent out and he would not play ball. They said, "there are no soft jobs in the Navy in wartime."[52] He was sent to the Pacific where, as Richard Goldstein somewhat sarcastically relates, Brancato was placed in the pressure packed "non-soft" job of shortstop for the Navy in the 1944 "Little World Series." Brancato made an errant throw that allowed Joe Gordon to score the winning run in the Army's 6–5 victory.[53]

Pete Suder moved from third to short to replace Brancato. He was an improvement over "no soft jobs," hitting .256 with 4 homers and 54 RBIs. Suder had a nice 13-year career with the A's, leading the league in fielding in '47 and '51.

Don Richmond— Richmond, who hit only .200 in his only prewar season, came back in 1946 and 1947. He appeared at-bat only 83 times combined in the two seasons hitting .290 and .190 respectively. He left the majors for 4 years before coming back with a short 34 at-bat career with the Cardinals in 1951 hitting .088 to end his stay in the show.

Ray Poole— Poole was hitless in his 2 pinch-hit appearances in 1941. He returned to the majors for one last season in 1947, getting 3 pinch hits in 13 tries.

Sam Chapman — Sam Chapman had an impressive 4-year stint with the A's before the war, hitting 80 homers in that time period. His incredible 25–106–.322 season in 1941 would be sorely missed by Philadelphia. He returned for 9 games in 1945 before being selected to his only All-Star game in 1946, hitting .261 with 20 homers.

Although he would never regain his form of 1941, Chapman would hit 94 homers between '46 and '50. He left the game in 1951 after being traded to Cleveland for Allie Clark and Lou Klein. He hit only .215 with 6 homers and he was done.

This was truly a case of what could have happened if there was no war, a great career that might have been if the service did not take up his absolute peak years. Chapman was at 1,329 hits when he went into the service, and with the approximately 650 hits he missed in the war, had a decent shot at 2,000. Sam also would have an outside shot at 250 homers, as he was only 70 away.

Mike Kreevich, who was picked up in the off-season from the White Sox with Jack Hallett for Wally Moses, took over for Chapman in center field.

Kreevich replaced him in name only as he hit only .255 and 1 homer, a far cry from Chapman's performance in 1941. Kreevich would be sent of to the Browns the next season.

Rankin Johnson— Johnson was the son of the Federal League pitcher of the same name. His major league career lasted only 7 games as he went 1–0 with the A's in 1941 before being called to arms.

Porter Vaughan— Vaughan started 15 games in his 1940 rookie season with Philadelphia going 2–9 with a 5.35 ERA. He tossed only 22 innings in '41 before going to war as his ERA ballooned to 7.94. He had a very abbreviated postwar career as he gave up a hit and hit a batter before being pulled. It would be the end of his major league career.

NATIONAL LEAGUE

1942 St. Louis Cardinals
106–48–0 GB

1941	*1942*
1B-Johnny Mize	Hopp
2B-Creepy Crespi	Crespi
SS-Marty Marion	Marion
3B-Jimmy Brown	Whitey Kurowski
OF-Enos Slaughter	Slaughter
OF-Terry Moore	Moore
OF-Johnny Hopp	Stan Musial
CA-Gus Mancusco	Walker Cooper
PI-Lon Warneke	M. Cooper
PI-Ernie White	Johnny Beazley
PI-Mort Cooper	Lanier
PI-Max Lanier	Harry Gumbert

The Cardinals improved on their second place finish in 1941 with an influx of rookies led by future Hall of Famer Stan Musial. Musial, who hit .426 as a late season call up in '41, allowed the Cards to deal Johnny Mize to the Giants as he took over the starting job in left field, with Johnny Hopp moving over to first. Another rookie, Whitey Kurowski, took over the starting spot at third while Johnny Beazley went 21–6 in his freshman year.

While it was the rookies that helped the Cardinals win the pennant, it was starter Mort Cooper who stole the show. After a 13–9 campaign in 1941, Mort came up with a 22–7 mark, lowering his ERA almost in half to a microscopic 1.78, and won National League Most Valuable Player Award.

With all the outstanding performances, it still took a Herculean effort in August and September to win the pennant. Brooklyn started out 70–30 with a 10.5 game lead by mid–August. St. Louis would come on strong, going 43–8 to end the season, a streak that started off with a sweep of Brooklyn. They caught the Dodgers by September 12th and won by 2 games, before defeating the Yankees in 5 to win it all.

Unfortunately, this was to be the last season in St. Louis for its architect Branch Rickey as he resigned on October 29th to take a job with the Dodgers.

Who Left for the War	*Who Replaced Them*
OF-Walter Sessi	
PI-Johnny Grodzicki	

Walter Sessi — Walter "Watsie" Sessi was 0 for 13 in his rookie season of 1941. After the war, he returned in 1946 to go 2 for 14, hitting his only major league homer, before ending his career.

Johnny Grodzicki— Impressively starting his career in 1941 by giving up only 6 hits in 13 innings, Grodzicki went into the service, where he would be hit with shrapnel while parachuting into Germany five weeks before V-E Day. He would wear a steel brace on his leg when he returned in 1946, but was not effective, throwing only 27 innings between 1946 and 1947 with ERAs of 9.00 and 5.40 respectively before leaving the majors.

1942 Brooklyn Dodgers
104–50–2 GB

1941	*1942*
1B-Dolph Camilli	Camilli
2B-Billy Herman	Herman
SS-Pee Wee Reese	Reese
3B-Cookie Lavagetto	Arky Vaughan
OF-Dixie Walker	Walker
OF-Pete Reiser	Reiser
OF-Joe Medwick	Medwick
CA-Mickey Owen	Owen
PI-Kirby Higbe	Higbe
PI-Whit Wyatt	Wyatt
PI-Luke Hamlin	Curt Davis
PI-Hugh Casey	Ed Head

Although not as well known as the 1951 squad which blew a 13½ game lead, this team nonetheless was up by 10½ in mid–August when it fell in a season that was every bit as disheartening as the one 9 years later.

After winning their first National League pennant in 21 years the previous season, Brooklyn got off to an impressive 70–30 start in '42. It wasn't as much that the Dodgers choked, ending the year at 34–20, but the Cardinals playing unbelievable ball, finishing 43–8 and winning the crown by 2 games.

Even though they won four more games than they did the year before, several key Dodgers did not perform up to their levels of the prior campaign. First baseman Dolph Camilli had a solid 26 homer, 109 RBI, .252 average season, far short of his 34–120–.285 performance the year before. The outfield trio of Pete Reiser, Dixie Walker and Joe Medwick all had nice seasons, but again fell off the pace of 1941.

It was truly a season that despite all the positive things cannot be considered a success. They were just one step behind.

Herman Franks— Franks began his career in 1939 going 1 for 17 for the Cardinals, before being sold to Brooklyn in 1940. After two seasons backing up Mickey Owen in '40 and '41, he left for his military commitment.

Who Left for the War	*Who Replaced Them*
CA-Herman Franks	
CA-Don Padgett	
3B-Cookie Lavagetto	Arky Vaughan
OF-Joe Gallagher	
OF-Tommy Tatum	

Herman returned to the majors in 1947 with the Phillies and batted only 116 times in the next three years with Philadelphia and the Giants before leaving the game under the Mendoza line, hitting .199 for his career. As bad a hitter as Franks was, he was a decent fielder, accumulating 16 fielding runs in 188 games.

Herman would go on to have a decent 7-year managerial career with the Giants and Cubs. He finished with a 605–521 record and four second place finishes.

Don Padgett— Padgett began his time in the show as the starting catcher for the St. Louis Cardinals in 1937, hitting an impressive .314 with career highs in homers with 10 and RBIs with 74. He would follow that up, almost breaking the elusive .400 barrier in 1939, hitting .399 in 233 at-bats with a .554 slugging percentage.

The North Carolina native would slump to .242 and .247 in 1940 and 1941 respectively before entering the Navy.

While in the Navy, he played for the Norfolk Naval Training Station Squad with the likes of Dom DiMaggio and Phil Rizzuto.[54] After returning in 1946, he played with the Dodgers, whom he was sold to in December of 1941 right before he went into action. Padgett would play three seasons as a reserve with the Dodgers, Braves and Phillies, the highlight being a .316 season for Philadelphia in 1947, before leaving the majors with a .288 career average.

Cookie Lavagetto— Harry "Cookie" Lavagetto came up with the Pirates in 1934 as a utility infielder before being sent to the Dodgers with Ralph Birkofer for Ed Brandt. With the Dodgers, he would take over the starting second base job in 1937, hitting .282 before being moved over to third the following campaign.

Beginning with his move to third, Cookie reeled off four straight All-Star game selections, having his best season in 1939 with career bests in homers with 10, RBIs 87 and a .300 average. He would slump to .257 in '40 and .277 in '41 before entering the military.

Returning four years later in 1946, Lavagetto was not the same player, hitting only .236 in 242 at-bats, before his closing act the following season with an 18 for 69 performance. Despite the lackluster swan song, Cookie would have one of the most memorable moments in World Series history in 1947 destroying Bill Bevens' no hit bid in the ninth inning of

Game 4, doubling in the two winning runs in Brooklyn's 3–2 victory, a classic way to end a solid 10-year career.

The war took 4 seasons away from Lavagetto when he was arguably at his peak. Had there been no war he had a shot at breaking the 1,500 hit level (Cookie finished with 945) as he had 546 the 4 years before he left.

Replacing Lavagetto at third was Hall of Fame member Arky Vaughan, who was acquired in the off-season from the Pirates and moved from short to third. Vaughan would be selected to the All-Star game in 1942 despite his .277 average, the first time in 10 seasons he went below the .300 level. He would move over to short the next season where he picked it back up, leading the NL in runs with 112 and stolen bases with 20 while hitting .305. Vaughan would temporarily retire after the 1943 season, staying out of the game until 1947.

Joe Gallagher—"Muscles," as he was called, first showed up in the majors in 1939, going 10 for 41 with the Yankees, before being sent to the Browns midway during the season for Roy Hughes and cash. He hit .282 with the Browns the rest of the season as their starting left fielder with 9 homers in 266 at-bats.

He was traded to the Dodgers in May of 1940 for Roy Cullenbine and hit .267 combined in his last major league season. He would go off into the military, never returning to the show.

Tommy Tatum—Tatum was 2 for 12 in his only prewar season of 1941 for the Dodgers. After returning in 1947, he was hitless in 6 official trips to the plate for Brooklyn when they sold him to the Reds. Tatum hit .273 in 176 at-bats the rest of the way, including his only big league homer, which turned out to be his final year in the majors.

1942 New York Giants
85–67–20 GB

1941	*1942*
1B-Babe Young	Johnny Mize
2B-Burgess Whitehead	Mickey Witek
SS-Billy Jurges	Jurges
3B-Dick Bartell	Bill Werber
OF-Mel Ott	Ott
OF-Johnny Rucker	Willard Marshall
OF-Jo-Jo Moore	Babe Barna
CA-Harry Danning	Danning
PI-Hal Schumacher	Schumacher
PI-Cliff Melton	Bob Carpenter
PI-Carl Hubbell	Hubbell
PI-Bill Lohrman	Lohrman

Coming off a disappointing 75–79 season in 1941, Hall of Famer Mel Ott replaced Bill Terry as manager and led the Giants to a third place finish. The big move that helped spark New York was the acquisition of first baseman Johnny Mize from the Cardinals. The move looked poor at first as an injured shoulder in spring training hampered Mize. It got so bad that Branch Rickey even offered at one time to void the trade and take Mize back if GM Bill Terry was so inclined to do so.[55]

The Giants declined and it paid off big time as "The Big Cat" clocked 26 homers, drove in a league leading 110 runs and hit .305, heading an offense that led the senior circuit in homers with 109.

All in all it was a good season. Unfortunately it would be the last for a while, as the war would wreak havoc on this franchise in 1943, tumbling it all the way down to the cellar.

Who Left for the War	Who Replaced Them
CA-Jack Aragon	
2B-Burgess Whitehead	Mickey Witek
3B-John Davis	
OF-Morrie Arnovich	

Jack Aragon— Angel Valdes Aragon, a native of Havana, had a career not unlike the infamous Field of Dreams figure Moonlight Graham, playing in one game in 1941 without getting to the plate. It would be the only game of his major league career.

Burgess Whitehead—"Whitey" came up in 1933 and became a valuable utility infielder for the "Gashouse Gang" in St. Louis in 1934 and 1935, being selected to the All-Star game the latter season. It was after Burgess was dealt to the Giants in 1936 for Roy Parmelee, Phil Weintraub and cash that his career really took off, as he immediately became New York's starting second baseman.

Proving he was an all around player, Whitehead amassed 55 fielding runs his first two years in a Giant uniform, leading the league in fielding percentage in 1937 with a .974 mark. He also hit a very respectable .278 and .286 those two seasons, making the All-Star game again in 1937.

The fear of Cardinal GM Branch Rickey was that Whitehead was too small to play full time. That fear came to pass in 1938 as he missed the whole season as Burgess broke down completely, physically and emotionally.[56] It took a toll on his career as he hit under .240 in three of his final four seasons (the lone exception was in 1940 when he rebounded to .282).

After joining the Army Air Corps in 1942, Burgess would return for one last season with Pittsburgh in 1946, hitting .220 in 127 at-bats.

At 883 hits, it's fair to say that the war cost Whitehead the 1,000 hit plateau, but he was definitely on his way down after the breakdown so it is doubtful he would have been able to reach any higher level than that.

Replacing Whitehead in 1942 was Mickey Witek. Witek, who had started in his rookie season of 1940 at short, moved over to third and was a more than capable replacement hitting .260 and .314 in 1942 and 1943, leading the league in fielding percentage in '42 with a .978 mark. He would get 16 fielding runs in '43 before going off to the service himself.

John Davis— "Red" Davis played one major league season in 1941, going 15 for 70 (a .214 average) before heading into the armed forces.

Morrie Arnovich— "Snooker" Arnovich was a fine all around player in his 7-year major league career, hitting .287 with 42 fielding runs.

The best part of Snooker's career was played in the City of Brotherly Love where he patrolled left field for the Phillies to begin his career. After an impressive .313 in 48 at-bats in 1936, Arnovich took over the starting spot in 1937, hitting a career high 10 homers with a .290 average. Morrie would make his first All-Star game two years later in 1939 when he hit a career high .324, accumulating 15 fielding runs.

Slumping in 1940 after a .199 start, Arnovich was sent to the Reds for Johnny Rizzo where he rebounded to hit .284 the rest of the way. He was sold to the Giants before the 1941 season and went into the war following the season. The 36-year-old outfielder would return in 1946 for 3 at-bats before ending his stay in the majors.

1942 Cincinatti Reds
76–76–29 GB

1941	*1942*
1B-Frank McCormick	McCormick
2B-Lonny Frey	Frey
SS-Eddie Joost	Joost
3B-Bill Werber	Bert Haas
OF-Jim Gleeson	Max Marshall
OF-Harry Craft	Gee Walker
OF-Mike McCormick	Eric Tipton
CA-Ernie Lombardi	Ray Lamanno
PI-Bucky Walters	Vander Meer
PI-Johnny Vander Meer	Ray Starr
PI-Paul Derringer	Walters
PI-Elmer Riddle	Derringer

United Press International writer Jack Guenther made a bold call in the preseason claiming that Johnny Vander Meer would have "one of the best five records in baseball" in 1942. His reasoning was that because of the increased number of night games, the speed pitchers would have more of an advantage than the batters.[57] Whether or not that fact is true was debatable, but the things that truly were factual was that Vander Meer was a speed pitcher and he did in fact have one of the best seasons in baseball, going 18–12 with a 2.43 ERA, leading the NL in strikeouts by 34 with 186. The 36-year-old Ray Starr was also a pleasant surprise, coming to the Reds the prior year after an 8-year hiatus from the majors. He went 15–13 in 1942 with a 2.67 ERA.

Despite the heroics of Vander Meer and Starr, the Reds won 10 fewer games than the previous season, due to their anemic offense. They scored 89 less runs than in 1941, as no one past first baseman Frank McCormick, who had 89 RBIs, had more than 54 (Bert Haas)

Who Left for the War	Who Replaced Them
2B-Benny Zientara	

Benny Zientara— Zientara hit .286 in 21 at-bats his rookie season of 1941 before being the only Red to miss the entire 1942 season due to military duty. He returned to have two solid seasons in 1946 and 1947, hitting .289 and .258 respectively before falling off to .187 in his last season of 1948.

1942 Pittsburgh Pirates
66–81–36.5 GB

1941	1942
1B-Elbie Fletcher	Fletcher
2B-Frank Gustine	Gustine
SS-Arky Vaughan	Pete Coscarart
3B-Lee Handley	Elliott
OF-Bob Elliott	Johnny Barrett
OF-Vince DiMaggio	DiMaggio
OF-Maurice Van Robays	Jimmy Wasdell
CA-Al Lopez	Lopez
PI-Rip Sewell	Sewell
PI-Max Butcher	Bob Klinger
PI-Ken Heintzelman	Heintzelman
PI-Johnny Lanning	Butcher

"Fool me once shame on you, fool me twice shame on me" is an adage that has been believed throughout the ages. In the case of shortstop Arky Vaughan, it would have been good to forget the above statement.

The *Pittsburgh Press* believed that the reasons Vaughan was traded were twofold. First they could get a lot of good players in exchange for him, in the names of Pete Coscarart, Jimmy Wasdell, Luke Hamlin and Babe Phelps. The second was that they felt they got burned keeping Paul

Waner too long, refusing several great offers until it was too late. They didn't want to repeat the mistake by hanging on to Vaughan too long when they couldn't get good value for him.[58] Add that to the fact that he really didn't get along with manager Frankie Frisch, which was perhaps the main reason, and you see why the Bucs let him go.[59]

The good value they thought they got turned out to be an outfielder in Wasdell who hit 39 points off his '41 average at .259 and was sold to the Phils the next season; a 37-year-old pitcher in Hamlin who was 4–4, leaving the game in 1943 only to resurface with the A's in 1944; a catcher in Phelps who had a fine season hitting .284 with 9 homers in 257 at-bats, yet retired after the season; and Pete Coscarart, who stayed with the team until 1946, yet his .228 average in 1942 was hardly a match for Vaughan's '41 output of .318.

For his part, Vaughan hit .277 for the Dodgers before his fine comeback season in 1943 when he hit .305.

Overall it hurt the Bucs more than it helped as they lost 15 more games than the year before. They truly fooled themselves this time, shame on them.

Who Left for the War	*Who Replaced Them*
CA-Vinny Smith	
SS-Billy Cox	
PI-Bill Clemensen	
PI-Ken Jungels	
PI-Oad Swigart	

Vinny Smith— Vinny Smith's career was broken up into two short seasons. The first was in 1941 when he was 10 for 33 for an impressive .303 mark before he enlisted in the Navy and the second in 1946 when he hit .190 in 21 at-bats.

Billy Cox— The Pennsylvania native broke in with the Bucs in 1941, hitting .270 in 37 at-bats. Bigger things were expected from Cox, as he was earmarked for the shortstop job that was vacated by the departure of Hall of Famer Arky Vaughan.[60] Unfortunately for Billy, Uncle Sam stepped in and he went off to war.

Cox would suffer emotional problems while serving his country during World War II and it would take him some time to recover.[61] When he did, Billy came back in a big way, finally taking over the Pirate starting shortstop job in 1946 and hitting .290 in the process. He hit career highs in both homers, with 15, and RBIs, with 54, before being sent to the Dodgers with Preacher Roe and Gene Mauch for 37-year-old Dixie Walker, Hal Gregg and Vic Lombardi after the 1947 season. Cox would be moved to third when he reached Brooklyn and would become a cornerstone in the infield for those championship Dodger teams.

While Cox's average slid a little to .233 and .257 in 1949 and 1950, he would show off his fielding skills at his new position garnering 21 fielding runs those seasons while leading the NL in fielding percentage with a .957 mark in 1950.

Perhaps his best overall season was in 1953 when he smacked 10 homers with a career high .291 average while defensively he turned in what would also be a career high fielding percentage at .974.

Cox slumped in '54 to .235 and was sent packing, again with Preacher Roe (who then immediately retired) to the Orioles where he hit only .211 in 194 at-bats the first part of the 1955 season. Baltimore shipped him to Cleveland in June of that year with Gene Woodling for Dave Pope and Wally Westlake. Cox refused to report and immediately retired himself. (The Indians would be given $15,000 instead.)

What did the war cost Billy Cox statistically? It's really tough to say how he would have been so early in his career, but we do know that he would have probably been given the starting shortstop job his rookie season instead of Pete Coscarart, so there was a good chance he would have had four complete seasons to add to his record. He finished with 974 hits, so the 1,500 plateau was definitely within his reach. With 351 RBIs, he most likely could have risen to the 500 level. He hit 28 homers his first 4 seasons as a starter after the war, so getting to the 100 mark (he needed 34), was not out of the question either. Despite it all, Cox had a career he certainly could be proud of.

Bill Clemensen gave up only 7 hits in 13 innings for the Pittsburgh Pirates in 1941 before being drafted after the season. When he returned, Clemensen would toss two hitless innings before leaving the majors for good in 1946. Courtesy of the Pittsburgh Pirates.

Bill Clemensen— After a tough rookie season in 1939

when he gave up 32 hits and 20 walks in only 27 innings, Bill Clemensen had an impressive, although very abbreviated, 1941 season, giving up 7 hits in 13 innings, winning his only major league decision and an OBA of .159.

Clemensen was originally classified a 1B as far as the military goes, due to an auto accident that hurt his left arm.[62] His draft board in Santa Cruz then reclassified him a 1-A and off he went to war after the '41 season.

When he came back in 1946, he would throw only two hitless innings, striking out two. A great way to end a career that unfortunately never had a chance to happen.

Ken Jungels— Jungels did pitch in 5 seasons with the Indians and the Pirates between 1937 and 1941, although they were very short campaigns for "Curly," as he was called, accumulating only 25 games and 49 innings with a 1–0 record and 6.80 ERA over his career. He would not return to the majors after his time in the service.

Oad Swigart— Swigart's major league career encompassed two seasons with the Pirates in 1939 and 1940, both almost identical years. He gave up 27 hits in 24⅓ innings with 8 strikeouts and a 4.44 ERA in 1939, coming back with 27 hits given up in 22⅓ innings with 9 strikeouts for a 4.43 ERA in 1940. He would not return after the war.

1942 Chicago Cubs
68–86–38 GB

1941	1942
1B-Babe Dahlgren	Cavarretta
2B-Lou Stringer	Stringer
SS-Bobby Sturgeon	Lennie Merullo
3B-Stan Hack	Hack
OF-Bill Nicholson	Nicholson
OF-Phil Cavarretta	Dallessandro
OF-Dom Dallessandro	Lou Novikoff
CA-Clyde McCullough	McCullough
PI-Claude Passeau	Passeau
PI-Vern Olson	Lee
PI-Bill Lee	Olson
PI-Larry French	Hi Bithorn

Although both Bill Nicholson, who was arguably the greatest player in the game during the war seasons, and Phil Cavarretta would both go on to lead the Cubs to the pennant in 1945. They were really not ready to pull off that trick at this point and time of their careers.

Nicholson did have a nice season with 21 homers and 78 RBIs and Stan Hack and Lou Novikoff both hit the .300 plateau right on the nose, but the Cubs scored 75 less runs than they did in 1941.

Unfortunately the only things the Cubs did lead the National League in were hits given up at 1,447 and strikeouts with 607 (while hitting, sadly, not pitching). They did have a couple good performances on the mound though, as Claude Passeau led the way with a 19–14 record and 2.68 ERA.

Overall better things were soon to come, just not this year.

Who Left for the War	*Who Replaced Them*
1B-Eddie Waitkus	
PI-Walt Lanfranconi	
PI-Russ Meers	

Eddie Waitkus— As we will find out later on, there was in fact a Crash Davis who was the inspiration for the movie *Bull Durham* (well if not the inspiration for the movie, then the name). How does this apply to Eddie Waitkus? He would be one of the inspirations for *The Natural*, Bernard Malamud's first novel and later a much-beloved movie starring Robert Redford.[63]

It wasn't necessarily his career that Roy Hobbs was to mirror, although he played well with 1,214 hits and a .285 average (hitting only 24 homers, which Hobbs did in a week), but an episode where he was shot by a 19-year-old devotee in a Chicago hotel in 1949 when she decided if she couldn't have him no one should. The Nazis couldn't get Waitkus during the war, but Ruth Ann Steinhagen did and shot him in the chest after leaving an invitation for him at the desk to meet her in her hotel room.

Waitkus survived the attack, but missed the rest of the 1949 season, a year in which he was selected to his second All-Star game while hitting what was a career high .306. It was his first year in Philadelphia playing for the Phils after coming over from the Cubs in 1948 with Hank Borowy for Dutch Leonard and Monk Dubiel. The Phils had gotten Waitkus after his first All-Star season of 1948 where he hit .295.

The 1950 season would lead Eddie to his one and only World Series appearance, hitting .267 in 15 at-bats with a double in the Yanks' 4 game sweep of Philadelphia.

He started for the Phils at first the next two seasons before being sold to the Orioles for $40,000 in 1954. He came back to the Phillies midway in through the 1955 campaign where he hit .280 in 107 at-bats before ending his major league career.

What Eddie Waitkus missed in his career due to his participation in the war is a bit of a mystery. He had gone into the military after only 1 season in the bigs with Chicago, going only 5 for 28. When he returned in 1946, he was their starting first baseman and hit .304. When he would have entered that starting roll is debatable and the chance he would have gotten the 286 hits needed to reach 1,500 is also not a certainty. He was a two time All-Star though and more importantly, if not for him, perhaps *The Natural* would not be the classic movie that it is, and for that we should be forever grateful.

Walt Lanfranconi— Lanfranconi threw only six innings for the Cubs in 1941 before going off to the service. He returned in 1947 with the Braves in a bigger roll, with a 4–4 record in 64 innings pitched for a 2.95 ERA. It would be his last major league season.

Russ Meers— The "Babe," as he was called, gave up 5 hits in 8 innings of work for the 1941 Chicago Cubs before reporting to the military. He came back for a short time in 1946, before going 2–0 in 64⅓ innings in 1947, his last year in the show. Overall, Meers finished with a fine IP/H ratio of 83⅔/76 and an OBA of .251.

1942 Boston Braves
59–89–44 GB

1941	*1942*
1B-Buddy Hassett	West
2B-Bama Rowell	Sisti
SS-Eddie Miller	Miller
3B-Sibby Sisti	Nanny Fernandez
OF-Gene Moore	Paul Waner
OF-John Cooney	Tommy Holmes
OF-Max West	Chet Ross
CA-Ray Berres	Ernie Lombardi
PI-Manny Salvo	Javery
PI-Jim Tobin	Tobin
PI-Al Javery	Lou Tost
PI-Art Johnson	Tom Earley

They say in life timing is everything and for the 1942 Boston Braves, that statement couldn't be truer. If you look at their roster, they would possess four Hall of Famers, certainly enough to make a team competitive, if not contenders. In this situation, a closer look makes one realize just why they finished so poorly.

Hall of Famer number one was catcher Ernie Lombardi, who was purchased from the Reds and did not disappoint, leading the senior circuit in hitting with a .330 mark. Second up was 39-year-old outfielder Paul Waner, who was at the end of a fabulous career, but hit only .258, 75 points under his lifetime .333 mark. Waner did provide the Braves one bit of history though, as he got his 3,000th base hit on June 19th, ironically against his ex-mates, the Pittsburgh Pirates and Rip Sewell. Hall of Famer number three was Warren Spahn, who was in his first season in the show and gave up 25 hits in 15⅔ innings for a 5.68 ERA. The trick to the equation was Hall of Fame member number four. It was manager Casey Stengel, who was not at his managerial peak yet as he would be later on with the Yankees.

Add to this the irony that their best pitcher performance, being Jim Tobin who lost a NL high 21 games, came at the plate and not on the mound as Tobin hit three home runs in a single game, narrowly missing a record fourth. Put it all together and maybe now it's more understandable how they finished so poorly.

Who Left for the War	*Who Replaced Them*
INF-John Dudra	
2B-Bama Rowell	Sibby Sisti/Nanny Fernandez
PI-Bill Posedel	

John Dudra— Dudra has an impressive career mark of .360. Unfortunately, it came in only 25 career at-bats for the 1941 Braves.

Bama Rowell— Carvel "Bama" Rowell came up in 1939, before hitting an impressive .305 his first season as a starter in his official rookie year of 1940. He would have career highs in both homers and RBIs with 7 and 60 respectively in 1941 before entering the service.

If Eddie Waitkus was the inspiration for the shooting scene in *The Natural*, it was Rowell who inspired the moment where Roy Hobbs hits the clock on the scoreboard and shatters it all over the field. In 1946 at Ebbets Field, Bama smashed the Bulova clock atop the right field scoreboard sending glass all over Dixie Walker. It inspired Brooklyn native Bernard Malamud, who wrote *The Natural*, to include it in his novel.[64]

When he returned in 1946, Bama moved from second into left field and would hit well over the next three seasons with averages of .267, .280 and .276 before being sent in March of 1948 to the Dodgers with Ray Sanders and $40,000 for Eddie Stanky. Brooklyn would turn around and send Rowell to the Phils for only the waiver price. He would hit only .240 in 196 at-bats for the Phils in 1948 ending his career.

With 521 hits and four seasons out of baseball due to the war, Rowell had a decent shot at reaching 1,000 hits for his career as he was in his prime, having two nice seasons starting at second for Boston before going into the military. It wasn't a sure shot, but he did have a relatively good chance at the mark.

Stengel moved Sibby Sisti from third to second to replace Bama in 1942. He hit only .211, far under Rowell's output, before going into the service himself. Nanny Fernandez would take over the starting spot at third and hit .255 before also going into the armed forces.

Bill Posedel— Bill Posedel had a couple of nice seasons before the war going 15–13 and 12–17 for the sub par Braves in 1939 and 1940. He would slump to 4–4 in 1941 before the 34-year-old Posedel entered the service. His return was not kind to him as he gave up 34 hits and 13 walks in 28 innings in 1946 for a 6.99 ERA, his last major league season.

1942 Philadelphia Phillies
42–109–62.5 GB

1941	1942
1B-Nick Etten	Etten
2B-Danny Murtaugh	Al Glossup
SS-Bobby Bragan	Bragan
3B-Pinky May	May
OF-Stan Benjamin	Ron Northey
OF-Joe Marty	Lloyd Waner
OF-Danny Litwhiler	Litwhiler
CA-Bennie Warren	Warren
PI-Cy Blanton	Hughes
PI-Johnny Podgajny	Rube Melton
PI-Tommy Hughes	Johnson
PI-Si Johnson	Podgajny

Perhaps the most impressive thing about the Phillies in 1942 was the fact their middle infield of Danny Murtaugh and Bobby Bragan went on to manage their Keystone State counterparts in Pittsburgh. Other than that fact, they were pretty much a failure in almost every facet of the game.

They finished at the bottom of the heap in batting average and had 121 fewer runs than the next lowest in Boston. On the mound their team ERA of 4.13 was ½ run worse than the number 7 team, the Braves, who finished at 3.76.

Other than Danny Litwhiler's 9 homer, .271 average and Tommy Hughes' 12–18 record with a 3.06 ERA, there wasn't much to brag about.

Who Left for the War	Who Replaced Them
INF-Heinie Mueller	
OF-Jim Carlin	
OF-Joe Marty	Lloyd Waner
PI-Roy Bruner	
PI-Lee Grissom	
PI-Bill Hofman	
PI-Dale Jones	
PI-Hugh Mulcahy	Johnny Podgajny

Not that those two performances were much to be proud of, but it was the best Philadelphia could muster. Bottom line, they certainly can go down in the history of the game as one of the worst teams ever.

Heinie Mueller— Emmett "Heinie" Mueller broke into the majors in 1938, immediately moving in as the starting second baseman for the Phillies. After hitting .250 in his rookie season, Mueller would become a utility man extraordinaire, splitting time between second, third and in the outfield for the next three years. His best campaign would be his sophomore season of 1939 where he hit .279 with career highs in homers and RBIs with 9 and 43 respectively.

Mueller would slump to .227 in 1941 before heading into the military. He would not return after the war had ended.

Jim Carlin— Jim Carlin's entire career encompassed 21 at-bats in 1941, hitting .143 with a homer.

Joe Marty— After an impressive rookie campaign for the Cubs in 1937, hitting .290 in 290 at-bats, Marty would find himself traded to the Phillies after a .132 start in 1939 with Ray Harrell and Kirby Higbe for Claude Passeau. He hit .254 the rest of the way.

Joe would have his finest two seasons with Philadelphia in 1940 and 1941 as the starting center fielder, hitting .270 and .268 respectively, with a career best 13 homers in '40. He would head off to the military after the '41 season never to return to the majors.

Replacing Marty in center was veteran Hall of Famer Lloyd Waner. Waner was at the end of his fabulous career hitting 55 points below his lifetime .316 average at .261. He would retire for a season in 1943 before ending his career as a part time player with the Dodgers and Pirates in 1944 and 1945.

Roy Bruner— Bruner's career would last three abbreviated seasons between 1939 and 1941, losing all seven lifetime decisions. He tossed only 62⅔ innings in 19 games for a 5.74 ERA during those three campaigns.

Lee Grissom— After three part-time seasons with Cincinnati, throwing only 55⅔ innings between 1934 and 1936, Lee Grissom would crack into the starting rotation in 1937, making his only All-Star game despite his 12–17 record. Lee would have an impressive .232 OBA while leading the NL in shutouts with 5.

Grissom spent two more seasons as a starter/reliever with the Reds before moving on to New York in 1940 playing for both the Yankees and the Dodgers. In 14 games with Brooklyn in '40, he would have an impressive IP/H ration of 73⅔/59 with a .215 OBA.

Lee would be sent to the Phils in May of 1941 for Vito Tamulis. He would put a sour note on his career in Philadelphia, ending his time in the show with a 2–13 mark. It took his career mark from 27–35 to 29–48.

Bill Harman—The Virginia native lasted only one season in the majors in 1941, giving up 15 hits in 13 innings for a 4.85 ERA.

Dale Jones—"Nubs," as Dale Jones was called, pitched in only two major league games for the Phillies during the 1941 campaign, giving up 13 hits and 6 walks in only 8⅓ innings of work.

Hugh Mulcahy— Sometimes when it seems like things are going down into the path of obscurity, situations happen that turn life into a whole new direction; such was the case of Philly hurler Hugh Mulcahy.

The Brighton, Massachusetts, native came up with the Phils in 1935, where he met up with manager Jimmy Wilson who turned his pitching career around. "Jimmy Wilson, manager of the Phillies, made some changes in my delivery that would help me out. They sent me to Hazelton, Pa. in the New York–Penn League in 1936 where I was named Most Valuable Player of the league by *The Sporting News*."[65]

After the fabulous season of 1936, the Phillies came calling for good with a full time promotion in 1937. The right-hander began his career with an 8–18 record, leading the league with 56 games appeared in. It was a record that would subsequently cause the baseball writers to dub Mulcahy, "Losing Pitcher," in reference to the many times he would have the initials LP listed next to his name in the box score (losing pitcher).[66] It wasn't necessarily the fact that the Mulcahy was a bad pitcher — he was not. That led to his career record of 45–89 with a .336 winning percentage, which is among the 10 lowest of all time among pitchers who have 100 decisions or more. It was more that the Philadelphia teams he played on in his full seasons between 1937 and 1940 were 201–406 with an abysmal .331 winning percentage.

After a 10–20 record in 1938, Wilson commented on just how well the Philly pitcher did in fact play that season with a team that finished 45–105. "I had won 10 games. At the end of the year Jimmy Wilson, the manager, asked me how many games I won, I said 10, he told me to consider myself a 20 game winner."[67]

Nineteen forty would prove to be the high water mark for the man that would retire to the historic Beaver Valley area of Western Pennsylvania. Despite a 13–22 record with a career low 3.60 ERA for the pathetic Philly club, Mulcahy would be selected to pitch in his only All-Star game.

At the end of the season, his career mark stood at 42–82. He had the less than flattering moniker of "Losing Pitcher" and his baseball legacy basically would be stuck in neutral with one of the worst teams in the annuals of the sport. It was at this point that everything was about to change.

The day was March 8th of 1941 when Hugh Mulcahy would go from also ran to hero, as he became the first major league player to be drafted in the Army in World War II. Johnny Podgajny, who had a 6–14 record in 1942, would replace Hugh.

The Brookline pitcher would play in a few All-Star games during his tenure in the armed forces between 1941 and 1945, but his baseball play would be generally limited to pickup games here and there. Stationed overseas in New Guinea and the Philippines, the Philly hurler's major league life severely came to a crashing end for all purposes when he contracted dysentery while in New Guinea.

Mulcahy came back in 1945 and was a shell of his former self. "After missing about 5 years from baseball and losing 35 pounds from an illness in New Guinea, I lost the zip in my fastball which was my main pitch." The Philadelphia fastballer would further go on to joke that "Maybe I should have developed a knuckleball."[68]

The postwar major league seasons of 1945 through '47 would produce only a 3–7 record in 23 games with the Phillies and Pirates. After an unsuccessful stint, he would try and recapture the magic with Oakland in the Pacific Coast League and Memphis in the Southern League from 1948 to 1950.

Hugh Mulcahy went through his baseball career as a fighter who would not accept failure. He left it as a hero, forever being known as the first major leaguer to be drafted into the Great War, a war that cost him his cherished vocation.

2

1943

If baseball spent 1942 trying to decide whether or not it could even exist in the midst of World War II, then it spent the following season in 1943 aiming just to keep its head barely above water, juggling one soap opera after another in one of the most bizarre seasons on record. We were now smack dab in the middle of war ball, and every day brought with it a new adventure.

There would be a new ball that promised to reintroduce the era of the home run and instead ushered back the dead ball years. There was the saga of the Philadelphia Phillies, whom the National League had thought it had dug out of turmoil by naming William Cox its owner and president, only to expel him from baseball by year's end for gambling on his own team. To top that off, the teams, in an effort to restrict travel, moved their spring training sites from the warmth of the south to the cold of the north. The minor leagues were in disarray, dropping from 31 to only 9 operating leagues by season's beginning. Most important, though, the game lost its biggest superstars including Ted Williams, Joe DiMaggio and Enos Slaughter, who were now in a bigger battle playing for Uncle Sam. It certainly would be a weird season, although despite FDR's declaration the season before that the games shall continue, it was no certainty as we entered the new year that a game would even be played.

Three of the most pressing issues facing baseball before the new campaign began were:

A): Would we even have baseball in 1943?
B): How could baseball best restrict travel to cover war guidelines?
C): What to do with the financially strapped Philadelphia Phillies?

As was the case in 1942, there was still some lingering doubt over whether or not baseball was essential to the war effort. At the New York baseball writers' annual dinner in February, Commissioner Landis threw the first volley in favor of the continuation of baseball by saying, "As long as we can put nine men on the field, the game will not die." He further went on to state that "Let 60 million baseball fans raise their voice as to whether the game should or should not be played in these times."[1]

Former Republican presidential candidate Wendell Willkie came up to the dais with his defense of the national pastime stating, "I visited Africa and I toured China. I spoke to 30 American boys in African service and every single one of them asked first for news of baseball — how were the Dodgers and Cardinals making out." He went on, "They weren't interested in the depth of the Russian defense. They wanted to know how the World Series looked to me."[2]

Dodger GM Branch Rickey put his two cents in on the subject saying that "If 400 professional ballplayers, now classified at 3-A, can do a better job for our 130,000,000 people than at anything other than playing this game, then we want to know the way to do it. If there is a morale job to be done by baseball, these particular men must do it."[3]

The controversy over whether or not the remaining baseball players were more essential working in another field that was more pertinent to the war effort or playing baseball for the country's morale would go on for a couple more months. In the meantime, baseball would have to make decisions on how best to curtail travel within the schedule and in spring training.

One thing on the docket was a proposal to cut the schedule from the traditional 154 games down to 140, a level it had not been to since 1919.[4] Landis was not in favor of such a move and drafted a plan to help the sport get through this difficult controversy. It was as follows:

A): Train at home or as close as possible. Landis drew boundaries that the sites were to be north of Ohio and the Potomac rivers and east of the Mississippi River, with the exception of the St. Louis franchises, which could train in Missouri. This meant that the 11 clubs that trained previously in Florida would now give up the warmth for the cold of their hometowns.

B): Play a 154 game schedule that would begin on April 21 and end October 3.

C): Reduce man mileage wherever possible.

D): Voluntarily reduce the size of the traveling squads.[5]

Indiana would become the new Florida as 6 teams chose to train there. The clubs chose the following locations to train:

National League

Pittsburgh-Muncie, In.
St. Louis-Cairo, Ill.
Cincinnati-Bloomington, In.
New York-Lakewood, N.J.
Brooklyn-Bean Mountain, N.Y.
Philadelphia Hershey, Pa.
Chicago-French Lick Springs, In.
Boston-Wallingford, Conn.

American League

Cleveland-Lafayette, In.
Detroit-Evansville, In.
St. Louis-Cape Girardeau, Mo.
Washington, College Park, Md.
Chicago-French Lick Springs, In.
New York-Asbury Park, N.J.
Boston-Medford, Mass.
Philadelphia-Wilmington, Del.[6]

Next on the agenda would be the curious case of the Philadelphia Phillies. The City of Brotherly Love was the unfortunate home of the two worst franchises in major league baseball in the Phillies and Athletics. The worst of the lot was the NL squad, as the Phils were in dire financial straits as they entered the new year. President Gerald Nugent decided to have an early fire sale, first selling off pitcher Rube Melton to the Dodgers for $30,000 and Johnny Allen (Melton at first refused to report to Brooklyn before recanting his decision), then sending first baseman Nick Etten, one of the best players during the war years, to the Yankees, for $25,000 (later turning out to be only $10,000), Al Gettel and Ed Levy, a first baseman who failed in his attempt with the Phils 3 years earlier.

It soon became apparent that the National League would have to take over the franchise before Nugent ran it further into the ground. The Phillies, which *Pittsburgh Press* sportswriter Chester Smith aptly claimed, "Didn't have enough talent to put up more than a fair battle in a class B league"[7] were taken over by the league, despite Nugent's protests, by purchasing 4,690 of 5,000 outstanding shares in the team.[8]

The intent was to sell the club and there were several groups interested including one headed by 33-year-old New York lumber company executive William Cox and another by Hall of Fame owner Bill Veeck. Although some question the validity of Bill's bid, Veeck would claim later on that he was denied the franchise because he admitted to Landis, before purchasing the Club, that he intended to fill its roster with players from the Negro Leagues. This caused Landis, according to Veeck, to take the lesser bid of Cox.[9] Whether or not the story was true, the Phillies' long range prospects would have changed dramatically had Veeck played the Negro League greats and rather than lament the embarrassment of Phillie baseball in the 1940s, we might be talking one of the great dynasties in the history of the sport.

Nonetheless, on February 19th, Nugent handed over his stock to National League President Ford Frick and resigned his post of president of the club, unable to make his bills, including $132,000 that he owed to the league.[10]

Cox would win the battle of control and was given the keys to drive the franchise into respectability on March 20th. One of his first maneuvers was to try and retrieve Etten from the Yankees and have the trade voided. The two players the Phillies received, Levy and Gettel, refused to report to the club. The trade of course would not be reversed and Etten would go on to star for the Yankees over the next three years. What Philadelphia did receive as compensation though, were two new players, Al Gearhouser and Tom Padden.

Cox would temporarily breathe life into the moribund franchise as the club would make several trades, including one, sending Danny Litwhiler and Earl Naylor to the Cardinals for Coaker Triplett, Buster Adams and Dain Clay in an attempt to make the team more competitive. The trade would be a good one for the Phils, as Triplett and Adams would both start hitting .272 and .256 respectively with Clay being sent to the Reds. Litwhiler would hit .279 for St. Louis while Naylor never played in a Cardinal uniform.

As the season went on, the New York businessman would begin to turn a little Stienbrennian in his approach to the game, especially on two particular instances in 1943. The first was when he vehemently protested a game against the Cardinals, when he argued St. Louis made no effort to cover the field during a rainstorm with the Cardinals up 1–0 in the 8th. When Frick stated that the game would be played from the finishing point, which was the new rule, Cox was livid claiming it should be forfeited and took the case to Landis stating, "The game should be forfeited. If they don't like the rule, they should wipe it off the books. It will only encourage people like Mr. Breaden (Cardinal president) to continue such despicable actions."[11] Although he was thwarted in his attempt, Cox showed he would do whatever it took to win.

The second move was the way he handled the firing of manager Bucky Harris. The dismissal came out of the blue in late June. In fact Harris' successor, Fred Fitzsimmons, was on his way to take over the club before Bucky was even notified that he was gone.[12] It got so bad that before the game the next day, 24 players threatened to strike in protest to the firing and felt that Cox needed to explain his actions. They all believed in Harris' ability to manage and were shocked by the dismissal.[13]

Order was eventually restored as Fitzsimmons won his inaugural game as skipper. Cox attempted to explain why he ended Harris' tenure after 19 years as a major league manager, claiming that Bucky told the board if they didn't think he was doing a good job, let him go. Cox further claimed that Bucky said he didn't know why the Phils started losing after a good start and didn't know what to do about it.[14] Harris himself claimed he was puzzled by the move and denied having any problems with Cox.[15]

The tumultuous campaign came to a head when it was learned in November that Cox had been investigated for gambling on his own team. For months, Cox had told Landis that it was an associate of his that was making the bets and not in fact him. It eventually came to pass on November 3rd that Cox admitted making 15 or 20 bets of between $25 and $100 on the team. When Landis called him into New York to testify on his own behalf, Cox refused, claiming he had already resigned his post from the Phillies front office to spend more time attending to his war important industry. Landis replied by banning Cox from ever holding any position in baseball.[16]

In early December, Landis granted Cox a new hearing at the controversial owner's request. The lumberman claimed that he didn't bet on the games and was just testing the loyalty of an employee. He further went on to claim that the only bets he made were just friendly ones. Apparently with all the evidence pointing to the contrary, Landis made the following statement: "There is no escape from the conclusion, with such intelligence as I am endowed with — or inflicted with — that there is nothing I could do for Mr. Cox."[17]

With that, the Commissioner sent Cox on his way, banned from the game for life, and 28-year-old Robert Carpenter, Jr., was named the new president.

Aside from the problems of the Philadelphia Phillies, baseball was still at a crossroads before the season began and nothing was more problematic than the plight of minor league baseball.

Late in February, San Antonio of the class A-1 Texas league announced that it would cease operations until after the war. This announcement brought down the entire Texas League with it.[18]

All of the sudden, there were only nine minor leagues that were left to operate for the 1943 season — the International League, Pacific Coast League and the American Association in class AA, the Southern Association in class A-1, the Eastern League in class A, the Piedmont and Interstate leagues from class B and the Pony and Appalachian leagues in class D. The total would be an incredible decline from the two previous seasons of 41 operating leagues in 1941 and 31 the following year.

The minor leagues were now full of players who were either 4-F's or men that worked in war vital industries.[19] Although they would go on, the level of play diminished significantly.

As the minors were struggling to hold on, the major leagues solved a few of their problems when they released their schedule in mid–March that would be for the more traditional 154 instead of the 140 game proposition. They rearranged things so they could save 35,000 miles of travel versus the past campaign.[20]

The official green light that major league baseball could continue was given in a report by the Office of Civilian Supply (OCS) that claimed baseball and its counterparts in hockey and professional football were essential to the national morale and should go on.[21]

With everything a go for the new season, the players had something new and exciting to look forward to, a new baseball produced by Spalding. The ball would be made out of cork, surrounded by two layers of balata, made out of reprocessed golf balls, and Michigan long staple yarn inside the cover. It was conservatively estimated that the ball would be 10 percent livelier than its predecessor.[22]

As with everything else that happened during this most disappointing of seasons, the ball turned out to be inferior. Teams like the Chicago Cubs, who went 32 games and 1,120 at-bats before Bill Nicholson hit their first homer of the year on May 30th, would have severe power outages.[23] Instead of ushering in a new era of home runs, it gave way to a ball that was deader than any in history. When questioned as to why there were 11 shutouts in the first 29 games, a spokesman from Spalding would say that it's "too wet and too cold. In time the new ball will prove to be just as lively as the old one."[24] Luckily for the fans, baseball did take immediate action, using the remaining supply of baseballs from 1942, until a new supply, which Landis promised would return us to "rabbit ball" (a new hitting era), was ready.[25]

The problem with the dead ball was the balata, an elastic substance taken from tropical trees, added to cork, and fashioned into a core, in substitute of war-rationed rubber. The balata hardened with time and the balls consequently traveled short distances when struck.[26]

When the new ball was introduced, the results were instantaneous, as the Yankees would get 16 hits en route to a 13–1 shellacking of the A's. The Bronx Bombers would hit 3 homers that game, compared to the 7 that the entire American League had hit to that point.[27]

Despite the new ball coming to the rescue, over all in 1943, runs were still down versus 1942 by 301 (9,694 in 1943 compared to 9,995 the year before). Worse yet were the power numbers as there were only 895 homers hit during '43 compared to 1,071 the prior campaign, an incredible decrease of 176 shots.

With all the soap opera situations in mind, the main subject of the 1943 season was the players that were sent to war. In 1942, only 71 players with major league experience were in the armed forces; by 1943 that figure shot up to 219. The greatest players in the game, Ted Williams and Joe DiMaggio, would now be gone into the Army and Navy respectively.

Every day new headlines would bring more great players into the conflict as they would read, Cardinals Brown and Walker off to war, or the announcement that the Cardinal captain Terry Moore was sent or that of Sid Gordon of the Giants, inducted even though he was married and with a child. Even Dodger manager Leo Durocher was rumored to be going until he did not pass his physical.

Major league baseball would be lucky in the first two seasons of World War II having no players killed in action, but other sports would not be so lucky in 1943. College football lost its Heisman Trophy winner Nile Kinnick from Iowa who was stationed on an aircraft carrier as a pilot where he was believed to have been killed. Track and field also lost a member when French track star George Andre, a proud veteran of both World Wars, lost his life at 51 years old fighting with the French African Corps.

With all the tragedy that was going around, the game was still played. Despite everything, there was still some wonderful performances that happened between the lines along with a collection of bizarre occurrences, the first of which happened to the old general himself, Boston manager Casey Stengel, who would miss most of the 1943 season after breaking his leg when he was hit by a taxi on April 20th.

The other strange tale in the early season was that of Dodger pitcher Johnny Allen. Allen was at the tail end of a successful career that included a 20 win season with Cleveland in 1936, a 17–4 rookie year with the Yanks in 1932 and a 15–1 mark with the Indians in 1937. As much as he was known for being a great hurler, he also had a temper, which was put on display May 27th when Allen attacked umpire George Barr over a balk call. Allen would be suspended 30 days and fined $200 (a good amount at that point). Later that season, he was sent to the Giants where he retired the following year with a record of 142–75.

Traded with Allen to the Giants was Dodger slugger Dolph Camilli, who was mired in a season long slump. Rather than report to the cross-town rivals, Camilli retired from the game. It wasn't that he didn't want to play for the Giants, but that the 35-year-old veteran felt he didn't have it anymore. "I simply am not playing good ball so my usefulness apparently is over," Camilli stated.[28] The San Francisco native would eventually play one more season in 1945 when he finished his 12-year career with the Red Sox.

Camilli's retirement was just one of many such occurrences, both actual and rumored, in 1943. Probably the most notable was that of Lloyd Waner, who quit to help build planes for the war effort in the Douglas Aircraft Company.[29] Like Camilli, Little Poison would return again, playing two abbreviated seasons for the Dodgers and Pirates in 1944 and 1945. On the rumor front, when it came to retirements, were three major items; the first was Joe DiMaggio rumored to say he was done with baseball, then A's owner and skipper Connie Mack. Finally there was the strange tale of Yankees second baseman Joe Gordon. After a story was released that Gordon was "tired of baseball" and was going to work in the physical education department of the University of Oregon,[30] the nation was shocked. It was later revealed Gordon was just joking to a friend who apparently didn't realize it.[31] The irony was that Gordon would eventually be inducted into the armed forces and missed the following season anyway.

Pirate Rip Sewell, who was in the midst of a fine 21–9 campaign where he led the NL in wins, added to the strange parade on June 1st as he introduced what would be known as the eephus pitch. It was a toss that went anywhere from 18 feet to 25 feet in the air falling over the plate in a softball manner, most times unhittable. It would later on become Rip's trademark.

Slugger Rudy York would take over for Ted Williams and Hank Greenberg as the premier slugger in the American League for 1943, leading the circuit in homers and RBIs with 34 and 118 respectively. August would be his prime month as he celebrated the death of the balata ball and the introduction of the new rabbit ball, by pounding 17 homers in August, one off his major league mark of 18 set in 1937. York was not well known for his glove and that would serve the Tigers well in a game on June 18th as the first baseman went an entire game without a single putout, a very strange occurrence symbolic with the bizarre season that was taking place.

With the coming of July, came All-Star month. The game this year would be at Philadelphia's Shibe Park and would be the first night All-Star game in the history of the sport. The game was won by the AL on Bobby Doerr's 3 run second inning homer. Vince DiMaggio led the senior circuit with a single, triple and homer. On the previous night, a military

All-Star team managed by Babe Ruth defeated the Boston Braves 9–8 on Ted Williams' 9th inning homer.

There were two oddities on September 6th that could have only occurred under war conditions. The first was the mark of Cincinnati second baseman Woody Williams who collected 10 hits in a row over two games. Williams was in the majors after a 5-year hiatus, presumably due to the lack of baseball personnel. He would start for the Reds in 1944 and 1945 before leaving the majors after the '45 season when the players came back from the service. The other was the story of A's pitcher Carl Scheib. Schieb pitched in his first major league game at 16 years and 248 days, the youngest major leaguer ever, until Joe Nuxhall beat the mark the following season. He went ⅔ of an inning giving up 2 hits. Scheib would go on to have an 11-year career, all but the last three games with the A's going 45–65 with a 4.88 ERA.

Speaking of the A's, they went on to set their record of futility, losing an AL record 20 games in a row. They broke the streak against the White Sox, winning the second game of a double header 8–1.

At a game on September 24th, the Cubs drew what would be an all time low mark at Wrigley Field of only 314 patrons. This would be yet another down season through the turnstiles for the national pastime. Attendance was down over 1.3 million with a total of 7,465,911 compared to that of 8,553,569 in 1942. This was despite an amazing turnaround by the Phillies, who even with all that William Cox had done to the contrary, were able to boost their total from 230,183 to 466,975. No team was able to break the 700,000 barrier as the Dodgers led the way at 661,739.[32]

As the season ended with the Yanks gaining retribution over the Cardinals in the Fall Classic, there would be plenty of issues to be decided. As seemingly with the end of every war ball season, baseball would have to argue for its continued existence. Senator Scott Lucas of Illinois threw the first volley in the game's favor as he stated, "Servicemen in every part of the globe are interested [in the game]. Those in charge [of baseball] have been most generous to servicemen, admitting them to games and with the donation of athletic equipment for boys in the camps."[33]

He went on to point out how much baseball has donated to the cause through their war relief games, which like the year before were contested in almost every major league park with several entertaining events preceding the contest such as the Three Stooges performing at Forbes Field. Surprisingly enough nobody ever mentioned that the game should continue on the rare occurrence that the St. Louis Browns just might win the 1944 American League pennant. Well, we might just be getting a little ahead of ourselves.

Any hopes and dreams that the players had of returning to the warmer climates during spring training of 1944 were quickly dashed by Landis who announced in October that the sites would remain up north as they did in 1943.

Perhaps the strangest announcement of the post 1943 season was one that the baseball czar himself would state in December. Landis said, in reference to a meeting that actor/singer Paul Robeson had with the joint session of the major leagues, that major league teams were free to sign as many Negro League players as they wanted.[34] It was a hollow decree and meant little, as no African-American player would ever perform in the majors under the iron-fisted rule of Kenesaw Mountain Landis.

As far as the Negro Leagues themselves went, players such as Monte Irvin, Larry Doby, Willard Brown, Buck O'Neill, Lyman Bostock, Howard Easterling, Ted Strong, Connie Johnson, Sammie Hughes, Max Manning, Ford Smith, Joe Greene and Dick Seay would all miss time playing baseball as they went into the service in 1943. Leon Day, who drove an amphibious truck onto the beaches of Normandy, and Hank Thompson, who was wounded at the Battle of the Bulge, also left for the war in '43.[35]

In the pennant races, the Birmingham Black Barons, led by Lester Lockett and Bostock, who hit .412, won a close race in the Negro American League over the Memphis Red Sox while the Homestead Grays waltzed to the Negro National League crown with a 44–15 mark. The Grays' roster included Josh Gibson, coming off a nervous breakdown suffered on New Year's Day,[36] who would have a great year, hitting .449 with 22 homers (tops in the circuit by 14 over Newark's Lenny Pearson who finished second with 8), Cool Papa Bell and Buck Leonard.

The Grays would take the series, 4 games to 3 with 1 ending in a tie, by taking the 8th and deciding game, scoring six runs in the 8th and 9th innings to erase a 4–2 Birmingham lead.

During the campaign, the Negro Leagues' Chicago American Giants would face off against Johnny Mize, Barney McCoskey and the powerful Great Lakes Naval team. The Giants would amass 19 hits in a 7–3 victory.[37]

Cub owner Phillip Wrigley, Dodger boss Branch Rickey and lawyer Paul Harper started a league in 1943 located in the Midwest called the All-American Girls Professional Baseball League.

The circuit consisted of four teams from Kenosha and Racine from Wisconsin, Rockford, Illinois and South Bend, Indiana. The Racine Belles, led by home run champion Eleanor Dapkus, beat the Kenosha Comets, with 31–8 pitcher Helen Nicol, for the league title.[38]

All in all it was an exhausting, tumultuous season. Everything the major league owners tried to improve the game blew up in their faces.

Things would not get much better the following season, except a gift from the baseball gods that would be bestowed the fine patrons of St. Louis.

Starting Lineups and Who Went to War

AMERICAN LEAGUE

1943 New York Yankess
98–56–0 GB

1941	1942	1943
1B-Johnny Sturm	Buddy Hassett	Nick Etten
2B-Joe Gordon	Gordon	Gordon
SS-Phil Rizzuto	Rizzuto	Crosetti
3B-Red Rolfe	Frank Crosetti	Billy Johnson
OF-Tommy Henrich	Henrich	Bud Metheny
OF-Joe DiMaggio	DiMaggio	Johnny Lindell
OF-Charlie Keller	Keller	Keller
CA-Bill Dickey	Dickey	Dickey
PI-Marius Russo	Tiny Bonham	Chandler
PI-Red Ruffing	Chandler	Butch Wensloff
PI-Lefty Gomez	Ruffing	Borowy
PI-Spud Chandler	Hank Borowy	Bonham

Perhaps the 1943 Yankees could be considered the most curious team during the war years, and the most surprising one, even more than the 1944 Browns.

On paper, the losses to the armed service would be devastating: three Hall of Famers in DiMaggio, Rizzuto and Ruffing, four starters in all and one pitcher from the starting rotation. The cross-town rival Giants would have similar losses, not as severe though, and lose 30 more games than they did the previous year, whereas the Yanks would drop only five additional.

Was it the brilliance of manager Joe McCarthy that kept the ship afloat, was it the strength of the front office that was able to properly replace the pieces or was it the fact that the team had a championship spirit and knew what it took to win? Most likely it was a combination of all of the above.

Statistically, McCarthy was the greatest manager of all time, having the highest winning percentage and claiming more championships than any other skipper in history.

There were some shrewd moves along the way too. They got first baseman Nick Etten from the Phils for Tom Pidden, Al Gerhauser, Ed Levy, Al Gettel and $10,000. It seemed like a lot for a first baseman that hit 8 homers and a .264 average in 1942, but he was more than worth the price. This new war ball hero would smack 14 homers, knock in 107 and hit .271, an improvement over Buddy Hassett who managed only 5 homers with 48 RBIs.

Rookie Billy Johnson, who replaced Crosetti at third when the veteran moved to short, taking over for Rizzuto, had a great freshman season, with 94 RBIs and a .280 average. Thirty-six-year-old Hall of Fame catcher Bill Dickey would also have a big year, hitting .351. Other than that, the offense wasn't as potent as it had been the prior season, but it didn't have to be, as the league wasn't scoring as many runs. The Bombers dropped from 801 runs to 669, but lead the AL both seasons.

Joe Gordon was probably the biggest disappointment, coming off his controversial MVP performance of 18 homers, 103 RBIs and a .322 average, falling to 17–69–.249.

On the mound was the true Yankee strength this season, led by Spud Chandler who had his signature season, winning the league MVP award by going 20–4 with a league low 1.64 ERA. The team as a whole had an AL low 2.93 ERA. Each starter would come in under that mark as the other three — Bonham, Borowy and Wensloff— would record 2.27, 2.82 and 2.54 ERAs respectively.

New York would meet the Cards again in the Fall Classic and were able to get some revenge defeating St. Louis 4 games to 1 on the shoulders of Chandler's 2–0, 0.50 ERA performance.

All in all, true champions always rise to the top and the 1943 improbable run of the New York Yankees was a prime example of that.

Who Left for the War	*Who Replaced Them*
1B–Buddy Hassett	Nick Etten
SS–Phil Rizzuto	Frank Crosetti/Billy Johnson
3B–Hank Majeski	
OF–Joe DiMaggio	Johnny Lindell
OF–Tommy Henrich	Bud Metheny
OF–George Selkirk	
PI–Norm Branch	
PI–Randy Gumpert	
PI–Red Ruffing	Hank Borowy/Butch Wensloff

Buddy Hassett— Hassett came over to the New York Yankees with Gene Moore from the Braves for Tommy Holmes prior to the 1942 season, taking over for Johnny Sturm who had gone off to war.

Hassett, who played first and outfield for Brooklyn and Boston between 1936 and 1941, was good at the plate, hitting between .310, his rookie season, and .293 in his first four campaigns before slumping to .234 in 1940.

He did not possess much power, hitting only 12 career homers, 5 of which came in his last season of 1942, but did hit for a more than respectable .284 average. Buddy was also a good fielder, accumulating 45 fielding runs throughout his career. Although Hassett did not return to the majors after the war, he did have an opportunity to play with Ted Williams in the Navy's Flying Training program at the University of North Carolina during his time in the service.[39]

Replacing Hassett at first would be Nick Etten, a man who took advantage of playing during the war years to become one of the best in the game between 1943 and 1945.

Before coming to New York, Etten started for the lowly Phils with one decent season in 1941, hitting 14 homers with a .311 average. It was in the Big Apple where his star really shined.

After his opening act in 1943 with 17 homers, 107 RBIs and .271 average, finishing 7th in the MVP race, Etten would lead the league in homers in 1944 with 22 and bring his average up to .293.

Nineteen forty-five might have been his best season with 18 rockets, a league leading 111 RBIs with a .285 average.

Nick Etten went from the outhouse to the penthouse when he was traded from the Phillies to the Yankees prior to the 1943 season. He became a true war ball star, breaking the century mark in RBIs with 107 in 1943 and an American League high 111 in 1945. He would also lead the league in homers with 22 in 1944. He was out of the majors after the 1947 season. Courtesy of Photo File, Inc.

When the boys came home from the service the following year, Etten's performance fell far off his wartime levels hitting only .232 with 9 homers before being sent back to Philly, ending his major league career in 1947, hitting only .244 in 41 at-bats.

Phil Rizzuto — Scooter was truly one of the leaders of the great Yankee teams of the 1940s and '50s. He was a great fielding shortstop who in 1995 finally became a Hall of Famer.

Rizzuto burst on to the major league scene in 1941 hitting .307. After making the All-Star squad in 1942 and leading the league in fielding runs, he would go into the Navy.

Phil returned in 1946 where his average hovered between .252 and .275 for his first four seasons before having his marquee offensive year in 1950, hitting .324 with a career high 7 homers, leading the league in fielding at .982 and TPR at 4.0. He won the Most Valuable Player award in the American League. It would also be the beginning of four consecutive All-Star game selections.

His career coming to an end, Scooter dropped 76 points in batting average between 1953 and 1954 from .271 to .195. He would be out of the game two years later, being released in mid season of 1956 after only 52 at-bats.

Phil would finish his career with a .273 average and 86 fielding runs. Despite some criticisms on his election to Cooperstown, there was no disputing his importance to those great Yankee teams.

When Rizzuto went into the military, Frank Crosetti moved from third to short, hitting only .233. Crosetti was the starting shortstop with the Yanks prior to Rizzuto's emergence in '41 and was at the end of a 17-year career.

Billy Johnson took over at third for Crosetti and hit .280 with 94 RBIs in his rookie season of 1943. He would enter the military himself the next season.

Hank Majeski— In a long 13-year career, Majeski was a well-traveled third baseman, playing for the Braves, Yanks, A's, White Sox, Indians and Orioles.

Majeski was a .279 hitter in his career, but was better known as a good defensive fielder, leading the circuit in fielding percentage in 1947 with a record .988 percentage and in 1949 at .975. He would accumulate 49 fielding runs throughout his career.

After a strong rookie season in 1939 where he hit .272 in 367 at-bats for the Braves, Majeski would bat only 58 times over the next two seasons before going into the service.

He played in only 8 contests for the Yankees in 1946 before being sold to the A's.

It was in Philadelphia where Majeski would have his best three years, including a monster 1948 when he smacked 12 homers with 120 RBIs and a career high .310 average.

"Heeney" was sent to Chicago in 1950 where he had another fine year, hitting .309 for the White Sox before being returned to the A's in '51.

After 1951, Majeski would play only part time roles with Philadelphia and Cleveland before ending his career with Baltimore in 1955 hitting a combined .180 for the Indians and Orioles.

Joe DiMaggio— He was the third of four Yankee deities (Babe Ruth, Lou Gehrig and Mickey Mantle being the others). He played 13 seasons making 13 All-Star games. He was perhaps one of the greatest winners of all time playing in 10 World Series. He holds one of the most celebrated records of all time with his 56 game hitting streak. Through it all he was one of the greatest players in the annuls of the sport. His name was "Joltin'" Joe DiMaggio.

DiMaggio began his career in star fashion taking the American League by storm in 1936, hitting 29 homers, 125 RBIs and a .323 average. It would be the first of 7 consecutive 100 RBI seasons. He would hit .300 or better in 11 of the next 12 seasons.

His sophomore campaign was even better, leading the junior circuit in homers with 46 and runs with 151. He also knocked in a career high 167 with a .346 average.

Joe would have his much celebrated holdout before the 1939 season, looking for a raise from $15,000 to $45,000. After settling for $25,000 in April he was met by an unappreciative Yankee fan base. They would soon forget, as the King would continue to dominate the game he loved winning the batting crown at .381 and his first MVP award.

His second would come in his 56 game hitting streak year of 1941, a year when he led the AL with 125 RBIs. He also hit .356.

In 1942, the "Yankee Clipper" held out again as New York tried to cut his $37,500 salary in the midst of the war.[40] He would eventually settle for a $6,000 raise, slump to .305 and go off to the service himself before the next season.

Returning in 1946, Joe had his first sub 100 RBI season with 95 and his first sub .300 season at .290. He rebounded the next year with a 3rd and final MVP season by one point over the snakebitten Ted Williams, hitting .315.

In 1948 Joe led the league in homers with 39 and RBIs with 155. A year later, a painful bone spur and eventual operation limited DiMaggio to 76 games.

Nineteen fifty was the Clipper's last big hurrah. He hit 32 shots, knocking in 122 with a .301 average. He fell to .263 the next year and despite an offer of $100,000 to play only home games, DiMaggio would retire.[41]

Although he would miss 3 years to the war, it's doubtful Joe would have reached the magical 3,000-hit/500-homer plateaus. He would need 139 homers, an average of 46 per year, a level DiMaggio only approached once in 1937, his next highest was 39.

He was 786 hits away from 3,000. He would need an average of 262 a year, which meant for three years Joe would have had to hit the third highest seasonal hit total in the history of the game, the most of the 20th century. His previous high was 215 again in '37.

Although Joe DiMaggio was considered one of the greatest players of the game in 1942, he gave it up, as did millions of other American men, turning in his batting stance for that of a military man. Courtesy of Transcendental Graphics.

Maybe if DiMaggio was close to achieving either mark, he could have extended his career, but it's unlikely. The fact he couldn't play at the level he was accustomed to probably would have caused the proud DiMaggio to retire anyway. Regardless, he was one of the game's true giants.

Replacing Joe during the war years was Johnny Lindell. Lindell played 12 years with the Yanks, Cards, Pirates and Phillies until 1954.

He made the All-Star game in 1943 as he lead the AL in triples with 12, but his total numbers were nowhere near Joe's, hitting only 4 homers with a .245 average. Nineteen forty-four would be a little better as he had career highs in homers with 18 and RBIs with 103. He would crack the .300 plateau right on the button.

Tommy Henrich — "Old Reliable" started with the Yanks in 1937, hitting .320 in 206 at-bats. He would patrol right field in New York for the next few years, his average hovering around .270, except for 1940 when he cracked .300, hitting .307.

In 1941, Henrich found his power stroke smacking 31 homers. It was in the fall classic that season, when Tommy participated in one of the great moments in World Series history. After what appeared to be a strikeout ending the game in a Brooklyn victory, superb fielding catcher Mickey

Owen let the ball get behind him on the pitch and Henrich made it to first on the passed ball. The Yanks went on to steal the game 7–4 and win the world championship in 6 games.

Tommy made an All-Star appearance in 1942, before "Old Reliable" went into the Coast Guard. He came back in 1946 when his career would take off to a higher level.

The first season wasn't so impressive as he only hit .251, improving to .287 in '47, but 1948 would be a banner campaign as he was Mr. Extra Base Hit whacking 42 doubles, an American League leading 14 triples, 25 homers, 100 RBIs, a sparkling .308 average and a league high 138 runs. Henrich would finish 7th in the MVP vote that season.

Tommy slipped a little in 1949 before hurting his knee in 1950, which limited him to 76 games. He would retire after the season.

Henrich finished his career with 1,297 hits and with the approximately 400 hits he missed during his time in the service, would have certainly hit the 1,500 level. Tommy was only 17 homers away from 200, which again he certainly would have achieved.

Arthur "Bud" Metheny would be Henrich's replacement during the war and be pretty much a wartime player. His rookie year in 1943 was far below Henrich's output with 9 homers and a .261 average. It would be his best season.

Batting averages of .239 and .248 while filling in for Henrich in '44 and '45 pretty much was the complete Metheny career.

After Tommy came back in 1946, Metheny would get only 3 more at-bats and be gone from the majors.

George Selkirk— "Twinkle Toes" was the starting right fielder for the Yankees in the pre–Henrich days. The Canadian was a two-time All-Star who had some very nice years for New York during their power runs in the late '30s.

In his rookie year of 1934, Selkirk hit .313 in 176 at-bats. His sophomore year was his first as a starter, hitting 312 with 94 RBIs.

"Twinkle Toes" had his first All-Star appearance when he topped the 100 RBI mark with 107 in 1936. Selkirk would follow that up with a career high .328 average the following season.

His second All-Star game selection occurred in Selkirk's best season in 1939, hitting .306 with 21 homers, 101 RBIs and 103 runs with a league leading .989 fielding percentage.

George would be a regular for one more season before slumping to .220 and .192 consecutively in 1941 and '42. Selkirk did not return after the war.

He was only 190 hits away from 1,000, but in 1942 George looked to be at the end of his career, so the mark looks mostly unachievable.

Norm Branch— Although the Bronx Bombers suffered severe losses in

1943, Norm Branch was not one of them. Not that "Red" had no success, he was 5–1 his rookie year in 1941 with a 2.87 ERA and an OBA of .224. 1942 was not so kind as he was 0–1 with a 6.32 ERA in 15⅔ innings. He would not return to the majors after the war.

Randy Gumpert— Randy Gumpert's career can really be broken down into two distinct parts. The first was as a young 18-year-old with the A's between 1936 and 1938 when he had three mostly unsuccessful years with ERAs of 4.76, 12.00 and 10.95. He would stay out of the majors until his return from the armed forces in 1946 when Gumpert had his marquee season going 11–3 with a 2.31 ERA and .229 OBA for the Yankees.

He did not match the success for the next couple years until he surfaced with the White Sox in 1949, winning a career high 13 games.

Inconsistency again would plague Gumpert as he fell to 5–12 the next season, recovering to 9–8 in 1951 and being selected to his only All-Star game.

The 1951 season would be the beginning of the end as the White Sox sent him to Boston in 1952 for Don Lenhardt, Mel Hoderlein and Chuck Stobbs. He would go 1–0 in 10 starts before being sent to Washington where he ended his career.

Red Ruffing— He was a gutsy player who was a great outfield prospect before he lost four toes in a mining accident as a teenager and turned to the mound.[42] Ruffing was also a pitcher, like Gumpert, who had two distinctly different careers, one with the lowly Red Sox, which he looked nothing like a future Hall of Famer, and one with the Yankees that secured his place in Cooperstown.

Twenty-year-old Charles Herbert Ruffing came up unimpressively with Boston in 1924, giving up 17 runs in 23 innings. He would have a pathetic 39–99 record with the Sox between 1925 and 1930 with ERAs between 3.89 and 6.38, including consecutive 20 loss seasons of 25 and 22 in 1928 and 1929. Immortality was not on his mind, except that of the greatest losing pitcher in the history of the game.

Ruffing's world would change after an 0–3 start in 1930, being sent to the powerful Bronx Bombers for Cedric Durst and $50,000. He went 15–5 the rest of the way. It was only the second time in his career to this point that Red had more strikeouts than walks, as his K/BB ratio was 117/62.

Nineteen thirty-two was his first banner year as he went 18–7 with a 3.09 ERA, leading the junior circuit in strikeouts with 190 with a league low OBA of .226. Things would just keep getting better as he won 20 games for the first time in 1936, the first of four consecutive 20 win seasons.

Perhaps his finest year was in 1938 when Ruffing checked in with league best 21 wins and a winning percentage of .750. Red also had a league high TPI of 4.2. It was his first of five consecutive All-Star appearances.

The 1942 season would mark the last All-Star game selection for Ruffing with a 14–7 record for the AL Champs. In that season Red would take a no-hitter into the sixth inning of Game One in the Fall Classic. The World Series was an area where Ruffing always excelled with a 7–2 mark.

Despite the fact he was 38 years old and missing four toes, Ruffing was sent off into the armed service where he entertained the troops playing ball in Long Beach and Honolulu.[43]

When he came back in 1945 at the age of 41, Red would throw shutout ball for 6 innings against the A's in his first game, ending with a 7–3 record and 2.89 ERA. Time would stand still the next season as Ruffing was off to a phenomenal 5–1 start, 1.77 ERA and .171 OBA before breaking his kneecap, in effect ending his career. He went 3–5 in 1947 with the White Sox before hanging them up with an impressive 273–225 mark, not too bad for a man that began his career 60 games under .500.

The war most definitely cost Ruffing the 300-win plateau. He won 29 games the 2 years before the war and if you take into consideration the half year he missed in 1945 and the fact he looked like he was no where near a downtrend in his career before the broken knee cap in 1946, then 27 wins certainly would have a certainty.

Taking Ruffing's place in the #3 slot during the war was Hank Borowy, who moved up from #4. He went 14–9 in 1943 with a 2.82 ERA, not far off Red's performance. Butch Wensloff would replace Ruffing in the rotation sliding into the #4 slot.

Wensloff would have a 2.54 ERA himself in his rookie year of '43, finishing 13–11. He would be sent into the battle two years later.

1943 Washington Senators
84–69–13.5 GB

1941	1942	1943
1B-Mickey Vernon	Vernon	Vernon
2B-Jimmy Bloodworth	Ellis Clary	Gerry Priddy
SS-Cecil Travis	John Sullivan	Sullivan
3B-George Archie	Bobby Estalella	Clary
OF-Buddy Lewis	Bruce Campbell	Case
OF-Doc Cramer	Stan Spence	Spence
OF-George Case	Case	Bob Johnson
CA-Jake Early	Early	Early
PI-Dutch Leonard	Bobo Newsom	Wynn
PI-Sid Hudson	Hudson	Dutch Leonard
PI-Ken Chase	Early Wynn	Milo Candini
PI-Steve Sundra	Alex Carrasquel	Mickey Haefner

A 22 game improvements despite losing 11 players into the armed service lifted the Washington Senators from 7th place into the spot right behind the Yankees.

When you look at the list of the players that left, you find one of the reasons for the increase is they only lost one starter, Bruce Campbell, who left midway in the 1942 season, and replaced him with George Case. They also acquired a legitimate major league star in Bob Johnson.

On the mound, the team lost only one starter in Sid Hudson who was ably replaced by veteran Dutch Leonard as the number 2 pitcher. There were no Rizzutos, Williams or DiMaggios that left.

Offensively, the Senators scored 12 more runs than the year before, which was significant when you take into account the fact that runs scored were way down across both leagues. George Case led the way, scoring 102 of Washington's entire output of 666 runs, hitting .294 and leading the American League in steals with 61.

As good as the offense was, the reason the Senators improved so dramatically can be found in their pitching staff. As a team they reduced their team ERA from 4.59 in 1942 all the way down to 3.19. They were led by future Hall of Famer Early Wynn, who after a disappointing 1942 showed what he eventually became, posting an 18–12 mark with a 2.91 ERA.

Another reason for the vast pitching improvement was a shrewd trade they made with the Browns getting war ball great Johnny Niggeling and Harland Clift for Ellis Clary, Ox Miller and cash. Niggeling, whose best years came during the war years, went 4–2 in 6 starts giving up only 27 hits in 51 innings with a 0.88 ERA. In three of the six starts, he threw shutouts.

It was only a one year run in the first division for the Senators, but it proved that one of the key strategies to succeed in war ball was to pray you didn't lose any valuable players.

Who Left for the War	*Who Replaced Them*
CA-Al Evans	
SS-Frank Croucher	
3B-Stan Galle	
OF-Bruce Campbel	George Case/Bob Johnson
OF-Al Kvasnak	
PI-Lou Bevil	
PI-Sid Hudson	Dutch Leonard
PI-Bill Kennedy	
PI-Walt Masterson	
PI-Phil McCullough	
PI-Maxie Wilson	

Al Evans— Before entering the Navy in 1942, Al Evans was finally getting some significant playing time, getting 223 at-bats after accumulating only 205 in his first three seasons.

A 2 for 22 performance in 1944 after his comeback gave way to a 6-year period in which Smith was a semi-regular catcher for Washington, batting between .235 and .271. He led the league in fielding in 1949 with a .992 percentage although he had–16 fielding runs.

Boston picked him up in 1951 where Smith went 3 for 24 and was gone from the majors.

Frank Croucher—" Dingle" had an every other year inconsistent career for the four years that he played in the majors.

The first season in 1939, Frank started at short for the Tigers, hitting .269 before going 6 for 57 (a .105 average) the next season.

Year number 3 would find Croucher getting back his starting position hitting .254 in 489 at-bats.

The Senators would pick him up with Bruce Campbell in 1942 for Johnny Bloodworth and Doc Cramer. A sore arm would limit "Dingle" to 65 at-bats, hitting .277, before going into the Navy.

Stan Galle— a 2 for 18 mark in 1942 would be both the beginning and the end for the man born Stanley Joseph Galazewski.

Bruce Campbell — The Chicago native would have a fine 13-year career before he became a Washington Senator, hitting an impressive .290 primarily for the Browns, Indians and Tigers.

Coming up with the White Sox in 1930, Campbell was dealt to the Browns with Bump Hadley for Red Kress. The move would certainly be a shrewd one for St. Louis as he would have two of his most productive offensive seasons with 14 homers, 87 RBIs and a .287 average in 1934 before breaking the century mark in RBIs the following year with 106 and a career high 16 rockets.

Cleveland came calling next, giving up Johnny Burnett, Bob Weiland and cash for the left-handed slugger in 1935. With the Tribe, Campbell would enjoy three consecutive .300 seasons, his only three, not including the .500 and .412 marks he posted in 27 at-bats his first two years with the White Sox.

Illness limited him to only 308 at-bats in 1935 although hitting .325, and it continued to plague him in '36 as he only accumulated 172 at-bats, again eclipsing .300 with a .372 mark. He recovered for the 1937 season, posting a .301 average.

After a couple more seasons with Cleveland and Detroit, the Senators picked him up after the 1941 campaign along with Croucher.

The Army Air Corps would come calling midway in his only season

Bruce Campbell played for the Washington Senators when the .290 lifetime hitter answered his call to arms after the 1942 campaign. When he returned there was no spot on the team for him. He challenged Clark Griffith and eventually won, being awarded the equivalent of his major league salary in 1942. Courtesy of Photo File, Inc.

in Washington as he hit .278 in 378 at-bats.

As nice a career as Campbell had, he is most noted for the stance he took against baseball after the war ended. Irritated with the fact that he was cut in spring training upon his return from the military, Campbell hooked on with the minor league Buffalo Bisons and went to the American Veterans of World War II to help him file a grievance against the majors and retrieve the difference between his $9,000 salary and the one he was receiving from the Bisons. Buffalo then released him. He announced his formal complaint soon afterwards and wanted to push the issue so other GI's wouldn't receive the same treatment.

Senator owner Clark Griffith met with him and came up with a compromise, getting him a spot in Minneapolis and making up the $5,000 difference in salary. [44]

Getting back to the business of wartime ball, George Case would move from right to left, replacing Campbell, which he did so successfully, leading the AL in steals for the 5th consecutive year with 61, scoring 102 runs and hitting .294, an All-Star performance. The man who was named for our first president, George Washington Case hit .250 and .294 his last two war seasons ending his career with a .282 average and 349 stolen bases.

Bob Johnson, a 7 time All-Star, who hit .296 and 2,051 hits in 13 years, was obtained by Washington for Bobby Estallela to replace Case in right and in essence replacing Campbell in the outfield. His time in Washington was disappointing as he had career lows with 7 homers, 63 RBIs and a .265

average. The Senators unfortunately sold him to Boston the next season where he came back to life with marks of 17–106–.324 and a league leading .431 on base percentage.

Al Kvasnak — In 1942 Kvasnak had a career best 2–11 performance. It was his career best because it was his only season in the majors.

Lou Bevil — Bevil went 0 for 1 in his 1-year major league career in 1942, giving up 11 walks and 9 hits in 9⅔ innings with a 6.52 ERA.

Sid Hudson — Coming out of the blocks fast in his career, Hudson reeled off a 17–16 rookie season in 1940 before being selected to two consecutive All-Star appearances, then going off to serve his country.

He would come back in 1946, pitch 9 more seasons, but except for a 14–14 record in 1950, would never sport another winning record again. He would have a 3.60 ERA in 1946, and then would range between 4.09 and 5.88 the next five years.

Midway in 1952, after a year in which he went 5–12 giving up a .302 OBA, Gordon was dealt to the Red Sox for Randy Gumpert and Walt Masterson. The Tennessee righty would go 9–13 as a part time starter the next two seasons, before ending his major league career with a .406 winning percentage and a 104–152 record.

Veteran pitcher Dutch Leonard replaced Hudson, who left for the military after a 1942 season, in which he went 10–17 with a 4.36 ERA. It's actually a misnomer that Leonard replaced him, as Dutch was the number 1 pitcher in 1941, breaking his ankle early in the '42 season and was limited to 5 starts.

Leonard finished the '43 season with an All-Star appearance despite his 11–13 record and a 3.28 ERA. Emil "Dutch" Leonard would finish the war years with a 31–21 record in '44 and '45, including a great 17–7–2.13 year in 1945. He would go on another 7 years compiling a lifetime 191–181 record.

Bill Kennedy — After a less than imposing 0–1–8.00 ERA start to his career in 1942, Bill Kennedy would return after his stint in the Armed Forces to pitch 23 games between 1946 and 1947. After 6.00 and 8.10 ERAs respectively, Kennedy would be out of the majors.

Walt Masterson — Masterson had a 14-year career that was as up and down as a nasty roller coaster, but equally as deceptive.

His final mark was 78–100, yet he had an impressive 1649⅔/1613 IP/H ratio. Very impressive when you consider he had a .438 winning percentage. Such was the prize for pitching with poor teams.

One prime example was 1940, Walt's second season. He finished 3–13, a pathetic .188 winning percentage, yet had a 130⅓/128 IP/H and a .257 OBA.

He returned halfway during the season in 1945 and had a 1.08 ERA in 25 innings. When he returned, Masterson was mainly a reliever, but made two All-Star appearances in 1947 and 1948 despite records of 12–16 and 8–15. Again hidden in those records were good OBAs of .234 and .247.

Masterson was dealt to Boston in 1949 for Sam Mele and Mickey Harris. He would have a cumulative 15–11 record in his 3½ years in the Red Sox bullpen, before the Senators got him back with Randy Gumpert for Sid Hudson.

The Philadelphia righty would have one more good season in 1953, going 10–12, a 3.63 ERA and another nice .232 OBA. Three years later he ended his major league career with Detroit.

Phil McCullough— McCullough's trip to the majors lasted one game in 1942. He gave up 5 hits and 2 walks in 3 innings of work.

Max Wilson — Wilson had a very tough rookie year for the Phillies in 1940, giving up 16 hits and 13 runs in 7 innings of work. He was much more impressive his next season in the big leagues, which was 1946 for the Senators. This time it took him 12⅔ innings to give up 16 hits. His ERA fell from 12.86 to 7.11; nonetheless it was his last season.

1943 Cleveland Indians
82–71–15.5 GB

1941	1942	1943
1B-Hal Trosky	Les Fleming	Mickey Rocco
2B-Ray Mack	Mack	Mack
SS-Lou Boudreau	Boudreau	Boudreau
3B-Ken Keltner	Keltner	Keltner
OF-Jeff Heath	Oris Hockert	Roy Cullenbine
OF-Roy Weatherly	Weatherly	Hockett
OF-Gee Walker	Heath	Heath
CA-Rollie Hemsley	Otto Denning	Buddy Rosar
PI-Bob Feller	Bagby	Bagby
PI-Al Milner	Mel Harder	Smith
PI-Al Smith	Smith	Allie Reynolds
PI-Jim Bagby	Chubby Dean	Harder

Cleveland was another club that improved, not because of an influx of talent, but because they were lucky enough to keep the military losses to minimum, losing no starters to the cause.

Finishing on the plus side of .500 with an 82–71 record, 7 games better than the year before, the Indians lost only seven players to the military. The three most important were Jim Hegan, Bob Lemon and Eddie Robinson. They were all very early in their careers and had little effect on the club's total performance at this time.

Lemon was the only Hall of Fame member of the group and was still an infielder, three years away from beginning the pitching career that would eventually send him off to Cooperstown.

Like most other teams that improved during this low scoring season of 1943, they did it by maintaining their offense, scoring 10 more runs than in 1942, and improving themselves significantly on the mound, lowering their team ERA from 3.60 to 3.15.

Jeff Heath led the way offensively, smacking 18 homers and knocking in 79. One nice deal that the Tribe pulled off did help the team at the plate, acquiring catcher Buddy Rosar and outfielder Roy Cullenbine from the Yankees for Roy Weatherly and Oscar Grimes. Rosar and Cullenbine both contributed, hitting .283 and .289 respectively, numbers 1 and 3 on the club.

On the rubber, 35-year-old Al Smith was the king, as the southpaw went 17–7 with a 2.55 ERA. Allie Reynolds led the league in strikeouts with 151. One of the Tribe's best hurlers, Mel Harder, would break his wrist during the season.

Although Cleveland would only lose seven players to the war before the season, four would be selected during the year as Hank Edwards, Gene Woodling, Pete Center and 1942's # 4 starter Chubby Dean all were taken by Uncle Sam.

Who Left for the War	Who Replaced Them
CA-Jim Hegan	
1B-Eddie Robinson	
3B-Bob Lemon	
OF-Buster Mills	
PI-Harry Eisenstat	
PI-Tom Ferrick	
PI-Joe Krakauskas	

Jim Hegan — When he left for the military after the 1942 season, Jim Hegan had logged only 1½ seasons in the majors, a total of 217 at-bats. When he came back, he went on to play 15 more seasons and become one of the greatest defensive catchers the game has ever seen.

Despite only hitting a career .228, Hegan made 5 All-Star teams, including 4 in a row between 1949 and 1952 when he hit .224, .219, .238 and .225 respectively. It wasn't the bat that he was truly appreciated for, but his spectacular defensive play.

Hegan would finish his time in the big leagues with an impressive 149 fielding runs, 44th on the all time list and second among catchers to Pop Snyder, leading the circuit twice in fielding percentage in 1954 and 1955.

Jim would occasionally show glimpses of power as he did for the 1948 world champs, smacking 14 shots. He also accumulated 22 fielding runs that year.

After a run of 11 consecutive years starting behind the plate, Hegan would be reduced to a backup role in 1957. He would then make the rounds to Detroit, Philadelphia, San Francisco and Chicago, before retiring after 43 at-bats with the Cubs in 1960.

Eddie Robinson— The 4 time All-Star would end up having a very productive 13 year career for the Indians, White Sox, Senators, A's, Yankees, Tigers and Orioles, but like Hegan and Lemon, his star would not shine until after his military service was complete.

In his one pre-induction season in 1942, Robinson would go 1 for 8. He cracked the starting lineup in 1947 and would hit 16 homers with 83 RBIs for the 1948 championship Indian club.

The first of many trades Eddie was involved in turned out to be a good one for Cleveland as the Indians acquired Early Wynn and Mickey Vernon from Washington for Robinson, Joe Haynes and Eddie Klieman.

Robinson made his first All-Star appearance in 1949, hitting 18 homers with a .294 average, but it was after a trade with the White Sox that he really took off. Nineteen fifty-one and 1952 were Eddie's banner seasons as he hit 29 homers, 117 RBIs and a .282 average the first season and 22–104–.296 the next, both times being selected again for the All-Star team.

He would be shipped to the A's in 1953 where he continued his good hitting ways, breaking the 100 RBI barrier again with 102.

The Yanks came calling next in an 11-player deal that included Vic Power. Thinking Robinson would be a good fit, the 33-year-old Texas native began a downtrend in his career, hitting only 3 homers. He would rebound a bit in 1955, cracking 16 in only 173 at-bats, but that was it. After two more seasons with five different teams, Eddie Robinson's major league career came to an end.

Bob Lemon— Brought up as a third baseman in 1941, Robert Granville Lemon had little success in his chosen profession, going a combined 1 for 9 in his first two major league seasons. It was in his stint in the Navy when Lemon's baseball altering moment occurred. While playing with his service team and their three star pitchers were hurt, Manager Billy Herman decided to put him on the mound. Bob had impressed enough people that he was named to pitch in the service All-Star series.[45]

When he returned, the Indians moved him to the outfield where Lemon continued his struggles. It was at that point when some players, including Ted Williams, remembered how he pitched in the military and convinced skipper Lou Boudreau to give him a shot on the mound. A reluctant Lemon agreed to the move, which proved to be a sound decision, probably saving his major league career.[46]

Lemon would reel off seven consecutive All-Star appearances, seven 20-win seasons (including 1950, 1954 and 1955 when he led the AL) and a 4-time leader in TPI in 1948, 1949, 1954 and 1956.

His best year was his 23–7 masterpiece in 1954 with a 2.72 ERA and a 5th place finish in the MVP voting.

After a final 20 win season in 1956, Lemon's career would come crashing as he lasted only two more seasons, combining for a 6–12 record in 1957 and 1958. With a 207–128 career mark, Lemon would be honored with his induction to Cooperstown in 1976.

Despite the fact he lost three years to the war, Lemon would probably be the only player who couldn't argue that the war cost him numbers or hurt his career. Had he not gotten the opportunity to pitch in the service, chances are he would have been remembered as a little used outfielder/third baseman, who was just a blip on the baseball scenery. Most likely, you would have never seen his plaque in the Hall of Fame.

Buster Mills — "Bus" Mills played seven years in the majors and had the dubious distinction of playing for six different teams his first six seasons. The only one that had him for two years would be the Indians.

His first season in Cleveland was 1942 when he hit .277, his second after the war in 1946 when Mills came up 22 times. Before that, he came up in 1934, playing for the Cards, Dodgers, Red Sox, Browns and Yanks before heading to the Tribe.

The Bus did have two seasons that he started, the first in 1937 with Boston, hitting .295 with 7 homers, the second in 1938 with the Browns where he hit .285. Despite his many travels, Mills would end up with a very respectable .287 career average.

Harry Eisenstat — Brooklyn's Harry Eisenstat came up with his hometown club in 1935 for three partial seasons and never had an OBA under .300. The Tigers would be his next stop and Eisenstat would have his best season in 1938, going 9–6 with a 3.73 ERA in the Motor City.

He would then have the distinction of being traded to Cleveland with cash for aging superstar Earl Averill. The southpaw would stay with the Indians for the duration of his career. In 1942 he had a career low 2.45 ERA in 47⅔ innings despite his inflated .304 OBA. Eisenstat would then go off to serve, never returning to the big leagues.

Tom Ferrick — The one thing Tom Ferrick would not lack in his career was the mileage he would put on his suitcase. In his nine-year career, Ferrick would end up with the A's, Tribe, Browns, Senators, Yankees and Senators once again.

He began in the majors in 1941 throwing a career high 119 innings before the Indians got him on waivers. It would prove to be a nice pickup.

In what was probably his marquee season in 1942, Ferrick gave up only 56 hits in 81⅓ innings, a low .200 OBA and a miniscule 1.99 ERA, also a career low. He would go into the Navy after that season where he would pitch on the Great Lakes Naval team with the likes of Bob Feller and Virgil Trucks. After the war, Ferrick bounced around from team to team, having some success as a full time reliever until the Yanks picked him up in June of 1950 in an eight man swap with the Browns that included Stuffy Stirnweiss and $150,000. He would go 8–4 in 30 games for the world champs. The true highlight of the season was throwing one scoreless inning and picking up a win in Game 3 of the World Series.

Washington would then acquire the Lima, Pennsylvania, native and he would be out of the majors after the 1952 season.

Joe Krakauskas — Baseball players are not an export that Canada produces excesses of, but pitcher Joe Krakauskas was one of them.

Hailing from the city of Montreal, Krakauskas broke into the big leagues in 1937 with the Washington Senators. Joe had a good sophomore year in 1938 when he held opponents to a .220 average, giving up only 99 hits in 121⅓ innings and 104 strikeouts.

When Krakauskas got his one chance to be a regular starter, going 11–17 in 29 starts in 1939, it would prove to be his high water mark. Nineteen forty was not so kind as he finished 1–6 with a 6.44 ERA, then being sent to the Tribe for future manager and Jackie Robinson nemesis Ben Chapman.

The young Canadian would go 1–2 in 15 games for Cleveland in the two years before his stint in the armed forces.

Nineteen forty-six was Krakauskas' comeback season, although he couldn't regain his early career magic going 2–5 with a 5.51 ERA. It proved to be the end of his major league stay.

It was a truly curious season for the White Sox. They lost 13 players to the military before the season, and unlike the Indians and Senators, they lost some pretty important ones, three everyday players and a starting pitcher who led the league in ERA. Two more players, including Don Kolloway, the starting second baseman, would leave before the 1943 season had come to its conclusion. If you put it all together, the last thing one would expect is the club would actually improve over the previous season, but that's exactly what happened as they finished a whopping 16 games better at 82–72, ½ game out of third place.

1943 Chicago White Sox
82–72–16 GB

1941	1942	1943
1B-Joe Kuhel	Kuhel	Kuhel
2B-Bill Knickerbocker	Don Kolloway	Kolloway
SS-Luke Appling	Appling	Appling
3B-Dario Lodigiani	Bob Kennedy	Ralph Hodgin
OF-Taffy Wright	Wally Moses	Moses
OF-Mike Kreevich	Hoag	Thurman Tucker
OF-Myril Hoag	Wright	Guy Curtright
CA-Mike Tresh	Tresh	Tresh
PI-Thornton Lee	John Humphries	Humphries
PI-Eddie Smith	Smith	Dietrich
PI-Johnny Rigney	Bill Dietrich	Orval Grove
PI-Ted Lyons	Lyons	Smith

Unlike the other teams that improved, the Sox did pick it up offensively, led by shortstop Luke Appling who had a monster season, leading the American League in hitting with a .328 average. He also had 80 RBIs, which was the best on Chicago by a wide margin (Ralph Hodgin, who replaced Bob Kennedy at third, had 50 to finish in second). Hodgin also had a nice season, hitting .314.

Thurman Tucker and Guy Curtright did an adequate job filling in for Myril Hoag and Taffy Wright, hitting .235 and .291 respectively.

As a team, they only picked up one point in their collective batting averages — .247 to .246 — but were able to score 35 more runs, a significant amount when you consider the lack of run production in 1943 compared to the previous season.

This wasn't to suggest they didn't improve on the mound; they shaved off .3 from their team ERA. Ted Lyons, who led the AL in ERA in 1942, was replaced nicely by Orval Grove, who led the staff with a 15–9 mark and a 2.75 ERA. Gordon Maltzberger was the top man out of the pen, leading the junior circuit with 14 saves. He also had an impressive ERA of 2.46.

It truly was a curious year. Whether or not it was superior scouting or just plain dumb luck, the White Sox truly had a year to be proud of.

George Dickey — Dickey started with the Boston Red Sox in 1935 and 1936, going 1 for 34 in his first two seasons. "Skeets" would be gone from the majors until 1941 when he reappeared for the White Sox, hitting .200 in 55 at-bats.

After a .233 performance in 59 games for the 1942 season, Dickey was off to the service. He returned in 1946 for two more years, getting a career high 211 at-bats and 27 RBIs his last season in the majors in 1947.

Jake Jones — Struggling before going into the military, Jones was 3 for

Who Left for the War	Who Replaced Them
CA-George Dickey	
1B-Jake Jones	
2B-Roy Schalk	
SS-Leo Wells	
3B-Bob Kennedy	Ralph Hodgin
3B-Dario Lodigiani	
OF-Val Heim	
OF-Myril Hoag	Thurman Tucker
OF-Dave Philley	
OF-Sammy West	
OF-Taffy Wright	Guy Curtwright
PI-Ted Lyons	Eddie Smith/Orval Grove
PI-Len Perme	
PI-Johnny Rigney	
PI-Ed Weiland	

31 in '41 and '42. After two reserve seasons in 1946 and 1947 upon his return, Jones was sent to Boston for Rudy York, where he came alive hitting 16 homers with 76 RBIs the rest of the '47 campaign (it gave him a total of 19–96 for the entire season).

He would accumulate only 105 at-bats in 1948, his final major league year.

Roy Schalk— Schalk was 3 for 12 in his rookie season of 1932 for the Yankees; he would not reappear in the majors for 12 years.

After serving one year in the military in 1943, Schalk would take over second base for the wartime White Sox, hitting .220 and .248 in 1944 and 1945. He would not return to play in the postwar era.

Leo Wells— Wells hit .194 in his rookie year of 1942. He would play only one more season, in 1946, after he returned from the armed service, hitting .189 in 127 at-bats for Chicago.

Bob Kennedy— Breaking in with the Sox in 1939, Kennedy would crack the starting lineup in 1940 at the young age of 19, hitting .252. Falling off to .206 the next season, Kennedy would regain his position in 1942, hitting .231, leaving before the season came to a close to serve Uncle Sam.

Kennedy returned in 1946 and played with Chicago for 2½ seasons before being sent to Cleveland in the middle of 1948 for Al Gettel and Pat Seerey. It would give Bob a chance to play in his only World Series, going 1 for 2 with an RBI for the champs.

His days with the Indians would be his best as he hit .276 and .291 in 1949 and 1950, slamming a career high 9 homers in both seasons.

Kennedy stuck with Cleveland until 1954 when he was sent off to Baltimore for Jim Dyck. After that he bounced back to Chicago, Detroit and Brooklyn where he finished his career hitting .129 in 31 at-bats in 1957.

Robert Daniel Kennedy ended up with a 16-year career batting average of .254.

Ralph Hodgin took over for Kennedy at third with Jimmy Grant in 1943 and 1944. Offensively, Hodgin was an improvement, hitting .314 and .295 respectively, splitting time at third and the outfield. He would join the service himself in 1945. Jimmy Grant played 51 games at third in 1943, hitting .259, before being sold to Cleveland in midseason.

Dario Lodigiani — Lodigiani began his career in Philadelphia with the A's, hitting .280 and .260 in 214 games between 1938 and 1940.

He was sent to the White Sox in 1942 for Jack Knott, hitting .239 in 1942 and .280 in 59 games in '42. Dario would return in '46, hitting .245 in 155 at-bats before leaving the majors a .260 lifetime hitter.

Val Heim — A 9 for 45 performance with a double and triple and 7 RBIs in 1942 would constitute Heim's entire career.

Myril Hoag — Hoag enjoyed a 13-year career that included stops with the Yankees, Browns, White Sox and the Indians.

After 5 seasons as a backup in New York between 1931 and 1936, Hoag broke in as a semi-regular in '37, hitting .301 in 362 at-bats. A year later, he was sent to the Browns with Joe Glenn, for Oral Hildebrand and Buster Mills. His first season with the Browns, Hoag made the All-Star team, hitting .295 with a career high 10 homers and 75 RBIs.

The White Sox purchased Hoag in 1941, making him the starting right fielder hitting .255 before moving him to center the next season where he hit .240.

He went into the armed service the next season where he remained until 1944 when Myril returned to the Windy City. Hoag was sold to the Tribe early in the '44 season and ended his trip in the big leagues a year later hitting .211 for Cleveland.

Replacing him in center was Thurman Tucker. Tucker was in his official rookie year after coming up 24 times in 1942. He hit only .235, a little off Hoag's pace, but would be selected to the All-Star game in 1944, hitting .287, while leading all AL outfielders in fielding percentage at .991 as he was an improvement over Hoag in the field, accumulating 18 fielding runs that season. Myril's career high was only 0 as he had -67 for his career.

Dave Philley — Dave Philley would come up a grand total of 9 times before he joined the Army in 1943. When he returned, he would become the White Sox' everyday center fielder by 1947.

Nineteen forty-eight and 1949 would be Philley's best seasons in the Windy City, hitting .287 and .286 respectively. He also was sharp in the field in 1948, accumulating 15 fielding runs. In 1950, Dave showed a little power, smacking a career high 14 homers.

The following year he was sent to the A's with Gus Zernial for Paul Lehrner and the great Minnie Minoso. Philley broke .300 for the first time in 1953 as a regular hitting .303.

He went to Cleveland next in 1954, hitting 12 homers, although slumping to .226 for the AL champions. Philley played in his first World Series that season going 1 for 8.

Nineteen fifty-five began an odyssey for Dave that would take him to Baltimore, Chicago (the Sox again), Detroit, Philadelphia (the Phils), San Francisco and Baltimore once again over an 8-year period, finishing things in 1962 as a .270 hitter with 1,700 total hits.

Probably the highlight of Philley's career was his record of 9 consecutive pinch hits between 1958 and '59.

Sammy West— Sammy was a well rounded player, as impressive a center fielder as he was a hitter, leading the AL twice in fielding percentage, accumulating double digits in fielding runs on 5 different occasions with a total of 93 in his 16 year career. On the offensive side, West would finish only one point off the magical .300 plateau at .299 ending with 1,838 hits.

Breaking into the starting lineup in 1928, West hit .302 while leading the junior circuit in fielding percentage at .996.

Nineteen thirty-one was his greatest season, hitting a career best .333, knocking in 91, also tops in his time in the majors. West would also accumulate another career high that season in fielding runs with 21.

Slumping a little in '32, although posting good numbers with a .287 average and 83 RBIs, Sammy was sent packing to the Browns with Lloyd Browns, Carl Reynolds and $20,000 for the great Goose Goslin, Fred Schulte and Lefty Stewart.

The left-hander would spend 5½ years in St. Louis, making four All-Star teams, hitting .300 on four occasions and leading the league in fielding percentage a second time at .989 in 1935.

West was returned to Washington in 1938, starting for one year before being reduced to a backup roll in 1940 and 1941. He would go to Chicago where he hit .232 in 151 at-bats. Sammy went into the Army the next season and came back as a coach, his playing days complete.

The war probably had no effect on West's career. With the minimal at-bats he was receiving by that point in time, it's doubtful he would have gotten the 162 hits needed to eclipse 2,000. With his batting average dropping as the years went on, the chances of him raising that career mark one point were probably remote.

Taffy Wright— Taft Wright was a player whose time away from the game during the war might have cost him the greatness he might have truly deserved.

He was a .311 hitter over the course of his 9-year major league career, but when he went into the Air Force in 1942, Taffy was coming off consecutive seasons of .350, .309, .337, .322 and .333. There's no telling how far Wright would have gone with his three years he lost to the war back.

In his rookie year of 1938, Taffy hit a career high .350 with a .517 slugging percentage for Washington. After his .309, 93 RBI season in 1939, Wright was sent to the White Sox with Pete Appleton for Gee Walker. It was a fortuitous trade for Chicago as the North Carolina native hit .337 his first season in 1940 with 88 RBIs. He would top that in '41 with his best overall year, hitting a career high 10 homers with 97 RBIs and a .322 average.

When Taft returned from the Air Force in '46, the momentum was gone as he slumped to .275. He reached .324 in 1947 but slumped the next year to .279. He was sent to the A's, where he finished his career hitting an abysmal .235 in 1949.

Taffy Wright was truly a casualty of war as the momentum he had going by 1942 was completely gone by the time he returned in 1946.

Replacing Wright in right field was Guy Curtright. Curtright was a true war ball player, having three solid years between 1943 and 1945, hitting a respectable .291 in 1943 — not quite to Wright's level though.

After the players returned for the war, Guy became a part time player, hitting .200 in 55 at-bats his final season in 1946.

Ted Lyons— He was a pitcher that lasted 21 years in the game, all with the White Sox, and was 46 years old when he pitched his last game. Lyons was a pitcher who injured his arm in 1930 and went from being known for his fastball to a man with a nasty knuckler, going on to play 11 more seasons.[47]

After he was brought up to Chicago in 1923, Lyons would not get off to a Hall of Fame start, going 12–11 in his first full season in 1924 with a horrendous 216⅓/279 IP/H ratio and a miserable 72/52 BB/K mark with a .322 OBA. The next season would be dramatically different.

Ted led the league in wins with 21 and shutouts with 5. His ERA dropped from 4.87 to 3.26. The Hall of Famer had arrived.

Nineteen twenty-seven would turn out to be Lyons' marquee season as he went 22–14, again leading the AL in wins. He also had a 2.84 ERA and a TPI that led the junior circuit with a 5.2 mark.

After winning 20 games for a third time in 6 years, Lyons hurt his arm in spring training and had a miserable 1931 campaign going 4–6. Ted would learn the knuckle ball, among other pitches, and go from a blazer to a junkball specialist. After struggling to a 31–49 record the next 3 years, Lyons found his groove again in 1938 with a 15–8 record and

3.02 ERA. Four years later in 1939, the Hall of Famer would receive his only All-Star game selection with a 14–6, 2.76 ERA season.

At 41 years old in 1942 and the great game being depleted by the war losses, Lyons would have one last big season with a 14–6 record and a career low, league-leading ERA of 2.10. He topped the AL in TPI for a second time with a 4.0 mark. Amazingly at 42, Ted would enlist in the Marines and see fighting up close and personal in the South Pacific.[48]

In 1946, Lyons would be effective for the last 5 games of his career with a 2.32 ERA and .235 OBA, yet losing 4 of his 5 complete games. Ted then retired and took over the reins of the club as manager. He was elected to the Hall of Fame in 1955 with 260 wins.

What did the war cost Lyons? His shot at 300 wins would have been a little bit of a reach, but still very possible. He had won 38 games in his previous 3 seasons, although his 14 wins in 1942 came in a war season. The reason one may believe he still had a chance to reach that level was he was still an effective pitcher in 1946 when he returned.

The other factor that comes into play, when considering Ted's shot at 300 wins, was the fact you don't have to assume what Lyons would have done if there were no war. He made the decision to go into the service, he could have pitched in three war ball seasons if he would have chosen, which would have given him a even that much more a realistic shot at 300.

Eddie Smith replaced Lyons at the #4 spot in the rotation in '43. He was 11–11 with a 3.69 ERA, much off Lyons '42 pace. Smith had been the # 2 man in 1942 so it was Orval Grove that actually replaced him in the 4-man rotation. Grove would move in quite nicely, finishing 15–9 with a 2.75 ERA and .239 OBA.

Making the All-Star team in 1944, Grove would be 43–36 for the Sox during the war years and 20–37 in all other seasons, ending his 10-year major league career in 1949.

Len Perme— The Cleveland native had an impressive short war season in 1942, giving up only 5 hits in 13 innings. After the war, he threw only 4⅓ innings in 1946, giving up 4 runs, 6 hits and 7 walks his last season.

Johnny Rigney— Rigney came up with the Sox in 1937, becoming a permanent member of the rotation in 1939 going 15–8 in 29 starts. He would follow that up going 27–31 in 1940 and 1941 with 3.11 and 3.84 ERAs, respectively.

Getting off to a 3–3 start, giving up a miniscule .185 OBA in 59 innings, Rigney was called to the armed service where he played on the Great Lakes Naval team.

There would be a 5–5 record upon his return in 1946 and an impressive

1.95 ERA in 50⅔ innings in 1947, but that would be it, 1947 would be his last season.

Ed Weiland— Edwin Nicholas Weiland was called up in 1940 tossing 14⅓ innings. His last year before the war in 1942, Weiland gave up 18 hits and 3 walks in 9⅔ innings. He would not return to the majors after the war.

1943 Detroit Tigers
78–76–20 GB

1941	1942	1943
1B-Rudy York	York	York
2B-Charlie Gehringer	Jimmy Bloodworth	Bloodworth
SS-Frank Croucher	Billy Hitchcock	Joe Hoover
3B-Pinky Higgins	Higgins	Higgins
OF-Bruce Campbell	Ned Harris	Harris
OF-Barney McCosky	Doc Cramer	Cramer
OF-Rip Radcliff	McCoskey	Dick Wakefield
CA-Birdie Tebbetts	Tebbetts	Paul Richards
PI-Bobo Newsom	Al Benton	Trout
PI-Hal Newhouser	Dizzy Trout	Virgil Trucks
PI-Tommy Bridges	Hal White	Newhouser
PI-Johnny Gorsica	Newhouser	White

The Tigers used the 1943 season for continuing to build a powerhouse pitching staff and trying to retool their offense in an effort to get over the loss of Hank Greenberg and continue their quest back to the top of the American League standings.

Detroit led the AL in average, hitting at a .261 clip. They were led by Rudy York's monster season in which he topped the junior circuit in homers, 34, and RBIs with 118.

Dick Wakefield, in his official rookie season, replaced Barney McCoskey and had a wonderful year, leading the league in hits with 200 and doubles with 38 while hitting .316.

The team made a significant improvement in runs scored, getting 43 more than the previous season.

Detroit's pitching staff again finished second in the league ERA race leading the AL in strikeouts with 706. Other than the Yankees and Browns, they were the only other American League team with more strikeouts than walks with a 706/549 K/BB ratio.

Dizzy Trout was tops in the circuit in wins with 20 and sophomore Virgil Trucks was a key element improving from his rookie year with a 16–10 record. Hall of Famer Hal Newhouser, who would have a monster 1944, finished the year a miserable 8–17, although his record wasn't indicative of his performance. He had a very respectable 196/163 IP/H ratio and struck out 144.

Detroit's war losses would be heavy, as they lost 11 players including Hall of Fame second baseman Charlie Gehringer, who was at the tail end of his career, starting catcher Birdie Tebbetts, pitcher Al Benton, outfielder Barney McCosky and shortstop Billy Hitchcock. Through it all, the replacements did a very adequate job of filling in, and the pitching staff was turning into one of the powerhouses in the league. Better times were coming.

Who Left for the War	*Who Replaced Them*
CA-Hank Riebe	
CA-Birdie Tebbetts	Paul Richards
IN-Murray Franklin	
2B-Charlie Gehringer	
2B-Dutch Meyer	
SS-Billy Hitchcock	Joe Hoover
SS-Johnny Lipon	
OF-Hoot Evers	
OF-Barney McCosky	Dick Wakefield
OF-Bob Patrick	
PI-Al Benton	Dizzy Trout/Virgil Trucks

Hank Riebe— Harvey "Hank" Riebe played four seasons as a backup catcher for Detroit. His rookie year in 1942 was also his best offensive season, hitting .314 in 35 at-bats before going into the service.

After a 0 of 7 return in 1947, Riebe would hit only .194 and .182 respectively in 95 at-bats, his final seasons of 1948 and 1949.

Birdie Tebbetts— George Tebbetts, more commonly known as "Birdie," came up with the Tigers in 1936, hitting .303 in 33 at-bats. He broke into the starting lineup in 1939 and played in his one and only World Series the following season. After hitting .296 in 1940, Tebbetts went hitless in 11 at-bats for the AL champs.

Birdie would be selected to his first two All-Star games in 1941 and 1942, before being selected into the service.

Tebbetts returned to the Tigers in 1946 where he hit .243. He got off to a 5 for 53 start in '47 and was shipped off to the Red Sox for Hal Wagner. He would hit .299 the rest of the season for Boston.

Things improved greatly for Birdie as he was selected to his third and fourth All-Star games the next two seasons, hitting .280 and .270 in '48 and '49 respectively with a career high 68 RBIs in 1948.

Nineteen fifty would be Tebbetts' last season in Boston and it would be a fine year, hitting career highs in homers, 8, and average .310 in 268 at-bats. He was sold to Cleveland the following year and finished his career after the 1952 season with a .270 lifetime average and 1,000 hits on the dot.

Thirty-five-year-old Paul Richards took over for Tebbetts during the

war. He had been out of the majors since 1935 and came to the Tiger starting line hitting .220 in 1943.

Richards would hit .237 and .256 in '44 and '45, holding the job until
Birdie came back. When Tebbetts returned, Richards would hit only .201
in 139 at-bats his last year in the majors.

Murray Franklin— Murray "Moe" Franklin played two seasons for the
Tigers in 1941 and 1942, with the majority coming in '42 hitting .260 in
154 at-bats (he would come up only 10 times in '41) with 2 homers.

He served in the Navy and played with Hugh Casey and Pee Wee
Reese for the Naval Air Station team.[49] After he came back, he would not
play again in the majors.

Charlie Gehringer—"The Mechanical Man," as Charlie Gehringer was
called, had a wonderful 19-year career which included 2,839 hits, 1,427
RBIs, a .320 lifetime average, a .404 career on base percentage and a trip
to the Hall of Fame in 1949.

Charlie was called up in 1924, accumulating only 31 at-bats in two
years, before taking away the starting spot at second from Frank O'Rourke
in 1926. Three years later in 1929, Gehringer would have his first great
year leading the AL in runs, 131, hits, 215, doubles, 45, triples, 19, and fielding percentage at .975, the first of seven times he would lead the American League in that category. Charlie would also hit 13 homers and knock
in 106 with a .339 average that season. The 131 runs and 106 RBIs would
represent one of 12 and seven times he would top the century mark in
those respective categories in his career.

Nineteen thirty-three would represent Gehringer's first selection to
the All-Star game (it was the first game ever). It would be his first of six
selections in a row. Nineteen thirty-four was another wonderful year as
he hit .356 with a lifetime high of 127 RBIs, leading the league with 134
runs and 214 hits. Even more impressive was his .379 average in Detroit's
seven game loss to St. Louis in the World Series. Charlie would have
another great series the next season, hitting .375 in leading the Tigers to
the world championship over the Cubs.

After hitting 60 doubles in 1936, the sixth highest figure of all time,
Gehringer would get his only career batting title in '37, hitting .371 with
209 hits, the 7th and last time he would achieve the 200 hit plateau.

The Mechanical Man would hit .300 for the next three seasons, before
slumping to .220 in 1941. Gehringer rebounded a bit, hitting .267 in 1942,
but in a reduced role. Charlie then enlisted in the Navy where he achieved
the rank of Lieutenant Commander.[50] Gehringer played his last, as he
would not return after the war.

Losing time in the service really did not do anything to Gehringer's career stats. Had there been no war, Gehringer probably would have sat the bench in a reserve role as his career was all but done in 1942. It's doubtful he would have gotten enough at-bats to reach the 3,000 hit mark.

Regardless, he ended his career as one of the greatest second basemen of all time.

Dutch Meyer—After appearing for one game for the Cubs in 1937, Lambert Dalton Meyer got a chance to play with the Tigers in 1940. After two sub par years as the backup second baseman, Meyer would hit .327 in 56 at-bats for the '42 Detroit club, before going into the service.

He was traded to the Indians with Dan Ross and Roy Cullenbine before the 1945 season began and would have his greatest year ever, playing in 130 games, hitting .292 with 7 homers, 48 RBIs and a .418 slugging percentage, although registering -32 fielding runs during baseball's last wartime season.

Nineteen forty-six would prove to be Meyer's swan song, as he slumped to .232 and was out of the majors.

Billy Hitchcock—The much traveled William Clyde Hitchcock began his career as the Tigers regular shortstop in 1942, hitting only .211 in 280 at-bats with a sub par .944 fielding percentage before going off to the service.

He was immediately sold to Washington when he returned after 3 games in Detroit, hitting only .210 for the season. He was sent to St. Louis to play for the Browns the next season in 1947, but despite his move to second base, he only hit .222. After going to the Red Sox in 1948, his fourth team in four major league seasons, Hitchcock was sent to the A's in 1950 for Buddy Rosar, where he enjoyed his best success in the majors. He was moved to third in 1951 and responded with a .306 career high average, before trailing off to .246 in a lifetime best 407 at-bats in '52.

He was sent back to Detroit in 1953 where he ended his career ironically hitting .211, the same average he hit for the Tigers in his rookie season.

Joe Hoover moved in at short, replacing Hitchcock in the starting lineup during the war. He played three seasons in the majors, all during war seasons. His .243 average between '43 and '45 was a much more effective output than Hitchcock had in 1942. Defensively, he was about Billy's equal at the time, as Hitchcock would become much better later in his career. Although Hoover had a mediocre .939 percentage, he did accumulate 15 fielding runs in 1944.

When the war ended, so did Hoover's career, as he was out of the big leagues after 1945.

Johnny Lipon—"Skids," as he was known, was a backup shortstop in 1942, hitting only .191, although accumulating 7 fielding runs in only 34 games. When he returned, he would take over the starting shortstop spot in the post–Hitchcock Era in Detroit, hitting .290 his first full season with the Tigers in 1948.

Probably his finest season was in 1950 when he scored a career best 104 runs as well as lifetime tops in hitting, .293, and RBIs with 63. Two years later, "Skids" was dealt to the Red Sox in a huge trade with All-Star pitcher Dizzy Trout, Hall of Famer George Kell and Hoot Evers for Walt Dropo, Bill Wight, Fred Hatfield, Johnny Pesky and Don Lenhardt. He would endure a disappointing season, hitting only .211 but leading the league in fielding at .981.

After being bumped around from Boston to the Browns and finally the Reds, Lipon's career came to an end following a single at-bat in 1954.

Hoot Evers— Walter "Hoot" Evers would go hitless in 4 at-bats in his only season in 1941 before entering the military. When he returned, Evers would become a star shifting between left and center for the Tigers.

After a couple decent seasons in 1946 and 1947, Hoot broke out in a big way in the 1948 season, making his first All-Star appearance on the heels of a .314, 103 RBI season. As good as '48 was, 1950 proved to be Evers' high-water mark season as he made his second and final All-Star game leading the AL in fielding at .997 and triples with 11. Evers would also establish career highs with 100 runs, 170 hits, 35 doubles, 21 homers, 103 RBIs, a .408 on base percentage, a .323 average as well as a .551 slugging percentage. It would prove to be the beginning of the end.

Hoot would slump to .224 in 1951 before being sent to Boston as part of a mega deal (please refer to Johnny Lipon for details). The thought process for Boston was that Evers would come back to form and replace Ted Williams while the splendid splinter fought in Korea.[51] A broken finger limited him to a .264 average.

Evers would spiral down, going to the Giants, Tigers, Orioles, and Cleveland in his last three seasons, finishing with 1,055 hits, 98 homers and a .278 average.

What the war statistically cost Hoot was at best 100 homers. He really didn't get his career going in high gear until 1947. Nineteen forty-two through 1945 probably would have been minimal numbers. Nevertheless, it was certainly a career to be proud of.

Barney McCosky— As soon as McCosky hit center field, and later left in 1942, he became a regular in the Tigers' lineup, hitting .311 in 1939 with 20 steals.

The next year he really broke out in the Tigers' AL championship season, hitting .340 with a .408 on base percentage. He led the AL in hits with 200 and triples with 19. In the Fall Classic, Barney hit .304 in 23 at-bats and had a .467 on base percentage.

After two solid seasons, William "Barney" McCosky went into the military. In his return season in 1946 he slumped badly in his first 25 games, hitting .198 before being sent to the A's for George Kell. He would catch fire the rest of the season, hitting .354 for Philadelphia the rest of the way, and .318 overall.

McCosky hit .326 in 1948 before hurting his back in the off-season and retiring from the game.[52]

He came back in 1950, but was not the same player, hitting .240 in a part time role. Jumping from the A's to Cincinnati to the Tribe as a reserve, Barney retired for good after the 1953 season, accumulating 1,301 hits and a phenomenal .312 average.

The war didn't cost McCosky as much statistically as a displaced vertebra did in 1948. Being in the military probably cost him about 500 hits, but the seven or eight years that the back injury cost him (remember he was only 32 at the time), also cost him a shot at 3,000 hits and a possible place in Cooperstown.

Dick Wakefield became the Detroit left fielder in 1943 his official rookie season and would lead the league in hits with 200 and doubles with 38, hitting .316. He would have a career high batting average in 1944 of .355, before leaving for military service himself.

When they both returned in 1946, Wakefield retained his position in left and McCosky went to the A's. Barney would rebound and be a superior player although let's not forget the Tigers did get Hall of Famer George Kell for him.

Bob Patrick— Patrick's entire career in 1941 and 1942 consisted of just 15 at-bats and 4 hits for a .267 average. He would crack a homer in 1942, though. Patrick would not return to the majors after his stint in the military.

Al Benton— The start of Al Benton's career with the Philadelphia A's was very unforgettable. He started out good enough, going 7–9 in his rookie year of 1934 with a fine IP/H ratio of 155/145, although he did walk 88, but his sophomore year of 1935 was a disaster as he gave up 110 hits and 47 walks in 78⅓ innings.

Benton was out of the majors until 1938, when he was sold to the Tigers. He led the league in saves with 17 in 1940 before his breakout season of 1941. He made his first All-Star team, winning 15 and losing 6, leading the junior circuit in OBA of .221. He made the All-Star game again in 1942 despite a 7–13 record before going off to serve.

Nineteen forty-six would prove to be his best season ever upon his return with a 13–8 record and a brilliant ERA of 2.02. An 11–7 record in 1947 would be his last big year before being sent to the bullpen full time by 1948. He was sold to Cleveland the next season in 1949 and had a 9–6 record, 10 saves, a 2.12 ERA and .238 OBA. Three years later, Benton finished up his career with the Red Sox, ending with a 98–88 mark.

Dizzy Trout became the number 1 starter in Detroit, moving up from the 2 spot, and would have back to back monster seasons, going 20–12 before his incredible 27–14 season in 1944 with a league leading 2.12 ERA. He also had an 8.8 TPI, 10th highest of all time.

Replacing Benton in the rotation was the great Virgil Trucks, who was 16–10 before leaving for the service. Overall this was a situation where his replacements made the team much stronger.

What did serving in the war cost Al Benton? Well, he was only 2 victories shy of 100, so he would have easily achieved that mark ending up perhaps in the 120–130-victory range as he was just coming into his prime.

1943 St. Louis Browns
72–80–25 GB

1941	1942	1943
1B-George McQuinn	McQuinn	McQuinn
2B-Don Heffner	Don Gutteridge	Gutteridge
SS-Johnny Berardino	Vern Stephens	Stephens
3B-Harland Clift	Clift	Clift
OF-Chet Laabs	Laabs	Mike Chartak
OF-Walt Judnich	Judnich	Milt Byrnes
OF-Roy Cullenbine	Glenn McQuillen	Laabs
CA-Rick Ferrell	Ferrell	Frankie Hayes
PI-Elden Auker	Auker	Steve Sundra
PI-Bob Muncrief	Johnny Niggeling	Galehouse
PI-Bob Harris	Galehouse	Bob Muncrief
PI-Denny Galehouse	Al Hollingsworth	Hollingsworth

In 1943 the St. Louis Browns, who would ride to their only title in 1944, took a temporary bump in the road, as they dropped from 82 wins down to 72.

The offense was probably the biggest catalyst for the fallback as they dropped from 730 runs scored to 596. The pitching remained about the same, falling from a team ERA of 3.60 to 3.42, but in a low run production season such as 1943 was, the improvement was negligible.

Probably the biggest fall off was third baseman Harland Clift, whose production of 108 runs, .274 average, .399 on base percentage and 55 RBIs in 1942 became 43 runs, .232 average, .301 on base percentage and 25 RBIs in 1943. Clift had injured his eye during the season and was sent packing with # 3 starter Johnny Niggeling to the Senators for Ellis Clary, Ox Miller and cash.

It would not necessarily be a good trade for the Browns, as Clary would hit .275 in 69 at-bats for St. Louis while Clift would improve to .300 with Washington. Ox Miller would have a 12.00 ERA in 6 innings while Niggeling would help the Senators with a 4–2 record and 27 hits given up in 51 innings.

On the positive side, Vern Stephens would continue to lead offensively with 22 homers and 91 RBIs, hitting .289. Thirty-three-year-old Steve Sundra would lead the way with a 15–11 record and 3.25 ERA. Nels Potter, who would be a hero in the '44 championship, chipped in at 10–5 with a 2.78 ERA. Niggeling, who was a star in '42, was only 6–8 before the trade.

It was a bit of an ugly scene now, but 12 months from this date, things would turn from disgust to ecstasy.

Who Left for the War	Who Replaced Them
1B–Chuck Stevens	
2B–Johnny Berardino	
OF–Walt Judnich	Milt Byrnes
OF–Glen McQuillen	Chet Laabs/Mike Chartak
PI–Pete Appleton	
PI–Frank Biscan	
PI–Hooks Iott	

Chuck Stevens— Chuck Stevens would go 2 for 13 in 1941 with the Browns before entering the service.

After his return in 1946, Stevens would enjoy 2 seasons as the starting first baseman, one in '46 when he hit .248 and led the league in fielding percentage at .995 and the other in '48, hitting .261. It would be his last season in the majors.

Johnny Berardino— More famous for playing Dr. Steve Hardy on the TV soap *General Hospital* than his 11-year baseball career, "Bernie," as he was known, nevertheless was a fine infielder.

Most of Johnny's success would come before he left for the service as he began things off in 1939 as the starting second baseman for the Browns.

Not really considered a power hitter for most of the time he was in the show, Bernie would have a one time burst in 1940, smacking 16 of his lifetime 36 homers that season. He also chipped in with 85 RBIs and a .424 slugging percentage after being moved to short. After a career high 89 RBIs in 1941, Berardino would be called to arms midway through the next campaign.

St. Louis put Johnny back at second when he returned in 1946. He remained a starter for two more seasons, hitting .265 and .261 respectively, before being moved to the Tribe. Before he went to Cleveland, the Browns tried first to trade him to Washington where Berardino threatened to retire and go into the movies. John "unretired" after Landis voided the deal. Two weeks later on December 9, 1947, he would agree to go to the Indians in exchange for Catfish Metkovich and $50,000. The bad part about the trade was Metkovich had a broken finger and was returned to Cleveland for another $15,000.[53]

Berardino would not be the same player as he labored as a reserve during the last four years he spent in the big leagues, bouncing around from Pittsburgh, to the Browns, back to Cleveland and a return trip to the Pirates, hitting between .094 and .227 for those seasons. His career ended after 1952 with a lifetime .249 average.

Walt Judnich— Nineteen forty was Walt Judnich's rookie season, and it was a fabulous one at that, leading the AL in fielding percentage at .989, smacking 24 homers, knocking in 89 with a .303 average. The center fielder would have two more solid campaigns in 1941 and 1942, going 14–83–.284 and 17–82–.313 respectively, leading the circuit again in fielding percentage in '42 at .991 before serving his country during the war.

Returning in 1946, Judnich would start two more seasons for the Browns. With his production off those two years, hitting only .262 and .258, St. Louis traded him to Cleveland in 1948 with Bob Muncrief for Dick Kokus, Joe Frazier, Brian Stephens and $25,000. Although Judnich's production would continue to slide, hitting .257 with 2 homers in 213 at-bats, he would get to play in his only World Series for the champs, going 1 for 13 against the Braves.

His career ended after the next season with Pittsburgh, hitting only .229 in 1949, but he would finish things with an impressive lifetime .281 average.

The three years Walt lost to the war didn't cost him major statistics, but he probably would have gotten at least 400 more hits, reaching the 1,200 hit plateau. He was only 10 homers shy of 100, which is certainly a level he could have easily attained. It wasn't out of the realm that Judnich would have smacked at least 60 at the pace he was at, which would have put him at 150.

Milt Byrnes replaced Walt in center for the 1943 season. He would play only three seasons, 1943–45, starting each year. "Skippy," as he was known, was just below Judnich's batting average output, hitting .280, .290 and .249 respectively, but only hit 16 homers in three years, which was Walt's yearly output. Byrnes did lead the majors in fielding percentage in 1943 at .997.

When the players returned from the service in 1946, Byrnes was out of the major leagues.

Glen McQuillen — Glen "Red" McQuillen was a decent hitter before he went into the military, hitting .284 in his rookie year of 1938 for the Browns in 116 at-bats. He would not return to the majors again until 1941, but broke into the starting lineup in left field for the 1942 season hitting .283 with 12 triples.

When he returned in '46, things would be different as he was back on the bench, hitting only .241, before finishing his career in 1947 going hitless in one at-bat.

Chet Laabs moved over to left to replace McQuillen for the 1943 season and made his only All-Star game, hitting only .250, but becoming a more productive power hitter than Red was, smacking 17 homers with 85 RBIs. He would become a reserve after that season.

Mike Chartak moved into the outfield replacing Laabs in right, hitting only .256, but again with decent power numbers for a low scoring season with 10 homers. He would come up only 72 times in 1944, his last season.

Pete Appleton — Pete "Jake" Appleton became a frequent traveler in his 14-year major league stay, which began impressively in Cincinnati with a 1.82 ERA in 29⅔ innings in 1927.

Jake would move around from the Reds to Cleveland, then the Red Sox and Yankees before arriving with the Senators in 1936, which was the crown jewel season of Appleton's career. He went 14–9 with a 3.53 ERA and a .254 OBA. His time with Washington was the best of his career, winning 34 of his lifetime 57 victories between 1936 and 1939.

His next move was to the Windy City with the White Sox as he was sent with Taffy Wright for Gee Walker. In Chicago, Appleton was reduced to a full time reliever before being sent to the Browns in 1942 and going into the military.

He would return from the service in 1945 to pitch for one last season, throwing 23 innings between St. Louis and Washington winning his only decision that season.

Frank Biscan — "Porky" had a great beginning for the Browns in 1942, going 0–1, but giving up only 13 hits in 27 innings for a 2.33 ERA and .143 OBA, before serving Uncle Sam.

His return to the majors in 1946 and 1948 would not be as impressive as he had a 1–1 record with a 5.16 ERA the first season and 6–7–6.11 his last major league year in 1948.

Hooks Iott — Clarence "Hooks" Iott came up in 1941 tossing only 2 innings. His second and final major league season came 6 years after his first in 1947, giving up 15 hits and 14 walks in 8⅔ innings for St. Louis before moving on to the Giants midway during the season, pitching a little better with a 3–8 record, giving up 67 hits and 52 walks in 71⅓ innings for an unimpressive 5.93 ERA (although much improved from the 16.20 ERA he sported for St. Louis the first part of the year).

1943 Boston Red Sox
68–84–29 GB

1941	*1942*	*1943*
1B-Jimmie Foxx	Tony Lupien	Lupien
2B-Bobby Doerr	Doerr	Doerr
SS-Joe Cronin	Johnny Pesky	Skeeter Newsome
3B-Jim Tabor	Tabor	Tabor
OF-Lou Finney	Finney	Pete Fox
OF-Dom DiMaggio	DiMaggio	Catfish Metkovich
OF-Ted Williams	Williams	Leon Culberson
CA-Frankie Pytlak	Bill Conroy	Roy Partee
PI-Dick Newsome	Tex Hughson	Hughson
PI-Charlie Wagner	Wagner	Yank Terry
PI-Mickey Harris	Joe Dobson	Newsome
PI-Lefty Grove	Newsome	Dobson

There were two things we found out about the Red Sox in 1943: Ted Williams did certainly deserve the MVP award the year before as without him, they tumbled from 93 wins and second place all the way down to 68 wins and 7th position. The second fact was Leon Culberson was no Ted Williams.

After a year of upheaval on the subject of the Splinter's controversial draft deferment, Ted finally took his triple crown and went off into the military. Culberson was the heir apparent in name only, hitting only 3 homers, 34 RBIs and a .272 average, compared to Williams' 1942 output of 36–137–.356.

Certainly if Culberson was no Ted Williams, then Catfish Metkovich was no Dom DiMaggio in center, as the Catfish hit .246, 40 points below Dom's.

A third important member of the team that went off to serve his country was shortstop Johnny Pesky, who hit .331 and scored 105 runs in 1942. Skeeter Newsome took over and could only muster up a .265 average with 48 runs scored. Things were so tough that it forced manager Joe Cronin to hold off retirement and use himself as the backup shortstop hitting .312 in 77 at-bats. Add it all together and they dropped from 761 runs in '42 to only 563 the following season. Their collective team batting average fell from an AL high .276 to .244.

On the rubber was not much more impressive as the prior season's ace, Tex Hughson, fell from 22 wins to a 12–15 mark, although still having a good 2.64 ERA.

Thirty-four-year-old Mace Brown was a beam of light, coming out of the bullpen with a 6–6 record with 9 saves and a 2.12 ERA.

To, date, along with the 1942 version of the Detroit Tigers, this would have to be considered the most devastating defection of players into the military.

Who Left for the War	*Who Replaced Them*
1B-Paul Campbell	
2B-Tom Carey	
SS-Johnny Pesky	Skeeter Newsome
OF-Dom DiMaggio	Catfish Metkovich
OF-Andy Gilbert	
OF-Ted Williams	Leon Culberson
PI-Bill Butland	
PI-Charlie Wagner	Yank Terry

Paul Campbell— After appearing in only one game with no at-bats in 1941, Paul Campbell would go 1 for 15 and head into the military after the 1942 season.

Nineteen forty-six would not be much better in his return season as he went 3 for 26. Campbell was then released and picked up by the Tigers for the 1948 season, where things would improve for the North Carolina native, as he was a semi-regular hitting .278 in 255 at-bats. It would be Campbell's swan song, as he would return for only 1 hitless at-bat in 1950, his last one in the majors.

Tom Carey—"Scoops" would start off his major league career as the starting second baseman for the St. Louis Browns between 1935 and 1937, hitting a very respectable .291, .273 and .275 in 1,271 at-bats.

Carey was shipped off to the Red Sox after the 1938 season for Johnny Marcum. After hitting .242 in 161 at-bats in 1939, Scoops would come up only 84 times in the next three seasons before being sent to serve Uncle Sam.

The year 1946 would bring Carey his final 5 major league at-bats, with one single.

Johnny Pesky— Pesky would hit .307 in his fabulous career, a career that if not for the war might have taken him to a whole other level in baseball annuals, perhaps even Cooperstown.

He had one of the greatest rookie seasons ever, leading the AL in hits with 205 and hitting .331, second to teammate Ted Williams after taking over at short for manager Joe Cronin in 1942. He then would find himself in the military playing for the North Carolina Naval Pre-Flight School team.[54]

When he returned, Johnny picked up right where he left off, leading the league in hits again with 208 and finishing third in batting average with a career best .335 mark. He was selected to his one and only All-Star game that season, also performing in his one Fall Classic, hitting .233 in the seven game loss to the Cardinals as Pesky just missed throwing out Country Enos Slaughter at the plate with the winning Game Seven run in the famous mad dash.

In 1947, Johnny led the junior circuit again in hits a third and final time with 207 ending with a .324 average. After dropping to .281 in 1948 when he moved to third, Pesky would go on again to finish above .300 the next three seasons.

Johnny moved back to short in 1951 when he suffered with a bad back.[55] He would slump to .149 in 1952 before being sent to the Tigers in a huge 9-man deal (see Detroit's Johnny Lipon for details).

In his 2½ years with Detroit, Pesky's play deteriorated as he was moved to second and hit .254 and .292 for the Tigers in 1952 and 1953, before a .176 early season in 1954 found him being sent to Washington where he ended his career hitting .246 his final season.

Pesky was not only a great hitter but a fine fielder, accumulating 77 fielding runs before his back injury in 1951 where he had -34 the rest of the way.

The back injury did cost him as much as going into the service, but at the pace he was on, he would have gotten 600 hits which would have lifted him over 2,000 (he ended up with 1,455) and potentially would have lifted his average over .310, borderline Hall of Fame numbers, but he definitely would have been considered.

Skeeter Newsome replaced Pesky at short in 1943. The 12-year veteran came to Boston in 1941 and hit .265 and .242 in 1943 and 1944. It was respectable, but nowhere near the output of Pesky. Newsome shifted to second in 1945 before being sent to the Phils.

Newsome was also a solid defensive player, accumulating 78 fielding runs throughout his career, including 47 during his time with the Red Sox during the war.

Dom DiMaggio—"The Little Professor," as he was called, not only was Joe's little brother, but was a seven time All-Star, a .298 career hitter and one of the greatest defensive center fielders of all time, accumulating 101 fielding runs, finishing third all time in chances per game with 2.99 and third in putouts per game at 2.82. All this was a testament to the fabulous range that the Professor had.

Dom was a starter from the beginning and a great leadoff man, hitting .301 in his first season of 1940. He would be named to two consecutive

All-Star appearances in 1941 and 1942, hitting .283 and .286 respectively, with 117 and 110 runs and career high 14 homers in 1942.

DiMaggio was sent to the Navy after the 1942 campaign where he played for the Norfolk Naval Training Team.[56] He would return to the majors in 1946, making his third All-Star appearance with a .316 average and playing in his lone World Series hitting only .259.

After setting the American League record for putouts in 1948 with 503, Dom would go on a hitting streak of his own in 1949, taking it to 34 games, far short of Joe's mark but nonetheless impressive.[57]

The year 1950 was DiMaggio's greatest offensive season, leading the AL in runs with 131, triples with 11 and stolen bases with 15. He would go on to hit a career high .328 that year. After leading the league in runs in 1951 with 113, the Professor would play only one more full season before leaving the game for good in 1953.

He finished with 1,680 hits and without the war would most definitely have cleared the 2,000 hit level, with an outside chance of raising his lifetime batting average the two points he needed to reach .300. DiMaggio gets consideration now by the Veterans Committee for the Hall of Fame, but with the stats he missed with the war, he would have a much better case for inclusion. The point must be debated, though — was DiMaggio the greatest defensive center fielder of all time? Unless you can emphatically say yes, like you could in the case of Bill Mazeroski, his offensive stats might be just too low with or without his service time in the military to be properly considered for Cooperstown, Joe's brother or not.

Replacing Dom in center was the infamous Catfish Metkovich. Catfish was a .261 lifetime hitter in 10 major league seasons and had similar speed to DiMaggio, stealing 33 bases from 1943 to 1945, but Dom was superior offensively as Metkovich hit .246, .277 and .260 in his 3 seasons. Defensively, Metkovich was not in the Professor's range as his -28 fielding runs were testament to, before he was moved to 1st base in 1945.

Andy Gilbert— Gilbert's career lasted 12 at-bats, going 1 for 11 in 1942 and hitless in 1 at-bat in 1946 for the Sox.

Ted Williams— What can be said of the Splendid Splinter that has not already been said? He hit .344 for his career, was a 16 time All-Star, hit 521 homers in 19 seasons, led the league in hitting 6 times, runs 6 times, homers on 4 occasions, RBIs 4 seasons, slugging percentage 8 years and on base percentage 12 times. He truly can make the case to be if not the greatest hitter of all time, then certainly in the top three. His loss to the military in 1943 was as devastating to the Red Sox as Greenberg's was to the Tigers a year earlier. It took his team from pennant contenders to bottom dwellers.

He came into the majors in a big way in 1939, hitting 31 homers and leading the AL in RBIs with 145, accumulating a .327 average. His first monster season was in 1941, becoming the last player to date to eclipse the .400 mark, going 6 for 8 on the final day of the season raising his average from slightly under .400 to .406 (although if he sat out that game, the number would have rounded up to .400).

Nineteen forty-two brought Williams his first triple crown, leading the circuit in homers with 36, RBIs with 137 and average at .356. He also was tops in runs, 141, walks, 145, on base percentage at .499 and slugging with a .648. His TPR was obviously the best in the league at 8.0. His team finished in second place primarily because of Ted, yet shockingly enough he lost the MVP award to Yankee second basemen Joe Gordon who arguably was not even the MVP of his own team. This would be the first of many times his poor relationship with the media would rear its ugly head.

After a yearlong odyssey of Ted trying to get a military deferment, Williams went off to the Navy and became a pilot. Upon his return to the majors in 1946, Ted would win his first MVP award leading the Sox to the World Series, although his .200 average probably cost Boston the title.

The Splinter won another triple crown in 1947 with 32–114–.343 marks, again remarkably losing the MVP award to Joe DiMaggio by a single vote. He did win a second MVP honor in 1949, leading the AL in homers, 43, RBIs, 159, runs, 150, walks, 162, on base percentage at .490 and slugging with a .650 mark. He just missed a third triple crown, finishing percentage points behind George Kell at .343 in the batting race.

Williams would break his elbow in the 1950 season and went back in the military in 1952. He took an active role in Korea, flying 39 bombing missions, crash landing on at least one occasion.[58]

Returning in 1954, Ted hit .345. He would go on to lead the AL in hitting two more times with .388 and .328 marks in 1957 and 1958. He would hurt his neck in '59 and hit under .300 for the only time in his career, slumping to .254. Ted retired after the next season, hitting a homer in his final at-bat.

The Splinter was truly one of the great hitters and if we look at what he could have done if not for his two stints in the military, it would have been mind-boggling. Add in the 560 hits he missed during the Second World War and about the 300 hits he missed in Korea and he would have reached the 3,500 hit plateau, 6th of all time. In homers, his 521 are impressive enough, but he could have very easily gotten at least another 150 between the two wars and moved to 671, ahead of Willie Mays into third place. Add to that the approximately 570 RBIs and he would have been the all time leader in that category at 2,400.

Replacing him during World War II was Leon Culberson in 1943 and Bob Johnson, who was purchased from Washington, in '44 and '45. Culberson hit .272 in 1943 with 3 homers, a far cry from the Splinter's output. Johnson did better with 17 shots, 106 RBIs and a .324 average in 1944, but dropped off to .280 in 1945, his last year in the majors.

Bill Butland— Butland played in 4 major league seasons with the Red Sox, three part-time and one that can go down in the books as a solid season. Brought up in 1940 for 3 starts, Butland didn't appear back in the majors until 1942. He went 7–1 that season, giving up 85 hits and 33 walks in 111⅓ innings. His ERA and OBA were spectacular at 2.51 and .206 respectively. It was at this point he went into the military.

When he returned in 1946, the magic was gone as he would throw only 18⅓ more innings in 1946 and 1947, giving up 26 hits and 13 walks.

He never got the chance to see if he could add to his special season of 1942, although to be fair the three non war seasons he pitched in were his worst years, and 1942, Bill's marquee campaign, was during a war year.

Charlie Wagner—"Broadway" Wagner would get knocked around pretty good in his first three seasons between 1938 and 1940. Although he was 5–4, he would give up 141 hits in only 104⅓ innings with ERAs of 8.35, 4.23 and 5.52. The year 1941 would be the season that Wagner would break out, going 12–8 with a 3.07 ERA, improving his IP/H ratio incredibly, at 187⅓/175. The K/BB ratio was not as impressive at 51/85. Broadway would win a career high 14 games the next season again with an impressive IP/H at 205⅓/184 and an unimpressive K/BB at 52/95. Charlie would go into the military after the season ended and pitch for the Norfolk Naval Training Station.[59]

Wagner returned in 1946, losing the momentum he had going in '41 and '42, with a 5.87 ERA in 30 innings. It would be his last big league year.

Replacing Charlie in the rotation was Yank Terry. Lancelot "Yank" Terry was as good as Wagner in ERA at 3.52 in 1943 and OBA .242, but with a much worse offensive team, he could only muster up a 7–9 record. Terry blew up a little in 1944 with a 4.21 ERA, before being relegated to the bullpen in'45, his last major league campaign.

There was no pulling punches with this team. While their City of Brotherly Love counterpart, the Phillies, were making all the headlines with their controversial owner, the A's were continuing to perfect the art of bad baseball.

They were the only team in the American League to eclipse the 4.00

1943 Philadelphia Athletics
49–105–49 GB

1941	1942	1943
1B-Dick Siebert	Siebert	Siebert
2B-Bennie McCoy	Bill Knickerbocker	Suder
SS-Al Brancato	Suder	Irv Hall
3B-Pete Suder	Buddy Blair	Eddie Mayo
OF-Wally Moses	Elmer Valo	Johnny Welaj
OF-Sam Chapman	Mike Kreevich	Jo Jo White
OF-Bob Johnson	Johnson	Bobby Estallella
CA-Frankie Hayes	Hal Wagner	Wagner
PI-Phil Marchildon	Marchildon	Jesse Flores
PI-Jack Knott	Roger Wolff	Harris
PI-Les McCrabb	Lum Harris	Wolff
PI-Bill Beckman	Dick Fowler	Don Black

ERA barrier, a real feat in a non-hitting season, and had the circuit's only 20 game loser in Lum Harris, who was 7–21.

War losses were heavy for the team, losing 13 players before the season began and 7 more by the end of the 1943 pennant race, including starting outfielder Johnny Welaj, who was hitting at a .242 clip at the time, and a young Elmer Valo. Prior to the season though, they only lost one everyday player in Buddy Blair. You can't squeeze blood from a stone, and this team had that same problem with talent.

It wasn't only war losses that helped bury this team; they helped it out as they sent their best offensive player, Bob Johnson, to the Senators for Bobby Estalella. Estalella was probably their best offensive player with 11 homers, 63 RBIs and a .259 average, compared to Johnson's 13–80–.291 average in '42 (although Johnson himself would slump with the Senators at 7–63–.265).

On the mound, the loss of number one man Phil Marchildon was felt, although rookie Jesse Flores did have a very respectable 12–14 record and 3.11 ERA in his stead.

There would be some improvement for this team in 1944, but bottom line, it was a long way to the early seventies when the A's would retake baseball again. As for now, it was just bad.

Jim Castiglia— The young lefty played one partial season for the A's in 1942, going 7 for 18 for a nice .389 average, before entering the armed forces.

George Yankowski— After a 2 for 13 performance in 1942 for Philadelphia, Yankowski would go into the service. He would return seven years later for one last shot in the bigs, hitting only .167 in 18 at-bats for the White Sox in 1949.

Who Left for the War	*Who Replaced Them*
CA-Jim Castiglia	
CA-George Yankowski	
2B-Crash Davis	
SS-Jack Wallaesa	
3B-Buddy Blair	Eddie Mayo
OF-Eddie Collins	
PI-Fred Caligiuri	
PI-Joe Coleman	
PI-Dick Fowler	
PI-Bob Harris	
PI-Jack Knott	
PI-Phil Marchildon	Jesse Flores
PI-Bob Savage	

Crash Davis— Although he was perhaps the inspiration for the lead character in the movie "Bull Durham," this Crash spent more that just "a cup of coffee" in the majors (of course he was also a second baseman instead of a catcher).

Davis was only a .230 lifetime hitter in 3 major league seasons between 1940 and 1942, compiling the majority of his statistics in the first war ball season of 1942. He hit .224 that year with his only 2 homers in 272 at-bats (he would only amass 444 at-bats in his entire career).

Although Crash didn't go through his minor league career chasing the all time home run record, he did play in the Carolina League after the war for 6 seasons, setting the all time league record with 50 doubles in 1948, being named to the All-Star team at second for the Durham Bulls.[60]

Hopefully he got his own Susan Sarandon after his career was through.

Jack Wallaesa — Hitting a career high .256 in his official rookie season of 1942, Wallaesa went into the service before returning to the majors in 1946. He would hit .196 and .195 in 399 at-bats for the A's and the White Sox in '46 and '47 before bowing out with a lifetime .205 mark in 1948.

Buddy Blair— Louis "Buddy" Blair had a nice rookie year with the A's in 1942 as the 32-year-old third baseman hit .279 with 5 homers and knocking in 66 in 484 at-bats. Unfortunately that was his entire career. After going off to war, he would not return to the majors.

Blair's replacement at third was Eddie "Hot Shot" Mayo, who had been out of the majors since 1938 with the Braves. The good fielding Mayo would hit far under Blair's output with a .219 average, but would lead the junior circuit in fielding with a .976 percentage. It would be his only season with the A's as he was dealt to the Tigers the next season where he led the AL in fielding runs with 29.

As far as Blair goes, it's questionable how effective his career would have been had there been no war. When he got his shot in '42, he was 32, replacing Benny McCoy, the 25-year-old starter who left to serve Uncle Sam himself after the 1941 season. One has to wonder if he ever would have made the big leagues at all if not for the war.

Eddie Collins— We can make one point perfectly clear when it comes to the career of Eddie Collins. This was not the Hall of Famer of the same name, it was his son. Other than playing for the same team which the senior Collins found greatness in the early part of the century, there would be no similarities in their careers as junior hit only .241 in 274 at-bats over a 3 year span between 1939 and 1942, which encompassed his entire major league career.

Fred Caligiuri— After a 2–2 debut with a 2.93 in 43 innings for the 1941 edition of the A's, Caligiuri would toss only one more season, in 1942, going 0–3 with an ERA that hovered at 6.38. He would then go off in the military, never returning to the major leagues.

Joe Coleman— His record before the war was 0–1 in 1941 for the father of the pitcher of the same name who played in the 60s and 70s.[61] When he returned in 1946 Joe Coleman's fortunes in the majors would definitely take a swing upwards.

After an abbreviated 0–2 season in 1946, Coleman would break into the starting rotation with the A's in 1947, before making the All-Star game in 1948 with a 14–13 record. He would sport a similar record in '49, going 13–14 with a 3.86 ERA in a career high 240 innings.

The next three campaigns would not be kind to Coleman as he primarily went back into the bullpen, going a combined 4–15 with ERAs of 8.50, 5.98 and 4.00 respectively.

Coleman went to the Orioles in 1954 with Frank Fanovich for Bob Cain. It was there he had a one season resurgence with a 13–17 mark and career low 3.50 ERA. He would be out of the majors after the next season with a lifetime 52–76 record.

Dick Fowler— Breaking in with Philadelphia in 1941, Dick Fowler earned a spot in the rotation for the 1942 campaign and finished with a 6–11 mark before going into the armed service. He returned in the latter half of the 1945 season, becoming the only Canadian to toss a no-hitter, completing a 1–0 gem against the Browns at Shibe Park nine days after he was discharged.

After a 9–16 record in '46 he finally got on the plus side of .500 in '47 with a 12–11 record and a career low 2.81 ERA. He would also post a .249 OBA that season. Fowler would follow his '47 campaign with 2 consecutive 15 win seasons, going 15–8 and 15–11 in 1948 and 1949. The bottom would then fall out on the right-hander.

He hurt his arm in 1950 and could not regain his prior form, posting a 1–5 mark to go with a 6.48 ERA. Two seasons later he was out of the majors, ending his stay with a 66–79 record.

Bob Harris—Wyoming native Bob Harris began his big league career in 1938 for the Tigers. He was promptly traded in the middle of the next year in a 10-player deal with the Browns that included Bobo Newsom and Chet Laabs. Harris would find his way into the Browns rotation before the season was over, finishing the year 4–13.

Compiling seasons of 11–15 and 12–14 over the next two years in St. Louis with ERAs of 4.93 and 5.21 respectively, Bob was sent to the A's following a 1–5 start in 1942. He would match his Brown record and finish his last pre-military season 2–10. With a lifetime mark of 30–52 in hand, Harris went into the service where he pitched for the powerhouse Great Lakes Naval Team.[62]

When he returned after his time in the Navy, Harris would be cut by the A's and signed in the American Association. He demanded to be paid the difference between his major league and minor league salary, which was $3,300. The dispute was settled with Harris receiving his pay after a meeting with Connie Mack, the club lawyer, Harris and a U.S. Attorney by the name of Gerald Gleason.[63]

Jack Knott— Jack Knott enjoyed a fine 11-year career with the Browns, White Sox and A's, finishing with an 82–103 record. His rookie season of 1933 was probably Knott's most unforgettable as he ended the campaign with a 1–8 mark in St. Louis. Better times were soon to come.

As a part time starter/reliever in 1934 for the Browns, he finished 10–3 before an 11–8 record with an AL best 7 saves in '35. The following campaign in 1936 would result in one of the worst seasons a pitcher with over 150 innings would endure as a finished 9–17 with a 7.29 ERA. Worse yet, his OBA was .330 as he gave up 272 hits in only 192⅔ innings.

Two years later in 1938 he was sent to the White Sox for Billy Cox. Knott enjoyed two decent seasons on the south side with matching 11 win seasons of 11–6 and 11–9.

His next stop was in the City of Brotherly Love with the A's, where he would win a career high 13 games before slipping to 2–10 in 1942 and going to serve Uncle Sam. While in the Army, Knott would be injured at the Battle of the Bulge and earn a battlefield commission.[64]

After his time in the service, he would return for three more games in 1946 before ending his big league stay.

Phil Marchildon— A native of Canada and player with the Toronto Maple Leafs of the International League before being brought up by the Athletics, Phil "Babe" Marchildon's fine baseball career would certainly be overshadowed by his heroic times fighting for the Royal Canadian Air Force.[65]

Babe would have a fine rookie season in 1941. Despite his 10–15 record, with a 3.57 ERA, he had a fine 204/188 IP/H ratio. Marchildon won 17 games the next season before entering the service.

It was in the RAF where Phil carved his name in history, being shot down over Denmark on August 17th, 1944, landing in the North Sea. For hours he swam before being picked up and turned over to the Germans. He would be sent to a prison camp for the duration of the war and lost over 40 pounds while in captivity. [66]

Returning from the service a more serious man and suffering from a nervous condition induced from his captivation by the Nazis,[67] Marchildon came back nonetheless bravely to the majors in 1945 and would have a career year in 1947 with a 19–9 record and all time low ERA of 3.22 with an outstanding 276⅔/228 IP/H ratio.

Things would immediately go downhill for Phil, slumping to 9–15 in 1948 before suffering a sore arm in '49. He was gone from the majors a year later after tossing ⅓ inning with the Red Sox. He left the game a true hero and was elected to the Canadian Hall of Fame in 1993.

Replacing Marchildon in the rotation in 1943 was rookie Jesse Flores. Flores pitched nicely for the A's, going 12–14 with a 3.11 ERA. During the next two seasons Flores would pitch well with a 16–21 record and a nice 377/352 IP/H ratio. Jesse finished his 7-year career at 44–59 with a lifetime 3.18 ERA.

Bob Savage — John Robert Savage pitched only 30⅔ innings in 1942 with the A's before entering the Army. While serving in Italy, Savage was wounded on November 5th, 1943, and awarded the Purple Heart. He was thought to be the first major leaguer injured during the war while in the military.

He returned in 1946, going a cumulative 11–25 in '46 and '47 before being sent to the pen full time in 1948, where he came up with a nice 5–1 mark although he had a poor 6.21 ERA. He would last one more season in the majors in 1949, finishing his career at 16–27.

Starting Lineups and Who Went to War

NATIONAL LEAGUE

They say a franchise is only as strong as its minor league system (at least before the free agency era that was true). During World War II, that fact would double in importance as the Cardinal farm system, which was the strongest during the time, would help them replace the mass

1943 St. Louis Cardinals
105–490 GB

1941	1942	1943
1B-Johnny Mize	Hopp	Ray Sanders
2B-Creepy Crespi	Crespi	Lou Klein
SS-Marty Marion	Marion	Marion
3B-Jimmy Brown	Whitey Kurowski	Kurowski
OF-Enos Slaughter	Slaughter	Musial
OF-Terry Moore	Moore	Harry Walker
OF-Johnny Hopp	Stan Musial	Danny Litwhiler
CA-Gus Mancuso	Walker Cooper	W. Cooper
PI-Lon Warneke	M. Cooper	M. Cooper
PI-Ernie White	Johnny Beazley	Lanier
PI-Mort Cooper	Lanier	Harry Gumbert
PI-Max Lanier	Harry Gumbert	Howie Krist

military defections and lead them to three National League pennants and two world championships in four years. This would especially come into play in 1943.

After an incredible comeback in '42 to steal the NL crown away from the Dodgers, the defending world champions would lose Enos Slaughter, Johnny Beazley, Creepy Crespi and captain Terry Moore before the season began, all important cogs in the Cardinal machine, yet win 105 games and ease into a repeat National League pennant by 18½ games. Stan Musial, who moved over to right to take over for Slaughter, won the MVP award, leading the league in hits with 220, doubles, 48, triples, 20, batting average at .357 and slugging percentage .562. Walker Cooper also excelled, picking up 38 points on his '42 average at .319

The infield was led by Ray Sanders, who took advantage of his time during the war years to have three tremendous seasons. He started at first hitting .280 with 11 homers. Sophomore third baseman Whitey Kurowski improved to .287, co-leading the Redbirds with 13 homers (along with Musial).

The 1942 MVP Mort Cooper would have another fabulous year, finishing runner-up to Musial in the MVP race with a 21–8 mark and 2.30 ERA. Max Lanier would fill the void left by Johnny Beazley, nicely going 15–7 with a very miniscule 1.90 ERA. The team as a whole led the NL in strikeouts with 639, shutouts at 21 and a low 2.57 ERA. Although it was truly a fabulous year, the Cards would go down quietly in the Fall Classic as the Yankees would get their revenge in 5 games.

Despite all the successes with the St. Louis farm system, they would still see the writing on the wall, as the minors were being more depleted by military defections than the big leagues and even they were starting to hurt. Desperately, they took an ad out in the *Sporting News* stating, "The

Cardinal organization needs players. If you are a free agent and have previous professional experience, we may be able to place you to your advantage on one of our clubs. We have positions open in our AA, A, B, and D classification clubs. If you believe you can qualify for one of these good baseball jobs, tell us about yourself."[68] Such was life in baseball during the war.

Who Left for the War	Who Replaced Them
2B-Creepy Crespi	Lou Klein
SS-Jeff Cross	
OF-Erv Dusak	
OF-Terry Moore	Harry Walker
OF-Enos Slaughter	Stan Musial/Danny Litwhiler
PI-Johnny Beazley	Max Lanier/Howie Krist
PI-Whitey Moore	

Creepy Crespi— After two full seasons with the Cardinals as the starting second baseman in 1941 and 1942, where he hit .279 and .243 respectively, Crespi went off to serve in the Army.

While in the Army, Crespi would break his leg while playing for the team at Fort Riley. As he was in the hospital recuperating, Creepy engaged in a wheelchair race where he would crash and break the same leg in a different place. After the second break, Crespi's career in the majors was over.[69]

Replacing him was Lou Klein, who had a wonderful 1943 season hitting .287 his only year as a starter with 7 homers and 62 RBIs. He would go off to serve the following year.

Jeff Cross— Before going into the service, Jeff Cross would go 1 for 4 with an RBI in his first major league game. When he came back in 1946, he would play in three limited seasons with the Cards, coming up only a combined 138 times for a sub-par .162 average. He would be gone after a 2 for 20 performance with Chicago in 1939.

Erv Dusak— After a poor pre-draft career where he hit only .143 and .185 respectively in 41 at-bats for the 1941 and 1942 campaigns, "Four Sack" Dusak came back in 1946 and would see some significant playing time over the next three seasons (he had 914 of his 1,035 lifetime at-bats during that time period).

The year 1947 would prove to be his best year, hitting .284 with 6 homers for St. Louis. Erv slumped to .209 the next season and would never recover. His major league career would end after the 1952 season where he hit .222 in 27 at-bats.

Terry Moore— The Alabama native was one of the finest center fielders of his time before he went off to war. Hall of Famer Leo Durocher said of Moore, " I don't see how they can rank anyone better than Moore. If a ball

Terry Moore was the undisputed captain of the great Cardinal teams of the late 1930s and early 1940s. He would go off to war after the 1942 season and return 3 years later. He was one of the greatest defensive outfielders of his time. Courtesy of Photo File, Inc.

is in the air, he'll get to it. Nobody can do better than that."[70]

Moore led the senior circuit in fielding in 1939 with a .994 percentage. He was no slouch at the plate either, hitting between .288 and .304 from 1939 to 1942 including back to back 17 homer seasons in '39 and '40. He would be selected to four consecutive All-Star games during that time period.

What was more important to the Cards than his spectacular defense and solid offensive contributions were his leadership skills. As the captain of the 1942 world champs, Moore was widely given credit by his teammates for being the catalyst behind the title. Harry Walker said that "We were a close team and Terry Moore was a lot of that.... We traveled by train and had more time together, but Terry was our captain and respected by everybody on the club. He would do more talking to the players than the manager did, everyone respected him for that."[71]

After the war, Terry would return in 1946 for three seasons with St. Louis, but would never again reach the levels that he did prior to the war. "I was a much better player before I went into the war than when I came back,"[72] he would say. After a sub par .232, 4 homer 18 RBI season in 1948, Moore was gone from the majors.

Replacing him in center was Walker. Harry turned out to be a better hitter than Moore, hitting .295 to Terry's .288. Although Walker was a good fielder, he wasn't the equal of his fellow Alabama native.

Enos Slaughter — The future Hall of Fame member was just coming into his prime when duty came calling early in 1943. He was coming off a season when he led the National League in hits with 188 and triples with 17. His .318 batting average and 98 RBIs were a pivotal part of the Cardinals' championship run in '42. During his time in the service, Enos played ball to help entertain the troops.

Keeping physically sharp during his stay in the service helped Slaughter when he returned in 1946, beginning a string of eight consecutive All-Star appearances by leading the senior circuit with 130 RBIs. He also hit .300 with a .465 slugging percentage in another St. Louis championship run.

The 1946 World Series gave Enos the moment he is best remembered for. After being hit in the elbow by Joe Dobson of Boston in Game 5 (an injury that would turn out to be a broken elbow), Slaughter would win the series in the seventh and deciding game. With the game tied at 3 in the 8th, Slaughter singled and with two outs, Harry Walker singled on a hit and run. Center fielder Leon Culberson would hit the cutoff man Johnny Pesky who looked back Walker. In the meantime Slaughter kept hustling and beat the throw home for the winning run.

Country, as he was also known, was a great clutch hitter driving in 100 runs in both 1950 and 1952 with less than 15 homers each season, the only major league player to accomplish that feat twice.

After his 10th All-Star game selection in 1953, Slaughter was dealt to the Yankees for Bill Virdon and Mel Wright. The demoralized ex–Cardinal would not be the same ballplayer, shuttling between New York and Kansas City for the next six seasons, although he did have one more banner season in 1955 for the A's, hitting .322 (.315 for the whole season including his time with the Yankees).

Enos was sold to Milwaukee in 1959 and after hitting only .171 for the Braves and Yankees he promptly left the game he loved.

Country was selected to the Hall of Fame in 1985 by the Veterans Committee and was considered a controversial selection by some. If you look at what statistics he missed by the war, he probably would have accumulated 450–500 hits, giving him over 2,800 in his career and about 230 RBIs, putting him over 1,500. At that point, he becomes a more logical choice. One thing no one disputes, though, is his guts and desire.

The great Stan Musial replaced Slaughter in right and had an MVP season in 1943 leading the senior circuit in hits, doubles, triples, batting average, a stellar .357 and slugging at .562. Danny Litwhiler took over Musial's place and in essence replaced Enos in the outfield. Litwhiler was the Phillies' representative in the All-Star game in '42 and came over from Philadelphia with Earl Naylor for Buster Adams, Coaker Triplett and Dain

Clay in June. He would not be the offensive force of Slaughter, hitting .279 with 7 homers and 31 RBIs, yet was a force with his glove.

Johnny Beazley — Johnny Beazley was coming off one of the greatest rookie seasons of all time in 1942 when he left for the armed forces. He was 21–6 with a 2.13 ERA for the world champs on top of two victories versus the Yankees in the World Series.

While in the military, Beazley would pitch for a team from the Army Air Transport Command in Tennessee that included Hugh "Losing Pitcher" Mulcahy.[73] Unfortunately, Johnny would also hurt his arm after a superior officer ordered him to pitch before he was ready. He was never the same again.[74]

After his return in 1946, Beazley went 7–5 with an ERA that ballooned to 4.46 in 18 starts. He was sold to the Braves in April of 1947. Johnny would pitch only 13 more games for Boston over the next three years and ended his career at the conclusion of the 1949 season.

He was replaced as the number 2 man in the rotation by Max Lanier, who did a wonderful job in 1943 with a 15–7 mark and a sparkling 1.90 ERA. Max won 108 games in his career, but the 47–29 mark he had during the war years were by far his peak. Since Lanier was already in the 4-man rotation in 1942, Howie Krist was the man who actually took Beazley's spot. Krist was a magnificent 23–3 in '41 and '42 before being moved up where he was 11–5 in 1943. The next season he went into the military himself.

Whitey Moore — Moore's career with the Cardinals lasted exactly nine games and 12 innings in 1942 before he went off to war, which was his last season in the majors. Prior to that he pitched 6½ years with the Reds, compiling a 30–28 record. His best season was 1939 when he finished 13–12 in 24 starts. Control was not his forte as his career K/BB ratio was 228/292.

1943 Cincinnati Reds
87–67–18 GB

1941	1942	1943
1B-Frank McCormick	McCormick	McCormick
2B-Lonny Frey	Frey	Frey
SS-Eddie Joost	Joost	Eddie Miller
3B-Bill Werber	Bert Haas	Steve Mesner
OF-Jim Gleeson	Max Marshall	Marshall
OF-Harry Craft	Gee Walker	Walker
OF-Mike McCormick	Eric Tipton	Tipton
CA-Ernie Lombardi	Ray Lamanno	Ray Mueller
PI-Bucky Walters	Vander Meer	Vander Meer
PI-Johnny Vander Meer	Ray Starr	Walters
PI-Paul Derringer	Walters	Riddle
PI-Elmer Riddle	Derringer	Starr

The Reds would still be a season away from being totally annihilated by the military draft, but 1943 was mild on that front as they lost only six players with one starter. The result was an 11 game improvement and a rise to second place in the National League.

First baseman Frank McCormick would lead the way for the otherwise anemic Red attack, hitting .303. Eddie Miller, who was picked up in the off season from the Braves for Eddie Joost, Nate Andrews and $25,000, led Cincinnati in RBIs with 71 and was an All-Star selection despite a .224 average.

The pitching staff was still the key to the team and was led by Elmer Riddle's 21–11 season with a 2.63 ERA and Johnny Vander Meer's league leading 174 strikeouts. Bucky Walters was a disappointing 11–11, but proved to be much more successful under the lights as he compiled an 8–1 record in night games.[75] During the day, he did not finish nor win a game at Crosley Field. Despite the Red hurlers' triumphs, Cincinnati did suffer some control problems, as was the case for the rest of both leagues with the war going on. In 1942 they had a 616/526 K/BB ratio, by 1943 the second place Red Legs fell to 498/579. Vander Meer was probably the biggest offender, going from 186/102 in '42 to 174/162 the next campaign in '43. He led the league in both categories. Despite the wildness, 1943 could be considered a true success.

Who Left for the War	*Who Replaced Them*
CA-Ray Lamanno	Ray Mueller
1B-Eddie Shokes	
OF-Eddie Luken	
OF-Howie Moss	
OF-Clyde Vollmer	
PI-Ewell Blackwell	

Ray Lamanno — Lamanno was the man who took over behind the plate when the great Ernie Lombardi was traded to the Braves before the 1942 season. The California native had decent power numbers, hitting 12 homers in 1942, but he was not one of the top defensive catchers as he was listed with -11 fielding runs for the season.

When Ray returned from the service in '46, he was selected to his only All-Star game. After two more seasons when he hit .257 and .242 respectively in 1947 and 1948, Lamanno's career in the majors was over.

Replacing Ray at catcher in 1943 was Ray Mueller, who came back after a three-year absence from the big leagues. Mueller just about matched Lamanno's '42 average, .260 to .264, and was close in homers, 8 to 12, but was much better defensively as he had 20 fielding runs. The "Iron Man," as he was known because of his major league record 155 games behind the plate in 1944, would go off to fight after the '44 season.

Eddie Shokes— Shokes' prewar career was all of one at-bat in the 1941 campaign. He did return for one more season in 1946, hitting .120 in 83 official times to the plate for the Reds.

Eddie Lukon—"Mongoose" looked like he had a promising career in 1941, hitting .267 in 83 at-bats for the '41 Reds. He came back from the service in 1945, going 1 for 8 before combining for 512 of his 606 career at-bats in 1946 and 1947. He showed decent power, hitting 12 and 11 homers but a .205 average at the end of 1947 signaled the end of his time in the show.

Howie Moss — After being shutout in his first season in 1941, going 0 for 14 for the Giants, Moss didn't improve much when he returned in 1946, hitting .121 with Cincinnati and Cleveland, finishing his career with a .097 batting mark.

Ewell Blackwell of the Cincinnati Reds was just a young pitcher in 1942 when he was drafted into the Army. He would come back to win 82 major league games. Courtesy of the Cincinnati Reds.

Clyde Vollmer— Vollmer would come back after a shaky start with the Reds (.093 average in 1942) to have nine solid years with the Reds, Senators and Red Sox after the war. His top year was with Boston in 1951, slugging 22 homers with 85 RBIs.

After a .256 performance in 47 at-bats with Washington in 1954, his time in the majors was done.

Ewell Blackwell — With the 1942 Cincinnati Reds, Blackwell was a young pitcher who tossed only 3 innings in 2 games. After his return from the military in 1946 where Blackwell would serve in the Army's 71st division infantry under General George Patton, he made a name for himself.[76]

The tall, lanky pitcher would have a very intimidating fastball that made Ewell "the toughest pitcher for me to hit,"[77] according to Hall of Fame slugger Ralph Kiner.

"The Whip's" official rookie season in '46 began a streak of six consecutive All-Star selections despite his 9–13 record. He finished with a 2.45 ERA that season and led the senior circuit in shutouts with 5. This would be only a preamble to his marquee season of 1947 when he led the NL in wins with 22, complete games, 23, strikeouts, 193, to finish second in the MVP race. He not only compiled a 22–8 record and 2.47 ERA, but also came within two outs of becoming only the second man ever (and second Red for that matter) to throw two consecutive no-hitters. After tossing one against the Braves in a 6–0 win, Ewell threw 8⅓ innings of hitless ball the next time out versus the Dodgers before Eddie Stanky singled up the middle in the 9th.

After 17–15 and 16–15 marks in 1950 and 1951 respectively, Blackwell fell to 3–12 and was traded to the Yankees for Jim Greengrass, Johnny Schmitz, Ernie Nevel, Bob Marquis and $35,000. After 13 games with New York in a year and a half, The Whip was sent to A's in 1952 where he threw 4 innings and left the game with a career 82–78 record.

1943 Brooklyn Dodgers
81–72–23.5 GB

1941	1942	1943
1B-Dolph Camilli	Camilli	Camilli
2B-Billy Herman	Herman	Herman
SS-Pee Wee Reese	Reese	Vaughan
3B-Cookie Lavagetto	Arky Vaughan	Frenchy Bordagaray
OF-Dixie Walker	Walker	Walker
OF-Pete Reiser	Reiser	Augie Galan
OF-Joe Medwick	Medwick	Luis Olmo
CA-Mickey Owen	Owen	Owen
PI-Kirby Higbe	Higbe	Higbe
PI-Whit Wyatt	Wyatt	Wyatt
PI-Luke Hamlin	Curt Davis	Davis
PI-Hugh Casey	Ed Head	Head

Star first baseman Dolph Camilli voluntarily retired in the middle of the 1943 season when he refused a trade to the Giants[78] (he would return in 1945 after a year in the military for one last season with the Red Sox), such was the life of the Bums from Brooklyn that season.

It wasn't that the team was decimated by the draft although they lost arguably their two best players in Pete Reiser and Pee Wee Reese. Perhaps the main reason for the 22 game fall of was the collapse of their once proud pitching staff.

The group which formed a strong starting rotation led by Kirby Higbe and Whitlow Wyatt had the league's third best ERA in 1942 at 2.85 with a K/BB ratio of 612/493 and an impressive IP/H mark of 1,398⅔/1,205. This year would be different as the same group shot up to an ERA of 3.89 in a non-hitting season and a K/BB ratio of 588/637 (they went from the third least walks to the leading the league with the most). The IP/H mark was good, but a little short of '42 at 1369⅔/1230.

Whit Wyatt was able to maintain his excellence at 14–5 with a 2.49 ERA while Higbe's ERA mark shot up from 3.25 to 3.70. Curt Davis, who broke his finger during the season, increased from 2.36 to 3.78 and Ed Head shot up slightly from 3.56 to 3.66. One of the biggest losses to the staff was the ravaging of their fine bullpen. Hugh Casey's 6–3 record, 2.25 ERA and 13 save performance in 1942 was replaced by Les Webber's 2–2, 3.81 and 10 save mark. Larry French also took his 1942 15–4 record and miniscule 1.83 ERA to the service.

Dissension also corrupted the fortunes of the Dodgers in 1943 after Leo Durocher suspended pitcher Bobo Newsom for not listening to the Lip on how to pitch to Pirate Vince DiMaggio, before Joe's brother slapped a double. The team believed Durocher was really mad at Newsom for complaining about Bobby Bragan, who was thought to be one of Leo's favorites. Arky Vaughan and Joe Medwick turned in their uniforms in protest and Dixie Walker would offer his up before cooler heads prevailed and the Dodgers would eventually take the field for their next game. The episode had to take its toll on the club and Newsom, who was also involved in attacking an umpire that year for calling a balk, was eventually banished to the Browns for Fritz Ostermueller and Archie McCain.[79]

Finally, on a positive note, the team did lead the National League in runs scored by 37 with a total of 716 to the Cards' 679. They were led by second baseman Billy Herman who hit .330 and had the distinction of knocking in 100 runs while hitting only 2 homers. Hall of Famer Paul Waner had a rebound season of sorts, hitting .311 in 225 at-bats.

Who Left for the War	Who Replaced Them
CA-Cliff Dapper	
SS-Pee Wee Reese	Arky Vaughan/Frenchy Bordagaray
SS-Stan Rojek	
3B-Lew Riggs	
OF-Pete Reiser	Augie Galan
OF-Johnny Rizzo	
PI-Hugh Casey	
PI-Larry French	
PI-Chet Kehn	

All in all it was a team on the decline. It would take new GM Branch Rickey a few years to right the ship, but once he did it, the Dodgers would have success unseen by the franchise in their long and storied history.

Cliff Dapper— Cliff Dapper's career lasted only for the 1942 season as he went 8 for 17, a .471 average, with 1 homer and 9 RBIs for a phenomenal .706 slugging percentage.

Pee Wee Reese— Before the war Reese was a young shortstop on the way up, making his first All-Star game in his third season of 1942 before spending three years in the military. After playing in the Navy, the little general came back in 1946 with an improved stroke, to lead the great Dodger teams of the late '40's and '50's into the history books.

He was certainly one of the great leaders of that team, which he showed in 1947 by befriending a young Jackie Robinson when all around the man who broke the color barrier were making vicious taunts which made his life a miserable hell. His teammates took Reese's gesture to heart and began to rally around Robinson.

Reese ran off a string of nine consecutive All-Star selections between 1946 and 1954 and found himself a little more power, hitting double digits in homers seven times including a career high 16 in 1949 when he also led the league in runs with 132, finishing 5th in the MVP vote.

Pee Wee would eventually crack the .300 barrier in 1954, hitting .309. The world championship year of 1955 would be the Louisville native's last big season, with 10 homers, 61 RBIs and a .282 average. Reese would have two more sub par years in Brooklyn before joining his team in Los Angeles for 59 games before retiring to coach.

His .269 average may not rate with the greats, especially not with today's trio of Derek Jeter, Nomar Garciaparra and Alex Rodriguez, and the time he lost in the war probably only cost him about 350–400 hits, which would have exceeded the 2,500 plateau, but in his era of Rizzuto and Boudreau, Pee Wee rated among the best if not in fact the best and certainly was deserving of a spot in the Hall of Fame.

Replacing Reese was fellow Hall of Fame member Arky Vaughan, who moved over from his one-year stint at third with Brooklyn. Vaughan rebounded from his 1942 season hitting .305, leading the league in runs with 112 and stolen bases with 20. He would temporarily retire after 1943, coming back for 2 more seasons in '47 and '48. Frenchy Bordagaray, a former outfielder, moved into Vaughan's spot with a host of others when Arky filled Pee Wee's Slot. He hit .302 before taking over full time at third in 1944 and 1945. Defense was not Frenchy's forte as he had a -46 fielding runs and a very poor .886 fielding percentage in 1945 alone, his last major league season.

Stan Rojek—In 1942, Stan Rojek went off to the armed forces after one game as a pinch runner to start his major league career. When he returned, he played only two seasons in a part time role for the Dodgers, appearing only 127 times, hitting .277 and .262 respectively.

He was sold to Pittsburgh in 1948 where he enjoyed his best success starting for the Bucs in both '48 and '49, hitting a career high .290 his first season.

Danny O'Connell took over his spot at short in 1950 as he was sent to the Cards for Erv Dusak and Rocky Nelson (of 1960 world champion Pirate fame) early in 1951. He hit .274 in a part time role before being sent to the cross town Browns in 1952 where he went 1 for 7 in his final big league season.

Lew Riggs—The bulk of Lew Riggs' career was as a starting third baseman with the Reds between 1935 and 1938 when he amassed a total of 39 fielding runs, and a selection to the 1936 All-Star game his second year as a starter when he hit 6 homers and had a .257 average. Billy Werber would replace Riggs at third as Lew was reduced to a reserve role in 1939 and 1940, coming up a grand total of 110 times before being sent to Brooklyn before the '41 season for Pep Young.

He remained with the Dodgers two years prior to leaving for the military after 1942, where he played in a reserve role, hitting a career high .305 for the NL champs in 1941.

Riggs returned to the majors in 1946, but played in only one more major league game going 0 for 4.

Pete Reiser—He was one of the greatest talents to ever play the game, but his reckless style put him on the shelf more times than he would care to remember and cost him what could have been a career for the ages.

Reiser crashed into a wall in July of 1942 and landed in the hospital after he collapsed in the locker room. It would leave him with dizzy spells the rest of his life. In 1947, he crashed into the concrete wall at Ebbets Field and was injured so badly he was given his last rites.[80] This was the career of Pete Reiser. Those who saw him play would never forget his talent. Those who never did cannot appreciate his greatness.

After breaking in with Brooklyn in 1940, Reiser showed how brilliant he could be his first season as a regular in 1941, leading the National League in hitting at .343, doubles with 39, triples 17, runs with 117 and slugging at .558. He helped lead the Dodgers to their first World Series since 1920. The lefty finished second to Dolph Camilli in the MVP vote that season.

He was continuing his spectacular play in 1942, challenging the .400 plateau when his crash occurred. When he returned from the injury, his average dropped to .310 as he was not the same, although Pete was selected to his second consecutive All-Star game.

Reiser went into the military after the '42 season where in true Reiser style, he fell into a ditch chasing a ball at Camp Lee in Virginia and hurt his shoulder. When he came back in 1946, he hit .309 and made the mid-summer classic for the third time. It would be the last time Pete hit .300. After his serious injury crashing into the wall in 1947, Reiser would start to go downhill, as injuries would catch up to him. He was sent off to Boston in 1949 for Mike McCormick and would bounce around from the Braves to Pittsburgh and Cleveland before ending things up in 1952 when he hit .136 for the Indians.

He finished with a .295 average and the war might have cost him between 450 to 500 hits, which would have put him over 1,200 for his career. In true Reiser style, he probably would have found a way to hurt himself again so we really can't say his time in the military cost him too much as far as his major league career goes.

Replacing Pete in 1943 was Augie Galan. The Dodgers picked up Galan in 1941 as a reserve. Although his production was not up to Reiser's level, he did make two consecutive All-Star games in 1943 and 1944, hitting .287 in '43 with 9 homers.

Johnny Rizzo — Rizzo's last year in baseball was his only season in Brooklyn in 1942 when he hit .230 in 217 at-bats. After that he left for the military and never returned to the majors. He did have some success earlier in his career, breaking in with the Pirates in 1938, hitting a career high .301 as the starting left fielder with 23 homers and 111 RBIs.

He dipped to .261 his second season, before slumping to .179 at the beginning of the 1940 season. By May of 1940, he was sent to Cincy for Vince DiMaggio, a trade that would turn out to be a good one for the Pirates. He was then sent to the Phils later in 1940 where he found his stroke again, hitting .292 with 20 homers the last 103 games of 1940 and finishing the year at .283. He slumped to .217 the next season before he was sold to the Dodgers in '42.

Hugh Casey — Casey's most notable accomplishment in baseball was his moment in the fourth game of the 1941 World Series versus the Yankees. It was Casey who threw the infamous pitch that got past Mickey Owen on a third strike swing by Tommy Henrich, allowing Henrich to go to first on what would have been the third out in the 9th inning of a Dodger victory. The Yanks would go on to steal the game 7–4 and win the Series in 5.

Before that moment, Casey broke in with the Cubs for a short time in 1935. Four years later in 1939, Hugh would pitch in his first full season going 15–10 with Brooklyn, sporting a 2.93 ERA. As a dual starter/reliever with the Dodgers in 1940 and 1941, Casey would win 25 games before being sent to the bullpen full time in 1942, becoming one of the first truly successful men at his new craft.

Hugh went 6–3 in his new roll with a league leading 13 saves for a sparkling 2.25 ERA before leaving for the Navy the following year. During the 1942 season, the Dodgers went to Havana for some exhibition games. It was during this trip when Casey, who enjoyed getting into trouble, apparently took on Ernest Hemingway and got into a violent fight. As teammate Kirby Higbe put it, "the furniture really took a beating."[81]

After his return from the military in 1946, Casey had his best season with an 11–5 record, 5 saves and a career low 1.99 ERA. He led the league with 18 saves in '47, before imploding the following year with an 8.00 ERA. The Georgia native would finish his career in 1949 with the Bucs and Yankees, going 4–1 in Pittsburgh before his 8.22 ERA in 4 contests with New York.

The Hugh Casey story would not have a happy ending as he took his own life two years after his retirement, supposedly despondent over the breakup of his marriage.

Larry French— French had a long and solid 14-year career as a starter in the majors, finishing with a final mark of 197–171.

He began with the Pirates in 1929, with Bert Blyleven–like records (double digits in both wins and losses). He twice won 18 games with Pittsburgh in 1932 and 1933 and took 17 games his first year as a starter in 1930. The southpaw was dealt to the Cubs with Freddie Lindstrom for Guy Bush, Jim Weaver and Babe Herman in 1934. He would have six nice seasons in Chicago, going 18–9 in 1936 and 15–8 in '39 before being selected to his first All-Star game in 1940.

After a disastrous 5–14 mark in 1941, he was put on waivers and picked up by Brooklyn. The California native would have his finest season in 1942 as a spot starter with the Dodgers, going 15–4 with a league leading winning percentage of .789 and a career low ERA of 1.83. He would leave for the Navy after the season. The 35-year-old pitcher, worried that he would be too old by the time his stint in the armed forces ended for him to get his 200 wins, petitioned the Navy to allow him to pitch during his time off so he could achieve that career mark he desperately wanted. French even offered to donate his entire salary to the naval relief. Not wanting to start a waterfall of similar requests, the Navy turned him down.[82] French would go on to participate in he invasion of Normandy and become a lieutenant commander.[83]

His premonition turned out to be factual as it was to late for him to pick up where he left off and French would never pitch in the majors again, the war definitely costing him the mark he so cherished. Larry would remain in the reserves and would fight in Korea. By the time he finished his military career in 1969 he was a captain.[84]

Chet Kehn—Before going to the armed service, Chet Kehn's career lasted all of 7⅔ unsuccessful innings where he gave up 6 runs and 2 homers.

1943 Pittsburgh Pirates
80–74–25 GB

1941	1942	1943
1B-Elbie Fletcher	Fletcher	Fletcher
2B-Frank Gustine	Gustine	Coscarart
SS-ArkyVaughan	Pete Coscarart	Gustine
3B-Lee Handley	Elliott	Elliott
OF-Bob Elliott	Johnny Barrett	Barrett
OF-Vince DiMaggio	DiMaggio	DiMaggio
OF-Maurice Van Robays	Jimmy Wasdell	Jim Russell
CA-Al Lopez	Lopez	Lopez
PI-Rip Sewell	Sewell	Sewell
PI-Max Butcher	Bob Klinger	Klinger
PI-Ken Heintzelman	Heintzelman	Wally Hebert
PI-Johnny Lanning	Butcher	Butcher

Perhaps it was the fact that the team just matured a little and improved naturally, or more than likely it was that the Pirates virtually went untouched by the war in 1943. Whatever it was, the Bucs improved 16 games over 1942 to finish at 80–74 and nudge into the first division.

The pitching staff made the most dramatic improvement, lowering their team ERA from 3.59 to 3.09, second in the National League. Rip Sewell, practitioner of the infamous eephus pitch (a pitch that floated high in the air like a softball), led the senior circuit in wins with 21 and came in with a sparkling 2.54 ERA. The entire starting rotation of Sewell, Bob Klingler, Max Butcher and Wally Hebert would all finish with ERAs under 3.00. Add into the mix Johnny Lanning, 4–1–2.33 and Jack Hallett, 1–2–1.70, both of whom left for the military in the middle of the season, and you had a powerful staff.

Offensively, the Pirates were also vastly improved, scoring 84 more runs than they did the previous campaign, leading the league in triples with 73 and stolen bases at 64. Third basemen Bob Elliott, one of the great stars during the war years, led the way with 101 RBIs and a .315 average. Infielder Frank Gustine also was a force, improving his '42 average by 61 points (.229 to .290). Despite the fact Vince DiMaggio led the NL in strikeouts,

Who Left for the War	*Who Replaced Them*
2B-Ed Leip	
OF-Cully Rikard	
PI-Ed Albosta	
PI-Ken Heitzelman	Wally Hebert
PI — Lefty Wilkie	

Rip Sewell of the Pittsburgh Pirates was not only one of the best pitchers during the war years, but was a very creative one also, coming up with a toss called the eephus pitch. It was a softball like pitch that arched high in the air coming down right at the perfect time over the plate. It was a toss that proved too tempting to many a player and baffled many more than those who figured it out. Courtesy of the Pittsburgh Pirates.

he also had a fine season, leading the team in homers with 15. He also chipped in 88 RBIs.

The military would take a bigger bite out of the Bucs in 1944, but in the meantime, it was nice to be in the first division again.

Ed Leip — The Trenton native played in parts of four seasons for the Senators and Bucs between 1939 and 1942, amassing only 62 at-bats and a .274 average. He would not return to the majors after the war.

Cully Rikard — After two part-time seasons in 1941 and 1942, hitting .200 and .192 respectively in 72 cumulative at-bats, Rikard would come back for one more season after the war in 1947 hitting .287 in 324 times to the plate. A nice way to end Rikard's short career in the show.

Ed Albosta — Ed Albosta pitched one year before the war in 1941 with Brooklyn and one year after with Pittsburgh in 1946, both unsuccessful ventures.

His '41 season saw Albosta give up 9 runs and 8 walks in 13 innings. He would pitch more in '46, tossing 41 frames, yet still with little success, giving up 34 runs and 35 walks before making his major league exit.

Ken Heintzelman — Heintzelman, who once won 20 games with the Pirate D farm club in nearby Jeannette in 1936,[85] came up to stay in 1940 after three abbreviated seasons between 1937 and 1939. He would accumulate a 27–30 mark in his three years as a starter in 1940 through 1942 and his ERA would read like a roller coaster, going from 4.47 down to 3.44

and ballooning back to 4.57 before he went into the service after the '42 campaign.

Heintzelman would return in 1946 with a 8–12 record and respectable 3.77 ERA before collapsing early in the 1947 season, being touched for 11 runs and 6 walks in 4 innings of work for the Pirates. His major league career given up for dead, Ken would be rescued by the Phillies where he would have a marquee season in 1949 going 17–10 and a career low ERA of 3.02 (if you don't count his 2.00 in 9 innings of work in 1937). It would be the beginning of the end for Heintzelman, as he would fall to 10–24 between 1950 and 1952, leaving the game after the 1952 season.

Wally Hebert replaced Ken in the rotation. After having three largely unsuccessful seasons with the Browns between 1931 and 1933, with a combined 11–25 mark, Hebert would return to the majors after a ten-year absence to go 10–11 in 1943 with a nice 2.98 ERA. It would be a nice swan song to Hebert's career.

Lefty Wilkie — Wilkie began his time in the big leagues in 1941 with a 2–4 record before going 6–7 in 107 innings of work in '42. He would go into the military, returning in 1946 to throw 7 more innings, giving up 13 hits and 9 runs in his final major league season.

1943 Chicago Cubs
74–79–30.5 GB

1941	*1942*	*1943*
1B-Babe Dahlgren	Cavarretta	Cavarretta
2B-Lou Stringer	Stringer	Eddie Stanky
SS-Bobby Sturgeon	Lennie Merullo	Merullo
3B-Stan Hack	Hack	Hack
OF-Bill Nicholson	Nicholson	Nicholson
OF-Phil Cavarretta	Dallessandro	Peanuts Lowrey
OF-Dom Dallessandro	Lou Novikoff	Ival Goodman
CA-Clyde McCullough	McCullough	McCullough
PI-Claude Passeau	Passeau	Passeau
PI-Vern Olson	Lee	Bithorn
PI-Bill Lee	Olson	Paul Derringer
PI-Larry French	Hi Bithorn	Ed Hanyzewski

The emergence of Bill Nicholson, who was perhaps the best player during the war seasons, and Phil Cavarretta helped the Cubs improve 6 games over 1942, despite the fact they lost 10 players to Uncle Sam.

The team batting average shot up 7 points to .261 as they scored 41 more runs than the previous campaign. Nicholson led the senior circuit in homers with 29 and in RBIs by 28 over the man who came in second, Bob Elliott, with 129. He also hit .309 and was second in the league in slugging at .531. Cavarretta hit 8 homers as his average shot up 21 points to .291. The 34-year-old Ival Goodman also had a nice season, hitting .320.

On the rubber, Hi Bithorn and his 18–12–2.60 season led the Cubs. Right behind him was Claude Passeau, who chipped in with a 15–12–2.91 mark. As a group, in a season where walks outdid strikeouts, this club had a very impressive 513/394 K/BB ratio.

Who Left for the War	Who Replaced Them
CA-Marv Felderman	
CA-Bob Scheffing	
CA-Benny Warren	
2B-Lou Stringer	Eddie Stanky
SS-Bobby Sturgeon	
3B-Cy Block	
OF-Marv Rickert	
PI-Emil Kush	
PI-Vern Olson	Paul Derringer
PI-Johnny Schmitz	

Marv Felderman—"Coonie" had a very short career, going 1 for 6 with 4 strikeouts and a walk in 3 games for the 1942 Chicago Cubs.

Bob Scheffing — Scheffing had a short career in the majors before being called into the service, hitting .242 in 132 at-bats in 1941 before slumping to .196 the following season.

When he returned from the military, he would improve drastically. He started in 1947 and 1948 for Chicago, hitting a career high .300 in '48. After a 3 for 16 start to start the 1950 season, Scheffing was sent to Cincinnati for Ron Northey. He was sent to the Cards a year later, hitting .111 (.236 for the year including his time in Cincinnati) and ending his time in the big leagues.

Benny Warren— Although listed as a Cub and on the Chicago roster when he was called into the military after the 1942 season, Benny Warren never actually played a game for the Cub franchise. He started for the Phils between 1940 and 1942 after his callup in '39, hitting .246, .214 and .209 respectively. He was picked up by Pittsburgh on waivers in '42 where he did not play, before being sold to the Cubs.

After the war, he was put on waivers by Chicago where the Giants took him in 1946. A year later after a 1 for 5 performance, he was gone from the majors.

Lou Stringer— As a rookie in 1941, Lou Stringer took over the starting position at second, hitting .246 with an impressive 20 fielding runs. Lou would almost double his home run total in 1942 before leaving for the military hitting 9 (he hit only 5 the year before) while his average dropped a little to .236.

When he returned for the 1946 campaign, Stringer would share his spot with Don Johnson, before being picked up by the Red Sox. It was in Boston where his major league career came to a quick end, batting only 69 times between 1948 and 1950.

Eddie Stanky would replace Stringer in 1943 and hit .245 with 12 fielding runs in his rookie campaign, before being replaced by Johnson in 1944, who was an offensive improvement over Stringer, hitting .278 and .302 in '44 and '45, when Stanky was sent to Brooklyn.

Bobby Sturgeon — Sturgeon was the starting shortstop for the Cubs in his rookie year of 1941 when he hit .245 in 433 at-bats. He hurt his leg in 1942 and gave way to Lennie Merullo.

Upon his return from the service, Sturgeon would have his best year ever hitting .296 in a part time role. After another campaign in Chicago, he was traded to the Braves for Dick Culler. He would play the 1948 season in Boston, hitting .218 in 74 at-bats before his time in the show was over.

Cy Block — After a successful opening act in which Block hit .364 in 33 at-bats in 1942, the Brooklyn native would answer his call to arms. He returned in 1945, but would appear in only 20 official at-bats in '45 and '46 before his career was over. Despite the brevity of his time in the majors, Block finished his career on the plus side of .300, hitting .302.

Marv Rickert — "Twitch" came up with the Cubs in 1942 in an abbreviated manner, playing in only 8 games. He would return in 1946 in a much more expansive role hitting .263 in 392 at-bats. Rickert fell off to .146 in 1947 before being sold to the Reds. Cincinnati would then turn around and send Marv to the NL champion Braves in 1948 for Danny Litwhiler. He had his best campaign the following season in 1949, hitting .292, before being sold to Pittsburgh who turned around and sold him to the White Sox early in 1950. Rickert would hit .237 in his final season that year.

Emil Kush — His six-year Cub career included two prewar abbreviated seasons in 1941 and 1942 where he combined for 6 innings and 3 hits with 1 run given up. After he returned in 1946, Kush would enjoy four much fuller seasons.

Perhaps his best year was in '46 where he posted a 9–2 mark with a career low ERA of 3.05 in 129 innings. He had another banner campaign the following year in '47 with an 8–3 record. He fell off his last two seasons with a combined 4–7 record in '48 and '49. Regardless of the falloff, Kush ended his career with a fine 21–12 mark.

Vern Olson — After being called up in 1939, where Vern tossed 7⅔ scoreless innings, the Oregon native would go on to have three solid seasons as a starter for Chicago before he would go off to the military.

His best season was his official rookie year of 1940, winning 13 games

with a fine 2.97 ERA and career low .260 OBA. The southpaw would follow up with a 10–8 mark in '41 before falling to a 6–9 record with a lifetime high 4.49 ERA.

After the war Olson would pitch in only 5 more major league games
in 1946, giving up 9 walks and 10 hits in 9⅔ innings before he was finished.

Paul Derringer would replace Olson as the number three man in the
rotation. Derringer, winner of 223 games in his 15 year career and starter
of the first night game ever while with the Reds,[86] went 10–14 in 1943 before
finishing with a fine 16–11 mark in 1945, his final season in the bigs.

Johnny Schmitz — Schmitz is another pitcher who would have a short
major league career before really breaking out when he returned. "Bear
Claw" would go 5–7 in 1941 and 1942 as a starter/reliever before he went
off to fight. When he returned, Johnny enjoyed a 5-year stint as a staple
in the Cubs rotation.

He was selected to his first All-Star game in 1946, leading the league
in strikeouts with 135 and a .221 OBA. His second selection to the big game
came in his best season in 1948 when Schmitz finished with a 18–13 record,
a 2.64 ERA and a NL low .215 OBA.

After two more seasons when he combined for a 21–29 mark, Johnny
was sent to Brooklyn along with Rube Walker, Andy Pafko and Wayne Ter-
williger for Bruce Edwards, Joe Hatten, Eddie Miksis and Gene Hermanski. It would be the beginning of a six year odyssey that would find Bear
Claw moving from Chicago to Brooklyn, to the Yankees, Cincinnati, Washington, Boston and Baltimore, where he ended his career in 1956 with a
93–114 mark. Most of his success during that time period came with the
Senators where he enjoyed a banner campaign of 11–8–2.91 in 1954.

1943 Boston Braves
68–85–36.5 GB

1941	1942	1943
1B-Buddy Hassett	West	Johnny McCarthy
2B-Bama Rowell	Sisti	Connie Ryan
SS-Eddie Miller	Miller	Whitey Wietelmann
3B-Sibby Sisti	Nanny Fernandez	Eddie Joost
OF-Gene Moore	Paul Waner	Chuck Workman
OF-John Cooney	Tommy Holmes	Holmes
OF-Max West	Chet Ross	Butch Nieman
CA-Ray Berres	Ernie Lombardi	Phil Masi
PI-Manny Salvo	Javery	Javery
PI-Jim Tobin	Tobin	Tobin
PI-Al Javery	Lou Tost	Nate Andrews
PI-Art Johnson	Tom Earley	Red Barrett

Unlucky 13 was the call of the 1943 Boston Braves as they lost 13 players to the military, including two of the biggest pieces of their 1948 National League championship club in Johnny Sain and Warren Spahn. On the positive side, this was war ball and others were losing a great deal of players too. So with it all, it was still possible for Boston to win 8 more games than the year before. On top of the 13 who departed, starting first baseman Johnny McCarthy and young relievers Bill Donovan and Ray Martin would also leave before the season was done.

Despite all the movement, the pitching staff gave up ½ run less per game than in 1942. Led again by Al Javery and Jim Tobin, the Braves not only reduced the team ERA, but they gave up 78 less walks than the year prior. Nate Andrews would lead the league in losses with 20, yet would have a sparkling 2.57 ERA and a great IP/H ratio of 284/253.

McCarthy, who had a troubling season despite his .304 average, as he broke his leg and was taken into the military, led the offense. Kerby Farrell, who took over for him, could manage only a .268 mark. No other offensive starter came within 30 points of McCarthy, as Tommy Holmes was next at .270. It got so bad that the remainder of the infield, Connie Ryan, Whitey Wietelmann and Eddie Joost would hit just .212, .215 and .185 respectively.

Even though things looked pretty pathetic at the time (even manager Casey Stengel broke his leg and missed a portion of the season), 1948 was just around the corner. In the meantime, the Braves would have to settle for the second division the next few years.

Who Left for the War	Who Replaced Them
INF-Skippy Roberge	
1B-Buddy Gramp	
1B-Max West	Johnny McCarthy
2B-Sibby Sisti	Connie Ryan
3B-Ducky Detweiler	
3B-Nanny Fernandez	Eddie Joost
OF-Frank McElyea	
PI-Tom Earley	Red Barrett
PI-Art Johnson	
PI-Frank LaManna	
PI-Johnny Sain	
PI-Warren Spahn	
PI-Ace Williams	

Skippy Roberge — Joseph "Skippy" Roberge was a utility infielder that-batted .215 in 339 at-bats in 1941 and 1942 for the Braves. The year 1946 found him getting his career highs in batting average at .231 and homers with 2 in his comeback and final major league season.

Skippy was by all means a decent fielder as he finished every year with positive fielding runs.

Buddy Gremp— Lewis "Buddy" Gremp saw his playing time increase in his first war season of 1942 after two abbreviated years in 1940 and 1941. He hit .217 in 207 at-bats before leaving for the military.

During the war, he played with Ted Williams, Johnny Pesky and Johnny Sain at the University of North Carolina Naval pre-flight training program. He would not return to the majors after his time in the Navy. [87]

Max West— West was a solid hitting outfielder/first baseman for the Braves in 1938 through 1942. After a fine rookie year where he smacked 10 homers and knocked in 63, he broke out big time in 1939, hitting 19 shots with 82 RBIs and a career high .285 average. In 1942, West moved to first where he hit 16 homers with a .254 average.

When he came back in 1946, Max was sent to the Reds for Jim Konstanty and cash and slumped to .212. He was out of the big leagues until 1948 when he finished up his career hitting .178 in his final big league campaign.

Johnny McCarthy took over for West at first in 1943 and hit .304, although not able to match Max's power, hitting only 2 homers. He went into the service by midseason.

Sibby Sisti— The war cost Sebastian "Sibby" Sisti his best years as a major league ballplayer. He started with the Braves in 1940 and 1941, hitting .251 and .259 his second and third years in the league respectively. Boston moved him to second from short the following season and Sisti slumped to .211.

After returning from the military in 1946, Sibby was mainly a reserve player. He did have one more good season in 1951, hitting .279 in 362 at-bats. Sisti fell to .212 in 1952, and was out of the majors two seasons later.

Connie Ryan replaced Sisti at second, making the All-Star game in 1944 with a .295 average after a sub par 1943, hitting only .212.

Ducky Detweiler— In 1942, Detweiler impressed the Braves, hitting .318 in 44 at-bats. He would only receive one more major league at-bat in 1946, going hitless. He left the majors with a .311 career average.

Nanny Fernandez— Froilan "Nanny" Fernandez started his career as the starting third baseman with the Braves in 1942, hitting .255 with 6 round trippers and 55 RBIs.

He returned in 1946, matching his rookie season average at .255 in 372 at-bats before slumping to .206 the next season. He was sent to

Pittsburgh in 1950 where he spent his last season hitting a career high .258 and matching his big league best of 6 homers in 198 at-bats.

Eddie Joost was brought over to Boston before the 1943 season to replace Fernandez from the Reds with Nate Andrews for $25,000 and Eddie Miller. He would have one of the worst seasons of his career, hitting .185 in 421 at-bats. Eddie retired for one season in 1944 before coming back to hit .248 in 141 at-bats in 1945.

Frank McElyea— McElyea had a very short 0 for 4 season in 1942, his only season in the majors.

Tom Earley— After three abbreviated years with Boston between 1938 and 1940 where Earley was a combined 4–4 in 67⅓ innings, he broke out in what would arguably be his career season in 1941 with a 6–8 record and 2.53 ERA. He also had a minuscule .233 OBA. As the number four starter in 1942, Earley slipped back a little, going 6–11 with a much higher ERA of 4.71. When he returned from the military, he would pitch only 11 more games, finishing with a 2–1 record.

Taking Earley's spot in 1943 was Red Barrett. Red would prove to be a more than adequate replacement despite his 12–18 record, with a 3.18 ERA and a 255/240 IP/H ratio. He was with the Braves until 1945 when he was dealt to the Cards for Mort Cooper.

Art Johnson—"Lefty" would pitch three years with the Braves between 1940 and 1942. Sandwiched in between two 6-inning seasons was a 7–15 performance for the 1941 campaign in 183⅓ innings. He would not return to the majors after going into the military.

Frank LaManna— Frank LaManna, one might say, was an Art Johnson clone, as he would come up with a 5–4 mark in 72⅔ innings in 1941 with a fat 5.33 ERA sandwiched around two 5 game seasons in 1940 and 1942. Like Johnson, 1942 was his last season.

Johnny Sain— When Johnny Sain left the Braves in 1942 for the navy he was a young rookie pitcher, having gone 4–7 in 40 appearances, 37 in relief. Upon is return in 1946, he would become a full blown superstar, winning 20 games in 3 consecutive years, 1946 through 1948, making the All-Star game in '47 and '48. He would lead the National League in complete games in '46 and '48, innings pitched in 1948 and wins that same year.

Sain would receive most of his fame helping pitch the Braves to the NL crown in 1948 with a 24–15 record and a 2.60 ERA. He was tops in the circuit in TPI at 5.4, finishing second to Musial in the MVP vote. Sain started the opening game in the Fall Classic, pitching the Braves to a 1–0 victory over Bob Feller and the Indians.

Despite the success of '48, perhaps Sain's best season was in his return year of 1946 where he was 20–14 with a fantastic 2.21 ERA and an impressive .230 OBA. He led the circuit that season in TPI with 5.9.

Johnny fell to 10–17 in 1949 before rebounding with another 20 win campaign in 1950, although he would hurt his shoulder that season, which resulted in his poor 5–13 performance in '51.

Sain was sent to the Yanks for Lew Burdette and $50,000 in 1952. The Arkansas native would have a few decent seasons in New York, going to the All-Star game in 1953 with a 14–7 mark before adapting well to his new relief role in '54 leading the league with 22 saves.

He was sent packing to the A's the next year with Enos Slaughter for Sonny Dixon and cash. He would go 2–5 the rest of the way and call it quits at the end of the campaign, finishing with a 139–116 mark.

Sain became a very successful pitching coach after his career with the Yanks, Tigers, Twins, Angels, White Sox and Braves, helping pitchers such as Whitey Ford, Jim Kaat, Denny Mcclain, Wilbur Wood and Jim Perry win 20 games.[88]

Warren Spahn—Like Sain, Spahn left the Braves for the military a young kid having thrown only 15 very unimpressive innings, giving up 25 hits with a 5.74 ERA. When he came back, Warren won more games than any other left hander in history with 363, won 20 games 13 times, including leading the league on 8 occasions. He would pitch in 14 mid-summer classics, 3 World Series, including the 1957 world championship season. Spahn would win the Cy Young Award in 1957, while leading the NL in ERA 3 times, strikeouts on 4 occasions, and TPI 5 times. As impressive as this all was, perhaps his most memorable performance was at the European Theater during World War II. Warren fought with the 176th combat engineers battalion in the Battle of the Bulge. He was awarded the Bronze Star for his participation in the taking of the Rhine Crossing Bridge. Spahn also got the Purple Heart after being hit with shrapnel.[89]

Upon his return from combat, Spahn showed glimpses of what he would be, finishing 1946 at 8–5 with a 2.94 ERA. After that he would reel off 20 wins in 6 of the next 8 seasons. Despite all the accolades Spahn gets for his performance with Johnny Sain in 1948 ("Spahn and Sain and pray for rain"), it actually was one of his worst seasons finishing at 15–12 with a 3.71 ERA, his highest until 1964. Spahn would win 20 games the next three campaigns before a 14–19 mark his last year in Boston in 1952.

The Braves moved to Milwaukee the next season and Warren responded with his best campaign, leading the league with 23 wins and a NL low ERA of 2.10 (which was also a career low), a .217 OBA and a 7.3 TPI. He would finish 6th in the MVP race, the top pitcher in the voting (there was no Cy Young Award at this point).

In Spahn's 12 seasons in Milwaukee, he would win 20 games on 9 occasions, including his Cy Young winning year in the Braves' world championship season of 1957. He finished that year with a league leading 21 victories, the first of five consecutive times he would lead the league in that category. In the World Series, Spahn would not be his best, losing Game 1, 3–1, to Whitey Ford before winning Game 4, 7–5 on a 3 run shot by Eddie Mathews in the 10th.

Warren won 126 games over the next 6 years before the wheels would come off. After a 23–7 record with a 2.60 ERA in 1963, Spahn would fall to 6–13 the following season. The Buffalo southpaw would be sold to the Mets in 1965 where Spahn made the statement, "I'm probably the only player to play for Stengel before and after he was a genius" (referring to Stengel also being his manager for the Braves in 1942).[90]

After a 4–12 mark for the hapless Mets, Warren went to the Bay to finish out his career with San Francisco in 1965.

The war cost many their careers or places in history, and many think that Spahn would have joined Cy Young and Walter Johnson as the only men to win 400 for a lifetime, but it might have been more difficult than one considers. It is true that barring injury, he would have easily passed Grover Cleveland Alexander and Christy Mathewson, who were 10 wins ahead of him at 373, but he was not impressive in 1942, so to crack the starting rotation, especially if there had been no war between 1943–45, would have been no certainty and 37 wins would have been difficult.

Of course this is all conjecture and Spahn might have caught fire immediately and not only cracked 400, but also beat Walter Johnson's 417 wins, but chances are, it would have been 1944 or 1945 before he realistically got into the rotation. Nonetheless, war or not, Spahn goes down as one of the greatest southpaws of all time, if not the greatest.

Ace Williams — Robert Fulton Williams' career lasted about as long as a single Warren Spahn outing, 9 innings. He threw them all in 1940, giving up 21 hits and 12 walks for a mind numbing 16.00 ERA. He got one last shot in 1946, hitting a batter and giving up a hit to the only two batters he faced.

⚾   ⚾   ⚾

It was truly an embarrassing franchise at this point and time in history, that had a season full of soap opera like twists and turns. You didn't know what was coming next. The Phils lost 11 players to the armed forces, yet the talent was so thin they actually won 22 more games than they did the year before and still had a bad season. The ownership saga that lasted the whole season had the opportunity to turn itself around had they been

1943 Philadelphia Phillies
64–90–41 GB

1941	*1942*	*1943*
1B-Nick Etten	Etten	Jimmy Wasdell
2B-Danny Murtaugh	Al Glossup	Murtaugh
SS-Bobby Bragan	Bragan	Glen Stewart
3B-Pinky May	May	May
OF-Stan Benjamin	Ron Northey	Northey
OF-Joe Marty	Lloyd Waner	Buster Adams
OF-Danny Litwhiler	Litwhiler	Coaker Triplett
CA-Bennie Warren	Warren	Mickey Livingston
PI-Cy Blanton	Hughes	Schoolboy Rowe
PI-Johnny Podgajny	Rube Melton	Al Gearheauser
PI-Tommy Hughes	Johnson	Tex Kraus
PI-Si Johnson	Podgajny	Dick Barrett

sold to Bill Veeck, who intended to field the team with a host of Negro League players. He felt the risk was too great and Judge Landis turned around and sold it to William Cox, a vocal George Steinbrenner type owner whom Landis would have to throw out of the league by the end of 1943 because he gambled on his own team — such was the saga of the Philadelphia Phillies.[91]

Truth be told, there are some who dispute Veeck's story, but if it was true, imagine what might have happened if he did buy the team. Not only would the Phils have been a vastly improved club with the injection of several Hall of Fame talents, they might have competed for a world championship, not only in 1943, but for years after that. Their history might have been up there with the Yanks and Cardinals, rather than the one they have today as one of the least successful franchises in the annals of the game.

To take matters one step further, had they taken several Negro League players in 1943, they might have cost the Dodgers their fabulous run during the late 40s and 50s, taking the endless supply of Negro League players that the Dodgers were the first to tap into. It also begs the question how Jackie Robinson would have truly performed if the Phils had taken Negro Leaguers ahead of him and he hadn't been under the constant pressure of being the first. There is some thought that the pressure made him a better player.

On the reality side of things, the team the Phillies did put on the field was vastly improved both on the mound and at the plate. The rotation of Rowe, Barrett, Gerheauser, and Kraus had ERAs of 2.94, 2.39, 3.60 and 3.16, an immense improvement over the previous season, but the major plus was in the offense.

The team that could only muster up 394 runs in 1942 jumped to 571 in this campaign. Ron Northey led the way smacking 16 homers, hitting .278. Second baseman Danny Murtaugh was also having a fine year, hitting at a .273 clip when Uncle Sam took him before the year was out.

Despite all the plusses, this was still a bad team. Imagine how one decision can affect an entire future, had they only sold the team to Veeck.

Who Left for the War	Who Replaced Them
CA-Bill Peterman	
INF-Hal Marnie	
1B-Ed Murphy	
SS-Bill Burich	
OF-Ed Freed	
OF-Ernie Koy	
PI-Frank Hoerst	
PI-Tommy Hughes	Schoolboy Rowe
PI-Gene Lambert	
PI-Sam Nahem	
PI-Ike Pearson	

Bill Peterman — Bill Peterman holds the dubious mark of having the highest batting average in the *Baseball Encyclopedia*; move over Ty Cobb. Peterman singled in his only major league at-bat in 1942 ending his career with a perfect 1.000 average, and you can't do better than that. Moonlight Graham would certainly be jealous.

Harry Marnie — Sandwiched in between sub par .180 seasons of 1940 and 1942, Marnie had a respectable 1941, when he hit .241 in 158 at-bats. He was a decent fielder who accumulated 19 fielding runs in only 96 career games, all of which occurred before the war.

Ed Murphy — 1st baseman Ed Murphy's 28 career at-bats all occurred in 1942. He had 7 hits and 2 doubles for a lifetime .250 average.

Bill Burich — Burich had a nice abbreviated rookie campaign in 1942, hitting .287 in 80 at-bats. After returning from the war in 1946, Burich got only one at-bat where he would go hitless in his last major league official time at the plate.

Ed Freed — The Pennsylvania native's career was also confined to one season, 1942. He did have some success, going 10 for 33, with 3 doubles and triple. Yes Virginia, Ed Freed can make the claim of being a lifetime .300 hitter, finishing with a .303 mark.

Ernie Koy — Koy was one Phillie draftee that wasn't a one or two year blip on the major league map. He started out with the Dodgers in 1938, having a wonderful rookie season, hitting .299 with 11 homers.

After falling off the next couple seasons, he was sent to St. Louis with

Sam Nahem in 1940 and hit .310 the rest of the way with the Cards. Koy fell to .200 the next year and was sold to the Reds, before going to Philadelphia in 1942 where he hit .244 in 258 at-bats. He would not resume his major league career after the war.

Frank Hoerst— Southpaw Frank Hoerst was just coming into his own when the war interrupted his career. Coming up in 1940, "Lefty" would go 3–10 in 1941 before a 4–16 mark the following year, which was a little deceiving as his IP/H ratio was 150⅔/162. Not a great mark, but better that the 4–16 record would indicate.

Returning from the armed forces in 1946, Hoerst would go a combined 2–7 in 79 innings in '46 and '47, which would be the last two years of his major league career. The overall Hoerst pitching line: 10–33 with a 5.17 ERA.

Tommy Hughes— Although he had his first two full seasons the same time as Frank Hoerst, the comparison would end there, as Hughes was truly a casualty of war. He would go 9–14 his rookie season in 1941 before becoming the Phils' number one starter the following year. Despite his 12–18 mark in 1942, Hughes had a nice 3.06 ERA and a wonderful 253/224 IP/H ratio.

When Hughes returned from action, he would receive only 28 starts in 1946 and 1947, and could not recapture his prewar momentum, going 10–20. Tommy was sent to the Reds in 1948 for Bert Haas and would finish his once promising career that season going 0–4, giving up 43 hits in 27 innings for a 9.00 ERA.

Replacing Hughes in 1943 as the number one starter was former Detroit superstar Schoolboy Rowe. Rowe would go 14–8 with a 2.94 ERA, nicely replacing Hughes in the spot. Schoolboy himself would go into the service following this season.

Gene Lambert—Lambert had a cup of coffee in the majors for the Phils, throwing a combined 10 innings in 1941 and 1942 before leaving for the service. It would be his only 10 major league games.

Sam Nahem — After breaking in with Brooklyn in 1938, Nahem was sent to St. Louis with Ernie Koy, Carl Doyle, Bert Haas and $25,000 for Joe Medwick and Curt Davis. He would show some promise in 1941 for the Cards with a 5–2 record and 2.98 ERA before being sent over to the Phils in '42. With Philadelphia he would fall to 1–3 before heading into the Armed Forces. Upon his return he would get one last opportunity to pitch in 1948, but his ERA ballooned to 7.02 in 59 innings and his career would be over.

Ike Pearson — The problem with playing for a poor team was your won-loss record would not have a chance to be too spectacular; such was the case of Ike Pearson.

In his first three seasons from 1939 to 1941, Pearson combined for a 9–41 record. After a 1–6 performance in 1942, Ike was called to arms. He returned in 1946 and throw only 14 innings for the Phils. After a year hiatus from the league, Pearson would toss 23 games for the White Sox in 1948 to finish his career.

Ike would go only 3–3 in his postwar years, but a .500 record sounds awfully impressive when you consider he had a .180 prewar winning percentage.

1943 New York Giants
55–98–49.5 GB

1941	1942	1943
1B-Babe Young	Johnny Mize	Joe Orengo
2B-Burgess Whitehead	Mike Witek	Witek
SS-Billy Jurges	Jurges	Jurges
3B-Dick Bartell	Bill Werber	Bartell
OF-Mel Ott	Ott	Ott
OF-Johnny Rucker	Willard Marshall	Rucker
OF-Jo-Jo Moore	Babe Barna	Joe Medwick
CA-Harry Danning	Danning	Gus Mancuso
PI-Hal Schumacher	Schumacher	Melton
PI-Cliff Melton	Bob Carpenter	Johnnie Wittig
PI-Carl Hubbell	Hubbell	Ken Chase
PI-Bill Lohrman	Lohrman	Rube Fischer

There was little question over what National League team the war affected most in 1943, the once proud New York Giants.

Three everyday players and two pitchers in the starting rotation went off to serve their country which would cause the Giants to tumble 30 wins from the year before, falling from third place to last, behind the lowly Phillies.

Johnny Mize, who had a wonderful 1942 season as probably the best first basemen in the senior circuit, Willard Marshall and Harry Danning were all gone. The team, which scored 675 runs in 1942, was reduced to 558. Mickey Witek was one of the lone bright spots as his average shot up from .260 to .314. Joe Orengo and Sid Gordon combined to try to replace Mize, but could only muster up 92 RBIs between them, compared to Mize's 1942 output of 110. Gus Mancuso only had a .198 mark which was 80 points under Danning's, although Hall of Famer Ernie Lombardi would share time behind the plate and hit .305. Manager Mel Ott also slumped badly after leading the NL in homers in '42 with 30, only hitting 18 with 47 RBIs for a .234 average.

On the mound, things would also go downhill badly. Except for Ace Adams, who was 11–7 with a 2.82 ERA, everything went bad as the team

ERA shot up almost 20 percent from third in the league at 3.32 to last with a 4.08.

In the topsy-turvy war years, 1943 would be one season New York would love to forget.

Who Left for the War	Who Replaced Them
CA-Harry Danning	Gus Mancuso
CA-Charlie Fox	
1B-Johnny Mize	Joe Orengo
1B-Babe Young	
SS-Buddy Blattner	
OF-Willard Marshall	Johnny Rucker
PI-Bob Carpenter	Johnny Wittig
PI-Dave Koslo	
PI-Hal Schumacher	Cliff Melton

Harry Danning — He was affectionately called " Harry the Horse," but his fine career with the Giants would end after his call to arms in 1942.

He came up with New York in 1933, which started a 4-year run where Danning would be a part time catcher with the Giants. He would improve to .288 in 1937 as he took over the starting reins. This was a prelude to a run of 4 consecutive All-Star game selections between 1938, hitting .306, .313, and .300, respectively, the three seasons between '38 and '40. Nineteen forty would prove to be his marquee year as he also smacked 13 homers and knocked in 91.

The Horse would fall off in 1941, dipping to .244 before rebounding in his last major league season in 1942 at .279. He ended his career with a fine .285 average.

Replacing him behind the plate in 1943 was the veteran Gus Mancuso. "Blackie" was sold to the Giants by the Cardinals in the middle of 1942, and was at the end of a fine 17-year career, which included two All-Star game selections. His best days were behind him as he could only muster up a .198 average, 67 points under his career mark. After improving slightly to .251 in 1944, he was sent to the Phils, where he retired after the 1945 season.

Charlie Fox — His lifetime average was an impressive .429, although it only came in 7 at-bats for the Giants in 1942, which would be "Irish's" one and only time in the show.

Johnny Mize — The "Big Cat's" major league career started off with a very impressive 1936 campaign for the Cardinals, where he hit 19 homers with 93 RBIs and a .329 average. It would be the first of nine straight years where Mize would eclipse the .300 plateau. The second season, in 1937, he hit .364 and was selected to play in his first All-Star game.

Nineteen thirty-nine was the first true breakout season for the Big Cat as he led the senior circuit in homers with 28, average at .349, slugging with a .626 mark and a TPR of 4.2. He finished second that season in the MVP race to Bucky Walters.

Mize would come up big again the next season, finishing as the MVP bridesmaid again, this time to the Reds' Frank McCormick, as he again won two ends of the triple crown, leading in homers again with 43 and RBIs with 137. He would win his third consecutive slugging crown that season at .636.

With his home run production down a bit in 1941, and his increasing contract conflicts with GM Branch Rickey becoming a problem,

The war cost Johnny Mize his shot at becoming a member of the 500-homer club. He would become the first left-handed hitter to break the 50 home-run barrier with 51 in 1947 and eventually entered the Hall of Fame.

the 28-year-old Mize asked for, and was given, a trade.[92] He was sent to the Giants for Ken O'Dea, Bill Lohrman, Johnny McCarthy and $50,000. Things were not good for the Big Cat at first as an injured shoulder threatened his season and there was even talk of the trade being voided.[93] The Giants luckily held on to the Georgia native as he led the NL again in RBIs at 110 and slugging at .521.

Mize was called to duty the next season and would play with a team in the 14th Naval District in Hawaii. Major league greats Virgil Trucks, Johnny Vander Meer and Pee Wee Reese would all join Johnny on the squad.[94]

After his return season in 1946 in which he hit .337 despite a broken hand that limited his play, Mize went on to have his best power season ever in 1947, becoming the first lefty ever to crack the 50 home run mark in a season with 51, tying Ralph Kiner of Pittsburgh for the lead, and had the outright NL high in RBIs with a career best 138.

Two years later in 1949, Mize's home run production dropped to 18 with a .263 average, which precipitated his sale to the cross town Yankees. He spent his last four seasons as an effective player off the bench, although still possessing his legendary power as he smacked 25 homers in only 274 at-bats in 1950.

He retired three years later after 1953 with lifetime marks of 2,011 hits, 359 homers and a .312 average. Despite the lack of Hall of Fame stats, Mize was elected by the Veterans Committee to Cooperstown in 1981, and when you look at the heavy toll the war took on his career numbers, it would turn out to be a wise decision. The three years prior to his induction, Johnny smacked 87 homers and would hit 99 after his return. Had the Big Cat gone injury free in his three seasons he spent in the service, he probably would have hit between 95–120 homers and definitely would have topped the 2,500 hit mark. Five hundred homers would have been a tough mark to get to, but nonetheless, when you put all those numbers together, you have one of the greatest power hitters of all time.

Replacing Mize at first in 1943 was the infamous Joe Orengo. Orengo was bought from the Cardinals in 1941 and was nowhere near Mize's level, hitting only .218 with 6 homers. He was sent to the Dodgers midway in 1943 in the famous Dolph Camilli trade (the one in which Camilli refused to report to the Giants and retired) and was out of the game after the 1945 season when the players returned from the war.

Babe Young— After going hitless in his only plate appearance of 1936, Babe Young would return to the majors three years later in 1939, hitting .307 in 73 at-bats. He was here to stay.

Norman Young followed that campaign with his two best seasons, smacking 17 homers for 101 RBIs and a .286 average in 1940, followed by a 25–104–.265 season the next year. Babe struggled in 1942, and the rest of his career for that matter, except in 1947 after he was sent to the Reds and hit 14 homers with 79 RBIs and a .283 average (it was .275 for the entire season if you take into consideration the 1 for 14 he was before the trade with the Giants).

Young played only one more season in 1948, hitting only 2 homers in 241 at-bats for the Reds and Cardinals. One could say that the war took Babe Young's prime years from him, but when you looked at the fact that he seemingly was on a downtrend in 1942, I don't know if it really had that much of an effect on his total numbers.

Buddy Blattner— A 1 for 23 performance in St. Louis in 1942 was a truly inauspicious start to Robert Blattner's baseball career.

After that season, he was sent to the Naval Training Station in Bainbridge, Maryland, where he showed himself not only to be a good ballplayer, but an accomplished tennis player, playing in exhibition matches with the great Bobby Riggs.[95]

When he returned in 1946, Buddy moved into the starting second base position with the Giants and hit .255 with 11 homers. The 27-year-old St. Louis native would be replaced by Bill Rigney the next season and would be reduced to only 117 at-bats over his final two years with New York and Philadelphia, finishing with a .247 lifetime mark.

Willard Marshall— He was an All-Star in his rookie season of 1942 before being sent off to war, hitting 11 homers for the Giants. His career would not reach its full swing until he returned from his time with Uncle Sam.

After a decent 1946 season, Marshall would have a career year in 1947, more than doubling what would be his second highest homer total of 17 in 1953, with 36. He also knocked in 107 with a .291 average and his second All-Star game appearance. His third and final trip to the midsummer classic would be his final year with New York, in 1949, as he would hit for a career high .307, the only time he would top the .300 plateau.

Marshall would spend his remaining major league seasons with the Braves, who got him from New York with Sid Gordon, Buddy Kerr and Red Webb for Alvin Dark and Eddie Stanky in a trade that gave the Giants their starting middle infield for their 1951 championship run, and the Reds.

He had two more decent seasons, one with Boston in 1951 with 11 homers and a .281 average, and one with Cincinnati in 1953 with a 17–62–.266 performance. He retired after only 112 at-bats with the 1954 and 1955 White Sox.

Johnny Rucker took over for Marshall in 1943 and would hit .273. He would start for two more seasons and would be out of the majors after 1946 a career .272 hitter. Although the Alabama native almost had an identical average when compared to Marshall (.272 to Willard's .274), he was nowhere near the same power hitter, only getting 21 lifetime homers, 15 less than Marshall had in his best year. His -12 fielding runs compared to Marshall's 20 showed Rucker not to be the superior fielder either.

Bob Carpenter— Classify Bob Carpenter as a young pitcher who lost the momentum of a good start to his career due to the war. He was brought up in 1940 and broke into the rotation the following season in 1941 when he won 11 games in each of the next two seasons before he was called into the military.

Only 29 years old when he returned from his time in the service, Carpenter would not enjoy the success after the war as he did before it. His ERA, which was 3.15 in 1942, ballooned to 4.85 in 1946. He would throw only 10 innings in 1947 with the Cubs and Giants to finish his once promising career.

Johnny Wittig would take over for Carpenter in 1943 and would not meet with the same success, going 5–15 with a 4.23 ERA. He would enter the military himself the next season.

Dave Koslo— Dave Koslo's star would not truly shine until he returned from the armed forces in 1946. After entering the majors in 1941, holding his opponents to a spectacular .202 OBA in 3 impressive starts, Koslo would slump the next season at 3–6 before entering the military.

He returned in '46 going 14–19, which what would be the beginning of a run where he won double digits in six of the next seven seasons, the only exception an 8–10 mark in 1948.

His career year would be the following season in 1949. Despite a sub .500 record at 11–14, which should come as no surprise, being Koslo had a 92–107-lifetime mark, Dave led the senior circuit with a 2.50 ERA and a 4.2 TPI. He would win 33 games over the next 3 seasons before collapsing to 6–12 in 1953, his ERA bulging to 4.76.

The Giants sold Koslo to Baltimore in 1954 where he gave up 20 hits in 14 innings. He would end his major league career a year later with the Braves.

Hal Schumacher—coming up to the Giants for two difficult seasons in 1931 and 1932, "Prince Hal" would explode onto the scene in 1933, leading the Giants to the world championship with a 19–12 mark and 2.16 ERA. He would lead the league with a .214 OBA and an All-Star game appearance in the initial midsummer classic.

The year 1934 would be another great season with Hal's only 20-win campaign as he went 23–10, helping himself at the plate with 6 homers. A second All-Star game appearance awaited him in 1935 finishing with a 19–9 record that gave him a 61–28 mark his first three seasons as a starter.

With his best seasons behind him, Schumacher would settle into a seven-year streak where he won between 11 and 13 games including 13 in four consecutive seasons between 1937 and 1940.

After serving as an officer on an aircraft carrier in the war,[96] Schumacher would return for one more season in 1946 at the age of 36 where he finished up at 4–4. He retired with an outstanding 158–121 lifetime record and became an executive vice president with the Adirondack Bat Company.

Cliff Melton would replace Schumacher as the number one man in the Giant rotation in 1943. Melton, who won 20 games his first season in 1937, went 9–13 with a nice 3.19 ERA for the last place club. He would finish up his career the following season with a 2–2 record.

3

1944

As 1944 came to pass, the game had proven it could survive during this time of conflict, even while it was running with mostly 4-F's and aging veterans. The quality of play had slipped immeasurably, yet it was certainly providing the country with the morale boost that FDR had envisioned two years before.

Unlike the two prior war ball seasons, which were filled with one controversy after another and several important decisions that were meant to keep the national pastime alive, this campaign would see the best that the sport had to offer, yet it wouldn't overshadow the serious events that were taking place overseas.

There would be one of the most fabulous pennant races in baseball's annals, complete with a surprise champion and a World Series in which both combatants came from one city (which wasn't New York or Chicago). We would also see a battle for the future of minor league baseball, very young teenagers making their mark in the game like they hadn't in the past and wouldn't in the future, and the czar who had brought the major leagues from the brink of extinction due to the 1919 Black Sox scandal all the way back to the pinnacle of success it had enjoyed currently, pass away five days before his 78th birthday. D-Day would finally come as the war would enter its most dangerous time period with several professional ballplayers leaving the fields of play for the battlefields, where some would be injured, captured and lose their lives in the line of fire. The game between the lines would take a serious backseat to the events around the globe.

Baseball was still more than a decade away from experiencing the financial boom of the West Coast, but Clarence Rowland, president of the Los Angeles Angels and soon to be Pacific Coast League president, was a man ahead of his time.[1] His idea was simple — in lieu of purchasing a current major league team and taking them to the coast, he wanted to convince his fellow PCL owners to form a third major league.

The idea was novel, but not really feasible as the league would find out a year later when they tried to go forward with their plan. Despite the fact it was the premier minor league circuit in the land, its parks were not of major league quality or size. The attendances, led by the Angels with 362,677 (which would only have been greater than one current major league team, the Boston Braves, who drew 208,691), were not really up to the par of the big leagues either.

Such was the case of the minor league baseball in 1944. After 23 leagues folded the previous season, the bottom had definitely been touched as the class D Ohio State League had started up again, raising the total operational leagues up to 10. The debates that raged were not just how to supply the minors with players during this manpower short time, but how would the future of the institution unfold as the incredible amounts of ex-players would soon return from the war? How would the new face of minor league baseball come to pass?

National Association president W.G. Bramham, who had survived a potential ousting the year before by allowing leagues that had been suspended during the war to vote on whether he should continue his post or not, was concerned with just how to restructure the suspended leagues after the war was over. He wanted to make the leagues more compact with an emphasis on local rivalries.[2] Washington Senator owner Clark Griffith was concerned over the stockpiling of minor league teams and players by certain major league clubs, and proposed a limit of only owning three teams, all above class A with the emphasis on having the lower leagues operate as independents.[3]

Jack Zoller, general manager of the Detroit Tigers, had a controversial plan that would allow the National Association to scout and develop players, while the major leagues would only be allowed to control 50 players each.[4] The majors would then have to purchase the players from the minor league team when a player was ready to be promoted. This would avoid a major league team from denying them "the privilege of earning a major league salary," as the richer clubs would do when they hid a prospect in their deep minor league systems, or having lesser teams rush a prospect up before his time.[5] Zoller feared that at some point, if things did not change, all the good (or rich) teams would corner all the best prospects.

One of the most vehement detractors to the plan was Branch Rickey, president of the Dodgers. As concerned as he was at the time in filling his current minor league rosters, Rickey, who had built the Cardinals into a power by stockpiling minor leaguers and certainly intended to do the same in Brooklyn, wanted to keep things status quo. "It is utopian. He has the wrong approach to the entire question and (the plan) does not interest me."[6]

Zoller's plan, of course, would never come to fruition and the minors for the time being would go on as they always had (although it would eventually evolve into the system we have today which is certainly more along the lines of what that great visionary Clark Griffith saw). What happened was that the minor leagues would go on an incredible boom after the war, flexing back up to 41 leagues.

Minor league baseball wasn't the only struggling entity around with a two-fold problem: how to fill the current rosters in the face of the war and what to do with the influx of several returning veterans. Currently, more manpower was needed abroad and the selective service was down to just two main classifications, 1-A, men eligible to go into the service, and 4F, men unable to physically perform as soldiers, which encompassed the majority of major league players during the time period (along with players over 38 years old).[7]

There was also the controversy of whether or not to use players in the one remaining classification 2B, men who stayed home to work in war related factories.[8] Two teams, the St. Louis Browns and the Philadelphia Athletics, both expressed interest in using these players on a part time basis when they were off, usually on the weekends (had the players played full time, they would have been subjected to the draft). The Yankees' Ed Barrow and Brooklyn's Rickey were both opposed to using these players. It was generally thought that this subject would need the full permission of Commissioner Landis, which he would soon give.[9] This decision was to open the door for players such as Frank Crosetti, Hal Wagner and Denny Galehouse, all of whom were working in war factories.[10]

On top of all the other manpower problems, Washington was considering using all 4F's in a labor battalion, a decision that certainly would have been the end of baseball during the war.[11] Luckily for the game, the 4F's were allowed to continue to play.

The lords of baseball also had the task of deciding what to do with the players when they returned from the service. They came up with a plan that would give the players their salaries at the level it was when they went into the armed forces. They then were to give the player a "fair" chance to make the parent club and if they weren't successful, were to be placed at a level at least one classification above the one they were obtained at.[12]

Being that most of the game's stars were still abroad, at least for one more season, there was still the undertaking of filling the 1944 rosters. One thing that would begin to occur was the signing of underage players.

Joe Nuxhall of the Cincinnati Reds became the youngest player in major league history when he threw his first game on June 10th, 1944, at the young age of 15. Although he gave up 5 runs in ⅔ of an inning, Nuxhall would go on to win 135 games. Courtesy of the Cincinnati Reds.

First there would be Joe Nuxhall of the Cincinnati Reds. Nuxhall debuted on June 10th when the Reds were down 13–0; they inserted the 15-year-old into the game. He had an awful performance, giving up 5 runs on 2 hits and 5 walks in ⅔ of an inning.[13] The happy ending is Nuxhall would end up winning 135 major league games after he returned to the show in 1952.

Next up was a 16-year-old high schooler by the name of Tommy Brown. Brown began his career with the Dodgers on August 3rd a bit more successfully than Nuxhall, as he doubled and scored a run.[14] Although he did not have as fine a career as the Cincinnati hurler, Brown nevertheless played nine seasons, hitting .241.

The minors would also have their teenage phenom, such as a 17-year-old pitcher by the name of Mario Picone. Picone, who played for Bristol (the New York Giants) of the Appalachian League, struck out 28 in a 19-inning game versus Johnson City on June 15th.[15] The New York native would have a short 13 game, three season major league career with the Giants and Reds between 1947 and 1954.

Yes, 1944 would certainly provide the nation with several strange moments as well as those that were thrilling and poignant. One such moment was the no-hitter by Boston Brave Jim Tobin, who was more famous at that point for hitting 3 homers in a game than his pitching. He would throw his gem against the Dodgers on April 27th. With the achievement, Tobin would become one of the few knuckleballers ever to achieve such a feat.[16] The Brave hurler would toss another no-hitter, in a 5 inning,

7–0 masterpiece against the Phillies in the second game of a doubleheader on June 22nd that was shortened due to darkness.[17]

An incident of a note occurred during the '44 campaign, when former A's shortstop Sam "Red" Crane was released from prison late in the year. Crane was a little used shortstop who hit .208 in 495 at-bats for 4 teams in seven major league seasons. He ended his stay in the show in 1922 and seven years later was convicted of second degree murder for shooting a former girlfriend who was out on a date in a Harrisburg café while Crane was inebriated. He was freed after serving 15 years of an 18–36 year conviction and more than anything else, wanted to see a night game.[18]

It was appropriate that Crane wanted to see a night game as most fans of the sport concurred, making them a big hit. The fans loved them and the attendance stats proved to be very beneficial. At the midpoint of the season, Pittsburgh had reported that it had drawn more fans for its ten night games than it did in all of the combined day contests.[19] It was decided in a joint meeting of the leagues in July that teams could play as many night games as they wanted for the remainder of the season, as long as they had permission of the visiting squad.[20] Rickey once again listed himself as a detractor as he said he would push for a strict limit of seven night games per team the following year.[21]

Another old controversy reared its ugly head, that of the creation of a new ball. As one recalls from 1943, a new ball was put into play with the hopes of ushering in a new era of home runs. It instead was deader than a doorknob and created an incredible void of offense. In 1944, Spalding announced that it was going back to making the centers out of synthetic rubber and a new cork, which would make the ball much livelier.[22] It did the job as 10,353 runs were scored compared to 9,704 from the previous campaign.

The Philadelphia Phillies chimed in with an effort that showed why they continually finished in last place as they thought they might change their bad luck by changing their nickname. Mrs. Elizabeth Crooks was the winner of a contest in which the name Blue Jays was chosen as the winner, not to replace the name Phillies, but to go along with it. The name was chosen because it was felt that the Blue Jay was a bird with a fighting spirit.[23] As it turned out, the Phils would have been better off getting superior talent in which to turn their fortunes around as they finished in their customary position of last place in the National League.

With all else that went on in baseball in 1944, probably the most important thing was the American League pennant race. Even though it was done with most of the game's stars gone, it still had all the makings of a Hollywood sports movie. It had the villains in the Yankees and the Tigers, two teams that were usually on the top, the team that couldn't quite get over the peak in the Red Sox and the big underdog in the St. Louis Browns, a team that had never won a crown in its history.

The Browns started off hot winning their first nine games, setting an American League mark for most wins at the beginning of the season. They were led by a collection of players such as Vern Stephens, the superstar slugging shortstop who led the junior circuit in RBIs with 109; Mike Kreevich, the only regular who hit over .300 at .301 yet would have to share his playing time with the one-armed outfielder Pete Gray one year later; Nels Potter, the war years star who was 19–7 with a 2.83 ERA yet would be more noted for being kicked out of a game and suspended for 10 more on July 2nd for throwing a spitter, the first player to be thrown out for such an incident[24]; and Sig Jakucki, the heavy drinking 6'2" 200 pound ex-marine who had been out of organized baseball for six years.[25]

By September 15th, the Yankees had taken over first place. The Bronx Bombers were a tremendous story themselves, losing every member of their Hall of Fame studded 1941 and 1943 world championship teams, yet were able to keep in the race for the better part of the season, falling off late in September to finish 6 games back.

Probably the main reason for their run at the crown was the one constant that stuck with them throughout the years, manager Joe McCarthy. While rival manager Jimmy Dykes claimed that McCarthy had "plain, uncanny luck," the *Sporting News* put it into proper perspective by saying that it wasn't luck that led McCarthy to greatness. It was his leadership and his ability to sort out the good ballplayers from the bad. They further went on to say that Joe was at his best staying cool in a tough situation when most others would panic. That's what made him successful.

The first contender to fall by the wayside was the Boston Red Sox. At the beginning of September, Boston was but 3½ games behind St. Louis in 4th place.[27] For the Red Sox, whose history is riddled with one unlucky break after another, 1944 would be no different. They had climbed back into a pennant race after a season in the second division, when the war reared its ugly head. The selective service took second baseman Bobby Doerr (15–81–.325), third baseman Jim Tabor (13–72–.285) and war years star pitcher Tex Hughson (17–5–2.26), all late in the campaign.

The last, yet most formidable contender was the Detroit Tigers. The Tigers had been mired in the second division since Hank Greenberg left in 1941. It looked like the streak would continue as they were in 7th place on July 13th.[28] It was at that time when Dick Wakefield temporarily returned from the service and led his team the way Greenberg once did. He smacked 12 homers, knocking in 53, while hitting .355 in only 78 games.

It picked up what was a mediocre offense, which was the perfect compliment to the dynamic pitching duo of Hal Newhouser (29–9–2.72) and Dizzy Trout (27–14–2.12).

Everything came down to the final weekend. The Tigers seemingly had the advantage, playing Washington, whom it had beaten 15 of 18 times, while the Browns had to take on the Yankees, a team it did not play well against. After Detroit won the opener of the Friday doubleheader, Washington came back to upset Trout and the Tigers in game 2. In St. Louis, the Browns swept Hank Borowy and Tiny Bonham of the Yanks as the AL was now all tied up. Saturday would bring wins by both contenders, leaving the games on Sunday to decide the crown.

The Senators' Dutch Leonard pitched Washington to a win over the Tigers and a very tired Dizzy Trout. In St. Louis it was all up to Jakucki to win the pennant for the Browns. A heavy drinker, Sig promised the team not to drink the night before the game. When the big hurler came into the locker room the next morning, trainer Bob Bauman smelled whiskey on his breath. When questioned on why he drank, Jakucki shot back, "I kept my promise, I promised Zack Taylor I wouldn't take a drink last night, but I didn't promise him I wouldn't take one this morning."[29] It wouldn't matter, as the Browns would come back from down 2–0 to win the game and the title in front of 37,815 at Sportsman's Park 3–2.

On the other side of the street (or the field for that matter, as they both shared the same stadium), the St. Louis Cardinals ran to a third straight National League pennant by 14½ games over the Pirates, setting up the all St. Louis World Series.

After taking a 2–1 lead in the best of seven final, the Browns would have their bubble burst as the Cards, led by Mort Cooper's 1.12 ERA in 16 innings, won three straight games to capture the world championship.

In the Negro Leagues, frustration was starting to set in as the majors were using teenagers and Cubans to fill their roster spots, while the one-armed Pete Gray was playing for the Memphis club in the minors. There was such a great selection of manpower in the Negro Leagues that it irritated the players that the all white major leaguers refused to admit them into their league. Chet Brewer responded, "The only thing a one-armed white man can do better than a two-armed black man is scratch the side that itches."[30]

The pennant race in the Negro American League was not real exciting as the Birmingham Black Barons ran to the crown by 8½ games over the Indianapolis/Cincinnati Clowns. They were led by Artie Wilson who hit .348 with 17 stolen bases, and Tommy Sampson, who led the league in homers with 7, although only hit .227. Alfred Saylor topped a tough mound corps, leading the circuit in wins with 14 and winning percentage at .737.

The race in the Negro National League was a little closer as the Washington/Homestead Grays beat the Baltimore Elite Giants by 5½ games. The Grays' star-studded lineup of Buck Leonard, Josh Gibson and Cool Papa Bell was led of course by the greatest catcher the game has ever known, Gibson. He hit .365 while smacking a league high 17 homers and 12 triples. Leonard chipped in with a .350 average, 9 homers, a circuit best 23 doubles and 7 triples. Third baseman Rev Cannady also had a nice campaign hitting .356.

In the World Series, the Grays made short work of the Barons. Led by Gibson's 8 for 16 performance, they beat Birmingham 4 games to 1.

While others were tragically dying across the ocean, Memphis pitcher Perry Moss did so in this country, showing not all problems were overseas. He was accidentally shot while playing cards and died when the doctor refused to treat him because of the color of his skin.[31]

There was a league in the Midwest that was showing great improvement while giving the people who saw it a new and entertaining brand of baseball; it was the All-American Girls Professional Baseball League. The AAGPBL had begun as a softball league a couple years earlier, but had decreased the ball by ½ inch to 11½ inches and had widened the distance between the bases from 65 to 68 feet in 1944 to become a baseball league.[32]

The attendance had increased 49 percent over 1943 and the league was now booming.[33] The Milwaukee Chicks, who had the best record in the league at 70–45 and won the second half title, played the Kenosha Comets, the first half winners, for the women's world championship. The Chicks, who were led during the season by Merle Keagle, the league leader in homers with 7 while hitting .264, 5th in the circuit, and Vickie Panos, who was 6th in the league at .263 coming over from South Bend, fell behind two games to none to the Comets, who had Eleanor Dapkus and her .273 average along with Canadian pitcher Helen Nichol, the best hurler in the league's two year history with a 17–11 mark in 1944 and a AAGPBL low 0.93 ERA. The Chicks would storm back to win 4 of the next 5 games and take the title.[34]

Baseball started to pick itself up again in 1944. Attendance was at 8,772,746, an improvement of over 1.3 million versus 1943, and the prospect of peace was starting to be talked about. Despite the positive things, the sport received a shot to the gut on November 25th as Commissioner Landis died of a heart attack in Chicago, five days short of his 78th birthday.[35]

He came into power in 1920 in the wake of the Black Sox scandal of 1919, replacing a three man national commission that had run the game since 1903.[36] Landis had made his name as a tough judge who was famous for fining Standard Oil over $29 million in 1907. His power was legendary in baseball, as every time someone threatened to have him ousted over his 24-year career as the baseball czar, he would hold up his contract and threaten to rip it up. This would inevitably cause the owners to cower in fear that he would actually quit and the threat would be over.[37]

As good as he was for the game, bringing it back from the edge of extinction to the to the top of the sports mountain and holding it strongly together during the very difficult war years, he also held it back in a manner that negated all the good. By keeping the Afro-American players from participating in the major leagues, he not only conspired to commit a grievous human rights violation but also lessened the quality of the league by not having some of the best players in the land participate. Three men came to the forefront immediately to replace him: NL boss Ford Frick, AL Chief William Harridge and secretary to Landis, Leslie O'Connor, who immediately said he was not interested.[38] Of course none of the men would receive the honor at that time (Frick would later get his chance in the asterisk years of Roger Maris), giving way to a former Kentucky Senator, who would right whatever wrongs Landis had administered.

As the baseball fans of this country enjoyed a phenomenal pennant race as well as the sport in general, the main event of 1944 came on June 6th as the Allied Forces landed on the beaches of France in what is known as D-Day. Baseball cancelled its games that day so that Americans had a chance to pray as over 5,000 professional players were playing in a more serious game in Europe, the Asian theater and all around the globe.

Several professional baseball players would perform valiantly on the beaches of France during the D-Day invasion. Former Dodger Larry French landed on Normandy and told the story saying, "The beach was plenty hot, 88 mm fire, mines wherever you stepped and the darnedest fireworks each night you can imagine." He further went on to say that "[the] first few nights we dove for our hole in the sand to get out of the way of the flak from the trigger happy sailors in the bay, but now we just stay in the tent.... Our tent is full of holes, but only one [of us] has been hit out of eight.... It really gives one plenty to think about."[39]

Minor leaguer John Pinder would give his life bravely in an attempt to rescue the radio equipment from his boat that was stranded 100 yards from the shore. It allowed the Allies to establish crucial radio contact from the French beaches and he would live long enough to see the radio parts set up and the air and sea backup support contacted.

The first time he went into the water to get the equipment, shrapnel hit him. As he went back into the water, which was engulfed in flames, he was shot in the head and was holding the left side of his face in his hand as he got more of the radio tools. After he set up the radio, he went back to get more equipment, and was blasted by more machine gun fire, yet continued to refuse treatment. John went on until he eventually was weakened and died. Pinder would receive the Congressional Medal of Honor posthumously on January 8th, 1945.[40]

There were many other ex-players who were in the other battlefields of Europe and in the Pacific, fighting the good fight. Nineteen forty-four would find several players injured; some gave up their lives while the enemy captured others. Two of the players that would make their marks as war heroes in '44 were A's star hurler Phil Marchildon and former Washington Senator catcher Elmer Gedeon.

Native Canadian hurler Phil Marchildon was the ace of the Athletics staff when he went into the Royal Canadian Air Force. His last season before joining the fight, Marchildon went 17–14 for a team that only won 55 games.

On his 26th mission over the Kiel Harbor, near the Danish Border, they were dropping mines in the harbor when a German fighter pilot shot him down. Phil would parachute out into the cold sea, when fishermen who were part of the Danish underground took him into a Danish fishing boat. Unfortunately as the boat came into shore, German soldiers were waiting and Marchildon was turned over to his new captors.

The Canadian was sent to Stalag Luft III, where life was, as expected, not so good. They were given to eat a diet that consisted of two dry pieces of black bread, grey potatoes, barley soup that was watered down and soup that not only had chunks of fat, but sometimes a pig's ear floating on top.[41]

As the war was coming to an end, the Germans, rather than give up their prisoners, took them out of the camp as the Allied Forces approached and marched them all over the German countryside. As the days went on, the German guards would give the prisoners more freedom. Marchildon was going from barn to barn when he would learn of his freedom on May 2nd, 1945, as he was "answering nature's call" after he contracted a case of dysentery. He noticed that the guards were gone as British troops came out of the woods to give him the good news.

Marchildon went back to his homeland and his soon to be wife Irene. It was apparent that his time in the prison camp had deeply affected him. Connie Mack continually tried to persuade him to come back to the club, but Marchildon was not so sure he wanted to play ball again. He just wanted to be left alone. He woke up often in the middle of the night frightened by horrid nightmares of his experience. He felt at peace in his small hometown and didn't know if he would ever have the courage to leave it.[42]

Phil did return though, his career lasting until 1950 that included his marquee season of 1947 when he went 19–9 with a career low 3.22 ERA.[43]

Elmer Gedeon's career was not as impressive as Marchildon's, yet his time in the service was inspiring and very memorable.

He was only 3 for 15 in his major league career, all in 1939 with Washington. Elmer joined the Air Force in 1941 and the following year while training in North Carolina, he was navigator on a B-52 that crashed as it took off. Gedeon was thrown from the plane, but returned to save his crew.[44] He was awarded the Soldier's Medal for his bravery, becoming the first major leaguer to be decorated.[45]

Gedeon would not be so lucky on April 20th, 1944. While flying his B-26, Elmer was hit by enemy fire over St. Pol, France. He crashed with his five crewmates, becoming the first major league player to lose his life in the war.

When the story of Elmer Gedeon is recalled, it makes the miraculous story of the St. Louis Browns pale in comparison. The Browns were a deterrent to the evils of war while Gedeon's tale was, in stark reality, a symbol of everything people should remember of those years, great men giving up their lives for the country's future.

Starting Lineups and Who Went to War

AMERICAN LEAGUE

1944 St. Louis Browns
89–65–0 GB

1941	1942	1943	1944
1B-George McQuinn	McQuinn	McQuinn	McQuinn
2B-Don Heffner	Don Gutteridge	Gutteridge	Gutteridge
SS-Johnny Berardino	Vern Stephens	Stephens	Stephens
3B-Harland Clift	Clift	Clift	Mark Christman
OF-Chet Laabs	Laabs	Mike Chartak	Gene Moore
OF-Walt Judnich	Judnich	Milt Byrnes	Byrnes
OF-Roy Cullenbine	Glenn McQuillen	Laabs	Mike Kreevich
CA-Rick Ferrell	Ferrell	Frankie Hayes	Red Hayworth
PI-Elden Auker	Auker	Steve Sundra	Jack Kramer
PI-Bob Muncrief	Johnny Niggeling	Galehouse	Nels Potter
PI-Bob Harris	Galehouse	Bob Muncrief	Muncrief
PI-Denny Galehouse	Al Hollingsworth	Hollingsworth	Sig Jakucki

The year 1944 was the midst of wartime baseball, but in the American League, the cream was rising back to the top. After a three-year hiatus, Detroit was now in the middle of a 4-way fight for the pennant as were the Red Sox. The Yankees, who were hurt by the defection of several Hall of Famers to the armed forces, weren't at the top, but they were still challenging for the crown. At the head of the pack though, was the surprise team of the first half of the 20th century, the St. Louis Browns.

The race went down to the wire with the Tigers, after Boston and New York had fallen off. They both had identical 87–65 marks going into the last weekend of the season. St. Louis had the tougher road, playing the defending world champion Yankees for two, while the Tigers faced off against the Senators. They both won their first games leading into the ultimate showdown, a tied race with one game left. The Browns would come up big; beating New York 3–2 while Detroit fell to Washington 4–1 giving St. Louis the improbable title, only during the war years.

Nels Potter was one of the cornerstones of the St. Louis Browns teams between 1943–45. He went 44–23 during those seasons (he was 48–74 the rest of his career). Potter was famous for being the first pitcher in major league history to be tossed from a game for throwing a spitter. Courtesy of Photo File, Inc.

One of the best pitchers during the time period, Nels Potter, led the way for the Browns with a 19–7 record and 2.83 ERA. He was backed up by Jack Kramer, who was a little used reliever until this magical season, with stats of 17–13–2.49, Bob Muncrief, 13–8–3.08 and war time phenom Sig Jakucki, the 34-year-old pitcher who had been out of the majors since his rookie season of 1936, finished with marks of 13–9–3.55.

The offense was vastly improved as they increased their run production from 596 in 1943 to 684 the following season. Vern Stephens who led the AL with 109 RBIs also cracked 20 homers. The 36-year-old Mike Kreevich, a reserve in '43, was tops on the team in hitting at .301.

The War Department would not have to worry about travel during the Fall Classic as the Browns went up against their St. Louis counterparts, the Cardinals. The Cards would win their second world championship in three years, but regardless of the outcome, 1944 would certainly prove to be the most special season in the history of their franchise, war time or not.

Who Left for the War	Who Replaced Them
CA-Hank Helf	
INF-Hank Schmulbach	
PI-Al Milnar	
PI-Fred Sanford	

Hank Helf— Hank Helf went 1 for 14 in his two prewar seasons of 1938 and 1940 for the Indians. When he returned from the service, he would play the majority of his career in 1946 for St. Louis, hitting .192 in 182 at-bats with 6 homers and a nice 12 fielding runs. He would finish his stay in the majors with a .184 lifetime mark.

Hank Schmulbach— Schmulbach had a Moonlight Graham career with a twist. He played in only one major league game, never getting to the plate, but did score a run as a pinch runner.

Al Milnar—"Happy" Milnar came up with the Indians in 1936 with an unimpressive 1–2 mark and 7.36 ERA. It would not be indicative of what would come between 1939 and 1941.

Milnar would have a combined 44–41 record during those seasons with his marquee year coming in 1940. Happy would go 18–10 that season with a selection to the All-Star game, leading the AL in shutouts with 4.

After falling to 6–8 in 1942, Milnar was sold to the Browns. He would pitch in only one season after returning from the armed service, going 1–1 in 5 games for the Browns and Phils, leaving the game with a career 57–58 record.

Fred Sanford— He didn't own a junkyard with his son, but after 9⅓ innings pitched in his only prewar season, Sanford would go off to serve his country before coming back for a decent postwar career.

In 1946 he came back starting only 3 games, 2 of which were shutouts. Fred cracked the starting rotation the next season, but could only muster up 7–16 and 12–21 records in 1947 and 1948.

Sanford was sent packing to the Yankees in 1949 with Red Partee for Sherm Lollar, Red Embree, Dick Starr and $100,000. He would enjoy two nice seasons as a starter/reliever for the Yanks with a combined 12–7 mark. He finished his career two years later in 1951 with a combined 4–10 record with New York, Washington and, ironically, the Browns.

1944 Detroit Tigers
88–66–1 GB

1941	*1942*	*1943*	*1944*
1B-Rudy York	York	York	York
2B-Charlie Gehringer	Jimmy Bloodworth	Bloodworth	Eddie Mayo
SS-Frank Croucher	Billy Hitchcock	Joe Hoover	Hoover
3B-Pinky Higgins	Higgins	Higgins	Higgins
OF-Bruce Campbell	Ned Harris	Harris	Jimmy Outlaw
OF-Barney McCosky	Doc Cramer	Cramer	Cramer
OF-Rip Radcliff	McCoskey	Dick Wakefield	Wakefield
CA-Birdie Tebbetts	Tebbetts	Paul Richards	Richards
PI-Bobo Newsome	Al Benton	Trout	Trout
PI-Hal Newhouser	Dizzy Trout	Virgil Trucks	Newhouser
PI-Tommy Bridges	Hal White	Newhouser	Rufe Gentry
PI-Johnny Gorsica	Newhouser	White	Stubby Overmire

There were many great duos that would go down in the history of baseball as leading their teams to the promised land — Ruth and Gehrig and Drysdale and Koufax were probably two of the most famous. In 1944 you certainly could add the names Hal Newhouser and Dizzy Trout to that list. Newhouser and Trout combined to win 56 of the Tiger's 88 games, losing 23 with a league leading 2.12 and 2.22 ERAs respectively. The two men would lead Detroit back to the top of the heap in the American League after an absence of three years in the first division, losing the junior circuit crown on the last day of the season to the Browns. They would go 1–2 in the MVP vote with Newhouser beating Trout by four votes 236–232. Without the two, the rest of the Detroit staff would combine to go only 32–43.

The Tigers improved 20 games over their 1943 performance, despite the fact they lost two starting pitchers in Virgil Trucks and Hal White and two everyday players in Jimmy Bloodworth and outfielder Ned Harris to the service.

Early on, it didn't look like Detroit would be one of the participants in this dramatic race for the pennant as they lost 12 of their first 13 home games.[46] In fact, as of July 13th, the Tigers were still mired in 7th place when outfielder Dick Wakefield would make his spectacular return.[47] Out since the end of the 1943 season when he entered the Navy's aviation cadet program, Wakefield returned when the curriculum was discontinued.[48] He went 9 for 24 his first week with 2 homers. Dick would finish the season hitting .355 with 12 home runs, before entering the service again at the end of the year and missing the 1945 season. Despite his abbreviated season, Wakefield finished 5th in the MVP vote behind his two teammates.

Rudy York would also lead the revamped offense, smacking 18 homers with 98 RBIs. Pinky Higgins also improved greatly, picking up 20 points in his average, going from .277 to .297.

In spite of all the improvement, Detroit would lose to the lowly Senators on the final day of the campaign, as the Browns would defeat the Yankees, winning the crown by one game. Frustrating as it was, the year was still a rousing success. Without the super duo though, Detroit probably wouldn't have made it out of the second division.

Who Left for the War	Who Replaced Them
2B–Jimmy Bloodworth	Eddie Mayo
OF–Ned Harris	Jimmy Outlaw
OF–Rip Radcliff	
PI–Virgil Trucks	Hal Newhouser/Rufe Gentry
PI–Hal White	Stubby Overmire

Jimmy Bloodworth— Jimmy Bloodworth was a fine fielding, average hitting second baseman with the Senators, Tigers, Pirates, Reds and Phillies during his 11-year major league career. He would finish with a .248 average, but would have 65 fielding runs, 89 occurring in his prime between 1939 and 1943 with — 23 coming after his return from the war in 1946.

Bloodworth broke in with the Senators in 1937, before breaking into the starting line-up as he hit .289 in 318 at-bats in 1939. Jimmy would hit .245 the next two seasons, leading the AL in fielding runs with 35 in 1941.

He was sent to the Tigers with Doc Cramer for Frank Croucher and Bruce Campbell following the '41 campaign. His average would hover in the .240s the next three years, although Bloodworth would show some rare power, hitting 13 homers in 1942. Nineteen forty-two also provided Bloodworth with a strange moment in the spotlight during a spring training game versus the Reds. Bloodworth hit an easy shot back to the box against Elmer Riddle. As Riddle and second baseman Lonnie Frey went after the ball, the national anthem came over the loudspeaker. Riddle and Frey stood at attention as Jimmy kept running towards first and was awarded a single.[49] Jimmy would set a batting record in 1943, although one I'm sure he wasn't proud of, hitting into 29 double plays, an American league mark that has since been broken.[50]

After returning from the service in 1946, Bloodworth was sold to the Pirates in December of that year. After hitting .250 for the Bucs, he was sent packing to Cincinnati, where he enjoyed his last season as a regular, hitting .261 with 9 homers in 1949. Bloodworth was sold to the Phillies in 1950, where he spent a year and a half before retiring in 1951.

Eddie Mayo was brought in from the A's in 1944 to fill in at second.

Before his stint with Philadelphia in 1943, he had been out of the majors since 1938. Mayo would be a carbon copy of Bloodworth in 1944, leading the league in fielding runs with 29, while hitting .249. He would hit career highs with a .285 average and 10 homers the following campaign, and a league high .980 fielding percentage. After giving way to Bloodworth in 1946, he recaptured his starting spot, when Bloodworth was sold to Pittsburgh following the season.

Ned Harris— Harris began his career in 1941, taking over the reins in right field the following season. After hitting .271 and .254 in 1942 and 1942, Harris would be taken by Uncle Sam. When he returned in 1946, Ned would receive only one more at-bat before leaving the majors.

Ten-year vet Jimmy Outlaw would take over for Harris in 1943 and hit .273 in 1944, splitting time between left and right. He moved over to left in 1945, again hitting in the .270s at .271.

Rip Radcliff— Radcliff was a 10-year vet in the majors, who finished with a career .311 average and 1,267 hits.

After a callup with the White Sox in 1934, Radcliff took over the starting left field position the following season, hitting .286 with a career high 10 homers. He had his breakout season the following year with a .335 mark and a trip to his only All-Star game. Rip spent the next three years in Chicago, hitting .325, .330 and .264 respectively before being sent to the Browns in December of 1939 for Moose Salters.

The trade would prove to be a wise move for St. Louis, as Radcliff hit a career high .342 in 1940, leading the American League in hits with 200. He was sold to Detroit the following season where he hit .317 after the trade in his last campaign as a starter. Rip would slump to .250 and .261 in 1942 and 1943, before going into the military. He would not return to the majors after the war.

There's not much the war cost Radcliff as far as statistics go. He was pretty much at the end of his career when sent into the military. He was 37-years-old and had just spent two seasons as a reserve for the Tigers. Regardless, anytime you play 10 years and finish with a plus .300 average, you've had a successful run in the majors.

Virgil Trucks— The long and illustrious career of Virgil "Fire" Trucks was like a strange roller coaster ride with plenty of surprising twists and curves.

Trucks had several great milestones; he was one of five men in baseball history to throw two 9 inning no-hitters in one season yet it came in a season in which he won only 5 games. There were 177 major league triumphs and victories in both a World Series and an All-Star game. On top of all the major league moments, he boasted perhaps the greatest year a minor league pitcher ever had. Throughout all the memorable times, perhaps his greatest achievement was serving his country in the armed forces.

In 1942 and 1943, Trucks broke in with the Tigers and had consecutive 14–8 and 16–10 records respectively for less than average teams. It was at that point the 27-year-old hurler gave up what could have been two productive years in his prime to join the Navy as a seaman first class. Stationed in Guam, he flew with a group of major league ball players from island to island in the South Pacific, entertaining the troops with baseball. "I just did what they told me to do. You didn't have a choice, so I did it [went into the Navy]," Trucks said with no regret about leaving his baseball career behind.[51]

After the Japanese surrender in 1945, the right-hander got his release from the military and gave the Tigers an early present by returning in time to start the last game of the season against the Browns. It was a different Tigers team that he came home to, one that was competing for the AL pennant. Trucks threw 5⅓ innings, giving up three hits and a run. Fellow war vet Hank Greenberg belted a ninth inning homer to vault the Tigers into the World Series 6–3.

With a two-year absence from the game behind him, manager Steve O'Neill gave "Fire" (which was the nickname they bestowed upon him for his blazing fastball) the ball for what would prove to be the most important game of the Birmingham native's illustrious career in the second tilt of the Fall Classic. Hall of Famer Hal Newhouser was belted in game one 9–0, so the pressure was really on Detroit and Trucks in Game 2. The Tiger hurler came up big as he pitched a complete game, 7 hit 4–1 victory. For the second time in as many outings, Greenberg came to the rescue again, hitting a three run blast in the fifth.

The championship was on the line when Trucks came out in Game 6. Unfortunately he would last only 4⅓ innings, giving up 4 runs, en route to an 8–7 loss.

Virgil reeled off four tremendous seasons in a row between 1946 and 1949 with a combined 57–45 record, including his breakout season of 1949 when Trucks went 19–11 with a 2.81 ERA, leading the league in strikeouts and shutouts with 153 and 6 respectively. Trucks played in his first All-Star game in Brooklyn that year, becoming the winning pitcher in an AL 11–7 triumph.

After a decent 1951 season in which the southerner would go 13–8, Trucks had probably the strangest season in major league history, finishing with an abysmal 5–19 record, yet 2 of his 5 victories would be memorable no-hitters.

The first one was a dramatic 1–0 victory over the Washington Senators, as Vic Wertz slammed a ninth inning shot for a 1–0 victory. "The first game was an easy no-hitter. Nothing but routine ground balls and pop-ups."[52] No-hitter number two would be anything but routine.

The Yankees' Hall of Fame shortstop, Phil Rizzuto, hit a ground ball to Tiger third baseman Johnny Pesky in the third inning. Pesky mishandled the easy bouncer and threw on to Walt Dropo a split second late. Official scorer John Drebinger ruled it an error only to inexplicably change the call to a single the next inning. After two innings of prodding from his fellow journalists, Drebinger called down to the dugout to ask Pesky his opinion of the play. Pesky swore he misplayed it and the play was changed back to error. The Tigers went on to win the game, ironically, 1–0, the same as the first.[53]

"There was an easy two hopper to Pesky, he bobbled it and I thought he threw him out at first," Trucks remembered. "When I came off the field it came up on the scoreboard as an error, then he changed it to a hit. It didn't bother me; I didn't figure it would be a no-hitter. Drebinger called the dugout in the 7th, Pesky told him it was an error and it [the call] was changed. I got on base in the 7th and the umpire said to me there's your no-hitter [implying it was a gift]. It made me mad because I wasn't pitching for a no-hitter. It was a tough season and I just wanted to win the game."[54]

An 11-year career with the Tigers came to a sudden halt in 1953 as they dealt him to the St. Louis Browns with Johnny Groth and Hal White for Owen Friend, Bob Nieman and Jay Porter. He would only stay with the team for half a season, but he would befriend a superstar by the name of Satchel Paige at a time when it still wasn't popular for white major leaguers to do so with former Negro League players. "He was one of the finest, greatest guys I've met. I went fishing with him a lot over the years and roomed with him down west when we were barnstorming. He was a great American."

With a decent 5–4 start in hand, the White Sox traded for Trucks in June of 1953 for Bubba Phillips. It was in Chicago that the old form was recaptured, winning 15 and losing 6 the rest of the way. It would be the only 20-win season Trucks would accomplish.

A second All-Star appearance was in the cards in 1953 as a reward for a great season, which ended up at 19–12 with a 2.79 ERA. He finished off the senior circuit in an 11–9 victory, earning a save.

After going 13–8 the next season, "Fire" would last only 3 more sub-par years for Detroit, Kansas City and the Yankees, who released him in spring training of 1959. Yankee assistant GM Lee MacPhail would offer him a scouting job in Japan, which would have made him more money than he ever made in the majors. Moving to the Orient was not an option and the long career had come to an end.

Working in a Chevy dealership in Kansas City was not the type of job that one of the greatest pitchers in the '40s and '50s would like to do, so when his old friend Paige called and wanted Trucks to join him barnstorming against a group of Cuban players that were in the Washington system, "Fire" jumped at the opportunity. "When Satch called and wanted to go barnstorming, I joined him immediately," the veteran hurler said. "The promoter offered us $650 a week, but we were lucky to get $250. The team we played was a bunch of 17 and 18 year old Cuban kids that belonged to the Washington Senators. We were in Beloit, Wisconsin, playing a game when Fidel Castro called for all Cubans to come home so they all left and went home I assume."[55]

Hal Newhouser took Trucks' spot as the number two starter, moving up from number three, and had an MVP season leading the Tigers back into the pennant race. Rufe Gentry would be the man that would actually replace Trucks in the rotation. He would go 12–14 in his only season as a starter in 1944, pitching in only 11 games the 4 other seasons he spent in the majors.

Hal White—Despite the fact Hal White had a 12 year major league career, he would peak early in his second and third year in the majors in 1942 and 1943, going 12–12 and 7–12 in two seasons as a starter, before going off to war.

White would return in 1946 to pitch nine more seasons, mostly with the Tigers, but his days as a starter were pretty much over. White only received 18 more starts in his final 266 appearances. Probably his best year coming out of the pen was in 1950, as he went 9–6 with an impressive OBA of .239 in 111 innings.

He left the Tigers after a 1–8 venture in 1952, being dealt to the Browns with Virgil Trucks. It was there that White would have probably the most unique thing about his career as he played for both St. Louis teams in one season, being sent from the Browns to the Cardinals in mid 1953. He was gone from the majors after the next season.

Stubby Overmire was the replacement for White in 1944. He went 20–20 in his two war ball seasons of 1944 and 1945 with ERAs of 3.07 and 3.88 a bit above White's output of 2.91 and 3.39 the two seasons prior. If the ERAs were only slightly higher, then the OBA's were significantly so as Stubby came through with substandard marks of .271 and .294 compared to Hal's .252 and .228. So overall, Overmire had an adequate season replacing White, but really didn't meet up to his production.

1944 New York Yankees
83–71–6 GB

1941	1942	1943	1944
1B-Johnny Sturm	Buddy Hassett	Nick Etten	Etten
2B-Joe Gordon	Gordon	Gordon	Stuffy Stirnweiss
SS-Phil Rizzuto	Rizzuto	Crosetti	Mike Milosovich
3B-Red Rolfe	Frank Crosetti	Billy Johnson	Oscar Grimes
OF-Tommy Henrich	Henrich	Bud Metheny	Metheny
OF-Joe DiMaggio	DiMaggio	Johnny Lindell	Lindell
OF-Charlie Keller	Keller	Keller	Hersh Martin
CA-Bill Dickey	Dickey	Dickey	Mike Garbark
PI-Marius Russo	Tiny Bonham	Chandler	Borowy
PI-Red Ruffing	Chandler	Butch Wensloff	Monk Dubiel
PI-Lefty Gomez	Ruffing	Borowy	Bonham
PI-Spud Chandler	Hank Borowy	Bonham	Atley Donald

Thankfully the New York Yankees still had manager Joe McCarthy. After losing several Hall of Famers and key players in 1943, New York gave up 37-year-old catcher Bill Dickey, superstar Joe Gordon and starting third baseman Billy Johnson to Uncle Sam while star outfielder Charlie Keller would spend the season in the Merchant Marines.

What was once a powerful lineup consisting of Keller, Gordon, Dickey, Phil Rizzuto, Joe DiMaggio and Tommy Henrich was now replaced with one of Hersh Martin, Stuffy Stirnweiss, Mike Garbark, Mike Milosovich, Johnny Lindell and Bud Metheny.

The Yankees' luck got so bad, they even lost catcher Rollie Hemsley and Spud Chandler to the military during the season while starter Butch Wensloff, reliever Johnny Murphy and shortstop Frank Crosetti would voluntarily retire. One would wonder how they even were able to field a team. Through it all, they not only were able to play, but succeed as they finished only 6 games behind the Browns for the AL pennant.

The surprising Snuffy Stirnweiss led the offense. Snuffy came out of nowhere to lead the junior circuit in runs with 125, hits, 205, triples, 16, and stolen bases with 55, also chipping in with a team high .319 average. War star Nick Etten led the AL in homers with 22 while the outfield duo of Martin and Lindell hit .300 and .302 respectively, with Lindell adding 18 homers and 103 RBIs.

Things weren't so pleasant on the mound as the team ERA ballooned from 2.93 to 3.39 in 1944. Ernie Bonham and Hank Borowy would continue to be the team leaders with stats of 12–9–2.99 and 17–12–2.64 correspondingly. The loss of reigning MVP Spud Chandler would be too much to overcome.

Overall, the team may not have been able to repeat as world champions, but thanks to McCarthy, who was at the top of his craft, they were able to remain very competitive.

Who Left for the War	Who Replaced Them
CA-Bill Dickey	Mike Garbark
CA-Aaron Robinson	
CA-Ken Sears	
2B-Joe Gordon	Snuffy Stirnweiss
3B-Billy Johnson	Oscar Grimes
OF-Roy Weatherly	
PI-Tommy Byrne	
PI-Marius Russo	

Bill Dickey— When you talk about the greatest catchers of all time, Bill Dickey is a name that always must be brought up in the conversation. Adept at both the plate and in the field, Dickey was selected to play in 11 All-Star games out of a possible 12 he was eligible for. He hit over .300 eleven times for a lifetime .313 mark while leading the league in fielding percentage on four occasions. To top it all off he was elected into baseball immortality as he entered Cooperstown in 1954.

Dickey broke into the starting lineup in 1929 after a 3 for 15 performance his first season. He hit .324, which would be the first of six consecutive times he broke the magical .300 level. Dickey would slump to .279 after that streak in 1935 before breaking out into a four-year ride where he would add some punch his game.

The Louisiana native would begin things with a 22 homer, 107 RBI, .362 average, .617 slugging percentage performance in 1936, using that as a prelude to arguably his finest season ever. Nineteen thirty-seven saw Dickey hit .332 with career highs in homers at 29 and RBIs with 133. He finished his onslaught in 1938 and 1939 with 27–115–.313 and 24–105–.302 seasons.

After Dickey's impressive four-year prime, where he hit 102 of his career 202 homers and 460 of a lifetime 1209 RBIs, the bottom fell out as the lefty hitter slumped to .247 in 1940 before rebounding to .284 and .295 the following two years.

Bill had one final big year in 1943 hitting .351 in 242 at-bats before heading into the Navy.[56] When the veteran catcher returned, he would play only one more season, hitting .261 while taking over as manager for the great Joe McCarthy in May, who had a conflict with the new boss of the Yankees, Larry MacPhail.[57]

Dickey was at the end of his career in the majors when he went into the Navy. About the only significant stat that he missed was the 2,000 hit plateau. Bill was only 31 hits shy and if nothing else that would have been a certainty.

Replacing Dickey in 1944 was Rollie Hemsley, who was hitting .268 when he was sent into the military, and Mike Garbark who was in his rookie year hitting .261. Garbark would play one more season the following year, slumping to .216 before leaving the game when the men came back from the service.

Aaron Robinson— Robinson was hitless in his only prewar season before returning to play eight more years with the Yankees, White Sox, Tigers and Red Sox.

After he came back, Robinson would hit .281, before having his marquee campaign in 1946, smacking career highs in homers, 16, RBIs, 64, and average at .297. Aaron would be selected to his only All-Star game in 1947 before providing the Yanks with two important pieces to their dynasty in the late 40s and 50s. He was traded to the White Sox for Ed Lopat, which opened up the starting catcher post for Hall of Famer Yogi Berra.[58]

The South Carolina native would play in Chicago for one season before being sent to the Tigers for another great, pitcher Billy Pierce and $10,000. Robinson had one nice year in the Motor City, hitting 13 homers in '49. He ended his major league career two years later in 1951 after hitting .205 with Detroit and Boston.

Ken Sears—"Ziggy" played two years in the majors, one with the Yanks in 1943, hitting .278 in 187 at-bats, the last in 1946 going 5 for 15 with the Browns.

Joe Gordon—"Flash" Gordon had a wonderful 11-year career as a member of the Bronx Bombers and the Indians. He was selected to nine All-Star games, finished with 54 fielding runs (he had 101 in his first seven seasons before tailing off with — 47 his last 4 years) and had a rare attribute for a second baseman, power. He averaged 23 homers a year when it wasn't popular for middle infielders to be power hitters.

Gordon would also be well known as being the only manager ever traded for another manager as the Indians swapped Gordon for Jimmy Dykes of the Tigers in 1960.[59]

Gordon was a star from the outset, slamming 25 homers with 97 RBIs in his rookie campaign in 1938. Flash improved to 28 homers, breaking the century mark in RBIs with 111 the following year, before hitting 30 and 103 in 1940.

The year 1942 would prove to be Joe's best year, putting together an 18 homer, 103 RBI, .322 campaign and a controversial MVP award over Ted Williams. Gordon slumped to .249 the next year before ending up in Hawaii with Joe DiMaggio and the Army's Seventh Air Force.[60]

The Los Angeles resident had his worst season when he returned in 1946, slumping to .210, which led to him going to Cleveland with Eddie

Backman for Allie Reynolds. It was with the Indians that Gordon reignited his career, having his best power year ever in the world championship season of 1948 with lifetime highs in homers (32) and RBI (124), finishing 6th in the MVP voting. It was Joe's last big hurrah as he finished his major league stay in 1951 after hitting 39 homers his last two years.

In the two campaigns Gordon missed due to the war, Joe would have had a chance to hit a couple of lifetime marks. He was only 47 homers away from 300, but that would have been a tall order being he hit 35 in the two years before the war and 40 in the two following. It's not that Gordon couldn't have done it, he certainly was capable as he had reached that number five times in consecutive seasons, 1938 and 1939 with 53, 1939 and 1940 with 58, 1940 and 1941 with 54, 1947 and 1948 with 61 and 1948 and 1949 with 52, but it wasn't necessarily a certainty. Other marks that were reachable were 1,000 runs; he was 86 short; and 1,000 RBIs as he was only 25 off that mark. One stat that was out of Gordon's reach was the 2,000 hit plateau; he was 470 short and never came close to doing that in two consecutive years.

More than ably replacing Flash was Snuffy Stirnweiss. Stirnweiss had his best two seasons ever in the war years of 1944 and 1945, leading the league in runs with 125, hits 205, triples 16 and stolen bases with 55, finishing 4th in the MVP vote. He did even better in 1945 as he was tops in the AL in runs again at 107 and average at .309, creeping up one more spot to third for the Most Valuable Player. Stirnweiss would steal 88 of his career 134 bases those two campaigns.

Billy Johnson— Johnson had a fine rookie season in 1943, hitting .280 with 94 RBIs while smacking only 5 homers, before going into the service.

"Bull," as he was known, returned in 1946, recapturing his starting position, and was selected to his first All-Star game in 1947 on the heels of a .285, 95 RBI season. He followed that up with a career high .294 campaign in '48, slumping to .249 the subsequent year.

Two years later in 1951, Johnson was sent to the Cardinals for Don Bollweg and $15,000 where hit a lifetime high 14 homers. Bull would be out of the majors two years later in 1953, a career .271 hitter.

There were two levels that Bull would have most likely hit had he not missed two seasons in the service; he was only 118 hits away from 1,000 and 13 RBIs short of 500. It was not a sure thing he would have made it to those marks, as without the war, it's questionable that Johnson would have slid into the starting role with Crosetti and Rizzuto there.

Oscar Grimes was the man who replaced Bull in '44, hitting .279 and .265 with a combined 9 homers and 91 RBIs in his two war years at third, roughly the 1943 output of Johnson.

Roy Weatherly—"Stormy," as he was known, was at the tail end of his 10-year career (where he was a .286 hitter) when he came over to the Yankees in December of 1942 with Oscar Grimes for Roy Cullenbine and Buddy Rosar.

Prior to that, he spent seven seasons with the Indians, beginning in 1936 when he hit a career high .335. After two sub par years in 1937 and 1938, Stormy again broke the .300 level hitting .310 in 323 at-bats.

Weatherly's best year was in 1940, hitting 12 of his lifetime 43 homers that year. He also knocked in a career best 59 runs while hitting .303. Roy spent two more years in Cleveland, then was traded to the Bronx, where he hit .264 before his trip to the military. When he returned, Weatherly played in only two abbreviated seasons in 1946 and 1950, coming up only 71 times, including 69 of which came in his final year with the Giants.

Tommy Byrne— Byrne would pitch in only 31⅔ innings before going into the Navy in 1944. While there he would pitch for the powerful Norfolk Training Station team with Johnny Rigney of the White Sox.[61]

Tommy returned in 1946 and three years later in 1949 had his finest campaign with a 15–7 record and league leading .183 OBA. He won 15 again the following season, making his only All-Star game, again with a nice .245 OBA. What isn't impressive about the two years was his wildness. Byrne would walk 339 over the two seasons while striking out only 247. In fact, his wildness would eventually cause Byrne to lead the circuit 5 times in hit batsmen.[62]

Tommy bounced around to the Browns, White Sox and Senators the next two seasons before returning to the Bronx in 1954. There he would have one final big season in 1955 going 16–5 for a league high .762 winning percentage. He left the majors two years later with a career 85–69 mark.

Would Byrne have reached 100 wins if not for his time in the military? Probably not as he really didn't come into his own until 1948, winning only 2 games his first three years.

Marius Russo—"Lefty" would have a nice beginning to his career, going 36–21 his first three seasons between 1939 and 1941, including back to back 14 win campaigns, the latter of which he made his only All-Star game as the number one starter for the world champions.

Marius would only win 9 more games the next two seasons, battling a sore arm in 1942 before entering the service, but had one shining moment in 1943, beating the Cardinals 2–1 in Game 4 of the World Series, giving up no earned runs and 7 hits. Marius would also hit two doubles and score a run.[63]

When he returned from the service, Russo pitched in only 8 more games, going 0–2 and giving up 26 hits and 11 walks in 18⅔ innings.

1944 Boston Red Sox
77–77–12 GB

1941	1942	1943	1944
1B-Jimmie Foxx	Tony Lupien	Lupien	Lou Finney
2B-Bobby Doerr	Doerr	Doerr	Doerr
SS-Joe Cronin	Johnny Pesky	Skeeter Newsome	Newsome
3B-Jim Tabor	Tabor	Tabor	Tabor
OF-Lou Finney	Finney	Pete Fox	Fox
OF-Dom DiMaggio	DiMaggio	Catfish Metkovich	Metkovich
OF-Ted Williams	Williams	Leon Culberson	Bob Johnson
CA-Frankie Pytlak	Bill Conroy	Roy Partee	Partee
PI-Dick Newsome	Tex Hughson	Hughson	Joe Bowman
PI-Charlie Wagner	Wagner	Yank Terry	Hughson
PI-Mickey Harris	Joe Dobson	Newsome	Emmett O'Neill
PI-Lefty Grove	Newsome	Dobson	Pinky Woods

Led by Bobby Doerr, who hit .325 with 15 homers and 81 RBIs, and Bob Johnson, who was purchased from the Senators and chipped in with a 17–106–.324 campaign, the Red Sox picked themselves up from the second division back to that of pennant contenders as they stayed in the race until late in the season when military callups broke up their run.

Pete Fox also cleared the .300 hurdle, hitting .315 as the offense was rejuvenated, leading the circuit in both average, at .270, and runs scored with 730.

Tex Hughson once again was the major force on the mound, going 17–5 with a league high .738 winning percentage and a miniscule 2.26 ERA.

As stated before, the military curtailed what looked to be a special season, taking Doerr and starting third baseman Jim Tabor who was hitting at a .285 clip with 13 homers and 72 RBIs. Boston would also lose lefty catcher Hal Wagner who was at .332 when he got the call. The mound corps was also devastated losing the ace of the staff, Hughson.

The losses might have cost Boston a shot at the pennant this season, but they would hurt more the next, sending them reeling back to the second division.

Who Left for the War	Who Replaced Them
CA-Danny Doyle	
PI-Mace Brown	
PI-Joe Dobson	Pinky Woods

Danny Doyle— Doyle was 9 for 43, a .209 average in 1943 which constituted his entire major league career.

Mace Brown — Mace Brown had a nice ten year career in which he would become one of the first truly full time relief specialists in the game.[64]

Brown broke into the game with the Pirates in 1935, quickly working into his role over the next two seasons. He would lead the NL in saves in 1937 with 7 before having his finest yet worst season ever the following year. Nineteen thirty-eight would bring a 15–9 mark in 51 games, a league high, and his only All-Star selection. Ironically this marquee campaign would end on a bitter note as he gave up the homer to Gabby Hartnett, more aptly known in baseball history as "the Homer in the Gloamin'," as it came in a darkened sky as the game was about to be called. It would cost the Pirates the pennant that season.[65] Brown would survive to throw 2½ more seasons in Pittsburgh, becoming the save leader again in the senior circuit for 1940 once more with 7.

He was sold to the Dodgers in April of 1941, playing for the NL champions the rest of the year before being purchased by the Red Sox. He would have some success with the Sox before the war, going 9–3 in 1942 and accumulating a career high 9 saves in 1943 with a 2.12 ERA in 93 innings with an excellent .222 OBA.

Mace would go in to the Marines the following year where he would achieve the rank of lieutenant and supervise two ball teams that the service put together with its Naval fleets in Hawaii, the Third fleet and the Fifth.[66]

When he returned, he pitched only one more season, going 2–0 in 1946 for Boston, finishing with a career low 2.05 ERA and a lifetime 76–57 mark.

Joe Dobson — After coming over from the Indians his second year in the majors in 1940 with Frankie Pytlak and Odell Hale for Jim Bagby, Gee Walker and Gene Desautels, Dobson quickly became an important member of the Red Sox starting rotation until 1950.

"Burrhead," as he was known, went 23–14 his first two seasons in Boston in 1941 and 1942, before slumping to 7–11 with a Red Sox team that was devastated by military callups. Dobson would return impressively in 1946, with a 13–7 record, with his highlight being a complete game 4 hit, no earned run, 8-strikeout masterpiece in a 6–3 victory over the Cards in Game 5 of the Fall Classic. He would pitch in 2 other games in relief, giving up no runs in his total of 12⅔ innings for the series.[67]

Joe had his two finest seasons in 1947 and 1948, winning a career high 18 games in an 18–8 season, before having his only All-Star game selection in '48 with a 16–10 mark. After two more seasons where Dobson was a combined 29–22, he was sent to the White Sox where he had his last big year, going 14–10 in 1952 with all time lows in ERA at 2.51 and OBA with a .222

mark. He would end his major league career 2 years later in 1954, back in Beantown throwing but 2⅔ more innings.

The war cost Dobson probably two career marks. He was 137–103 in his career, so chances are he would have won the 13 games necessary to top 150. Dobson also was only 8 strikeouts shy of 1,000, which would have fallen in only two or three more outings.

Pinky Woods replaced Dobson in the rotation and had 4–8 and 4–7 marks in 1944 and 1945. Pinky was truly a wartime player as his career would last from 1943 through 1945, ending with a 13–21 mark, a 3.97 ERA and a .272 OBA, all quite a bit less than the output of Dobson.

1944 Cleveland Indians
72–82–17 GB

1941	1942	1943	1944
1B-Hal Trosky	Les Fleming	Mickey Rocco	Rocco
2B-Ray Mack	Mack	Mack	Mack
SS-Lou Boudreau	Boudreau	Boudreau	Boudreau
3B-Ken Keltner	Keltner	Keltner	Keltner
OF-Jeff Heath	Oris Hockett	Roy Cullenbine	Cullenbine
OF-Roy Weatherly	Weatherly	Hockett	Hockett
OF-Gee Walker	Heath	Heath	Pat Seerey
CA-Rollie Hemsley	Otto Denning	Buddy Rosar	Rosar
PI-Bob Feller	Bagby	Bagby	Harder
PI-Al Milner	Mel Harder	Smith	Smith
PI-Al Smith	Smith	Allie Reynolds	Steve Gromek
PI-Jim Bagby	Chubby Dean	Harder	Reynolds

It certainly was not the offense that sent Cleveland reeling 10 games down versus 1943, as they led the league in hits with 1,458, scoring 43 more runs than the year before. It was the mound crew, whose ERA ballooned from 3.15 to 3.66, leading the AL in hits given up at 1,428 and walks given up at 621, which was 29 more than the second worst squad in Boston, that was primarily responsible for the downturn.

Steve Gromek, who replaced Jim Bagby when Jim entered the merchant marines, led the troubled group with a 10–9 record and 2.56 ERA. Bagby himself was in the midst of a poor 4–5, 4.33 ERA campaign when he left.

On the offensive side, Manager Lou Boudreau became the first player-manager to win a batting crown leading the league with a .327 average. He also was tops in the circuit with 45 doubles. Ken Keltner and Roy Cullenbine also had solid seasons, going 13–91–.295 and 16–80–.284 respectively.

Who Left for the War	Who Replaced Them
CA-Gene DeSautels	
INF-Ted Sepkowski	
OF-Hank Edwards	
OF-Gene Woodling	
PI-Pete Center	
PI-Chubby Dean	

Gene DeSautels— Gene "Red" DeSautels was a fine fielding catcher who had a long 13-year career with the Tigers, Red Sox, Indians and A's. He would only miss one season in the military and finish his time in the major leagues with a .233 mark and 31 fielding runs.

Red spent his first four years in the majors, between 1930 and 1933, with the Tigers playing in basically what was a very abbreviated role. He only came up 251 times, hitting only .191. With not much of a future in hand, he was sent to the Red Sox where he turned his career around and became a starter in Beantown.

After hitting .243 in 1937 with a league high fielding percentage at .993, Gene had his most explosive offensive season with a career high .291 average (a fluke season obviously as his next high was only .247) and 2 of his lifetime 3 homers in 1938. He fell back to .243 the next season before tumbling down to .225 in 1940. Gene was sent to the Indians in December of 1940 with Jim Bagby and Gee Walker for Frankie Pytlak, Odell Hale and Joe Dobson.

DeSautels would not reach the success he had in Boston, hitting only .201, .247 and .205 between 1941 and 1943, before heading off to war. He would spend only one season in the service returning for only 10 games with the Indians in '45, finishing his career with the A's the following season.

Ted Sepkowski— Sepkowski would have a very short 3-year career in the show, garnering only 6 hits in 26 at-bats for the Indians and Yankees.

Hank Edwards— With only 116 times at-bat in hand his first two season in 1941 and 1942, Hank Edwards finally got some significant time hitting .276 in 92 games in 1943 before being called to arms.

When Edwards returned in 1946, he would have his best big league campaign hitting .301, with a league leading 16 triples, 33 doubles and 10 homers for a .509 slugging percentage. He would turn up the power more in 1947 with a career best 15 homers and 59 RBIs.

Hank slumped in 1948 due to a shoulder injury before starting a 5-year odyssey where he went to the Cubs, Dodgers, Reds, White Sox and Browns. He would have a couple good years as a reserve, the best being 1950 with the Cubs hitting .364 in 110 at-bats.

Edwards ended his career a .280 hitter after finishing up with the Browns in 1953.

Gene Woodling— Woodling was a 4 time batting champ in the minors before breaking in with the Indians in 1943.[68] He would go into the service the following season, playing with the Great Lakes Naval team.[69] When Gene returned in 1946, he stumbled around a couple more years with Cleveland and Pittsburgh before ending up with the New York Yankees in 1949.

In the Bronx, Woodling would come into his own, platooning with Hank Bauer in left with one of the great dynasties of all time. Gene's best three seasons with the Yanks were between 1951 and 1953 when he hit .281, .309 and .306 respectively, with a combined 37 homers, leading the AL in fielding percentage in both '52 and '53 at .996 each season. He would also top the junior circuit in on base percentage at .429 in '53.

Gene went to Baltimore and back to Cleveland in 1955 and 1956 before having his finest offensive season ever in 1957. Woodling would set career highs in homers with 19, RBIs 78, average .321 and slugging at .521. He would find his way back to Baltimore in 1958, coming over with Bud Daley and Dick Williams for Larry Doby and Don Ferrarese. In Baltimore, he was selected to his one and only All-Star game in 1959 classic in a year he hit .300 with 14 homers and 77 runs knocked in.

Gene ended up in Washington where he hit .313 in 1961 before being reunited with Casey Stengel on the Amazin' Mets of 1962. He would end his career after '62 with a lifetime .284 mark in 17 seasons. Woodling would amass 1,585 hits and 830 RBIs during that time.

Pete Center— Marvin Earl "Pete" Center played two years before going into the service in 1942 and 1943 where he went a combined 1–2 in 25 games, 24 coming in '43 when he had an outstanding IP/H ratio of 42⅓/29 and equally impressive OBA of .201.

The last two seasons for Center would come after the war in 1945 and 1946. He would win 6 of his 7 career games in '45 before his swan song season in '46 where he was 0–2 with a 4.97 ERA.

Chubby Dean— Chubby would begin his time in the show in 1937, pitching in only 8 games for the A's his first two campaigns. He would settle into an extended relief role in 1939, going 5–8 in 54 games, 53 in relief. After 1½ more very poor seasons in Philadelphia where Alfred Lovill Dean went 8–17 with ERAs of 6.61 and 6.19, the Indians picked him up on waivers midway through the 1941 season.

In Cleveland, during the first war year of 1942, Dean enjoyed his most successful campaign. Despite his 8–11 record, Chubby reached career highs in both starts with 22 and innings pitched with 172⅔ while having career lows in ERA at 3.81 and OBA with a .261 percentage. After a 5–5 start in 1943, Dean would go into the service never to return to the big leagues. He would end things with an unimpressive 5.08 ERA, .288 OBA and a 30–46 record.

1944 Philadelphia Athletics
72–82–17 GB

1941	1942	1943	1944
1B-Dick Siebert	Siebert	Siebert	Bill McGhee
2B-Bennie McCoy	Bill Knickerbocker	Suder	Hall
SS-Al Brancato	Suder	Irv Hall	Ed Busch
3B-Pete Suder	Buddy Blair	Eddie Mayo	George Kell
OF-Wally Moses	Elmer Valo	Johnny Welaj	White
OF-Sam Chapman	Mike Kreevich	Jo Jo White	Estalella
OF-Bob Johnson	Johnson	Bobby Estalella	Ford Garrison
CA-Frankie Hayes	Hal Wagner	Wagner	Wagner
PI-Phil Marchildon	Marchildon	Jesse Flores	Bobo Newsom
PI-Jack Knott	Roger Wolff	Harris	Black
PI-Les McCrabb	Lum Harris	Wolff	Flores
PI-Bill Beckman	Dick Fowler	Don Black	Russ Christopher

As amazing as the rise of the St. Louis Browns was, perhaps not far behind was the sudden emergence from the tar pits of the Philadelphia A's.

After back-to-back 55 and 49 win seasons the first two years of war ball, the A's improved 28 games and finished in a tie for fifth place, the first time they had been out of the basement since 1939. Mack made several moves throughout the season, including trading catcher Hal Wagner to the Red Sox for outfielder Ford Garrison, who became a regular and hit .269. They were also able to get troubled 36-year-old pitcher Bobo Newsom from Washington for Roger Wolff.

The offense overall was enhanced, picking up 25 points in its average over 1943 by hitting .257. Catcher Frankie Hayes led the way hitting 13 of the team's 36 homers with a club high 78 RBIs.

If the offense was considered improved, then it was the pitching that made the most dramatic climb. They lowered the 1943 league worst 4.05 ERA to the third best in the AL at 3.26. Their K/BB ratio, which was 503/536, was incredibly improved to 534/390. The newly acquired Newsom, who finished at 13–15 with a 2.82 ERA, led the staff. Russ Christopher also had a nice year at 14–14–2.97. Perhaps the finest performance of all was that of 39-year-old rookie "Jittery Joe" Berry, who was 10–8 in 53 relief appearances with a league high 12 saves, 1.94 ERA and incredible .192 OBA.

The record 72–82 might not seem like it should be considered a watershed season, but for this rag tag collection, it was by far better than anyone could have imagined.

Who Left for the War	*Who Replaced Them*
1B-Bruce Konopka	
2B-Pete Suder	Irv Hall/Ed Busch
OF-Vern Benson	
OF-George Staller	
OF-Elmer Valo	
OF-Johnny Welaj	Jo Jo White/Fred Garrison
PI-Herman Besse	
PI-Charlie Bowles	
PI-Norm Brown	
PI-Lou Ciola	
PI-Tom Clyde	
PI-Everett Fagan	
PI-Bert Kuczynski	
PI-Sam Lowry	

Bruce Konopka— The Hammond, Indiana, native went 3 for 12 in 1942 and 1943 for the A's before going into the service. When he returned, he hit .237 in 93 official times at the plate in 1946, which would prove to be his final 93 career at-bats.

Pete Suder— Pete "Pecky" Suder was a proficient second and third baseman throughout his 13-year career, all of which came with the Athletics. He wasn't a great offensive player, hitting only .249, but did amass 1,268 hits. He wasn't Bill Mazeroski in the field, yet led the league twice in fielding percentage in 1947 at .986 and in 1951 with a .987 mark, both coming at second.

Suder broke into the majors in 1941 and immediately became a starter at third. He spent his second season a jack of many trades, playing 69 games at short, 34 at third and 31 at second, all the while hitting .256. Pete would slump to .221 in 1943 before heading into the service.

Pecky returned, hitting .281 in 1946, splitting time between short and third. He moved over to second the following season, where he would finally settle in. Pete's best offensive year came in 1949 when he hit .267 and career highs in both homers, with 10 (he only had a total of 49) and RBIs at 75. That was also the season he combined with Eddie Joost and Ferris Fain to help set the record for team double plays in a season with 217.[70]

The Aliquippa, Pennsylvania, native would not break .250 again until he hit .286 in 1953, a career best. Suder lasted only two more seasons, hitting only .203 in 287 at-bats for the 1954 and 1955 campaigns. He retired after the '55 season, although sticking around long enough to see the A's move from Philly to Kansas City.

Replacing Suder at second was Irv Hall, who moved over from shortstop. Three of Hall's 4-year career was during the war. He would hit .268, a bit better than Suder in 1944, before hitting .261 the following year. Irv proved to be a better fielder as he accumulated 26 fielding runs in 1945, which was a league high.

Ed Busch, who like Hall played only during the war years, took over Irv's spot at short, in essence replacing Suder in the infield. Busch would have a nice .271 average for '44, although he had a nasty -30 fielding runs. He hit .250 the following season, his last in the majors.

Vern Benson— Benson's prewar career was all of 2 hitless at-bats with the A's in 1943. After the conflict he would play one season with Philadelphia and three with the Cardinals. Benson would only come up 102 times in that span, finishing with a .202 career mark.

George Staller—"Stopper" Staller played one season for the A's in 1943. He hit .271 in 85 at-bats, including 3 homers. He would go into the service following the season, never to return to the show.

Elmer Valo— Valo would have a successful 20 year career, mostly with the A's, in the majors, hitting .282 for his career.

Born in Ribnik, Czechoslovakia, Valo broke into the starting lineup in 1942 after two abridged seasons. He would hit only .251 and .221 the following season before going into the military. When he returned in 1946, he was a better player, making his mark with three successive .300 seasons between '46 and '48.

Valo, who was not a power hitter, only accumulating 58 homers throughout his career, would show a rare bit of power in 1949 and 1950, knocking in a career high 85 runs the first season (30 higher than his second best of 55) and smacking 10 homers the next, the only time he would reach double figures in that category.

The Czech native would slump to .224 and .214 in 1953 and 1954 before hitting a lifetime high .364 in 1955. Valo remained with the A's for only 9 more games as he was sent to the Phils in 1956.

Elmer began his travel time at that point going from Brooklyn (and on to Los Angeles in the move), to Cleveland, then New York with the Yanks, Washington (moving to Minnesota with the team) and finally back to the Phillies, where he retired in 1961. If you can count successfully, that's eight cities in six years.

Elmer would probably be the only man to accompany three different franchises to their new cities as he went from Philadelphia to Kansas City with the A's, Brooklyn to Los Angeles with the Dodgers and Washington to Minnesota when the Senators became the Twins.

Valo missed only 2½ seasons due to the war, but the one figure it did prevent him from achieving was 1,500 hits. He was only 80 shy of the mark, which with the 250 to 300 hits that he missed, would have easily put him there.

Johnny Welaj— Welaj was a utility outfielder for the Senators between 1939 and 1941, hitting .253 in 512 at-bats. The war would provide him with one last opportunity to play in 1943 when Valo went off to the service. He would hit .242 in a career best 281 times up. After going into the military, Welaj would be done in the majors.

Herman Besse— Half of Besse's 5-year major league career came in 1942 when he went 2–9 in 133 innings. It wasn't a dream season, as he would give up 163 hits and 69 walks for a mercuric 6.16 ERA. He would throw only 109⅔ innings the rest of the time, finishing his career in 1946 with a 6.79 ERA and a .302 OBA.

Charlie Bowles— Bowles was a true war ball pitcher, pitching 2 seasons between 1943 and 1945 (he missed 1944 in the service). He would go a combined 1–4 in only 51⅓ innings.

Norm Brown— Brown's career lasted only 2 years, 1943, when he gave up no earned runs in 7 innings and 1946, losing his only major league decision.

Lou Ciola— The Norfolk, Virginia, native pitched only one season in the majors, going 1–3 in 1943 with a 5.56 ERA.

Tom Clyde— Clyde would give up an even 6 earned runs in 6 innings of work in 1943, his only major league season.

Everett Fagan— Fagan would get an opportunity that Clyde and Ciola would not have; he got to pitch one season after the war. He went 2–6 with the 1943 A's, coming back in 1946 to go 0–1. He retired with a 5.47 in 82⅓ innings.

Bert Kuczynski— Bert would go one season in 1943, losing his only decision in 6 contests for a 4.01 ERA and .336 OBA.

Sam Lowry— Lowry would throw only 21 innings without a decision in 1942 and 1943 for the A's. He would not return after his time in the military.

1944 Chicago White Sox
71–83–18 GB

1941	1942	1943	1945
1B-Joe Kuhel	Kuhel	Kuhel	Hal Trosky
2B-Bill Knickerbocker	Don Kolloway	Kolloway	Roy Schalk
SS-Luke Appling	Appling	Appling	Skeeter Webb
3B-Dario Lodigiani	Bob Kennedy	Ralph Hodgin	Hodgin
OF-Taffy Wright	Wally Moses	Moses	Moses
OF-Mike Kreevich	Hoag	Thurman Tucker	Tucker
OF-Myril Hoag	Wright	Guy Curtright	Eddie Carnett
CA-Mike Tresh	Tresh	Tresh	Tresh
PI-Thornton Lee	John Humphries	Humphries	Dietrich
PI-Eddie Smith	Smith	Dietrich	Grove
PI-Johnny Rigney	Bill Dietrich	Orval Grove	Ed Lopat
PI-Ted Lyons	Lyons	Smith	Humphries

Although it wasn't Shoeless Joe Jackson, the White Sox in 1944 were helped by a player who emerged from the wheat fields of Iowa, a man who by most accounts wore shoes, former Indian slugger Hal Trosky. Trosky, who had been out of the game since the end of 1941 due to chronic migraine headaches, had been farming in Iowa.[71] He had intended to come back with the Indians in 1943, but it never came through.[72] In the off-season the White Sox purchased him to replace Joe Kuhel who had been sold to the Senators.

Trosky didn't disappoint as he hit 10 of the Pale Hose's 23 homers. Unfortunately, it was the rest of the Chicago offense that did disappoint. As a team they scored 30 less runs than the year before, very much missing the potent bat of short stop Luke Appling who took his 1943 league leading .328 average into the military. Third baseman Ralph Hodgin did his part as he had a solid season, hitting .295.

The pitching staff didn't exactly come through either as their 1943 ERA of 3.21 shot up to 3.58. The IP/H ratio of 1,400/1,352 was now 1,391/1,411. Ed Lopat was the best of the lot going 11–10 with a 3.26 (he also had the highest batting average hitting .309) in his rookie year. Gordon Maltzberger was the strength from the bullpen with a 10–5 mark and a league leading 12 saves.

You put it all together and you see that Appling's loss had an effect on this team as it rolled from the first division all the way down to 7th place. Perhaps they needed to go back to Iowa and see if they could now pull Jackson out of a cornfield this time.

Who Left for the War	Who Replaced Them
2B-Don Kolloway	Roy Schalk
SS-Luke Appling	Skeeter Webb
OF-Frank Kalin	
PI-Eddie Smith	John Humphries/Ed Lopat

Don Kolloway—"Butch" Kolloway began his career in the Windy City in 1940 and started to become a force the following year. He hit .271, which would eventually be his career mark, and performed a feat unique to the game against the Indians on June 28th. He stole second, third and home, becoming one of only a few players in league history to accomplish the feat.[73]

Kolloway moved into the starting lineup the next year, when he led the league in doubles with 40; Butch slumped to .216 the next season before going into the military. He would return in 1946 and spend the next three seasons hitting on a very consistent basis, .280, 278 and .273 between '46 and '48 respectively. Despite his solid play, Don was sent packing to the Tigers early in 1949 for Vern Rapp.

After hitting .294 following the trade, Butch had his best offensive year ever hitting .289, equaling his career high with 6 homers and setting a lifetime best in RBIs with 62 as he was moved from second over to first in 1950. It would prove to be the beginning of the end as Kolloway slumped to .255 and .243 in a part time role.

He was sent to the A's for the 1953 campaign, where he would only come to the plate once to end his career.

The only level Butch really was close to was 500 runs as he was only 34 off that mark. He had 1,081 hits, so 1,500 would have been a little out of the question. At best he would have had 290–300.

Replacing Kolloway was Roy Schalk. Schalk, who had not been in the majors since 1932, returned from the service in 1944 to hit only .220 with -14 fielding runs. He would improve a little in '45, raising his average to .248 and 6 fielding runs, but was just a wartime replacement and was gone after the season was over.

Luke Appling— Luke Appling would hit .310 for his career, garner 2,749 hits with 1,116 RBIs and to round out his game, compile 73 fielding runs. He would win two batting titles, be selected to seven All-Star games, set league records for double plays, assists and putouts for a shortstop (all eventually broken by Luis Aparicio)[74] and deservingly be elected to the Baseball Hall of Fame in 1964. He would do all this without the benefit of ever playing in a World Series.

"Old Aches and Pains" spent his first two seasons as a reserve before becoming the starting shortstop in 1932; it was a position that only a call to the military could take away from him.

In 1933, he cracked the .300 plateau, hitting .322 with 85 RBIs. It would be the first of nine consecutive years he would stay above .300 (he did it 16 of the next 17 years that he played). Three years later in 1936, Appling was selected to play in his first All-Star game as he won his first batting title at what would be a career best .388 average. He would also set his personal record in RBIs, knocking in 128 on only 6 homers. It would be 43 RBIs, more than his second best season. Luke would finish second in the MVP vote behind the Iron Horse himself, Lou Gehrig.

After a .317 campaign in 1937, Appling would break his leg in spring training, missing a good portion of the season.[75] He recovered to play in the All-Star game the next three seasons, including a .348-year in 1940 when he accounted for 79 RBIs without a homer.

Luke slumped to .262 in 1942 before rebounding to win his second title in 1943 with a .328 mark. He would also lead the circuit in on base percentage at .419. Appling got his call to arms before the 1944 season and was stationed for the Army at Camp Lee, Virginia, where he was the manager/shortstop for the quartermaster team.[76]

He returned at the end of 1945 where he hit .368 in 18 games before having two more All-Star seasons in 1946 and 1947. Luke would raise his postwar .300 streak to five with .314 and .301 seasons in 1948 and 1949. The 43-year-old Appling would finally fall below .300 in 1950, hitting .234 and retiring from the game.

The war very legitimately cost Luke the 3,000 hit level. He needed 251 hits to reach it and barring injury, there is no reason he couldn't have attained that in the almost two seasons he missed. The two campaigns prior to his going into the military, he had 334 hits, the two full years afterwards he ironically had 334 also.

Replacing him at short was Skeeter Webb. Webb would play one season in Chicago, replacing him in 1944, and could only muster up a .211 average. It certainly was no question why the Sox missed "Aches and Pains" so much.

Frank Kalin — "Fats" Kalin would play only two seasons in the majors, one in Pittsburgh in 1940 and the last with Chicago in 1943. He would only have 7 at-bats in his career and never got a base hit.

Eddie Smith — Smith came into the show in 1936 before breaking into the Philadelphia A's rotation the following year and having a very strange season. He would go 4–17 in 1937 but had an impressive 196⅔/178 IP/H ratio and a decent .242 OBA, although he did walk 90 that year. The New Jersey resident had one more tough season in Philly before being picked up by the White Sox on waivers in 1939.

Smith had his best year in 1940 with his only plus .500 campaign at 14–9 with a 3.21 ERA and career low .228 OBA. He would follow that year up with two consecutive All-Star selections in 1941 and 1942. The second one in '42 came in a season where Smith lost 20 games. Eddie would go 11–11 in '43 before heading into the service.

Smith returned in 1946 with an 8–11 mark and 2.85 ERA. It would be his last good season, as he would fall to 2–6 with a 7.33 ERA in 1947 with both the White and Red Sox, leaving the majors with a 73–113 record.

Although Smith won 27 games in two consecutive years in 1940 and 1941, it's very doubtful he could have pulled the trick off in 1944 and 1945 had he not gone off to war, as the White Sox were just not a very good team. Had he done it though, it would have given him 100 wins in his career.

Replacing Smith in the number four slot in the rotation was Johnny Humphries. Humphries was a good pitcher who had been in the White

Sox rotation throughout the war years from 1942 through 1945. He went 8–10 in 1944 with a fine 3.67 ERA. Ed Lopat was the new man in the rotation as a rookie for Chicago and would have a combined 21–23 mark in his two war campaigns. He would of course go on to have a very successful venture with the Yankees after being sent there following the 1947 season.

1944 Washington Senators
64–90–25 GB

1941	1942	1943	1944
1B-Mickey Vernon	Vernon	Vernon	Joe Kuhel
2B-Jimmy Bloodworth	Ellis Clary	Gerry Priddy	George Myatt
SS-Cecil Travis	John Sullivan	Sullivan	Sullivan
3B-George Archie	Bobby Estalella	Clary	Gil Torres
OF-Buddy Lewis	Bruce Campbell	Case	Jake Powell
OF-Doc Cramer	Stan Spence	Spence	Spence
OF-George Case	Case	Bob Johnson	Case
CA-Jake Earley	Early	Early	Rick Ferrell
PI-Dutch Leonard	Bobo Newsom	Wynn	Leonard
PI-Sid Hudson	Hudson	Dutch Leonard	Haefner
PI-Ken Chase	Early Wynn	Milo Candini	Wynn
PI-Steve Sundra	Alex Carrasquel	Mickey Haefner	Johnny Niggeling

It would be a surprising 1943 season for manager Oscar Bluege and the 1943 Washington Senators, finishing in second place to the eventual world champion New York Yankees. When three pivotal members of that team, Mickey Vernon, Gerry Priddy and Jake Early went off to fight after the campaign concluded, the inevitable happened and they won 20 less games, finishing 1944 in the cellar.

The offense was much less productive; scoring 74 runs less than the previous year. They were able to purchase veteran first baseman Joe Kuhel from the White Sox in the off season to replace Vernon, but he was not as productive, knocking in only 51 batters compared to Vernon's 70 from '43. Despite it all, Stan Spence still put up big numbers, hitting .316 with 18 homers and 100 RBIs, finishing 8th in the MVP race.

The mound corps, led by Dutch Leonard, 14–14–3.06, southpaw Mickey Haefner, 12–15–3.04 and 40-year-old war phenom Johnny Niggeling, 10–8–2.32, fell back a little with their ERAs going up from 3.19 to 3.50. The most disappointing year was turned in by future Hall of Famer Early Wynn who, coming off his first All-Star game selection in '43, fell to 8–17 with a 3.38 ERA. The IP/H ratio, which was a fine 1,388/1,293 in '43, blew up to 1,381/1,410 in this fateful year.

The up and down Senators would become the most inconsistent major league team during this time period as they would eventually be lifted up to second place again the following season, but for the time being the cellar was not a fun place to be.

Who Left for the War	Who Replaced Them
CA-Jake Early	Rick Ferrell
1B-Mickey Vernon	Joe Kuhel
2B-Gerry Priddy	George Myatt
3B-Alex Kampouris	
3B-Sherry Robertson	
PI-Jim Mertz	
PI-Ray Scarborough	

Jake Early— Early was a catcher who was as much known for trying to keep hitters off their game, by consistently chatting with them when he was behind the plate, than anything else.[77] When he got to the plate, the 9-year veteran was a .241 lifetime hitter who basically peaked after his first three seasons.

As a part time catcher his first two seasons in 1939 and 1940, Early hit .262 and .257 while learning his craft. He took over the starting spot the following season and hit career highs in homers with 10 and batting average at .287. He would fall down to .204 the next season before rebounding in his last prewar campaign of 1943 to .258. Early was selected to his only All-Star game that year and caught the entire game.[78]

Jake would not be able to capture the same success when he returned, as he hit only .216 between 1946 and 1948 for the Senators ('46 and '48) and the Browns ('47), ending his career two years later in 1949 with Washington.

Replacing Early was catcher Rick Ferrell. Ferrell had been Early's predecessor in Washington before being sent off to the Browns. He returned to the capital just in time to miss the Browns' miraculous run. Nonetheless he would prove to be a most adequate replacement as he was selected to two All-Star games in 1944 and 1945 hitting .277 and .266 respectively. The 15-year veteran was at the end of his career and would be out of the game after the 1947 season.

Mickey Vernon— Vernon's 20-year career was full of many ironic twists and turns. He would lead the league twice in hitting, 1946 and 1953 (the second one tainted as his teammates got questionable outs in the last game of the year so he wouldn't have to bat as Mickey held the lead by the slimmest of margins[79]), yet in the years between, did not bat .300 once.

He set a major league record for most double plays by a first baseman and AL marks for putouts, assists and chances in a lifetime[80] and would lead the league four times in fielding percentage, yet lead the circuit in errors three times.[81] Through it all, Vernon collected 2,495 hits, 1,311 RBIs, a .286 career mark, played in four decades and was the favorite of President Dwight D. Eisenhower.[82]

After two reserve seasons in 1939 and 1940, Vernon took over the starting role at first in 1941, hitting .299 with 93 RBIs. He would slump a little the next two seasons before going into the Navy where he would play with the great Norfolk Naval teams.[83] Mickey won his first batting title upon his return, hitting .353 with a league leading 51 doubles in 1946 and was selected to play in his first All-Star game. He would slump the next two seasons before being sent to Cleveland with Early Wynn for Joe Haynes, Eddie Klieman and Eddie Robinson after the 1948 season.

He had a nice season for the Tribe in 1949, hitting .291 with 18 homers and 83 knocked in, but that was it as Washington brought him back in June of 1950 for Dick Weik.

Vernon would have a couple of nice years before breaking into his marquee campaign in 1953, winning his second batting title at .337, leading the circuit with 43 doubles and hit 15 homers with a career high 115 RBIs, finishing 3rd in the MVP chase to Al Rosen. It would be the beginning of a four year stretch when Vernon would show some unusual power, hitting 64 of his lifetime 172 homers, including a career best 20 in 1954, again leading the league in doubles with 33.

Mickey left the Senators for good following the 1955 campaign and spent the last five years of his career in Boston, Cleveland, Milwaukee and Pittsburgh. During that stretch, he would be selected to play in two All-Star games, one in his 15–84–.310 season for the Red Sox in 1956 and the last in 1958 for the Indians when he hit .293. His career ended in 1960 for the Bucs when the player/coach was given 8 at-bats for the world champions, giving him a career that went through four decades.

Had he not missed two years in the service, it's very unlikely that Vernon would have garnered the 505 hits he needed to hit the magical 3,000 level, as he never had more than 207 hits in his career. Mickey certainly would have made the 500 level in doubles, needing only 10 more and he had an outside chance of getting the 189 RBIs needed to shoot him up to 1,500. He had 156 in the two seasons preceding the war and 170 the two after.

Veteran first baseman Joe Kuhel was purchased from the White Sox to replace Vernon during the war. Kuhel would have a similar average to Vernon in 1944 and 1945, hitting .282 combined although his power numbers were not in the ballpark, hitting only 9 homers and 97 RBIs in the 2 years.

Jerry Priddy— Priddy may not have had the best reputation in the world, being known as an outspoken troublemaker who was later convicted of trying to extract a $25,000 payday from a shipping company by threatening to set off a bomb on a cruise ship.[84] What he was though was a fine fielding second baseman who accumulated 82 fielding runs during his 11 year career.

He came up with the Yankees in 1941 and 1942 before being sent to Washington with Milo Candini for Bill Zuber and cash. He would take over the reins at second in 1943, hitting .271 before going off to serve Uncle Sam. He would play in Hawaii during his time there before coming back in 1946.[85]

Gerry had two sub par seasons in the nation's capital and was sent off to the Browns where he would enjoy his best two seasons. In 1948 he would have career highs in both RBIs, 79, and average when he hit .296. Priddy would also come up with 24 fielding runs. Nineteen forty-nine was equally as impressive with 11 homers and a .290 average.

Despite his success, Priddy would go on to the Tigers for Lou Kretlow and $100,000. He continued his ways in 1950, hitting a career best 13 homers while accumulating what would also be a lifetime high 31 fielding runs. Priddy stayed with Detroit the remainder of his career, which would be only three more seasons. He broke his leg sliding into second in 1952 and was gone from the majors the following season.[86]

Probably the only career achievement Priddy missed during his time in the service was the 1,500 hit level. He needed 248, which was not out of the realm as he had 152 hits the year before he left for the service.

George Myatt replaced Priddy at second during the war. The 7-year veteran would have 1,028 of his career 1,345 at-bats during 1944 and 1945 where he hit .284 and .296 respectively. He was not as effective a fielder as Priddy was, having a -41 fielding runs during the two seasons.

Alex Kampouris— Kampouris was at the tail end of his career when he played with the Senators in 1943, before going into the war. He was a slick fielding second baseman who accrued 50 fielding runs in his career, including 28 in 1936.

The 9-year veteran began things off with the Reds in 1934, playing in Cincinnati for 4½ seasons. His best year with the Reds was also the best of his major league career, hitting lifetime bests in homers with 17 (he would only hit 45 in his entire career) and RBIs at 71 in 1937.

Alex was sent to the Giants midway in 1938 and hit .249 both seasons he was at the Polo Grounds.

Kampouris ended up in Brooklyn in 1941 and would never get back to a starting position that he enjoyed with the Reds and Giants, accumulating only 116 at-bats in 2½ seasons. He was sold to Washington in May of 1943 where he hit .207 in his final 145 at-bats

Sherry Robertson— Robertson's entire prewar career lasted all of 70 games and 156 at-bats in 1940 through 1943, hitting a combined .212. When the nephew of owner Clark Griffith[87] returned in 1946, he played seven more seasons, only one of which was over 100 games when he was moved to second base from left field and hit career bests in homers with 11 of his lifetime 26 and RBIs with 42.

After hitting a lifetime high .260 in 123 at-bats in 1950, he slumped to .189 the following year before being shipped off to the A's early in 1952, where he finished his major league career with a lifetime .230 mark.

Jim Mertz— Mertz was a one-year war ball pitcher in 1943 when he went 5–7 in 116⅔ innings with a nice .251 OBA. After going into the service he would not return to the majors.

Ray Scarborough— Scarborough would go 6–5 in two war seasons of 1942 and 1943 with the Senators before going into the service. When he came back in 1946, the curveballer would go on to have a nice 10-year career where he would win 80 games.

Ray went 13–24 in 1946 and 1947 before his two breakout seasons in 1948 and 1949. The North Carolina native would go 15–8 the first season with a career low 2.82 ERA and .233 OBA. He'd follow it up in 1949 with a 13–11 mark, his last full season in Washington.

The righty would be sent to the White Sox in May of 1950 with Al Kozar and Eddie Robinson for Bob Kuzava, Cass Michaels and John Ostrowski. He enjoyed his only All-Star game selection that year despite his 13–18 record and 4.94 ERA. Scarborough went off to Boston the next season and had his last nice year with a 12–9 record for the Red Sox in 1951.

Ray would go to Boston, the Yankees and Detroit the next two years, finishing his career after the 1953 season.

Although he won 20 games in successive years on four occasions, it's doubtful Scarborough would have accomplished that in 1944 and 1945 when he was in the service, most likely missing the 100 win plateau. He had not broken into the starting rotation when he left in 1943 and only had 19 victories in his first four seasons by the end of 1948. Nonetheless it was a decent 10-year ride in the show.

Starting Lineups and Who Went to War

NATIONAL LEAGUE

1944 St. Louis Cardinals
105–49–0 GB

1941	1942	1943	1944
1B-Johnny Mize	Hopp	Ray Sanders	Sanders
2B-Creepy Crespi	Crespi	Lou Klein	Emil Verban
SS-Marty Marion	Marion	Marion	Marion
3B-Jimmy Brown	Whitey Kurowski	Kurowski	Kurowski
OF-Enos Slaughter	Slaughter	Musial	Musial
OF-Terry Moore	Moore	Harry Walker	Hopp
OF-Johnny Hopp	Stan Musial	Danny Litwhiler	Litwhiler
CA-Gus Mancuso	Walker Cooper	W. Cooper	W.Cooper
PI-Lon Warneke	M. Cooper	M. Cooper	M.Cooper
PI-Ernie White	Johnny Beazley	Lanier	Lanier
PI-Mort Cooper	Lanier	Harry Gumbert	Harry Brecheen
PI-Max Lanier	Harry Gumbert	Howie Krist	Ted Wilks

While the rest of the baseball world was jumping up and down like a roller coaster out of control, the St. Louis Cardinals kept humming along like a finely oiled machine, winning 105 games, just like they did in 1943, capturing their third consecutive National League pennant and winning the world championship from their cross town rivals, the St. Louis Browns.

They would lose Lou Klein, Harry Walker, Jimmy Brown and Howie Krist from their '43 squad, yet would replace them nicely with Emil Verban, who hit a solid .257, Johnny Hopp, who moved to center and hit .336, and Ted Wilks, the 28-year-old pitcher that came out of nowhere to lead the league in winning percentage at .810, with a 17–4 mark.

The offense would continue to perk as they led the circuit in hitting at .275, slugging with a .402 mark and runs with 772, 93 more than the previous season. War ball star Ray Sanders continued to improve as he led the way with 12 homers, 102 RBIs and a .295 average. Marty Marion, who won the National League MVP by a single vote over Chicago's Bill Nicholson, hit .267 and led the circuit in fielding percentage at .972. Stan Musial was also a force topping the NL in doubles with 51, hits at 197 and slugging with a .549 mark, all the while hitting .347.

The pitching staff was no different, leading the senior circuit with an ERA of 2.68. Their awesome starting rotation consisted of Mort Cooper, 22.7–2.46, Max Lanier, 17–12–2.65, Harry Brecheen, 16–5–2.85 and Ted

Wilks, 17–5–2.64. Twenty-five-year-old George Munger was also solid with an 11–3 mark and miniscule 1.34 ERA when he was drafted into the armed forces.

In the Fall Classic, they had to scramble back from down 2–1 to win the final three games and their second championship in three years. Verban led the way offensively, hitting a healthy .412, but it was the pitching staff that told the story with a team ERA of 1.96 (the Browns would actually go them one better with a 1.49 mark). Cooper, again, was the man with a 1.12 mark and 16 strikeouts in 2 starts.

The Cardinals, during the war years, would be a blueprint for what a great farm system can do for you. Despite losing 10 players and three starters, they just kept chugging along, raising another bottle of champagne. War years or not, this is a dynasty that was truly worth celebrating.

Who Left for the War	*Who Replaced Them*
2B-Lou Klein	Emil Verban
2B-Jimmy Brown	
OF-Earl Naylor	
OF-Harry Walker	Johnny Hopp
OF-Johnny Wyrostek	
PI-Al Brazle	
PI-Murry Dickson	
PI-Howie Krist	Ted Wilks
PI-Howie Pollet	
PI-Ernie White	

Lou Klein — Half of Lou Klein's major league career would take place in his rookie season of 1943, when he took over at second for Creepy Crespi, after Crespi went into the service. Klein played every game for the Cardinals that season, hitting a very impressive .287, with 7 homers and 62 RBIs.

Klein would go off to war after the season, playing for the Coast Guard team at Curtis Bay, Maryland, returning late in 1945.[88] Unable to recapture the magic of his rookie season, Klein hit only .207 in 150 at-bats in 1945 and 1946.

Frustrated at not being able to recapture his starting position, the Louisiana native bolted for the Mexican League, and was banned by organized baseball.[89] He would be the first player allowed to return in 1949, as commissioner Happy Chandler would lift the ban against the league.[90] It wouldn't help Lou as he would play two more seasons in 1949 and 1951 for the Cards, Indians and A's, hitting .219 and .226 respectively.

In the bottom line, Klein's only successful season would be more because of when he got his opportunity to start — during the midst of war ball.

Replacing Klein in 1944 was Emil Verban. Verban would hit .257 and .278 starting in '44 and '45, leading the league in fielding percentage the latter season with a .978 mark as well as being named to the All-Star game that year.

Jimmy Brown— The switch-hitting North Carolina native was a jack of all trades when it came to playing the infield for the Cardinals during his 8-year career (the last season spent with Pittsburgh). In the 890 major league games he played, 392 were at second, 273 were at third and 235 were playing shortstop.

He broke into the show in 1937 as the starting second baseman, hitting .276. Jimmy eclipsed the magical .300 plateau the following season with a .301 average. After a couple of more successful campaigns, Brown would take over the starting spot at third in 1941. That season would see Jimmy hit a lifetime high .306.

As the war broke out, Brown would get 606 at-bats in 1942, being selected to his only All-Star game and knocking in a career best 71, despite only hitting 1 homer. Regardless of the amount of official plate appearances, Brown would split his season between second, short and third, never really settling into one spot or another.

Jimmy would have a disappointing 1943 season, hitting only .182, before leaving for the service. He would return in 1946, playing his last campaign in Pittsburgh. He would hit only .241, leaving the majors with a career .279 mark.

There were a couple of levels that Brown would have easily achieved had he not gone off to war. He had 980 hits, so the 1,000 hit plateau would have been a sure thing, although, as badly as he slumped in 1943, I don't know if he would have accumulated many more. Brown was only 35 runs away from the 500 level; again you would think that 35 runs wouldn't have been a daunting task, yet he only scored 6 in '43 and 23 in his return season of 1946, so it becomes questionable at that point.

Earl Naylor— Naylor was a decent fielding, poor hitting outfielder that came to the Cardinals in 1943 after a two-year jaunt with the Philadelphia A's. He would never play in St. Louis and finished his career a .186 hitter, going hitless in two at-bats with the Dodgers in 1946.

Harry Walker— Harry "The Hat" Walker was a .296 major league hitter, who was as colorful as he was good, never ceasing to talk about hitting during his life to anyone who would listen. He came from good breed, as Harry was the son of the pitcher Ewart "Dixie" Walker and brother to Cardinal Fred "Dixie" Walker.[91]

The Hat broke into the majors in 1940, coming up only 42 times his first two campaigns. He would hit .314 in a reserve role in 1942 before taking over in center for the departed Terry Moore in 1943. He made his first All-Star game that season, hitting .294 with a career best 53 RBIs.

Harry went off to the service after the season and would play ball for the Army in Fort Riley, Kansas, before taking over the reins as manager of the 65th division team in Germany, winning the European service title after V-E Day.[92]

Walker would also see some action in the war that wasn't of the baseball variety. He won the Bronze Star for his actions on a bridge going from Germany to Austria, when he shot three Germans as he was about to be shot. He also received a purple heart for some minor injuries he received.[93]

The Hat returned in 1946 to have one of his worst seasons ever, hitting only .237. The season did end on a bright spot, as Walker would strike the hit that scored Enos Slaughter on his famous mad dash to defeat the Red Sox in the World Series. He did not get off to a good start in '47 and was shipped to the Phillies with Freddy Schmidt for Ron Northey. He woke up in the City of Brotherly Love and hit .371 the rest of the year to win his only batting title at .363, thus becoming the only National League player to with a batting title with two different teams.[94] Harry would also lead the league in triples with 16, being selected to play in his second and last All-Star game.

After hitting .292 the following season, Walker would be traded to the Cubs for war ball star Bill Nicholson in 1949. He would end up going to the Reds before seasons' end having his final .300 season as a regular, hitting the mark right on the nose. (He would hit .308 in 1951, but only in 26 at-bats and .357 in 1955 in 14 times up.)

The Hat would return to the Cardinals where he would finish out his career in 1955.

Although not a definite, it is probable that Walker would have broken the 1,000 hit mark in his career as he fell just 220 hits short. The only other thing that Walker might have achieved was the .300 level, had he had two really good seasons.

Replacing Walker was Johnny Hopp. Hopp, who switched time between first and the outfield, replaced Harry magnificently in '44, hitting .336 while smacking a career best 11 homers and leading the circuit in fielding percentage with a .997 mark. He would follow that up with a .289 average while moving over to left.

Johnny Wyrostek — Wyrostek was a Cardinal in name only as he would never come to bat for the club in his 11-year career.

Before that was he was only a part time player with Pittsburgh hitting only .143 in 114 at-bats in 1942 and 1943. Afterwards his career really took off as the Cardinals, whose property he was at the time, sold him to Philadelphia in 1946. It was with the Phillies that he assumed the starting spot in center, hitting .281 with 17 fielding runs.

Wyrostek would spend the next season in Philly before being shipped off to the Reds with cash for Eddie Miller in 1948. Johnny would have his best season ever that year, hitting a career best 17 homers with 76 RBIs. He had his best success in Cincinnati being selected to two All-Star games in 1950 and 1951 where he had back-to-back seasons of 8–76–.285 and 2–61–.311 (the best average in his career).

The lefty was sent back to Philadelphia the following season where he ended his career after 1954 with a .271 lifetime mark.

It's hard to tell exactly what Johnny missed statistically due to his time in the service, being that he was a very limited player when he left, yet immediately was given a starting role after the war. He finished with 1,149 hits, 351 off the 1,500 level. This mark probably wouldn't have been achieved, as Wyrostek never had over 167 hits in his career. The other plateau was 500 RBIs. He was only 19 off that pace, but it all would depend on when Johnny would have started.

Al Brazle— After 8 years in the minors,[95] Al "Cotton" Brazle broke in with the Cards in 1943, finishing with an 8–2 mark and a microscopic 1.53 ERA. Cotton then entered the Army, serving at Camp Shelby in Mississippi, before going to the 65th Division in Germany where he fought and played with Harry Walker among others.[96]

He returned for the 1946 season and won 10 games or above for the next five seasons. Al's best two were in 1947 and 1949 when he went 14–8 with 2.84 and 3.18 ERAs respectively. Brazle would be sent to the bullpen in 1951, enjoying two solid seasons, going 12–5 in 1952 with a league leading 16 saves before leading the senior circuit again in saves the following year with 18. He would finish his time in the show following the 1954 campaign, falling 3 victories short of 100 with a 97–64 mark, which is obviously the one statistical achievement Brazle would have certainly attained had he not been in the service.

Murry Dickson— Dickson, who was called the "Thomas Edison" by Joe Garagiola because he had so many pitches, including a knuckler,[97] pitched 18 years in the majors, retiring in 1959, one year short of pitching in 4 decades.

He spent his career as a starter/reliever, splitting his games nearly down the middle (287 relief appearances, 338 starts,) but when he came up in 1939, he would spend the first four seasons starting only 15 of his first 69 games. He left directly after the 1943 season for the service, but would be given a 10-day pass from Fort Riley so he could pitch in the Series, which he would toss only ⅔ of an inning in Game 5.[98] He returned

in 1946 and won more than 10 games in each of the next 11 seasons, starting with the '46 campaign where he went 15–6 with a 2.88 ERA, leading
the league in winning percentage at .714.

After two sub .500 seasons, Dickson was sent to the Pirates for
$125,000, where he would continue his losing ways until 1951 when he won
20 games in a 20–16 year. His fortunes would reverse in 1952, as he would
lose 60 games over a three-year period with the lowly Pirates. Dickson
didn't pitch poorly during the time as he had a 3.57 ERA in '52 and was
selected to play in his only All-Star game in '53 despite his 10–19 mark.

Murry would be traded to Philadelphia in 1954 before heading back
to his original club, St. Louis, in 1956 when he went 13–8 after the trade
finishing 13–11 for the year. After trades to the A's, Yankees and back to
Kansas City, Dickson ended his long career at 43 after the 1959 campaign.

He would finish with a 172–181 mark and like Wyrostek, it's tough to
gauge what his time in the military meant to his stats as he really didn't
get into the rotation until 1946. He was 28 wins short of 200 which is
exactly what he won in '46 and '47, although again, he would have to have
been in the rotation in '44 to have a shot.

Howie Krist— Krist came up for two abbreviated seasons in 1937 and
1938 before being undefeated at 10–0 in his third campaign of 1941. He
would follow that up with a 13–3 mark, 2.51 ERA and .233 OBA before
breaking into the starting rotation in 1943. He went 11–5, again with an
impressive .233 OBA before heading off to fight.

When Krist would return from the military in 1946, it would prove
to be his last major league season, finishing at 0–2. He ended his career
with a 37–11 record for a magnificent .771 winning percentage.

Ted Wilks took over in the rotation for Krist and immediately was a
hit, with a 17–4 record in his rookie year of 1944, and a league high .810
winning percentage for a 2.64 ERA. He would have a good 2.93 ERA
the following season, but would fall to 4–7 while suffering from a sore
arm.

Howie Pollet— Pollet would enter the majors in 1941 with the Cardinals and have what looked to be one of the great seasons of all time in 1943,
before enlisting in the Army Air Corps in July.[99] He was 8–4 at the time
with an incredible 1.75 ERA (which as it turned out would lead the NL),
and even more remarkable .200 OBA, being selected to play in his first
All-Star game.

Howie returned in 1946, picking up where he left off by leading the
circuit in wins with 21, innings pitched, 266, and ERA at 2.10, finishing
4th in the MVP race and playing in his second All-Star tilt. He would have
two sub par seasons before winning 20 games again in 1949 with a 20–9

record and 2.77 ERA. Howie would lead the circuit in shutouts with 5 and be selected to his third and final midsummer classic.

After another sub par year, he was shipped to the Pirates with four players, including Joe Garagiola and Ted Wilks for Cliff Chambers and Wally Westlake. He would only go 14–27 in his 2½ years with the Bucs and was sent off to the Cubs in 1953. He could never recapture the success that he achieved in the late '40s and retired after the 1956 season with a 131–116 record.

Only 19 wins short of 150, there was a very good chance Pollet would have gotten to that mark as he seemed to be coming into his own in 1943, before he left for the Army.

Ernie White — Most of Ernie White's 7-year career would occur in his sophomore season of 1941, when he went 17–7 with a 2.40 ERA and equally as impressive .217 OBA.

He would spend the next two seasons in St. Louis with a combined 12–10 mark before going into the military.

When he returned to the game in 1946, he was sold to the Red Sox. White would accumulate an 0–3 mark in his 3 seasons in Beantown, before leaving the show following a 1948 campaign when he gave up only 13 hits in 23 innings for a .167 OBA and 1.96 ERA. Ernie would end with a 30–21 record and 2.78 ERA.

1944 Pittsburgh Pirates
90–63–14.5 GB

1941	1942	1943	1944
1B-Elbie Fletcher	Fletcher	Fletcher	Babe Dahlgren
2B-Frank Gustine	Gustine	Coscarart	Coscarart
SS-ArkyVaughan	Pete Coscarart	Gustine	Gustine
3B-Lee Handley	Elliott	Elliott	Elliott
OF-Bob Elliott	Johnny Barrett	Barrett	Barrett
OF-Vince DiMaggio	DiMaggio	DiMaggio	DiMaggio
OF-Maurice Van Robays	Jimmy Wasdell	Jim Russell	Russell
CA-Al Lopez	Lopez	Lopez	Lopez
PI-Rip Sewell	Sewell	Sewell	Sewell
PI-Max Butcher	Bob Klinger	Klinger	Butcher
PI-Ken Heintzelman	Heintzelman	Wally Hebert	Nick Strincevich
PI-Johnny Lanning	Butcher	Butcher	Preacher Roe

The Pittsburgh Pirates spent the first two seasons of war ball losing only 10 players into the military. They improved steadily, going 66–81 in 1942 and 80–74 the following season. What would happen in 1944 certainly would defy logic, yet this was war ball and anything was truly possible. They lost 13 players off their roster, yet vaulted up to second place in the senior circuit standings with a 90–63 mark. It would be truly a bizarre circumstance especially when one takes a closer look at exactly what they lost.

Perhaps the most important departure was that of Elbie Fletcher. Fletcher, with fellow Bucs Bob Elliott and Vince DiMaggio, was one of the most important hitters that Pittsburgh had. He would hit .289 and .283 in 1942 and 1943 and would be difficult to replace. Starting pitcher Bob Klinger, who had been 11–8 in '43 with a 2.72 ERA, would also be missed. Hank Gornicki, who had been a reliable starter/reliever with the Pirates the past two seasons and Johnny Lanning, who had been off to a strong start in '43 when he went into the military, were further key losses from the mound corps. Add into the mix the loss of top reserve outfielder Martin Van Robays, who hit .288 the previous season in 236 at-bats,

Hank Camelli's career with the Pittsburgh Pirates and Boston Braves occurred mainly during the war years. His best season was 1944 when he hit .296 in 125 at-bats for the Pirates.

and it was presumed the Pirates would fall into the second division.

Perhaps one of the main moves in spring training which helped put off the deluge was the acquisition of first baseman Babe Dahlgren, who was brought over from the Phils for Babe Phelps and cash. Dahlgren would go above and beyond the call of duty, leading a resurgent Pirate offense that scored 744 runs versus a total of 669 the previous campaign. Dahlgren hit a Fletcher-like .289, but would provide more power and production, hitting 12 homers and knocking in 101.

War years star third baseman Bob Elliott came up big with 108 RBIs and a .297 average. Jim Russell and Johnny Barrett would also significantly boost the Pirates' fortunes with Russell hitting .312 and Barrett leading the league in triples with 19 and stolen bases, swiping 28.

As in the past two seasons, Rip Sewell would lead the pitching staff, again winning 21 games, with a 21–12 mark. Nick Strincevich would nicely replace Klinger as he ended at 14–7 with a 3.08 ERA.

Although they did end up 14½ games behind the world champion Cardinals, paint this season a huge success for the proud men from the Steel City.

Who Left for the War	Who Replaced Them
CA-Bill Baker	
CA-Billy Sullivan	
1B Elbie Fletcher	Babe Dahlgren
SS-Alf Anderson	
SS-Huck Geary	
OF-Bud Stewart	
OF-Maurice Van Robays	
PI-Russ Bauers	
PI-Bill Brandt	
PI-Hank Gornicki	
PI-Jack Hallett	
PI-Bob Klinger	Max Butcher/Nick Strincevich
PI-Johnny Lanning	

Bill Baker— Baker would spend each of his seven years in the majors as a backup catcher, with a decent glove and occasional hitting prowess. He broke in with Cincinnati in 1940 and was sold to the Pirates the following season.

In Pittsburgh he had his best offensive season in 1943, hitting .273 with 26 RBIs in only 173 at-bats and a .365 on base percentage. Baker would head into the service after the campaign, only to return in 1946. After spending 1947 away from the majors, Bill was picked up by the Cardinals in 1948 and would hit a career high .294. He would be gone from the show after the following season.

Billy Sullivan— Son of the major league catcher by the same name,[100] Billy Sullivan would turn out to be a fine hitter in his 12-year major league career, accumulating a lifetime .289 average.

He broke in with the White Sox in 1931, hitting .316 his second season, splitting time between first, third, catcher and outfield. He would slump the next year before taking the tour of Ohio going to Cincinnati in 1935, before ending up in Cleveland the following year. Nineteen thirty-six would certainly prove to be his best overall offensive season, hitting a career best .351 while moving in to primarily the catcher's role.

Sullivan moved over to the Cardinals in 1938, becoming their regular catcher his first season and leading the league in fielding percentage at .990. He hit .289 the following year as he was shipped off to the Tigers.

Billy would clear the .300 mark again at .309 in 1940, playing in his one and only World Series. Despite the fact he was only 2 for 13 in the fall classic, Detroit did win it all, as Sullivan was a key part of the world championship.

The Windy City native was sold to Brooklyn in 1942, before going off to war. He would return in 1947 with the Pirates, where he finished his major league career hitting .255 in only 55 at-bats.

Sullivan was only 180 hits shy of 1,000, but in '42 he was pretty much at the end of his career and probably was going to come nowhere near that number.

Elbie Fletcher— Fletcher did not begin his professional baseball career through the ordinary channels that other players were subject to. He won a contest for the Boston High School player that would most likely make the big leagues as every member of his large family sent letters attesting to his baseball skills. The prize was a trip to spring training with the Braves and the rest was history.[101]

Fletcher would arrive in the show with the Boston Braves in 1934 and break into the starting lineup at first base two years later. He spent 2½ moderately successful years with the Braves before being sent to the Pirates in June of 1939 for Bill Schuster and cash. He hit .303 the rest of the way with 12 homers in 370 at-bats.

Elbie hit his prime with the Bucs, immediately achieving career highs in both home runs, 16, and RBIs, knocking in 104 in 1940. He also led the league in walks with 119 and on base percentage at .418.

The lefty would continue his winning ways leading the circuit a second consecutive time in 1941 with 118 walks and a .421 on base percentage and in 1942 he got on base at a .417 clip for his third successive crown in that category. The Milton, Massachusetts, native would be selected to his one and only All-Star game in 1943, showing he could not only hit, but field, as he led all NL first baseman with a .996 percentage. Defense was one thing he was known for, as he would end his career with 33 fielding runs, a high mark, especially for first baseman.

After the '43 campaign, Elbie would go into the Navy, playing successfully for the Bainbridge Naval Training Station in Maryland. He led the team in 1944 with a .344 average.[102]

Fletcher returned in 1946, hitting only 4 homers for a .256 average. He would be displaced the next season, when Pittsburgh acquired Hank Greenberg and was sent back to the Braves where his finished his career in 1949.

Elbie, who ended his career with a .271 average, 1,323 hits and a .384 on base percentage, most definitely would have gotten 1,500 hits if not for the war, as the 177 he was short was almost what he had per season in the two prior years.

Babe Dahlgren was the man who would replace Fletcher during the war years in 1944 and 1945. Dahlgren was 32 years old when the Pirates got him from the Phillies for Babe Phelps before the '44 season. He would have his best year ever with 12 homers and 101 RBIs. Babe came down to earth a little in '45, falling to 75 RBIs and a .250 average although leading the league in fielding that season at .996.

Alf Anderson— Alf Anderson was a poor fielding shortstop who had -21 fielding runs and a .936 fielding percentage in 124 games in 1941 and 1942. He wasn't much of an offensive force, as he would only hit .239 in that time period, before going off to the service. When he returned, Alf had only 1 hitless at-bat in 1946 before leaving the game.

Huck Geary— Eugene "Huck" Geary was a shortstop who hit only .160 in 188 at-bats for the Pirates between 1942 and 1943. They would be his only two major league seasons.

Bud Stewart— Stewart came up with the Pirates in 1942, hitting .242 in 355 at-bats his first two seasons, before going into the military. He would not return until 1948 when the Yankees traded him after 5 at-bats to the Senators for Leon Culberson and $15,000. He would immediately move into the Washington outfield, hitting .279 in 118 games. He enjoyed two more years in the nation's capital, hitting .284 and .267 respectively, before being sent to the White Sox in 1951.

Edward "Bud" Stewart hit between .267 and .276 in the three years before bowing in 1954 after a 1 for 13 performance.

Maurice Van Robays—"Bomber" was the man who dubbed Rip Sewell's famous pitch the eephus pitch when Sewell was asked by Bucco skipper Frankie Frisch what pitch he had thrown (Sewell's pitch was of course a softball like pitch that went 15–25 feet in the air). Sewell asked Van Robays what exactly was an eephus and when Van Robays responded, "Eephus ain't nothing." Sewell apparently liked the explanation and the name stuck.[103]

Van Robays' on the field exploits were impressive for the short time he played. He came up with the Bucs in 1940, hitting .314 in 27 games. He would move into the starting left field position the next season where he had a monster season, hitting .273 with 11 homers and 116 runs knocked in. Maurice continued his success the following season with a .282 average before slumping to .232 in 1942.

The "Bomber" hit .288 in 1943 before heading into the service. He was never the same as he hit only .212 in 1946, which turned out to be his swan song in the show.

Maurice was only 7 hits way from 500 so most certainly he would have achieved that mark in the two years he missed. The true crime, though, is that the two years away from the game took away what might have been a really triumphant career.

Russ Bauers— The bulk of Bauers' 8-year major league career would occur during the 1937 and 1938 seasons when he won 26 of his career 31 victories. After pitching one inning in 1936, Russ went 13–6 in his official rookie season with a 2.88 ERA. He followed that up with another solid campaign at 13–14–3.07, the year the Buccos came within an eyelash of the 1938 World Series.

Bauers hurt his arm in 1939, which would signal the end, for all intents and purposes, of his meaningful career. Russ pitched four more seasons though, 1940, 1941, 1946 and 1950, going a combined 3–6 in 113⅓ innings.

Bill Brandt— After tossing 23 innings in two seasons with the Pirates in 1941 and 1942, Brandt would win 4 of his 5 career victories in 1943, going 4–1 with a 3.14 ERA in 57 frames. He would not return after the war.

Hank Gornicki— Although Hank Gornicki threw a one-hitter in his first major league game on May 3rd, 1941, for the Cardinals versus the Philadelphia Phillies,[104] he would generally have most of his success in the war years for the Pirates after Pittsburgh got him on waivers 6 days before Pearl Harbor, December 1st, 1941.

Hank went go 5–6 in his official rookie season of 1942 but would have an impressive IP/H ratio of 112/89 with a .215 OBA and ERA of 2.57. He would fall off a little in 1943 with a 9–13 mark and his OBA bloated up to .286. After going into the service following the season, Gornicki returned briefly in 1946, pitching only 12 innings in 7 games.

Jack Hallett— Hallett would have a six year major league career, although he would toss only 77 games, mostly in relief, during that time. After three mostly unsuccessful seasons between 1940 and 1942 for the White Sox and Pirates, Jack had a successful moment in 1943 with a superb 47⅔/36 IP/H ratio with a .212 OBA and 1.70 ERA. He would go into the service before the '43 campaign was over, returning in 1946 where he tossed 115 of his career 277⅔ innings, going 5–7 with a 3.29 ERA.

Bob Klinger— Klinger's most notable moment in baseball was one I'm sure he would like to forget. He was the pitcher on the mound for the Boston Red Sox in 1946 when Enos Slaughter made his famous dash home for the winning run in game 7 of the World Series for the Cardinals.[105] Luckily for Klinger it was just a blip on what otherwise was a fine major league career.

He broke in with Pittsburgh in 1938 and promptly went 12–5 with a 2.99 ERA. He could not keep the momentum going and fell to 14–17 the following season with a 4.36 ERA in a career best 33 starts. After another unsuccessful venture, he went 9–4 in 1941.

Perhaps Klinger's best year in a Pirate uniform was in 1943 when the Missouri native was 11–8 with a nice 195/185 IP/H ratio and an ERA down to 2.72. He would go play for Uncle Sam following the season.

Bob's return in 1946 was successful as he was with the Red Sox and adapted very well to his new roll in the bull pen, finishing with a league high 9 saves and 2.37 ERA, playing in his only World Series. He would leave the majors after one more season with a lifetime mark of 66–61.

Replacing Klinger as the Pirate number two man in '44 was Max Butcher. Butcher moved up from the four spot and had two nice seasons in '44 and '45 of 13–11–3.12 and 10–8–3.03 although his OBA's were only at .273 and .277 respectively. He would leave the majors after 1945.

Nick Strincevich took over for Butcher and in essence was the replacement in the starting rotation for Klinger. He had two fabulous seasons for the Bucs, going 30–17 in the two war seasons after Klinger left. He would only win 46 games his entire career.

Johnny Lanning—"Tobacco Chewin' Johnny" came to the majors in 1936 with the Braves and promptly spent his first four seasons as fringe starter, going 25–31 with respectable ERA's of between 3.42 and 3.93.

Lanning was traded to the Pirates before the 1940 season for great hitting pitcher Jim Tobin (who would have the unique double in the war years of hitting 3 home runs in a game in 1942 and throwing two no-hitter's in 1944) and cash. After an 8–4 start in '40, he would start a career best 23 games the following season with an 11–11 mark and 3.13 ERA.

Johnny got off to a fabulous 4–1 start with an ERA of 2.33 in 1943, before he got the call to arms midway in the campaign. He would be back in the league late in 1945 and have a 4–5 season in 1946, mostly out of the bullpen. He went back to play for the Braves the subsequent season where he threw only 3⅔ innings and left the show with a career 58–60 record.

The draft caught up a little with the Cincinnati Reds in 1944, taking star pitcher Johnny Vander Meer as well as starting second baseman Lonny Frey. Despite those losses as well as starting right fielder Max Marshall, who was gone by mid season, the Reds actually improved two games, winning 89.

They were led by an awesome pitching staff headed up with a pair of 35 year olds that included Bucky Walters who led the senior circuit in wins with 23, as he went 23–8, and Ed Heusser who had a National League low

1944 Cincinnati Reds
89–65–16 GB

1941	1942	1943	1944
1B-Frank McCormick	McCormick	McCormick	McCormick
2B-Lonny Frey	Frey	Frey	Woody Williams
SS-Eddie Joost	Joost	Eddie Miller	Miller
3B-Bill Werber	Bert Haas	Steve Mesner	Mesner
OF-Jim Gleeson	Max Marshall	Marshall	Walker
OF-Harry Craft	Gee Walker	Walker	Dain Clay
OF-Mike McCormick	Eric Tipton	Tipton	Tipton
CA-Ernie Lombardi	Ray Lamanno	Ray Mueller	Mueller
PI-Bucky Walters	VanderMeer	VanderMeer	Walters
PI-Johnny VanderMeer	Ray Starr	Walters	Ed Heusser
PI-Paul Derringer	Walters	Riddle	Clyde Shoun
PI-Elmer Riddle	Derringer	Starr	Tommy de la Cruz

ERA of 2.38 in a 13–11 year. Clyde Shoun was able to replace Elmer Riddle, who left the team early on with a shoulder injury, by going 13–10. As a team Cincinnati would have an ERA below 3.00 as they came in at 2.98. They had a nice team IP/H ratio of 1398/1292, although their strikeout total without Vander Meer was a league low 369, about the level of a single Randy Johnson season.

Offensively, the team certainly wasn't a juggernaut, as they scored only 573 runs, which, next to the Phillies, was the lowest in the league. Regardless of the lack of offensive guns, there were three Reds who had pretty impressive seasons. First baseman Frank McCormick hit 20 of the team's 51 homers, knocking in 102 runs while hitting .305. Catcher Ray Mueller was the only other Cincinnati player in double figures in home runs with 10 as he hit .286. Eric Tipton also had some success, as he was the only other Red to top .300 at .301.

Bill McKechnie, the Cincinnati manager, proved his worth again keeping the ship not only afloat but still competitive as he was able to keep this team in the first division for the third consecutive year.

Who Left for the War	Who Replaced Them
CA-Dick West	
1B-Bert Haas	
1B-Hank Sauer	
2B-Lonny Frey	Woody Williams
OF-Frank Kelleher	
OF-Mike McCormick	
PI-Jack Niemes	
PI-Junior Thompson	
PI-Johnny VanderMeer	Bucky Walters/Ed Heusser

Dick West— Dick West played six abbreviated years with the Reds before being called into the service. His best season was in 1941, when he had 172 of his lifetime 299 at-bats. He would hit only .215 that season, 6 points under his career .221 mark. He would not return to the majors after serving in the military.

Bert Haas— After two very short seasons in 1937 and 1938 with the Dodgers, Bert Haas came over to the Reds in 1942 and immediately moved into the Reds' starting third base spot hitting .239. He would improve to .262 before heading into the war where he served his time in Italy.[106]

When Hass returned, he would take over at first, hitting .264 in 1946 before being chosen to play in his only All-Star game, garnering career highs in RBIs with 67 and batting average with a .286 mark. He would be sent to Philadelphia the next season for Tommy Hughes, where he continued his good hitting, ending after a .282 average in 1948.

Bert played only two more years in 1949 with the Phillies and the Giants and 1951 in the Windy City with the White Sox. He would finish with a .264 career average.

Hank Sauer— The slugging left fielder first broke into the majors with the Reds in 1941, coming up only 53 times in his first two seasons before heading into the Coast Guard.[107] He would return briefly in 1945 before coming back in 1948 with the kind of season that showed just how spectacular he could be. Hank hit 35 homers that season with 97 RBIs.

The Steel City native would get off to a poor start in 1949 before being dealt to the Cubs with Frankie Baumholtz for Peanuts Lowrey and Harry Walker. He would respond to his new surroundings by hitting 27 shots and knocking in 83 in his 96 games in Chicago that year, including 11 in his first month there.[108]

In the following season, Sauer was selected to his first All-Star game as he broke the century mark in RBIs for the first time with 103. Hank would receive his second and last All-Star selection two years later in 1952, leading the senior circuit in homers with 37 and RBIs with 121. He won the MVP award that year in a controversial election that picked a player from a team that finished fifth over the likes of Roy Campanella, Duke Snider and Pee Wee Reese (many felt that the various Dodgers who were candidates for the award actually split the votes giving Sauer the award).[109] It was the first time a player from the second division had won the award.[110]

Hank would slump the next season before hitting a career best 41 homers in 1954, breaking the century mark in RBIs for the third and final time with 103. 1954 proved to be the end of Hank Sauer's peak as he fell to .211 the next season, ending his career four years later.

Sauer was very close to several key plateaus as he was only 12 homers away from 300, 124 RBIs from 1,000 and 222 hits from 1,500. It's doubtful he would have reached any of those levels even had he not joined the military, as the tall slugger's career did not take off until 1948. Prior to that in three major league seasons, he hit only 7 homers, knocked in 29 and had but 49 hits.

Lonny Frey — Linus "Lonny" Frey broke in successfully with the Dodgers in 1933, hitting .319 in 135 at-bats. He would take over the starting shortstop spot the following season improving his average to .284 before hitting a career high 11 homers and 77 RBIs in 1935.

"Junior" was sent to the Cubs in 1937, before being sold to the Reds the following year where he would be selected to play in his first All-Star game in 1939, matching his lifetime high in homers with 11 while having his best average as a starter with a .291 mark. Frey would play in two consecutive World Series in '39 and '40, going hitless in 19 at-bats.

After 3 more seasons heading the spot at second in Cincinnati that included two more selections to the midsummer classic and leading the NL in fielding in both 1941 and 1943, Frey went into the military. When he came back, Lonny would only have one more significant season in 1946, hitting .246 in 111 games. He ended his career two years later with the Giants in 1948.

Frey, who had a lifetime .269 mark, was only 18 hits short of 1,500, which he most certainly would have gotten during the two years he missed due to the war. Lonny was 29 homers short of 100, but never hit more than 20 in two consecutive years, so it's doubtful he makes that number.

Taking over at second for Frey was Woody Williams. Although Williams was not as good a hitter as Lonny, hitting .240 and .237 in 1944 and 1945, he did have a solid season in the field during the 1944 campaign with 15 fielding runs and a league leading .971 fielding percentage.

Frank Kelleher — Kelleher was specifically a wartime ball player who had 110 of his 120 career at-bats in 1942, hitting only .182. He would not return to the show after going into the military following the 1943 season.

Mike McCormick — Myron "Mike" McCormick's career got off to a booming start in 1940, hitting .300, setting a major league record for most outfield putouts in a single World Series with 24. [111] It would be his pre-war highlight, as things would not come so easily afterwards. After a .287 average in 1941, he would break his leg in 1942 before leaving for the military early in 1943 after 15 at-bats.

Mike came back in 1946 and was sold to the Braves early on that year. He had a nice comeback year in 1948 when the Braves won the National League pennant, as he hit a career high .303. It was the beginning of the end for McCormick, hitting only .209 the following campaign after he was sent to the Dodgers for Pete Reiser. He would be gone two seasons later, hitting .288 with the Senators in 1951, which left the California inhabitant with a .275 lifetime mark.

Jack Niemes— Niemes would toss only 3 innings for the Reds in 1943, giving up 5 hits and 2 walks before heading to the service. He did not return after the war.

Junior Thompson— Most of the six year career for Eugene "Junior" Thompson came in his first two seasons in 1939 and 1940 when he went 13–5, which included a league high 8 relief wins[112] and a 2.54 ERA, followed by a 16–9 campaign with a nice 225⅓/197 IP/H ratio and .233 OBA.

He slumped in 1941 before rebounding with a nice 1942 year in which his IP/H ratio was a fabulous 101⅔/86 in 29 games, mostly in relief. Thompson would retire in 1943 before heading into the service.

Junior's return to the majors in 1946 would prove to be one of his best seasons. By this time he was a full time reliever for the Giants, with a magnificent 62⅔/36 IP/H and miniscule 1.29 ERA for a .190 OBA. It was Thompson's swan song as he left the majors after throwing in 15 games for New York the following year.

He was 3 wins short of 50, finishing with a 47–35 mark, which he certainly would have attained without the war. He was also 185 strikeouts short of 500 and that might have been a little more difficult. By the time he went into the service, he was pretty much a reliever, getting only 81 strikeouts in his two seasons preceding his entrance into the service. Taking into account, though, the season he retired, presumably because of the war, he might have had a third season in which he could have gotten to 500. Even with that extra campaign it still would have been tough.

Johnny Vander Meer— After a fine beginning in 1937, Johnny Vander Meer would etch his name forever in the history of the national pastime by tossing two consecutive no-hitters in 1938. The first game was a 3–0 classic versus the Braves, the second the first night game ever at Ebbets Field versus the Dodgers in front of 40,000 fans. "Double No-Hit," as he was soon to be dubbed, struggled in a 6–0 victory, walking the bases loaded in the ninth before an Ernie Koy hopper to third, which caused a force out at home, and a strikeout of Leo Durocher that gave the "Dutch Master" his second gem.[113] The season as a whole was a good one as Johnny finished 15–10, garnering his first All-Star game selection and a league leading .213 OBA.

The Dutch Master had fallen off the mound on a rainy day the following season that caused him to tear muscles in his shoulder, missing the rest of 1939 and most of 1940. He came back big in 1941 leading the circuit for the first time in strikeouts with 202 and a .214 OBA.

Vander Meer took very well to the war seasons, being selected to two All-Star games in 1942 and 1943 while going 18–12–2.43 and 15–16–2.87 both years. He would also win his second and third strikeout titles with 186 and 174 respectively and had OBA's of .208 and .224.

Johnny went into the military following the '43 season, playing for the 14th Naval district in Hawaii.[114] Returning in 1946, he was not quite the same pitcher. Vander Meer was 36–40 between '46 and '48 with his strikeout totals falling to 94, 79 and 120. After leaving the Reds in 1950 he pitched for the Cubs and Indians over the next two seasons before departing from the majors after 1951 with a 119–121 record, 1,294 strikeouts and a .232 OBA.

What Johnny could have achieved without the war was probably 150 wins, as he was on pace at the time to win that in a two year period. He also was 206 strikeouts short of 1,500 which he certainly would have been on pace to eclipse. Although the Dutch Master would have a nice career 2,104⅔/1,799 IP/H ratio, he would also be known for his wildness, as his K/BB ratio was 1,294/1,132.

Johnny Vander Meer of the Cincinnati Reds was the Randy Johnson of his time, leading the league in strikeouts in three successive seasons between 1941 and 1943. He was the only player in history to toss two consecutive no-hitters. Johnny had a successful career in the military as the star pitcher for the Samson Naval Base. Courtesy of the Cincinnati Reds.

Bucky Walters took over for Vander Meer as the number one man in the rotation in 1944 and responded with a magnificent 23–8 record and 2.40 ERA. He led the NL in wins, OBA at .219 and TPI with a mark of 4.9. Ed Heusser moved into Walters slot and replaced Johnny in the 4-man rotation. He had his best year ever in 1944 with a 13–11 mark and was tops in the National League with a 2.38 ERA.

1944 Chicago Cubs
75–79–30 GB

1941	1942	1943	1944
1B-Babe Dahlgren	Cavarretta	Cavarretta	Cavarretta
2B-Lou Stringer	Stringer	Eddie Stanky	Don Johnson
SS-Bobby Sturgeon	Lennie Merullo	Merullo	Merullo
3B-Stan Hack	Hack	Hack	Hack
OF-Bill Nicholson	Nicholson	Nicholson	Nicholson
OF-Phil Cavarretta	Dallessandro	Peanuts Lowrey	Andy Pafko
OF-Dom Dallessandro	Lou Novikoff	Ival Goodman	Dallessandro
CA-Clyde McCullough	McCullough	McCullough	Dewey Williams
PI-Claude Passeau	Passeau	Passeau	Hank Wyse
PI-Vern Olson	Lee	Bithorn	Passeau
PI-Bill Lee	Olson	Paul Derringer	Bob Chipman
PI-Larry French	Hi Bithorn	Ed Hanyzewski	Bill Fleming

After a horrid 1–10 start which caused manager Jimmy Wilson to lose his job, Charlie Grimm came in and stabilized the floundering franchise, leading them the rest of the way to a 74–69 record.

The team was still fueled by its offense as the wartime duo of Bill Nicholson and Phil Cavarretta belted the team to 702 runs, which was 70 more than they scored the previous season. Nicholson was the true horse, leading the league in home runs with 33, RBIs at 122 and runs with 116, while hitting a robust .287. He would finish only 1 vote behind St. Louis' Marty Marion in the MVP race. Cavarretta was tops on the team with a .321 average while knocking in 82 despite hitting only 5 homers. He would lead the senior circuit with 197 hits (tied with Stan Musial). Dom Dallessandro, coming off a poor 1943 campaign, came back big to hit .305, with 74 RBIs.

While offense was the key, pitching was the problem. Their ERA went up from 3.32 in 1943 to 3.59. They would lead the league in hits given up while compiling a sub par 1,401/1,481 IP/H ratio. Thirty-five-year-old Claude Passeau would once again lead the way with a 15–9 mark and an ERA of 2.89. Hank Wyse would step in to help replace the loss of Hi Bithorn and have a fine 16–15–3.15 season.

The Cubs had truly been a consistent team during the war years, consistently under .500, but with Charlie Grimm at the helm and the apparent offensive weapons in place, Chicago's fortunes would truly change 12 months from then as they would make their dramatic rise to the top of the heap.

Mickey Livingston— Thompson Orville "Mickey" Livingston was a well traveled catcher over the course of his 10 year major league career that began in Washington in 1938, going 3 for 4.

Who Left for the War	*Who Replaced Them*
CA-Mickey Livingston	
CA-Clyde McCullough	Dewey Williams
2B-Al Glossop	
OF-Charlie Gilbert	
OF-Peanuts Lowrey	Andy Pafko
OF-Whitey Platt	
PI-Hi Bithorn	Claude Passeau/Hank Wyse
PI-Lon Warneke	

It would be three more years before he resurfaced in the show with the Phillies, hitting only .229 in 2½ seasons between 1941 and 1943, before he was sent off to the Cubs for Bill Lee. Livingston would hit .261 the rest of the way with Chicago before getting his call to serve for Uncle Sam.

Mickey, who had a severe concussion when in the minors in 1939, began to suffer from severe headaches every time he put on a helmet, due to the earlier injury, so he would eventually be discharged and returned for the 1945 season where he had his most famous moment in the majors.[115] Livingston was the surprise player in the '45 Fall Classic, hitting .364 in 22 at-bats, knocking in 4 with 3 doubles in the 7 game loss to the Tigers.

It would be the height of Mickey's career as he would shuffle around from Chicago to the Giants, Braves and Dodgers his last five years mostly as a little used backup catcher, before finishing his career with a .238 life-time average after the 1951 season.

Clyde McCullough— McCullough was a fine defensive catcher, whose best seasons came during the war years.

After coming up in 1940 with the Cubs, McCullough took over the reins behind the plate in 1941, hitting .227 in 418 at-bats. He would take advantage of the war years to have two of his best offensive seasons, hitting .282 in 1942, including 3 solo shots in one game (he would only hit 5 homers all season),[116] before hitting .237 in '43.

He went into the military after the season and would return in time for the 1945 World Series, becoming only 1 of 2 people to play in a series without playing in the regular season when he went hitless in one at-bat.[117] He was selected to play in his first All-Star game in 1948, despite a .209 average. After the season he went to the Pirates with Cliff Chambers for Cal McLish and Frankie Gustine.

With Pittsburgh, McCullough enjoyed his best offensive season in 1951, hitting a career high .297 with 8 homers and 10 fielding runs. Clyde would be sent back to the Cubs in 1952, where he was selected to play in his second midsummer classic, hitting .258 for the season. After 3 years as a little used reserve, he was done with the majors in 1956.

The only achievement statistically that the war possibly cost the .252 career hitter was the 1,000 hit plateau. It would have been a tough nut to crack though as he was 215 hits shy. The most hits he ever had in back-to-back seasons were 190 in 1941 and 1942.

Replacing McCullough behind the plate was Dewey Williams. Williams would hit .240 in 1944 before raising it to .280 although he would get only 100 at-bats in '45, as Mickey Livingston would return from the service to take over the reins and hit .254.

Al Glossop— Glossop was a utility infielder that played with five different teams in five years in the majors.

The bulk of his career came in 1942 for the Phillies when he took over the reins at second, hitting only .225 in 454 at-bats. He would end up in Brooklyn the following season, slumping to .171 before heading into the military. He played only 4 games for the Cubs after he returned in 1946, going hitless in 10 at-bats ending his career.

Charlie Gilbert— Gilbert came from good baseball stock as his father Larry and Brother Tookie both played in the majors. Other than that, he basically was a very poor hitting reserve outfielder.

Coming up with Brooklyn in 1940 before heading to the Cubs the following year, Gilbert hit .184 and .150 in the two years prior to his going into the military. When he returned in 1946, Gilbert came up a career high 273 times and hit .234 for the Cubs and Phillies. He be gone from the majors after the next season.

Peanuts Lowrey— Harry "Peanuts" Lowrey had a fine second season in the majors in 1943 when he hit .292 with 63 RBIs. Lowrey would head for the military afterwards, coming back a year later in 1945, hitting .283 with career highs in homers with 7 and RBIs at 89. He hit .310 in his one and only World Series with a 9 for 29 performance.

Despite slumping to .257 in 1946, Peanuts did make his one and only mid summer classic. After 2½ more seasons in the Windy City, he was sent off to the Reds with Harry Walker for Frankie Baumholtz and Hank Sauer in 1949. He would be sent to the Cards a year and a half later where he had two solid seasons hitting a career best .303 in 1951, before turning in a .286 the following year. He would slump to .115 and .189 in 1954 and 1955 (with the Phillies the latter year) and leave the majors after the '55 campaign.

There were two statistical categories that Lowrey could have achieved if not for the war. He was 21 RBIs short of 500, which at the pace he was on, would have gotten 130–150 more and he had 1,177 hits, which put him 323 under 1,500. That mark would have been a little tougher as the most hits he had during a two-year period was 288.

Replacing Peanuts in the starting lineup was Andy Pafko. Pafko had two solid seasons during the war years, hitting .269 in 1944, being selected to his first All-Star game the following year as he hit .298 with 12 homers and a career high 110 RBIs.

Whitey Platt— Mizell "Whitey" Platt came up only 57 times in two seasons before the war for the Cubs. Afterwards he came back to the Windy City in 1946, not with the Cubs, but with their cross town rivals the White Sox, where he hit .251.

He went to the Browns in 1948 where he had his two best years in the majors, hitting .271 with 7 homers and 82 RBIs as the starting left fielder. He would follow that up with a .258 season in 244 at-bats in 1949, leaving the majors for good after the campaign.

Hi Bithorn— The Puerto Rican native had most of his successes during the war years in 1942 and 1943. After a 9–14 season in 1942, he had by far his marquee campaign in 1943 going 18–12 with a 2.60 ERA and .244 OBA in 30 starts, 7 of which ended up in a league leading 7 shutouts. He would head to answer his call to arms after the season was over.

When Bithorn came back in 1946, he was not the same pitcher, going 6–5 with a 3.84 ERA. Hi was gone after the next season, throwing only 2 innings in two games.

He would attempt a comeback in a Mexican winter league in 1952, when he was shot to death on New Year's Day.[118]

Claude Passeau dropped down to the number two man in 1944, taking Bithorn's place. Passeau had a fine 15–9 year with 2.89 ERA in 1944 before making the All-Star game in 1945 with a 17–9 mark while his ERA dropped to 2.46. Hank Wyse took over Bithorn's spot in the rotation as he replaced Passeau as the number one man. Hank went 16–15 in '44 before making his only All-Star game in his marquee season of 1945 with a 22–10 mark and 2.68 ERA.

Lon Warneke— After breaking into the show in 1930, the "Arkansas Hummingbird" would have his breakout season in 1932 with a league leading 22 wins, 2.37 ERA, .786 winning percentage and 4 shutouts. He would make his first midsummer classic the following season with an 18–13 mark and an ERA that dwindled to 2.00.

Warneke won 20 games in 1934 and 1935, and then was sent to the Cardinals in 1937 for Ripper Collins and Roy Parmelee. With St. Louis he would enjoy five consecutive years winning more than 13 games. His best two seasons in that time period were 1937 with an 18–11 mark and 1941, when he was selected to his 5th and last All-Star game, with a 17–9 record and 3.15 ERA.

He was sold to Chicago midway in 1942 before heading to the military after the 1943 season where he went 4–5. After returning in 1945, he went 0–1, retiring from the majors for good.

Lon finished his career with a 192–121 mark with a 3.18 ERA, .255 OBA and 1,140 strikeouts.

He was pretty much at the end of his career when he went into the service so it's rather doubtful he would have won the 8 games to win 200. Bill James had an interesting theory when discussing whether or not Warneke belonged in the Hall of Fame. He compared him to Dazzy Vance, who made the Hall in 1955. He claimed that despite the fact Warneke won only 5 less games and had a better winning percentage, Vance had more big, Hall of Fame type seasons, and James claimed that "big years get you in the Hall of Fame."[119]

1944 New York Giants
67–87–38 GB

1941	1942	1943	1944
1B-Babe Young	Johnny Mize	Joe Orengo	Phil Weintraub
2B-Burgess Whitehead	Mike Witek	Witek	George Hausmann
SS-Billy Jurges	Jurges	Jurges	Buddy Kerr
3B-Dick Bartell	Bill Werber	Bartell	Hugh Luby
OF-Mel Ott	Ott	Ott	Ott
OF-Johnny Rucker	Willard Marshall	Rucker	Rucker
OF-Jo-Jo Moore	Babe Barna	Joe Medwick	Medwick
CA-Harry Danning	Danning	Gus Mancuso	Ernie Lombardi
PI-Hal Schumacher	Schumacher	Melton	Bill Voiselle
PI-Cliff Melton	Bob Carpenter	Johnnie Wittig	Harold Feldman
PI-Carl Hubbell	Hubbell	Ken Chase	Ewald Pyle
PI-Bill Lohrman	Lohrman	Rube Fischer	Fischer

After the embarrassment of a last place finish in 1943, the Giants would improve slightly, winning 12 more games and moving up to 5th.

The biggest reason for the development was the increased offensive production. After scoring an anemic 558 runs in '43, New York would plate a much more acceptable 682 in '44, picking up 16 points in team batting average at .263. Hall of Fame player/manager Mel Ott, who hit 26 homers with a .288 average led the way. Another member of the Cooperstown elite, Joe Medwick, was purchased from the Dodgers in June of 1943 and would hit team highs in average at .337 and RBIs with 85. First baseman Phil Weintraub would also break the .300 barrier at .316.

The mound corps was headed by Bill Voiselle with a 21–16 mark, leading the National League in innings pitched at 313, walks with 118 and strikeouts at 161. Ace Adams again was a force out of the pen with an NL high 13 saves.

The Giants would continue their improvement the next season, but would still end the war years as New York's most disappointing team.

Who Left for the War	Who Replaced Them
2B-Mickey Witek	George Hausmann
3B-Dick Bartell	Hugh Luby
3B-Sid Gordon	
OF-Vic Bradford	
OF-Buster Maynard	
PI-Hugh East	
PI-Ken Trinkle	
PI-Johnnie Wittig	Harold Feldman

Mickey Witek— Witek was a solid all around player with the Giants from 1940 to 1943, before heading to serve his country.

He immediately moved into the starting second base position in his rookie season, hitting .256 while leading the league in fielding runs with 19. As good as Witek played that season, it was 1943 when his star really shone with a .314 average and a career best 55 RBIs while leading the league in putouts and assists for a second baseman, accumulating 16 fielding runs. On the negative side, he also led the circuit in errors that season.

Mickey went into the service afterwards, playing for the Curtis Bay Coast Guard team in Maryland.[120] He returned in 1946, and never achieved the kind of success he did in '43, hitting .248 in 444 at-bats between '46 and '47. He left the majors in 1949, singling in his only time up for the Yankees.

Witek hit .277 for his career, but really wasn't close to any significant levels statistically that could have been attained if not for his time in the service. Mickey was 405 hits shy of 1,000, so it was not likely he was going to make that number.

George Hausmann took over for Witek in 1944 and 1945, which really constituted 90 percent of his career. He hit .266 and .279 respectively with -2 fielding runs combined, far under Witek's career output of 34. Other than those two war years, Hausmann would play in only one other season, hitting .128 in 47 at-bats for the Giants in '49.

Dick Bartell— He was a fiery player that earned him the nickname "Rowdy Richard" and when his act ran tired, it got him traded six times during his 18-year career.[121] He came up with the Pirates in 1927 at the age of 20, making the team over a gentleman who would one day make the Hall of Fame, Joe Cronin.[122]

He captured the starting shortstop position in 1929, and would hit over .300 three times for the Bucs between 1928 and 1930 including a career high .320 in 1930.

Dick was sent to the Phillies in November of 1930 for Tommy

Thevenow and Claude Willoughby. It would prove to be a shrewd move for Philadelphia as he continued his good hitting ways with a .308 average in 1932 and a lifetime high 48 doubles. He made his first All-Star game in 1933 before hitting .310 the following year. Bartell was sent packing in November of that season to the Giants for 4 players and cash. It was here he would have arguably his best all around seasons.

Nineteen thirty-five proved to be a year that Bartell would flash some rare power. Despite a very sub par .262 average, he hit 14 of his lifetime 79 homers. The following year Rowdy Richard rebounded, hitting .298, but also showed what an effective fielder he could be, racking up 45 fielding runs to lead the league. He also had the best TPR in the circuit at 5.9 and hit .381 in his first Fall Classic with 3 doubles, a homer and 3 RBIs in the Giants' six game loss to the Yankees.

In 1937, Bartell put it all together in what was his marquee year, matching his career best with 14 homers, setting the mark with 62 RBIs and a .469 slugging percentage. He would once again be the best in the NL in fielding runs with 38 and TPR at 6.2, finishing 6th in the MVP vote and getting his second All-Star game selection. It proved to be the beginning of the end for the Chicago native, who would be sent to the hometown Cubs in 1939.

Dick spent one year there hitting .238 before heading off to the Motor City where he fared no better with a .233 mark in 1940 and .167 five games into the '41 campaign before being sent back to the Giants.

He started there for three years, going into the Navy and playing for the Bainbridge Naval Training Station team in Maryland in 1944.[123] Bartell would come back for 2 at-bats in 1946 before calling it a career.

The 18 years Rowdy Richard spent in the majors were largely successful. He hit .284 with 2,165 hits, a magnificent 178 fielding runs, which ranks 23rd all time and a 28.3 TPR which is 110th. It's doubtful Bartell really missed much in the time he spent in the Navy. He had 168 hits the two years prior to his induction and he needed 335 to make 2,500. One must also consider the fact that Dick may have gotten more playing time in '42 and '43 because of the lack of available players due to the war. The one area Bartell might have been able to improve was in fielding runs. He had 18 the year before he left. Had he only matched that in the two seasons he missed, he would have shot up to 18th ahead of Buddy Bell.

Is he a Hall of Famer? According to Bill James' Hall of Fame standard system, which ranks players on certain categories such as career batting average (1 point for each .005 points above .275 with a limit of 9 and 1 bonus point for hitting .300 in a career) and fielding (points given if played in the following positions over 1,000 games: 20 catcher, 16 shortstop, 14 second base, 13 third base, 12 center field, 6 right field, 3 left field and 1 first base) as well as nine other categories that add up to 100 points,[124] Bartell had 35 points which ranks him ahead of current Hall of Fame short-stops Phil Rizutto (25) and Joe Tinker (22). This doesn't mean so much that Bartell belongs in, but why the other two are in. James rates the average Hall of Fame member with 50 points (Honus Wagner leads all short-stops with 80 points); anybody under would be a considered marginal candidate.[125] One thing that James really does not properly take into account in his formula is fielding. How one feels about the fielding runs stat probably determines whether one believes Bartell is Hall of Fame caliber.

Replacing Bartell in 1944 was Hugh Luby. Luby, who broke in with the Phils in 1936, never to play again in the majors until 1944 with the Giants, hit .254 with 16 fielding runs in '44, which would be his last season in the show.

Sid Gordon— After two abbreviated seasons in 1941 and 1942, Gordon would get some significant playing time in 1943 going back and forth between third, first and left field, before heading into the Coast Guard for two years.[126] Sid would hit .293 in his return for the '46 campaign, taking over full time in left.

Two years later, in 1948, he would move to third and make his first All-Star team, cementing himself as one of the best power hitters in the game. He hit a career best 30 homers that year with 107 RBIs while garnering a .299 average and a .537 slugging percentage. He was selected to another All-Star game the following season before reluctantly being traded to the Braves with Buddy Kerr, Willard Marshall and Red Webb for Eddie Stanky and Alvin Dark, which turned out to be the middle infield for the Giants during that magic 1951 season.

Sid did not disappoint in Boston as he had back-to-back strong seasons at 27–103–.304 and 29–109–.287 respectively. His production slipped a bit the next two seasons, and he was sent to the Pirates in 1954 in a 7-player deal. Although his power would be curtailed in massive Forbes Field, he would hit a lifetime best .306 (for a full season as he hit .316 in 1942 in only 19 at-bats). Gordon hit only .170 in 47 at-bats in '55, before being sent back to the Giants midway through the season, where he ended his career.

There was perhaps one statistical level that Gordon could have achieved if not missing time due to the war. The .283 career hitter was 85 hits away from 1,500, which with the 119 he whacked in '43 would have made that virtually a lock. One plateau that would have been very difficult to get to was 1,000 RBIs. He finished at 805 and was not quite the power hitter in 1943 that he would turn out to be later in his career, so the best guess figure is he would have finished around 900–910.

Vic Bradford—Henry Victor Bradford was 1 for 5 in 1943 for the Giants, before going into the service. He would not return to the majors afterwards.

Buster Maynard—After coming up with the Giants in 1940, Maynard would achieve most of his career statistics in 1942 and 1943, hitting .220 in 583 at-bats with 13 homers in the two years combined. Buster would go 0 for 4 when he returned from the service in 1946, his last year in the majors.

Hugh East—East was 2–6 in his only three major league seasons, all with the Giants, before going into the service during the 1943 season.

Ken Trinkle—After a 1–5 start in 1943 for the Giants, Ken Trinkle would head into the service, returning in 1946. He would lead the NL in appearances with 48 and 62, in '46 and '47, finishing second in the league in saves with 10 the latter year. He finished his career in 1949 with the Phillies, ending up at 21–29 and a 3.74 ERA. Although his IP/H was not bad at 435⅓/442, his K/BB ratio was abysmal at 130/208, walking on average 4.3 batters every 9 innings.

Johnnie Wittig—"Hans" would go 5–10 in three seasons as primarily a reliever between 1938 and 1941 before getting his shot in the rotation in '43. He ended up with a 5–15 record and a 4.23 ERA before heading to answer his call to arms. Johnnie would toss only 2 innings in one game for the Red Sox when he returned in 1946, before leaving the big leagues.

Harry Feldman more than adequately replaced Wittig, going 11–13 and 12–13 in 1944 and 1945 with ERAs of 4.16 and 3.27 respectively.

1944 Boston Braves
65–89–40 GB

1941	1942	1943	1944
1B-Buddy Hassett	West	Johnny McCarthy	Buck Etchison
2B-Bama Rowell	Sisti	Connie Ryan	Ryan
SS-Eddie Miller	Miller	Whitey Wietelmann	Wietelmann
3B-Sibby Sisti	Nanny Fernandez	Eddie Joost	Damon Phillips
OF-Gene Moore	Paul Waner	Chuck Workman	Workman
OF-John Cooney	Tommy Holmes	Holmes	Holmes
OF-Max West	Chet Ross	Butch Nieman	Nieman
CA-Ray Berres	Ernie Lombardi	Phil Masi	Masi
PI-Manny Salvo	Javery	Javery	Tobin
PI-Jim Tobin	Tobin	Tobin	Andrews
PI-Al Javery	Lou Tost	Nate Andrews	Javery
PI-Art Johnson	Tom Earley	Red Barrett	Barrett

Things would be pretty much status quo for the Boston Braves as they spent another season in 6th place in the National League despite removing colorful Hall of Fame manager Casey Stengel in favor of Bob Coleman.

As the offense would be more plentiful in 1944 as a whole, so would it be for the men from Boston. They scored 593 runs in '44, only the 6th best figure in the league, yet a vast improvement over the 465 they plated the previous year. War star Tommy Holmes led a more powerful offense, which more than doubled its homer output from 39 to 79, with 13 homers and a .309 average. Butch Nieman also chipped in with a team high 16 shots. Starting second baseman Connie Ryan was hitting at a .295 clip when the service came calling for him.

Jim Tobin, as much known for his hitting as his pitching, led a staff whose team ERA ballooned from 3.26 to 3.67, with an 18–19 mark, also tossing a no-hitter. The 1943 ace Al Javery fell quite a bit back, finishing at 10–19 with a 3.54 ERA and tying the National League high in walks with 118.

With Casey or without, this team was destined to finish in sixth place as it did in 3 out of 4 war years.

Who Left for the War	*Who Replaced Them*
1B-Johnny McCarthy	Buck Etchison
OF-Sam Gentile	
PI-Bill Donovan	
PI-Ray Martin	
PI-Lou Tost	

Johnny McCarthy— McCarthy came up with the Dodgers in 1934, only receiving 87 at-bats in two seasons, before being sold to the Giants in 1936. He would take over for Bill Terry at first for two seasons in 1937 and 1938, hitting .279 and .272 respectively.

Johnny would lose his starting spot to Zeke Bonura in 1939 and spent the next three years getting into only 115 combined games. He would be part of the Johnny Mize trade in 1941, never playing one game with the Cardinals. McCarthy ended up in Boston in '43 and had his best season ever, hitting .304 with 24 doubles in 313 at-bats before breaking his ankle and then heading into the military.

The Chicago native would return for only 7 at-bats in 1946, before ending his major league career as primarily a pinch hitter with the Giants in '48.

The .277 hitter finished only 68 hits away from 500, which had he not gone to war, probably would have achieved that level.

Buck Etchison took over for McCarthy in 1944 and was a war years only player. He came up 19 times in 1943 before playing his first and last season as a starter, hitting .214 in 308 at-bats. He would be gone from the show afterwards.

Sam Gentile— Sam Gentile would hit a double in his only 4 major league at-bats in 1943.

Bill Donovan— Although he shared the same name as the great pitcher in the early 1900s (no apparent relation though), the comparison would truly end there. Bill would go only 4–6 in 1942 and 1943 with a decent 3.20 ERA before heading into the service and ending his big league career.

Ray Martin— After only tossing 3⅓ innings in 1943, Ray Martin would return from the service in 1947 to win his only major league decision. He would leave the league after 2 hitless innings in 1948.

Lou Tost— Most of the statistical portion of Lou Tost's career happened in his rookie campaign of 1942. He went 10–10 in 22 starts as the number three man with a 3.53 ERA.

The 32-year-old would pitch in only 3 games for the Braves in 1943 before moving on to Uncle Sam. He returned in 1947, tossing only 1 inning for the Pirates before exiting the majors for good.

1944 Brooklyn Dodgers
63–91 42 GB

1941	1942	1943	1944
1B-Dolph Camilli	Camilli	Camilli	Howie Schultz
2B-Billy Herman	Herman	Herman	Eddie Stanky
SS-Pee Wee Reese	Reese	Vaughan	Bobby Bragan
3B-Cookie Lavagetto	Arky Vaughan	Frenchy Bordagray	Bordagray
OF-Dixie Walker	Walker	Walker	Walker
OF-Pete Reiser	Reiser	Augie Galan	Goody Rosen
OF-Joe Medwick	Medwick	Luis Olmo	Galan
CA-Mickey Owen	Owen	Owen	Owen
PI-Kirby Higbe	Higbe	Higbe	Hal Gregg
PI-Whit Wyatt	Wyatt	Wyatt	Davis
PI-Luke Hamlin	Curt Davis	Davis	Rube Melton
PI-Hugh Casey	Ed Head	Head	McLish

The military proved to be a stronger adversary to Branch Rickey in his second year as head of the proud Dodger franchise as the losses of Kirby Higbe and Billy Herman to the service, not to mention the retirements of first baseman Dolph Camilli, who refused to go to the Giants when he was traded in 1943, and Arky Vaughan ended up tossing them into a deep hole in 6th place, 42 games out of first. A far cry from the 104 win season only two short years ago.

The powerful infield of Camilli, Herman, Pee Wee Reese and Vaughan was now replaced by one of Howie Schultz, the 6' 6½" first baseman who was ½ inch too big for the service,[127] Eddie Stanky, Bobby Bragan and Frenchy Bordagaray, three Hall of Famers and a great slugger for a group that combined to hit 17 homers.

It wasn't that the offense was completely poor, as Dixie Walker led the league in hitting at .357 and Augie Galan had 12 homers with a team high 93 RBIs while hitting .318 himself, but the pop that was the Dodger offense just three short years removed from winning the NL crown was now in ruins.

Worse yet was the pitching staff. The ERA went up from a 3.89 in 1943 to a league high 4.68 in '44, .39 higher than the next worst. Curt Davis and Rube Melton led the way with 10–11–3.34 and 9–13–3.46 seasons respectively. The once highly respected staff had a miserable 487/660 K/BB ratio, leading the circuit in walks by 73 over the Giants.

Despite all the problems, Leo Durocher and Rickey would soon find the mix to improve the team, but for now it remains one of Brooklyn's darkest moments when it comes to baseball.

Who Left for the War	Who Replaced Them
CA-Gil Hodges	
2B-Al Campanis	
2B-Billy Herman	Eddie Stanky
SS-Boyd Bartley	
OF-Gene Hermanski	
PI-Rex Barney	
PI-Dutch Dietz	
PI-Chris Haughey	
PI-Kirby Higbe	Hal Gregg
PI-Bill Sayles	

Gil Hodges— Although the Dodgers technically lost Hodges in 1944 due to the service, he was a catcher and only had 2 hitless at-bats in 1943. Gil did enlist in the Marines and fought in the battles that took place in Okinawa.[128]

It wasn't until 1947 that he arrived back in the majors, taking over the slot at first the following year. Nineteen forty-nine would prove to be Hodges' first breakout season as the slugger hit .285 with 23 homers and 115 RBIs, leading the circuit in fielding for first basemen at .995, all the while being selected to his first of seven consecutive All-Star games.

The next six seasons, Gil would show an incredible consistency, only dipping below 30 homers once, in 1955 when he hit 27, and never going below 100 RBIs.

Probably his best two seasons in the stretch were 1953, 31–122–.302, and 1954 when he had career highs in homers 42, RBIs 130, average .304 and slugging percentage at .579.

Hodges would fall a little in 1956, although he still hit 32 bombs, before coming back to play in his final All-Star game in 1957 on the heels of a 27–98–.299 campaign.

When the Dodgers made the move to the coast, so did Gil, but after two sub par seasons as a starter, he would spend his last two years with the Dodgers in 1960 and 1961 as a reserve.

Hodges returned to New York in 1962 to finish out his career with the Mets. He got into only 65 games in two seasons, although hitting the franchise's first homer,[129] before being traded to the Senators for Jimmy Piersall. Gil would never play again, instead becoming the manager. He strangely enough would be involved in one more trade, this time in 1967 for Bill Denehy and $100,000 to become the manager of the Mets, the team he, of course, led to the magical world championship of 1969.

Gil finished off his career with 1,921 hits, 370 homers, 1,274 RBIs, a .273 average and slugging at a .487 clip. He is often mentioned as a Hall of Fame candidate, but his career stats are not really on par in just about any category. Being that he probably would not have played with the Dodgers in 1944 and 1945, you really can't add anything to the total. Perhaps the main argument one had for Gil's candidacy is he had a very strong 7-year stretch between 1949 and 1955, hitting an average of 32 homers, 112 RBIs and a .284 average, very substantial, but considering he played 18 years, was not long enough.

Al Campanis— More famous for his controversial, yet successful run as Dodger GM, Campanis was a second baseman for the team, playing in the majors in 1943, going 2 for 20 before answering his call to arms. He would not return afterwards.

Billy Herman— Second baseman Hall of Famer Billy Herman came up with the Cubs in 1931, becoming the starting second base position in 1932, hitting .314.

Herman was selected to play in his first All-Star game in 1934 on the heels of a .303 season, which was a prelude into what was arguably his finest year ever. Billy would break out big leading the National League with career highs in hits with 227, batting average .341 and doubles at 57. He would also knock in 83 while leading all senior circuit second basemen with a .964 percentage, finishing 4th in the 1935 MVP race.

Over the next five years, between 1936 and 1940, Herman would continue to be one of the best second basemen in the game, making five more All-Star games to bring the streak to seven consecutive, hitting over .300 three times, including .334 and .335 in 1936 and 1937, leading in triples with 18 in 1939 and topping the league in fielding percentage two more times in 1936 and 1938.

Despite the superior play, manager Jimmie Wilson took over the club in 1941 and feared that Herman was a threat to take over his job if he didn't succeed. He dealt the star player to the Dodgers for Johnny Hudson, Charlie Gilbert and $65,000.[130] Wilson would fail until Charlie Grimm replaced him in 1944 while Herman would continue his streak of All-Star game appearances, which would end at 10 in 1943, and lead the Dodgers to the pennant in '41.

Herman continued to play well for Brooklyn, including a tremendous year in 1943, when he knocked in a lifetime best 100 (while smacking only 2 homers) and hitting .330. Billy would head into the Navy after the season, playing on the star-studded Great Lakes Naval team in 1944.[131]

He returned in 1946 and was traded at the midway point of the season to the Braves where he would hit .306 the rest of the way, while playing both second and first. Herman went to the Pirates after the season and hit only .214 in 1947, his last year in the majors.

His 2,345 hits, 1,163 runs, 839 RBIs and .304 average would be good enough to get him into the Hall of Fame in 1979, but take what he missed in 1944 and 1945 and those numbers would increase nicely.

He had 339 hits the two years preceding his time in the service and was only 155 short of 2,500. Best guess, even if he didn't reach those lofty numbers, was that he would have gotten 290–300 hits, finishing over 2,600 for his career. The 141 RBIs he was short of 1,000 would have been difficult but certainly achievable. He had 165 the two years prior, but it was the most he had in back to back seasons since 1935 and 1936, while he only had 50 in 1946. Most likely, it could be assumed that the 100 RBIs in 1943 were probably an aberration at that point and time of his career, so getting to 1,000 RBIs might not have come to pass.

Eddie Stanky took over for Herman when he went to the Navy, as the Dodgers were able to pick him up from the Cubs for Bob Chipman in June of 1944. Stanky was early in his career and would hit .273 and .258 in '44 and '45. He would be productive as he led the league in walks in 1945 with 148 that gave him a .417 on base percentage. He also led in runs that year at 128.

Boyd Bartley — Bartley would have one very unsuccessful year that encompassed his entire major league career in 1943, going 1 for 21 with the Dodgers.

Gene Hermanski — The Massachusetts native would enjoy a solid nine year career starting in 1943 when he hit .300 in 60 at-bats before heading into the armed service.

Gene came back in 1946 where he was a reserve outfielder in both '46 and '47, before taking over the Dodger starting right field spot in 1948. That year he hit 15 of his lifetime 46 homers while knocking in a career best 60 RBIs and hitting .290. While he had a good season at the plate, which would continue over the next two years as he would hit a combined .298 in '49 and '50, his defensive limitations would prove to be too much and his playing time would be cut almost in half.[132]

Hermanski was sent to the Cubs midway in '51, before heading to the Bucs almost exactly two years later in June of 1953 to end his career, hitting only .167 that season.

Rex Barney— Barney came up in 1943 before heading into the service to fight with the Army's 65th Division.[133] When he returned, he would tantalize baseball with both his fastball and his wildness.[134]

He would have only one truly solid season, in 1948, when he finished 15–13 with a 3.10 ERA and a .217 OBA. His K/BB ratio was 138/122, not great, but the only time he would have more strikeouts than walks in his career. To illustrate the point of his fastball's effectiveness and wildness, he had a 6-year career OBA of a miniscule .221, while his K/BB ratio was 336/410 (which was an average of 6.17 walks per nine innings). He finished his career at 35–31 after the 1950 season.

Dutch Dietz— Most of the statistical part of Dietz's 4-year career came in 1941 and 1942 with the Pirates; he was 7–2 in '41, mostly out of the pen, with a 2.33 ERA and .233 OBA. He would pitch a career high 134⅓ innings the following season with a 6–9 mark. After a 1–4 record with a 6.40 ERA in 1943, Dietz would serve his country, and his major league career was finished.

Chris Haughey—"Bud" would lose his only major league game while pitching for the Dodgers in 1943, giving up 5 hits and walking 10 in 7 innings of work.

Kirby Higbe— Walter Kirby Higbe came into the show in 1937 with the Cubs, before ending up in Philadelphia with the Phillies in 1939.

Higbe would have two nice years with the Phils, going 10–14 the rest of the way in '39 (he was 12–15 overall including his time with the Cubs), then making his first All-Star game the following year with a 14–19 mark while leading the league in strikeouts with 137.

Strapped for cash, the Phils sent him to Brooklyn in 1941 for Vito Tamulis, Bill Crouch, Mickey Livingston and $100,000. He proved to be a very valuable addition to their National League championship run. Higbe combined with Whit Wyatt to form an impenetrable 1–2 punch as he tied with Wyatt for the lead in wins going, 22–9 with a 298/244 H/IP ratio and a 3.14 ERA. Higbe would follow that year up with solid 16–11–3.25 and 13–10–3.70 campaigns in 1942 and 1943 before heading into Army where he played on a team in Manila known also as the Dodgers.[135] Kirby would see some battle also as he was a combat infantryman in the 86th Division where he almost was hit by German artillery shell while in a boat crossing the Danube.[136]

Higbe came back in 1946 and was selected to his second and last All-Star game with a 17–8 record and career low 3.03 ERA with a .229 OBA. It would prove to be the beginning of the end as he was sent to the Pirates with 4 other player including Gene Mauch and Dixie Howell for Al Gionfriddo and $100,000 in May of 1947, with one possible reason being he was a southerner who did not really like playing with Jackie Robinson, although he apparently would learn to respect the way Robinson played. [137] He ended up 13–17 before ending up the remainder of his career in the bullpen. Kirby would last only three more years, the best in 1948 with an 8–7 record and 3.36 ERA, before ending his career in 1950 with the Giants.

The South Carolina native finished at 118–101 and would have had a decent chance at reaching 150 victories if not for the war. He was 32 short, which with the 29 he won 2 years prior to his induction and the 30 he won the two after, put him in range of the mark. At 971 strikeouts, he most assuredly would have reached the 1,000-strikeout plateau (on the negative side he was actually closer to 1,000 walks finishing at 979).

Hal Gregg took over for Kirby in 1944, going 9–16 with a 5.46 ERA. He would improve the following season, having a career year going 18–13 with a 3.47 ERA and a selection to his only All-Star game.

Bill Sayles— Sayles would throw in only 28 major league games in his two major league seasons, 23 of them coming in 1943 when he was 1–3, his final career mark, with a 5.29 ERA in his tour of New York, for the Giants and Dodgers.

1944 Philadelphia Phillies
61–92–43.5 GB

1941	1942	1943	1944
1B-Nick Etten	Etten	Jimmy Wasdell	Tony Lupien
2B-Danny Murtaugh	Al Glossup	Murtaugh	Moon Mullen
SS-Bobby Bragan	Bragan	Glen Stewart	Roy Hamrick
3B-Pinky May	May	May	Stewart
OF-Stan Benjamin	Ron Northey	Northey	Northey
OF-Joe Marty	Lloyd Waner	Buster Adams	Adams
OF-Danny Litwhiler	Litwhiler	Coaker Triplett	Wasdell
CA-Bennie Warren	Warren	Mickey Livingston	Bob Finley
PI-Cy Blanton	Hughes	Schoolboy Rowe	Ken Raffensberger
PI-Johnny Podgajny	Rube Melton	Al Gerheauser	Charley Schanz
PI-Tommy Hughes	Johnson	Tex Kraus	Gerheauser
PI-Si Johnson	Podgajny	Dick Barrett	Bill Lee

After a remarkable 1943 campaign, twisting and turning with the soap opera that was owner William Cox, while ascending to the lofty heights of 7th place, the Phillies came crashing down to reality to re-conquer their rightful spot in last place of the senior circuit.

Ron Northey would lead the league's most anemic offense (only 539 runs scored, 54 runs less than the Braves, the league's second worst) with a monster season hitting 22 of the club's 55 homers while knocking in 104. Ted Lupien, who was picked up from the Red Sox on waivers, chipped in at .283, the same average as Buster Adams who also hit 17 homers.

The pitching staff was slightly improved over 1943, being led by the two new additions to the rotation, 13 game winners Ken Raffensberger (13–20–3.06) and Charley Schanz (13–16–3.32), who replaced Schoolboy Rowe and Tex Kraus, both of whom went into the military. Andy Karl was tough out of the bullpen with a 3–2 record, 2.33 ERA, .237 OBA and a wonderful 89–76 IP/H ratio.

The key to the Philadelphia's season was the contest the team ran to replace the Phillies as the official nickname. The Blue Jays ended up being the winner, although catcher Dee Moore thought if they truly wanted to change their luck, they should rename themselves the Philadelphia World's Champs, which was the name he submitted.[138] Despite the new name, the Phillies, or Blue Jays if you will, were the same. Long live the kings of the NL basement, at least during the war years.

Who Left for the War	Who Replaced Them
CA-Dee Moore	
2B-Danny Murtaugh	Moon Mullen
3B-Pinky May	Glen Stewart/Roy Hamrick
PI-Dick Conger	
PI-George Eyrich	
PI-Si Johnson	
PI-Tex Kraus	Al Gerheauser/Charley Schanz
PI-Andy Lapihuska	
PI-Schoolboy Rowe	Ken Raffensberger

Dee Moore— D.C. Moore was a little used catcher, who came up with the Reds in 1936 going 5 for 23 his first two years before returning to the majors in the war ball season of 1943. He played for Brooklyn and the Phillies that season, hitting .245 in 192 at-bats, before heading into the Marines.[139] He returned in 1946 with a 1 for 13 performance, which would be his last in a major league uniform.

Danny Murtaugh— The Chester, Pennsylvania, native, who would go on to manage the Pirates to world championships in 1960 and 1971, broke in with Philadelphia in 1941, hitting only .219, but led the National League in steals with 18. His average improved in each of the next two seasons to .241 in '42 and .273 the following year before heading into the service.

He returned in 1946 and came up only 27 times in the next two seasons with the Phillies and Braves. Murtaugh was sent to Pittsburgh following the 1947 campaign with Johnny Hopp for Jim Russell, Bill Salkeld and Al Lyons. Danny responded by breaking into the starting lineup, hitting .290 with 71 RBIs, almost double his next best season (37 in 1950). He followed that up with a career best .294 in 1950 before ending his time in the show in '52 where the .254 lifetime hitter batted only .199.

Moon Mullen would be the heir apparent to Murtaugh when he left for the war in 1944, hitting .267 in 464 at-bats his only season in the majors.

Pinky May— Merrill "Pinky" May, who was the father of 1971 World Series hero Milt May,[140] had a short yet very full career in the majors between 1939 and 1943. He hit .275 while accumulating 74 fielding runs and led the NL in fielding percentage in three of his five seasons.

After hitting .287 in his rookie season in '39, while having a senior circuit best .956 fielding percentage, May would be selected to play in his one and only All-Star game the following season, hitting a career best .293.

Pinky fell to .267 in '41, a season that would turn out to be his best defensive campaign ever, with National League highs in both fielding percentage at .972 and fielding runs with 25.

The year 1943 proved to be his last season in the big leagues and he went out with a bang, garnering his third fielding percentage title for third basemen at .963 while hitting .282 before answering his call to arms.

Glen Stewart would move from short to third in 1944, replacing May, and hit only .220 in what proved to be his last major league season. Ray Hamrick slid into Stewart's position at short, hitting a poor .205, although coming up with 20 fielding runs. Like Stewart, it would be his final year, as Hamrick would be called into the military before the season was over.

Dick Conger— Conger played for the Tigers, Pirates and Phillies between 1940 and 1943, accumulating a 3–7 mark (nine of the decisions coming is his 2–7 season for the Phils in '43) in 70 innings of work.

George Eyrich— Eyrich would pitch in only one major league season, 1943, giving up 27 hits and 9 walks in 18⅔ innings.

Si Johnson— After going 3–1 in his first three campaigns with the Reds between 1928 and 1930 for the Reds, Johnson would embark on a miserable five year run in which he would go a combined 43–85, including back to back 7–18 and 7–22 seasons in 1933 and 1934. He didn't exactly pitch poorly during the stretch, accumulating ERAs of 3.77, 3.27 and 3.49 between '31 and '33 (although it did balloon to 5.22 and 6.23 the following two years); he was just unfortunately with some very bad Cincinnati teams that usually were mired in the cellar.

Si would head off to the Cardinals in August of 1936 for Bill Walker. It was there he would probably enjoy his best season, going 12–12 with a 3.32 ERA.

Johnson was sold to the Phillies in 1940 and had another remarkable down period, going 18–45 between 1940 and 1942, before finishing his pre-war career with a fine 8–3–3.27 campaign in 1943. Si headed into the Navy where he would finally play on a winning team, the 1944 Great Lakes club.[141]

He returned in 1946, finishing his major league career with the Braves the following season, concluding with a lifetime 101–165 mark in 17 years.

By missing two years to the service, Johnson missed out on potentially hitting the 1,000-strikeout plateau. He ended up with 840 and accumulated 124 in the two seasons prior to his departure. Being he was pretty much at the end of his career, the 160 strikeouts he needed were probably just a little out of reach.

Tex Kraus—Jack "Tex" Kraus enjoyed his marquee season in his rookie year of 1943, going 9–15 with a 3.16 ERA as the Phillies' number three man. He would return in 1945, pitching one season with the Phils and one with the Giants in 1946, ending his major league career with a 15–25 mark.

Al Gerheauser slipped down into his spot in 1944, finishing up at 8–16 in 1944. Charley Schanz would take Gerheauser's spot as the number 2 man, in effect replacing Kraus in the rotation. He would have two unremarkable seasons in 1944 and 1945, going 13–16 before falling to 4–15.

Andy Lapihuska—"Apples," as he was known, would toss only 23 career innings in 1942 and 1943, going 0–2 for Philadelphia.

Schoolboy Rowe—Lynwood "Schoolboy" Rowe was as much known for his hitting (a .263 lifetime mark) as he was for his pitching. Regardless of that fact, he was very good at his number one craft, pitching.

After breaking in with the Tigers in 1933, Rowe would lead the Tigers to the World Series in 1934 on the heels of a 24–8 record which included an AL record tying 16 wins in a row. He would follow that up with a 19–13 mark, leading the junior circuit in shutouts with 6, garnering his first All-Star game selection and ending up in the Fall Classic once again, this time as a member of a world championship team.

Nineteen thirty-six would be the end of a great three-year run, finishing at 19–10 with a second All-Star game selection. He would hurt his arm in the subsequent campaign; it would be an injury that would plague him the next two seasons. Schoolboy would come all the way back in 1940 with a 16–3 season, leading the American League in winning percentage at .842.

Rowe was sold to the Dodgers in 1942 before they turned around and sold him to the Phillies. He would become Philadelphia's best pitcher in 1943, going 14–8 with a 2.94 ERA, showing what a good hitter he was by leading the NL in pinch-hit appearances, going 15–49, a .306 average. [142] Schoolboy would then head into the Navy where he was another key ingredient to the 1944 Great Lakes club.

He came back to the majors in 1946, accumulating an 11–4 mark with a career low 2.12 ERA before becoming the first player to perform in an All-Star game for both leagues when he came up as a pinch-hitter in the 1947 mid summer classic.[143] Rowe would end his career two years later in 1949.

He finished with a 158–101 record, missing about 25–28 victories due to his participation in the war. Rowe was only 87 strikeouts short of 1,000, which seemed like a very reachable total, as he would strike out 125 the two years after he came back.

Ken Raffensberger replaced Rowe as the number one man in 1944 with a 13–20 record, a 3.06 ERA and his only selection to the All-Star game. He would head into the military early in 1945 after an 0–3 start.

4

1945

On the positive side in 1945, it was becoming more apparent that the Nazi war machine was starting to wear down and it would be just a matter of time until the war would finally come to an end. In baseball terms that meant that baseball's greatest stars would soon return and bring the game back to some semblance of normalcy. In reality, what we would see in 1945, like in the previous war seasons, was anything but normalcy.

Before the season began, there would be two questions that would need to be answered:

- Who would be the man chosen to replace the recently departed baseball czar Kenesaw Mountain Landis, who passed away at the age of 78 the past winter?
- Would the government start pulling the 4-F's, the classification which encompassed the majority of major league players, into military service, all but destroying the game?

We would also see the death of one of the most beloved leaders this country had ever known, and the man that saved baseball in 1942, Franklin Delano Roosevelt.

While unfortunately there would also be more players suffering war injuries and losing their lives in the conflict, there were also several stirring comebacks, including that of Hank Greenberg, who took up where he left off, pulling the Tigers up by their collective tails and leading them to the world championship, as well as that of Lieutenant Bert Shepard, a minor league pitcher who despite losing his leg in the war would inspirationally pitch in a game for the Senators.

Perhaps the most important thing to happen in all the war years was the signing of Jackie Robinson, a move that would not only change the scene of professional sports as we know it, but in baseball terms, would open a clear path for Branch Rickey, the GM of the Dodgers who signed Robinson, to several Negro League stars such as Roy Campanella and Don Newcombe, the players that would take him to the National League dynasty he enjoyed in the late '40s to mid–'50s.

As with every other war season, 1945 would open up with owners making crucial decisions on the future of the game. This year's soap opera would be choosing the replacement for Landis, the man who completely controlled the game for over 20 years.

National League President Ford Frick was the frontrunner to fill the post when the owners met in February. Everything looked good until they opted to put the decision on hold until they first set the ground rules on what powers the new commissioner would have. Although Landis did a lot to restore the good name of the game after the 1919 Black Sox scandal, they felt he had too much power. The owners wanted to limit the new boss to more administrative and executive duties. Since Landis had the power to make any rules he wanted to, they wanted to take back some control and prohibit a new commissioner from having that kind of authority, which they did. Bottom line, they wanted the new commander of baseball to work with them, not a commissioner they worked for.[1]

The owners would also decree at this meeting that it would now take a ¾ approval of all teams to elect their new commissioner and not a simple majority. This would cause excessive campaigning among the candidates. At first, the man seemed to be Frick, whom it was reported that Rickey and the Giants' Horace Stoneham were supporting. Warren Giles of the Reds was the senior circuit's lone dissenter. He wanted outside help to come in and try and stem the seemingly growing tide of a labor union that the players were starting to become interested in (another man who was ahead of his time). He wanted 1944 Republican vice-presidential candidate John Bricker.[2]

A four man committee would be set up, Sam Breadon of the Cardinals, the Cubs' Phil Wrigley, Alva Bradley, the head man in Cleveland and Don Barnes of the Browns, to select worthy candidates for the owners to vote on.[3]

One man that came to the forefront was Admiral Robert Donohue, head of the Coast Guard, who was backed by Clark Griffith of Washington.[4] *The Sporting News* reported that Wrigley and Barnes could come around to Donohue's side, when they found out in a sample vote that Frick did not have enough votes to win.[5]

As it turned out, none of the above would be chosen. It would be a man who was mentioned for the post back in October of '44 when Landis was first hospitalized for a heart condition, Kentucky Senator Happy Chandler.[6]

One of the first problems to crop up during the Chandler administration was that of how to ward off the Selective Service from drafting

4-F players, which encompassed the majority of those who were in the majors. Without the 4-F's, baseball certainly could not continue. A couple of months earlier, Chandler, while serving in the Senate, had come out in support of baseball's continuance, claiming that "Baseball was worth continuing and that an Army reject would be more useful playing than fiddling around at something else."[7]

A work or fight bill had been in the Senate saying that 4-F's must either work in war important factories or go into the military. When the end of the war seemed inevitable, the Senate killed the bill, presumably saving baseball in 1945.[8]

Unfortunately, there were still some politicians that wanted ballplayers targeted for the draft and 4-F's such as Ron Northey, rejected three times because he couldn't hear out of one of his ears, Ray Mueller, rejected because of a stomach ulcer, Hugh Poland, a torn up ankle, and Danny Litwhiler, who had no cartilage in his knee. All found themselves strangely inducted into the service.[9]

In the event of the all out loss of 4-F's, baseball decided that it would be OK to take players from the American Legion. It was certainly a plan, but doubtful it would have been enough to save the game.[10]

Illinois congressman Melvin Price, a lifelong baseball fan, would come to the rescue of the national pastime, demanding that the drafting of ballplayers obviously unfit for duty be stopped.[11] Thanks to Price's diligence, the practice was stopped and the game would go on without a hitch.

The Congress and the president had done a lot during the war years to save the game, which is why it was particularly disheartening to the baseball establishment to learn of the death of one of the most beloved leaders ever to grace this land, Franklin Delano Roosevelt. He had certainly been the man most responsible for saving the game during this time period and the *Sporting News* was pushing for his induction to Cooperstown to rightfully honor him.[12] Despite their insistence and editorials, FDR of course would not make it in.

As the war was coming to an end, we were still reminded of all the horror that was still going on abroad. Such was the case of three men: New York Giants farmhand Fred Price, the professional player who spent more time in the service than any other, who would be injured fighting in the Philippines; Billy Southworth, Jr., from Toronto in the International League who after 25 successful bombing missions in Europe was ironically killed trying to land his plane at LaGuardia Field in Flushing, New York; and Harry O'Neill of the Philadelphia A's who became the second and final major league player to lose his life during the war.

Fred Price was a promising young first baseman out of George Washington University, whom the Giants signed and sent to Greenwood,

Mississippi, of the Cotton State League, before being promoted to Clinton, Iowa, of the Triple I league with future major leaguer Sid Gordon. Price would hit .253 in four minor league seasons before enlisting in the Army on October 30th, 1940, which made him the professional ball player who served the longest in the service, 5 years, 2½ months.[13]

Price, who had been released in October of 1941 after his one-year commitment, was still in the reserves when he was called back to active duty after Pearl Harbor and sent to the Asian Theater. His baseball record might not have been the thing legends are made from, but his war record was about to be.

While fighting on April 10th, 1945, at Cebu in the Philippine Islands, 1st lieutenant Fred Price was shot twice, first hit by shrapnel right below the right knee, a second time in the lower stomach.

"It was a frightening time for my mother," Dan Price said. "She hadn't heard from my dad for a month. She didn't get the letter until May informing her that my dad had been seriously injured and where to send the mail.

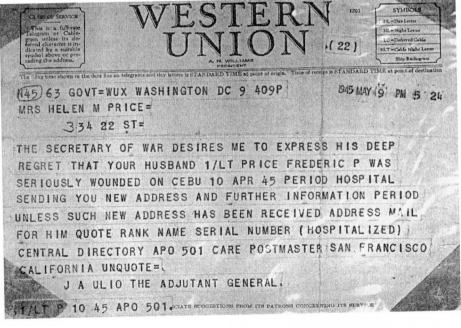

Fred Price was a promising first baseman in the New York Giant farm system when he entered the service before Pearl Harbor. He was injured in the Philippines and became the professional ballplayer who served the longest in World War II. His time serving his country would eventually cost him his dream of becoming a major league player. This is his official notice sent to his family telling them of his war injury. Courtesy of Daniel Price.

It was another month before she heard from him again."[14] Price would be laid up in the hospital for 2½ months recovering; he would not be able to walk the first two months of his stay.

The Brooklyn native received two Purple Hearts for his injuries. He more impressively was awarded three Distinguished Star awards, including the Bronze Star and a Philippine Liberation Ribbon. The most important thing to Price that he would receive was his designation as captain right before he was released. "His biggest thrill and pride in his life was that he went into the service a private and finished a captain," Daniel stated.[15]

In January of 1946, with his war injuries healed, he came home and reported to the Giants' spring training camp. Unfortunately there would be no spot on the team, as the Giants only would offer a position on their AAA minor league club. With a family now to worry about, Price did not want to go to the minors again. The war had cost Price what might have been a promising major league career.

Major Billy Southworth, Jr., the son of great Cardinal manager Billy Sr. and one of the first players to go into the service, would lose more than just a promising major league career, he would lose his life in the conflict.

Southworth, who was a Philadelphia Phillies farmhand with Toronto of the International League when he joined the Army Air Corps, had not only become a war hero, winning the Distinguished Flying Cross, three Oak Clusters and a Purple Heart, but was becoming something of a celebrity. Billy had met producer Hunt Stromberg at a fight in Hollywood and Stromberg, obviously impressed with Southworth, offered him a 10-year contract, which the major quickly signed.

After 25 successful bombing raids over Europe, Southworth crashed his plane while in Flushing, New York. Five men would survive the crash; unfortunately Billy was not one of them. A devastated Billy Sr. issued a simple classy statement, saying that the same tragedy had struck thousands of other American homes; in essence let's honor them all. A potentially fabulous life would not have a chance to unfold, as Southworth, who had an unlimited future and was about to be promoted to lieutenant colonel before his death, was only 27.[16]

Harry O'Neill would have a very limited career with the Philadelphia A's, playing in only one game in 1939 after he was signed by the A's immediately following his graduation from Gettysburg College, never coming to bat (a la Moonlight Graham).

O'Neill was sent to the minors following the season and would play with both Allentown and Harrisburg of the Canadian-American League.

The Philadelphia native would join the Marines where the lieutenant would fight valiantly in the battle of Iwo Jima, a fight where he sadly would lose his life, becoming only the second person with major league experience, the other Elmer Gedeon, to lose his life in the conflict.[17]

As V-E day came and went and the country was mourning those who had lost their lives while celebrating others who were returning home, many war vet ballplayers were also coming back, trying to pick up their lives where they left off. There were some comebacks that were inspirational because of the high levels of play they achieved upon their returns, while others were more stirring because of the obstacles they were able to overcome on their way back to the diamond.

Probably the one player who was most missed by his team during the conflict was Detroit Tiger Hank Greenberg. When he left to serve his country, he had just led the Tigers to the world championship in 1940. In the time between when he left and returned, Detroit had fallen into the second division until Dizzy Trout, Hal Newhouser and Dick Wakefield helped drag them to within a game of the pennant in 1944.

On July 1st, Greenberg would become the first player to return from the service and he did it in style, hitting a homer against the A's in a 9–5 Tiger win.[18]

It would be the first of many key moments for Greenberg during the year, the most important being the one that occurred on September 30th. It was the last day of the season and the pennant was on the line. Detroit was down 3–2 in the top of the 9th inning when Hank Greenberg came up with the bases loaded. Greenberg would lift a shot into the Sportsman's Park stands, giving the Tigers a 6–3 victory against the Browns and the American League crown.[19]

Sportswriter Fred Lieb probably summed up Greenberg's feat the best when he said, "It was fitting indeed that a returned serviceman should decide a pennant race with his bat, on the final day of the season. Military men around the world will glory in his feat."[20]

There would be two pitchers who returned from the war to pick up where they left off, while two others shook off horrific war stories to return to the fields of play.

Bob Feller was probably the best pitcher in the majors when he left to serve Uncle Sam. He returned on August 24th to 46,477 fans in Cleveland. Bob would not disappoint as Feller had a no-hitter thru 6⅓ innings on his way to a 4–2 victory over the Tigers, striking out 12 while giving up only 4 hits. He would finish the season with a 5–3 mark and a nice 2.50 ERA in 9 starts.[21]

Detroit Tiger hurler Virgil "Fire" Trucks had an even more dramatic return. After starting for Detroit in the final game of the season, Trucks got the nod to start in Game 2 of the Fall Classic. He pitched spectacularly in a complete game, 7 hit 4–1 victory over the Cubs.

The two pitchers who would suffer the rigors of war, Hugh Mulcahy and Phil Marchildon, made it all the way back to pitch for their clubs again in 1945.

Mulcahy, who was the first major league player to go into the conflict, suffered a bad case of dysentery while in the Philippines. He returned to the Phils and went 1–3 in 4 starts. Unfortunately, the onetime ace would be affected by the ailment, which took his fastball away from him, and he went only 2–4 over 18 games in the last two years of his major league career for Philadelphia and Pittsburgh.

Marchildon's comeback to the majors was a little more improbable. The Canadian hurler spent time in a German prisoner of war camp after being shot down over Denmark. He returned home beaten with shattered nerves. While it seemed at times he just wanted to find peace in the confines of his hometown, Phil returned on August 17th in Cleveland, one year to the day after he was shot down.

He pitched just 2 innings, giving up 4 runs, 4 walks and 2 hits, but despite the poor outing, the victory was in the fact he made it to the mound, a feat he could not even imagine just 12 months earlier.[22]

Phil Marchildon wasn't the only Canadian ballplayer to return to the diamond in 1945. Infantryman Dick Fowler, Marchildon's teammate on the A's, probably had the most dramatic return of all as he became the first and only Canadian to toss a no-hitter, completing a 1–0 gem against the Browns at Shibe Park nine days after he was discharged. It would be the only American League no-hitter during the war years.[23]

After a season of wonderful moments following the end of the war, perhaps the one that is most inspiring was the incredible story of Lieutenant Bert Shepard.

Shepard was a minor league pitcher in 1942 when he was called to arms as a pilot with the 55th fighter group in England.[24] He was flying a P-38 in a bombing run over Germany when he was shot down over a farm. Things seemed grim for Shepard as a group of farmers were prodding the unconscious pilot with a pitchfork. His luck would turn immediately when a kind German doctor by the name of Dr. Loidl chased the farmers away, arranging for Shepard to receive proper medical treatment, which meant amputating his leg and inserting a metal plate in his head.[25]

Shepard had been fitted with a special prosthetic leg and Washington's Clark Griffith signed him to play for the team. Although it was more a publicity thing than anything else, as Washington was in a pennant race and the probability of Shepard actually pitching was slight, he still practiced hard in the hopes of an opportunity.

An article in *The Sporting News* would show what a great attitude and sense of humor that Bert possessed. He was having problems keeping his sock up on the artificial limb, when the batting practice pitcher offered to get him a rubber band to keep the sock from falling. Shepard responded not to worry, "It would stop the circulation in my leg."[26]

Luckily, Bert would finally get his chance on August 14th, being sent into a game against the Red Sox. He would not fail as the lieutenant gave up 3 hits and a run in 5⅓ innings of relief. It was his only major league game, but more importantly it was a triumph to all who served in the conflict.

As inspiring as the story of Bert Shepard was, so was the incredible rise to the majors of one-armed outfielder Pete Gray to the St. Louis Browns.

Gray, who had lost his arm at the age of 6 falling off a wagon,[27] taught himself to play and eventually would realize his dream in 1943 when the Memphis Chicks of the Southern Association signed him. He would hit .299 before hitting .333 with 63 stolen bases the following season, a campaign in which he was named the league MVP.[28]

Pete would end up with the Browns the next season and might have been as influential in costing them a repeat of their title as anything else, according to author Mark Christman of the book *Even the Browns*, when he stated that the hitter who hit one to Gray would "...wind up at second base. I know that cost us eight or ten ballgames."[29] (The Browns of course only finished six games out that year.)

Perhaps the greatest day in Pete's short major league career occurred on May 20th when he went 4 for 8 against the Yankees in a doubleheader sweep for the Browns in which he made several outstanding catches in his 10 putouts.[30]

Gray would hit only .218 that season with no homers in 234 at-bats, but there were players who hit worse, and despite the fact it may or may not have just been a publicity stunt to play him so often, it was nonetheless every bit as exciting a story as there was during that time period.

On top of all the comebacks by players returning from the war, there were also several other interesting events that happened during 1945. One such moment was the dramatic rise of Red Sox rookie pitcher Dave "Boo" Ferriss. Ferriss, who had been recently discharged from the Air Corps before coming to the Red Sox, had started his career off with a 2–0 victory over the A's, pitching a 5-hitter while collecting 3 hits on his own.[31] He shut out the Yankees in his next turn, becoming only the fifth player at the time to start out his career with two consecutive shutouts.[32]

Ferriss would go on to establish a major league mark for consecutive shutout innings at the beginning of a career, 22, while taking it to the Tigers 8–2 on May 13th.[33]

When Boo defeated the Tigers 6–5 in 14 innings on June 15th, as the Red Sox came back down from 5–0, it would end an incredible run where Ferriss would defeat every American League club the first time he went against them.[34] Dave completed in unbelievable season in 1945 at 21–10.

The All-Star game was cancelled during the season and would be replaced by a series of interleague exhibition games designed not only to reduce travel, but also raise approximately twice the amount for the war effort than the special night games did the year before. On July 9th and 10th, the White Sox beat the Cubs 5–4. The Yankees knocked off the Giants 7–1, Cincinnati topped the Indians 6–0, the Red Sox would thrash the Braves 8–1, the Browns shut out the Cardinals 3–0, the Senators nipped the Dodgers 4–3 and in a game that drew only 4,835 in the battle of the cellar in Philadelphia, the Phillies won over the Athletics 7–6. The seven contests were attended by 169,880 in what was the forebearer to today's controversial interleague contests.[35]

In other memorable moments from 1945, Mort Cooper, perhaps the finest pitcher during the war years, was involved in a salary dispute with the Cards and would be sent to the Braves. Dodgers manager Leo Durocher would show his legendary temper again as he would hit a fan, John Christian, at Ebbets Field, giving Christian a broken jaw. The Yankees were the first team to finish a game without an assist, beating Cleveland 4–2. Tommy Holmes of the Braves hit in 37 consecutive games. The Dodgers' Tommy Brown became the youngest player to hit a homer at 17 years, 8 months and 14 days. Philadelphia's Vince DiMaggio hit a record tying 4 grand slams in 1945 and 42-year-old batting practice pitcher Paul Schreiber would pitch 3⅔ innings of relief on September 4th, appearing in his first big league game since 1923.[36]

Finally there would be a severe train accident on September 15th involving the Dodgers on a trip to St. Louis. Luckily only outfielder Luis Olmo, a cut right arm, and coach Charlie Dressen, a hurt right knee, would receive injuries, although engineer Charlie Tegtmeyer would be burned to death from flying gas.[37]

The season was coming to a close with two great pennant races. In the AL, the Tigers would survive a run by the Senators, beating them by a 1½ games while the Cubs finally knocked down the Cardinals, ending their string of three consecutive National League crowns.

It would be a fine World Series, going the complete seven games, with the Tigers coming out on the winning end, led by Greenberg's 2 homers, the only 2 the Tigers would hit, trouncing Chicago 9–3 at Wrigley Field in the final game. It came on the heels of a great Cub comeback in Game 6 where Stan Hack doubled in Bill Schuster with the winning run in an 8–7, 12 inning victory. It would be the Cubs' last trip to the Fall Classic to date.

From a business standpoint, 1945 had to be considered a great success. Attendance had shot up from 8,772,746 to 10,841,123, although discussion would begin on the possibility of moving teams from cities, where two teams or more currently existed. The main culprit would be St. Louis, where it was concluded that the city could no longer support two teams.[38] It was a correct statement, but it would be eight years until action was taken when in 1953 the Braves would move as the second banana in Boston to Milwaukee while in 1954 the Browns went to Baltimore and Philadelphia would lose the A's the following season to Kansas City.

Thirteen leagues were operating in the minors in 1945, and the prospect for a huge boom the following year came through, as 46 million fans would attend minor league games in 1946 compared to 10 million in 1945.[39]

If the attendance increase was impressive in the major leagues then the growth of the All American Girls Baseball League was that much more remarkable.

The AAGBL was in its third season after being founded by Phillip Wrigley, Branch Rickey and Paul Harper, and the attendance figures, which were at 259,000 in 1944, shot up to 450,000 in 1945. It caused Wrigley to take the circuit from a league ownership, where all franchises were owned by the league, to one more like the majors where each team was owned separately. Former baseball great Max Carey was at the helm of the AAGBL as they began play in '45.

Leading the regular season standings were the Rockford Peaches, who finished 5 games in front of the Fort Wayne Daisies. The Peaches were led by Dorothy Kamenshek, second in the league with a .274 average, and Margaret Wigiser, who was fourth at .249.

Helen Callaghan of Fort Wayne would top the circuit in hitting at .296 while Grand Rapids pitcher Connie Wisniewski was named player of the year with a 32–11–0.81 campaign, leading the league in both wins and ERA.

One change for the league in '45 was a change in the playoff format. In the past, the season was broken into two halves with the first half winner meeting the second half champs for the title. In this campaign, the race was for one complete season with the top four teams heading into the playoffs.

The regular season champs, Rockford, would beat Grand Rapids 3 games to 1 in the first round, while Fort Wayne outscored Racine 27–10 to also win in 4 games.

Although short, the finals turned out to be five classic games with 3 being decided by a single run and the other two by two runs. Unfortunately for Fort Wayne, Rockford would win every one run contest, taking the series 4–1.[40]

The Cleveland Buckeyes of the Negro American League and the Washington-Homestead Grays of the National League dominated the Negro Leagues, which were coming into the last chapter of their existence.

Winning by 14 games over the second place Birmingham Black Barons, the Buckeyes went 53–16 and were led by Sam Jethroe, who led the circuit with a .393 average and 10 triples, along with four other regulars who broke .300, Avelino Canizares, .314, Parnell Woods, .335, Buddy Armour, .325, and Ducky Davenport who hit .345. On the mound, Cleveland had the two best pitchers in the circuit with Willie Jefferson, 12–1, and George Jefferson at 10–3.

The perennial American League champs, the Kansas City Monarchs, had an off year at 32–30, but unveiled an outstanding shortstop that hit .345 with 5 homers, second in the league, by the name of Jackie Robinson.

To no one's surprise, the Washington-Homestead Grays took another National League pennant by 5½ games over the Baltimore Elite Giants, finishing 32–13, including a 20–2 mark at home. Hall of Famers Buck Leonard, .365, and Josh Gibson, .323, with a league high 11 homers (the equivalent of 60 in a full 550 at-bats, 154 game major league season), led the way for the Grays, while pitchers Roy Welmaker, 10–2, and Garnet Blair, 8–1, were the head of the class on the mound.

Even though the Philadelphia Stars finished in fourth place in the six team league, they still possessed three of the circuit's top four hitters with Ed Stone, .430, and Frank Austin, .398, at number one and two, while George Curry finished fourth with a .395 mark.

The World Series turned out to be no contest at all as the Buckeyes, led by Quincy Trouppe's .400 average, swept the Grays in four straight, the last two being shutouts.

With Happy Chandler now in charge, the hope that the Negro League players would now be permitted to join the white major leagues were rekindled when Chandler made the statement, "If a black boy can make it on Guadalcanal, he can make it in baseball[41]

Ironically, it was almost the Monarch's 38-year-old pitcher Chet Brewer that became the first player to break the color barrier in professional baseball. The Indians farm team in Bakersfield, California, wanted to sign Brewer. They had the approval of Commissioner George Trautman, but unfortunately Cleveland GM Roger Peckinpaugh shot down the idea.[42] That opened the door for Robinson to make history, which he certainly did on October 23rd, signing with the Brooklyn Dodgers.

Prior to the signing, Larry MacPhail, head man of the New York Yankees, voiced his opinion on the subject by pointing out why not only African-Americans had not yet been signed, but why the Yankees would not sign them in the future.

MacPhail reasoned that they had not been signed because organized baseball, including himself with Yankee Stadium, makes a good profit from the Negro Leagues using their fields of play; and the players are under contract to their owners and that contract should not be violated. He decided against signing them in the future because he felt there were not enough Negro League players who were of major league quality. He further said, "A major league player must have something besides natural ability. He must possess the technique, the coordination, the competitive aptitude and the discipline usually acquired after years of training in smaller leagues." Secondly, the Negro League players were currently under contract. Thirdly, he felt that the league could not exist without good players and to take them would cause the leagues to fold (which inevitably happened).[43]

Regardless of MacPhail's shortsighted opinions towards the Negro League players, Rickey went ahead and signed the Kansas City Monarchs star, assigning him to Montreal of the International League for the upcoming season.

Minor League czar W.G. Bramham highly criticized Rickey for the move questioning if the mixing of the races on the diamond would pan out in the long run and implied that Rickey considered himself the "Moses" of the African-American race.[44]

Rickey would reply by saying, it "left him cool considering the source. He's the master of the epithet."[45]

As far as the opinion of others, it was pretty much split with varying views. The standard thought of the players was (although certainly some had no problems while others were vehemently opposed), it was all right with them, as long as Robinson wasn't on their team. It caused an editorial in the *Sporting News* in which they said that "Those players of southern descent who gave out interviews blasting the hiring of a Negro would have done a lot better for themselves and baseball had they refused to comment. 'It's all right with me, just so long as Robinson isn't on our club'— the standard reply — is unsportsmanlike, and, above all else, un–American.

Meanwhile it would be well for the players to keep their opinions to them-selves and let the club owners work out this perplexing problem."[46]

While it might have been nice for the players to be quiet during this time, their bosses, the owners, certainly had no problem expressing their opinions. Horace Stoneham of the Giants was against the signing because he felt it wasn't fair to fill the open slots on rosters with anybody other than returning vets, while Clark Griffith did not support the signing because he didn't want to steal their stars under contract, therefore killing the Negro League themselves (like MacPhail he made money off the use of his stadium by the Grays, so perhaps he didn't want to destroy the money coming into his pocket).

William Benswanger of the Pirates was one of the few owners who did not oppose the move, claiming that it was the Dodgers' business and no one else's.

There was of course dissention in the minors as Texas League chief J. Alvin Gardner said that his league would not see a Negro League player as long as Jim Crow laws applied.

As far as the press went, there were a lot who were on Rickey's side, with some unique opinions. Ed McCauley of the *Cleveland Press* had a different slant, saying he wasn't sure if the dugout was the proper place to see if the races could work together, claiming that the dugouts of organized baseball who "...seldom operated on the highest level of mental maturity" might not be the proper place to seek the answer to racial harmony.

Dick McCann of the *Washington Times-Herald* somewhat naively felt that the players would accept Robinson if he proved he had the ability to play the game.

There was some support in the southern press as Frank Spencer of the *Winston-Salem Journal* said if he was qualified he should be given an oppor-tunity. Jack Hoerner of the *Durham Herald* voiced the opposing opinion when he balked at the idea, claiming that an African-American player was not going to be accepted in the southern leagues for a very long time.

Perhaps the one scribe who hit the nail on the head was a member of the African American press, Ludlow Werner, who wrote for the *New York Age*, "I'm happy for the event, but sorry for Jackie. He will be haunted by the expectations of his race." He further went on the state that Robinson could not afford a day off and "Lord help him with his fellow Negroes if he should fail them."[47]

Luckily for the Dodgers, Rickey and his race, he did not fail. The pressure of the above comment is perhaps something that Robinson felt every day of his career, although he performed with a skill and class that few will ever know or achieve.

In baseball terms, he hit .311 for his career and was elected to the Hall of Fame in 1962 on his first ballot. He would bring with him to the majors just about every Negro League star due to his outstanding success with the Dodgers, despite the fact he was under a complete duress that some say helped to prematurely end his life at the age of 53 in 1972. Robinson truly deserves every honor and attribute accorded to him and then some.

The war years were a dark time for the game and the nation in general, yet ironically the end of the time period brought with it perhaps the greatest moment the game had ever known. The signing of Jackie Robinson would finally make the great game truly, for once and for all, our National Pastime, one that now the entire nation could justly enjoy with pride.

Starting Lineups and Who Went to War

AMERICAN LEAGUE

1945 Detroit Tigers
88–65–0 GB

1941	1942	1943	1944	1945
1B-Rudy York	York	York	York	York
2B-Charlie Gehringer	Jimmy Bloodworth	Bloodworth	Eddie Mayo	Mayo
SS-Frank Croucher	Billy Hitchcock	Joe Hoover	Hoover	Skeeter Webb
3B-Pinky Higgins	Higgins	Higgins	Higgins	Bob Maier
OF-Bruce Campbell	Ned Harris	Harris	Jimmy Outlaw	Roy Cullenbine
OF-Barney McCosky	Doc Cramer	Cramer	Cramer	Cramer
OF-Rip Radcliff	McCoskey	Dick Wakefield	Wakefield	Outlaw
CA-Birdie Tebbetts	Tebbetts	Paul Richards	Richards	Bob Swift
PI-Bobo Newsom	Al Benton	Trout	Trout	Newhouser
PI-Hal Newhouser	Dizzy Trout	Virgil Trucks	Newhouser	Trout
PI-Tommy Bridges	Hal White	Newhouser	Rufe Gentry	Al Benton
PI-Johnny Gorsica	Newhouser	White	Stubby Overmire	Overmire

If Dick Wakefield was the man who brought the Tigers back into the pennant race in 1944 after his temporary return from the service, then Hank Greenberg did Wakefield one better, returning from his time with Uncle Sam to bring Detroit all the way back up the mountain, leading them to the 1945 world championship.

The veteran slugger hit a homer in his first game back on July 1st and never looked back. Greenberg took over in left field and would hit 13 homers with 60 RBIs and a .311 average in 78 games. More importantly, Hank would hit a dramatic grand slam in the top of the 9th inning on the last day of the season to beat the Browns 6–3, giving them the pennant.[48]

Rudy York, 18–87–.264, and Roy Cullenbine, who came over from the Indians in April for Don Ross and Dutch Meyer, 18–93–.277, were also key ingredients in the Tiger lineup.

The pitching staff, which was second in the league with a 2.99 ERA, was headed up once again by Hal Newhouser who finished with a league leading 25 wins, .735 winning percentage and an AL low 1.81 ERA, while winning his second consecutive Most Valuable Player award. Dizzy Trout had another strong season at 18–15–3.15, while Al Benton, 13–8–2.02, was lost to the team for a time with a broken ankle.

In the Fall Classic, Detroit, led by Greenberg's 2 homers, came back from down 2 games to 1, to win 3 of the last 4, capturing the world title against the Cubs.

Greenberg did put in his stake as the player who was most missed by his team during World War II. The year before he left they won an AL title as they did when he came back, while in the middle, they finished in the second division 2 out of 3 years. With all that going for him, there is little disputing of the above argument; he truly was missed more by his team than any other player in the service.

Who Left for the War	*Who Replaced Them*
3B-Pinky Higgins	Bob Maier
OF-Dick Wakefield	Jimmy Outlaw/Roy Cullenbine
PI-Johnny Gorsica	

Pinky Higgins— Michael "Pinky" Higgins was a fine .292 hitter throughout his 14-year major league career, which started in 1930 for the Philadelphia A's, although he was not much of a fielder, leading the AL in errors 3 times in his career, garnering a -131 fielding runs. He took over the starting reins at third in his official rookie season in 1933 when he hit .314 with 99 RBIs.

He was selected to play in his first All-Star game the following year, hitting a career high .330. After a second All-Star game selection in 1936, Higgins was sent to the Red Sox for Bill Werber. Pinky would eclipse the 100 RBI plateau in 1937 and 1938, his two years in Fenway, while going over .300 twice also. He also set a major league record of 12 straight hits in '38.[49]

Higgins would be sent to the Tigers in December of 1938 for 3 players that included Elden Auker. Even though he never topped .300 for the Tigers, he would come close twice, once in 1941 finishing at .298 and once in 1944, a season where he was selected to play in his third and final All-Star game, hitting .297.

Although he was not known as a power hitter, he did have decent home run numbers, hitting more than 10 on eight occasions including a high of 23 in 1935.

Pinky went into the Navy after the 1944 season where he played on the Great Lakes Naval team.[50] When he returned in 1946, he played in one more season, for Detroit and Boston where he hit .262 in 260 at-bats.

The Texas native, who was well known for his racist attitude,[51] finished with 1,941 hits, 59 short of the 2,000 mark, which he most certainly would have achieved if not for the war. He was 70 runs short of 1,000, which with the 79 he scored in 1944, was not out of the realm.

Replacing Higgins at third in 1945 was Bob Maier. Maier would hit .263 in his only major league season with 1 homer and 34 RBIs.

Dick Wakefield— Wakefield was given a $52,000 signing bonus coming out of the University of Michigan and looked like he would be worth every penny after the first couple years of his career.

In his official rookie season of 1943, Wakefield would lead the circuit in hits with 200 and doubles with 38 as he hit .316 before going into the Navy flight program.[52] After the program was cancelled he returned to Detroit in 1944 and led them in a way that no other had since Hank Greenberg. The Tigers were mired in 7th place on July 13th due to an anemic offense when he returned and lit a fire under them. He hit 12 homers with 53 RBIs and a .355 average in the last 78 games, leading the Bengals to a 2nd place finish, a game behind the Browns.[53]

He went back into the Navy again after the year and would play for that memorable Great Lakes team of 1944.[54] Dick was not the same player when he returned, hitting only .268 between 1946 and 1949 for Detroit. Wakefield would be sent to both the Giants and Yankees in 1950 and 1952, going only 1 for 4 his last two seasons combined.

The former Wolverine ended his career a .293 hitter, but some feel it was a lack of desire to play the game that cost him his place as one of the greats.[55] Consider that and the fact his two marquee seasons were during the war and perhaps one could deduce that the early success might have been a little overrated.

Taking over for Wakefield moving from left was Jimmy Outlaw. Outlaw would hit .271 with no power whatsoever, hitting no homers. Roy Cullenbine came over from the Indians early in the '45 campaign and would take over Outlaw's vacated spot in right. He had a fine year hitting 18 homers, knocking in 93.

Johnny Gorsica— A converted first baseman,[56] Johnny Gorsica broke in with the Tigers in 1940 finishing 7–7 in 20 starts. He would play in his only World Series that season, pitching nicely with a 0.79 ERA in 11⅓ innings.

After a 9–11 sophomore season in 1941, Gorsica went into the bullpen for two years before returning to the rotation in 1944, finishing 6–14 in 19 starts. Johnny would spend the 1945 season in the service and would return in 1946 to pitch in one more major league season, ending with a 2–0 mark, a 3.75 ERA and career low .208 OBA in 57⅔ innings.

1945 Washington Senators
87–67–1.5 GB

1941	1942	1943	1944	1945
1B-Mickey Vernon	Vernon	Vernon	Joe Kuhel	Kuhel
2B-Jimmy Bloodworth	Ellis Clary	Jerry Priddy	George Myatt	Myatt
SS-Cecil Travis	John Sullivan	Sullivan	Sullivan	Torres
3B-George Archie	Bobby Estalella	Clary	Gil Torres	Harlond Clift
OF-Buddy Lewis	Bruce Campbell	Case	Jake Powell	Lewis
OF-Doc Cramer	Stan Spence	Spence	Spence	George Binks
OF-George Case	Case	Bob Johnson	Case	Case
CA-Jake Early	Early	Early	Rick Ferrell	Ferrell
PI-Dutch Leonard	Bobo Newsom	Wynn	Leonard	Roger Wolff
PI-Sid Hudson	Hudson	Dutch Leonard	Haefner	Leonard
PI-Ken Chase	Early Wynn	Milo Candini	Wynn	Haefner
PI-Steve Sundra	Alex Carrasquel	Mickey Haefner	Johnny Niggeling	Marino Pieretti

The war years were the Senators' own personal roller coaster, finishing 7th, 2nd, 8th and finally 2nd in the four seasons.

Although it was not the offense that would lead the team to within 1½ games of the pennant, war hero Buddy Lewis returned from the service to hit a team high .333 in 68 games. The club as a whole would hit only 27 homers all season including one in their home field at Griffith Stadium, and that was an inside the park shot by Joe Kuhel (who hit 8 of the 27) on September 7th.[57]

The mound corps was superb with a league low 2.93 mark. Thirty-four-year-old Roger Wolff, who registered 20 of his 52 career wins that year, finishing at 20–10–2.12, led them. Dutch Leonard also chipped in with a 17–7 mark and 2.13 ERA.

In what was on one end probably a publicity stunt and on the other end one of the great moments in the war years, one-legged pitcher Bert Shepard, who lost his leg in the war and pitched with a prosthetic limb, tossed 5⅓ effective innings in his only major league game on August 14th, giving up only 1 run.

It would be a fitting way for the one of the majors' strangest teams to end their war years run.

Who Left for the War	Who Replaced Them
SS-John Sullivan	Gil Torres/Harlond Clift
3B-Eddie Yost	
OF-Stan Spence	George Binks
PI-Milo Candini	
PI-Vern Curtis	
PI-Bill LeFebvre	
PI-Early Wynn	Mickey Haefner/Marino Pieretti

John Sullivan— Sullivan was a light hitting, below average fielding shortstop who took over for the departed Cecil Travis when Travis was drafted after 1941, and held on to the starting shortstop job until he went to serve his country following the 1944 season.

He broke in with the Senators in 1942, hitting .235 before slumping to .208 his sophomore season, although he would knock in a career best 55 runs. Sullivan would hit .251 in 1944 before heading into the service.

John returned in 1946 as a backup with Washington for two seasons before ending his time in the show with the Browns in 1949, hitting .226 in 243 at-bats.

Gil Torres moved over from short to replace Sullivan. He hit .237 with a poor -21 fielding runs in 1945. Harlond Clift, who came over from the Browns late in 1943 with Johnny Niggeling, would take over for Torres at third and hit a pathetic .211 with 8 homers. It would be the last season in his 12-year career.

Eddie Yost— The 18-year vet — who was more known for drawing walks, accumulating 1,614 bases on balls, 8th highest in baseball history, compared to only 1,863 hits, than anything else in his career — was just a young rookie with only 14 at-bats in 1944 before heading into the service. When he returned in '46, he would lead the league in walks six times, on base percentage twice and doubles and runs one time each in the remaining 17 years he was in the show.

After going 2 for 25 in 1946, Yost took over the starting third base spot in 1947, with a .238 average. He would have his first breakout season in 1950, hitting .295 with 11 homers and a league high 141 walks for a .440 on base percentage. He would follow that up with a .283 average, an AL high 36 doubles and career high 65 RBIs.

Although he slumped to .233 in 1952, Yost would be selected to play in his one and only All-Star game. Eddie spent the next four seasons between 1953 and 1956 breaking the .400 on base percentage plateau each season.

"The Walking Man" as he was known, would also show he wasn't a bad fielder, leading the circuit in fielding percentage at .964 and .962 in 1958 and 1959. As impressive as that was, his -169 career fielding runs might suggest otherwise.

In December of 1958, Yost was sent to the Tigers in a 6-player deal. Eddie had a fine 1959 campaign as he topped the circuit in runs with 115, walks at 135 and on base percentage at .437 while batting .278. He followed that up by again topping the AL in walks and on base percentage with 125 and .416 respectively.

The year 1960 would be his last big season as he went to the Angels in '61, spending his last two years as a reserve.

Stan Spence— After a short two-year stint in Boston, playing for the Red Sox, Spence came to the Senators in 1942, immediately moving into the starting center field spot. He had a great year in '42, being selected to his first All-Star game while leading the AL in triples 15, hitting a career high .323.

Spence's marquee year was 1944, the year before he went into the service, being selected to his second spot in the midsummer classic, while hitting career highs in both homers, 18, and RBIs, 100, while clearing the .300 plateau for the last time at .316. He showed he was a fine fielder, accumulating 19 fielding runs.

Stan returned in 1946 and was chosen to play in his third and fourth All-Star games in '46 and '47, hitting .292 and .279 with a combined 32 homers and 160 RBIs. Spence was sent back to the Red Sox in 1948, where he slumped badly, coming in at .235. He would end his major league career the next season with the Browns hitting only .240.

The only career mark that Spence missed in his career due to his time in the armed forces was the 100-homer mark. The .282 career hitter ended up with 95 in his career and most certainly would have achieved that level.

George Binks would replace Spence as the starting center fielder in 1945 and was under Spence's production in 1944, hitting .278 with 81 RBIs while smacking only 6 homers.

Milo Candini— The best year in Mario "Milo" Candini's 8-year career was his rookie campaign of 1943 where he went 11–7 with a 2.49 ERA and .238 OBA. He would go 6–7 the next year before heading off into the service.

Milo was sharp in his comeback season of 1946, going 2–0 in 21⅔ innings with career lows in both ERA, 2.08, and OBA, .192. Things went quickly downhill afterwards, where he went a combined 7–7 his last five years with the Senators and Phillies, his ERA falling below 4.76 only once. Candini finished his career with a 26–21 mark and a 3.92 ERA, although his control would not be so good with a poor 183/250 K/BB ratio.

Vern Curtis—"Turk" Curtis would pitch in only 16 games in his 3-year major league career, going 0–1 with a 5.70 ERA.

Bill LeFebvre—"Lefty" LeFebvre would toss 6 games in 1938 and 1939 with the Red Sox, before leaving the majors. He would resurface with the Senators during the war years, going 2–0–4.45 in 1943 before a 2–4–4.52 campaign the next season, his last in the majors.

Early Wynn— As a young pitcher before going into the service, Wynn would have 3 fairly unimpressive seasons before breaking out with an 18–12–2.91 year in 1944. He would go into the army afterwards where he would play with the Manila Dodgers.[58] When Wynn returned, he went on to pitch 20 more seasons, winning 300 games, making six consecutive All-Star games and being given the ultimate honor in 1972, a selection to the Hall of Fame.

Wynn spent three more seasons in a Washington uniform after the war, going 33–39 before being traded to the Indians after the 1948 season with Mickey Vernon for Joe Haynes, Eddie Klieman and Eddie Robinson. It would be a fortuitous trade for Early as he was 72–87 at the time, far from being considered a future Hall of Famer. The move would be the sparkplug that would lead him to a 228–157 mark the rest of his career.

After a decent 1949, Wynn went 18–8 in 1950, leading the AL in both ERA at 3.20 and OBA with a .212 mark. "Gus," short for "Gloomy Gus,"[59] won 20 games the next two seasons, going 20–13 and 23–12 in 1951 and 1952. Arguably his best year was in the AL championship season of 1954 for the Indians, leading the league in wins with a 23–11 mark and a 2.73 ERA.

Early began his streak of six consecutive All-Star selections in 1955 and would enjoy another 20 win season in '56 with a 20–9 record. Wynn slumped to 14–17 in '57, prompting the Indians to send him to the White Sox for Fred Hatfield and Minnie Minoso.

Gus would have a few decent years in the Windy City, led by his clutch performance in 1959, sending the Sox to the American League crown with an AL high 22 wins.

The North Carolina native ended his time in Chicago in 1962 with a 7–15 mark, leaving him with 299 wins and no team to go to. The Indians came to the rescue the following season by giving him a shot, which paid off with his 300th win on July 13th against Kansas City.[60]

Although he did reach 300 wins, it's tough to know just how Early would have done in the war season that he missed. The Senators were a good team that season, so odds are as the number 2 or 3 man, which he was, Wynn could have won 15–18 games, which of course would have forced him not to have to go through that painful last season.

Replacing Wynn was Mickey Haefner, who slid down to the number 3 spot in 1945. He went 16–14 with a 3.47 ERA and .247 OBA. Marino Pieretti replaced Wynn in the rotation as a whole and the 24-year-old rookie would not disappoint, going 14–13.

1945 St. Louis Browns
81–70–6 GB

1941	1942	1943	1944	1945
1B-George McQuinn	McQuinn	McQuinn	McQuinn	McQuinn
2B-Don Heffner	Don Gutteridge	Gutteridge	Gutteridge	Gutteridge
SS-Johnny Berardino	Vern Stephens	Stephens	Stephens	Stephens
3B-Harlond Clift	Clift	Clift	Mark Christman	Christman
OF-Chet Laabs	Laabs	Mike Chartak	Gene Moore	Moore
OF-Walt Judnich	Judnich	Milt Byrnes	Byrnes	Kreevich
OF-Roy Cullenbine	Glenn McQuillen	Laabs	Mike Kreevich	Byrnes
CA-Rick Ferrell	Ferrell	Frankie Hayes	Red Hayworth	Frank Mancuso
PI-Elden Auker	Auker	Steve Sundra	Jack Kramer	Potter
PI-Bob Muncrief	Johnny Niggeling	Galehouse	Nels Potter	Kramer
PI-Bob Harris	Galehouse	Bob Muncrief	Muncrief	Jakucki
PI-Denny Galehouse	Al Hollingsworth	Hollingsworth	Sig Jakucki	Tex Shirley

The St. Louis Browns were the defending American League champions for the one and only time in their history, yet most of the talk around the league was not of their title defense but of the call-up of a young one-armed outfielder by the name of Pete Gray.

Despite the heartwarming story of Gray's dream season with the Memphis Chicks in 1944 and eventual call-up in 1945 with the parent club, he would only hit .218 in 234 at-bats and was considered more of a publicity stunt by some than a legitimate major league player, although his season with Memphis was worthy of a look by the Browns.

It wasn't just Gray that had a poor offensive season for the champs, as the team as a whole fell from 684 runs scored to 597 in 1945. They were led once again by Vern Stephens, who led the circuit with 24 homers with a team high 89 RBIs and .289 average. First baseman George McQuinn was the only player who was even in the ballpark with Stephens, hitting .277 with 61 RBIs.

If hitting was the problem, then pitching had to be considered the main reason that the Browns were able to stay in the pennant race. Nels

Potter again led the way not only on the mound with a 15–11 mark and a 2.47 ERA, but he had the highest batting average on the team at .304 in 92 at-bats. Bob Muncrief was also very sharp with his 13–4 record. The surprise story of 1944, Sig Jakucki would wear out his welcome late in '45 and be cut after a 12–10 performance, as he showed up on August 31st at Union Station, as the team was preparing to go to Chicago, in a very drunken state which apparently was the last straw in a series of insubordinate instances. They would bring up Cliff Fannin to replace him.[61]

All in all, despite the lack of offense and the fact they did not defend their crown, 1945 would bring an end to what was probably the most successful four year run in the franchise's history, at least the Browns

The defending American League champion St. Louis Browns brought up Pete Gray, who lost his arm in a childhood accident, in 1945. Although he would hit only .218 in 234 major league at bats, he proved to be a true inspiration. Courtesy of Photo File, Inc.

portion of it. Although things would get a lot better after the move to Baltimore, this would have to be considered the best of times for the team when it resided in Missouri.

Who Left for the War	Who Replaced Them
CA-Tom Turner	
OF-Al Zarilla	
PI-Denny Galehouse	
PI-Steve Sundra	

Tom Turner— Tom Turner was a little-used catcher, who primarily played most of his 5-year career with the White Sox during the war years.

Turner arrived in the majors in 1940, hitting .208 in 96 at-bats. He would be very consistent over the course of the next 3½ years with averages between .230 and .242, catching in 181 games during that time. He was traded to the Browns midway in 1944, hitting .320 in 25 at-bats for the American League champs, his last 25 at-bats in a major league uniform.

Al Zarilla—"Zeke" Zarilla, was a reserve outfielder in his second season for the 1944 American League Champion Browns, hitting .299 in 288 at-bats when he was called into the service.

He returned in 1946 and two years later would have his finest all around season. He was selected to play in his one and only All-Star game in 1948, setting career highs in hits, 174, homers, 12, doubles, 39, and average, .329.

Zarilla would slip a little the following season and would find himself shipped to the Red Sox for Stan Spence and cash midway in the season. Al's first full season in Boston during the 1950 campaign would prove to be his last meaningful year, hitting .325 with 74 RBIs. He would be shipped to the White Sox before 1951 and was never the same as he slumped to .257.

Zeke would spend his last two seasons in the show going from Chicago, back to the Browns and finally in a Red Sox uniform where he ended his career in 1952 hitting .194 in 67 at-bats.

With 975 hits, the .276 career hitter most certainly would have broken the 1,000 hit plateau had he not been called into the service. He had a decent chance of breaking the 500 RBI barrier, as he was 44 short. He had 45 the year before his callup and 43 the year after, so it certainly was a possibility.

Denny Galehouse—Galehouse would spend the first five years of his major league career, between 1934 and 1938, in Cleveland where he was a starter/reliever compiling a mediocre 25–29 record with ERAs never falling below 4.34.

Galehouse was sent to the Red Sox the following year with Tommy Irwin for Ben Chapman. His fortunes would not improve with 9–10–4.54 and 6–6–5.18 campaigns in '39 and '40. He was sold to the Browns following the 1940 season and while his records really did not progress much, his overall stats were very much improved.

After a 9–10 season in 1941, Denny won a career tying 12 games in 1942 before having perhaps his best overall season in 1943, finishing 11–11 with a career low 2.77 ERA and .255 OBA.

He would be allowed to take advantage of the new edict by Landis in 1944 of working in a war plant in Akron during the week and playing for the Browns on the weekend. He quit his job in the factory late in the season when told he wouldn't be drafted immediately, and went on to a 9–10 mark with a 3.12 ERA.[62] He was drafted following the season and would play with the Great Lakes Naval team.[63]

When Galehouse returned to the game after the war, he would toss only one more season with the Browns before being sold to the Red Sox early in 1947 where he went 11–7 with a 3.32 ERA after a poor start for St. Louis.

His last big moment in the majors was one of his worst ever as he was selected to pitch in the one game playoff for the American League pennant versus the Indians in 1948. He was shelled 8–3 and would only pitch in two more major league games, finishing his career at 109–118 with a 3.97 ERA.

Steve Sundra— Although Sundra would pitch the bulk of his career in the war years it would be his third campaign for the Yankees in 1939 for which his was most noted.

After finishing his official rookie year at 6–4, winning his last 4 games, Sundra reeled off 11 straight wins in '39 for a combined 15 wins in a row.[64] He would finish his marquee season at 11–1 with a 2.76 ERA.

Steve spent the next 2+ seasons unsuccessfully with the Yanks and Senators, going a combined 14–22 with ERAs over 5.00 before he was shipped off to the Browns early in the 1942 season with Mike Chartak for Roy Cullenbine and Bill Trotter.

Sundra finished 1942 with an 8–3 mark in St. Louis before going 15–11 the following season with his ERA at 3.25. He would head into the service early in the 1944 campaign and would pitch in only 2 more major league games when he returned in 1946.

1945 New York Yankees
81–71–6.5 GB

1941	*1942*	*1943*	*1944*	*1945*
1B-Johnny Sturm	Buddy Hassett	Nick Etten	Etten	Etten
2B-Joe Gordon	Gordon	Gordon	Stuffy Stirnweiss	Stirnweiss
SS-Phil Rizzuto	Rizzuto	Crosetti	Mike Milosovich	Crosetti
3B-Red Rolfe	Frank Crosetti	Billy Johnson	Oscar Grimes	Grimes
OF-Tommy Henrich	Henrich	Bud Metheny	Metheny	Metheny
OF-Joe DiMaggio	DiMaggio	Johnny Lindell	Lindell	Tuck Stainback
OF-Charlie Keller	Keller	Keller	Hersh Martin	Martin
CA-Bill Dickey	Dickey	Dickey	Mike Garbark	Garbark
PI-Marius Russo	Tiny Bonham	Chandler	Borowy	Bill Bevens
PI-Red Ruffing	Chandler	Butch Wensloff	Monk Dubiel	Bonham
PI-Lefty Gomez	Ruffing	Borowy	Bonham	Dubiel
PI-Spud Chandler	Hank Borowy	Bonham	Atley Donald	Borowy

Luckily for the Yankees, they were only 12 months away from restocking their roster with a collection of Hall of Famers, but for the time being Joe McCarthy would successfully make do with the collection of war years players that he was given, staying within 6½ games of the title in 1945.

The two best players that he would develop during this time were Nick Etten, who finished with 18 homers and a league high 111 RBIs while hitting .285, and Stuffy Stirnweiss who topped the circuit in runs, 107, hits, 195, triples, 22, stolen bases, 33, average, .309, and slugging at .476 while finishing third in the MVP race. Overall offensively, McCarthy would push enough buttons to help lead the Yankees to the highest run total in the American League at 676.

Second year pitcher Bill Bevens, more famous for losing his no-hitter in the 1947 World Series to Cookie Lavagetto and the Dodgers, who doubled with 2 outs in the ninth to not only break up the gem, but win the game 3–2, was in his second season and led the team with a 13–9 mark and 3.67 ERA. Hank Borowy, who was 10–5 at the time and had helped lead the team during the past 3 years, was sold to the Cubs in July and was a pivotal part in their run to the Fall Classic.

On a positive note, slugger Charlie Keller would return from the Merchant Marines to hit .301 and 10 homers in 44 games.

Overall, there was no team more devastated by the draft than the Yankees during the war. On paper it was a team worthy of the second division, but thanks to Joe McCarthy they never fell below 4th. That's why the games are not played on paper.

Who Left for the War	Who Replaced Them
CA-Rollie Hemsley	
PI-Al Lyons	
PI-Mel Queen	
PI-Jake Wade	
PI-Butch Wensloff	

Rollie Hemsley— Hemsley was a good defensive catcher who played for 19 major league seasons, being selected to appear in five All-Star games while accumulating 90 fielding runs.

Rollie broke in with the Bucs in 1928, having his best season his second year, hitting .289. He would be sent to the Cubs in 1931 before heading to Cincinnati and the Browns in 1933. St. Louis had picked him up on waivers, and it proved to be a masterful move as the Syracuse, Ohio, native would hit .309 in 1934 while accumulating a career high 23 fielding runs before making his first All-Star game the next year, a season in which he hit .290.

The catcher would enjoy one more All-Star season in 1936 before heading to the Indians in 1938 for Ed Cole, Ray Hughes and Billy Sullivan. He would make All-Star games number three and four in 1939 and 1940 combining a decent average, .263 and .267, with his wonderful fielding, leading the circuit in '40 with a .994 fielding percentage while combining for 15 fielding runs in the two years.

Hemsley headed back to Cincinnati for a half season in 1942 before going to the Yanks in midseason. He would take over for the recently drafted Bill Dickey in 1944, splitting time with Mike Garbark. Hemsley was selected to his fifth and final All-Star game that year, before heading into the service himself.

He would return in 1946, coming up only 142 times with the Phillies before ending his career in 1947.

Rollie was a .262 career hitter and the only mark his was close to was 1,500 hits. He was 179 off the pace, which being he was at the end of his career and never had more than 146 hits in any single season, would have been virtually impossible for him to reach.

Al Lyons— Al Lyons would pitch in only one prewar season, tossing in only 11 games with a 4.54 ERA. He would not pitch much more after he came back from the service, going 3–3 in 3 years with the Yankees, Pirates and Braves, finishing with a 6.30 ERA in 100 career innings pitched.

Mel Queen— Queen, the father of the Reds and Angels pitcher of the same name in the '60s and '70's, came up with the Yankees in 1942 while enjoying his best season ever in 1944. He went 6–3 with a 3.31 ERA and an impressive .227 OBA before going into the service.

He would return in 1946, heading off to the Pirates midway in 1947 where he pitched in 4½ fairly unsuccessful seasons, the best being in 1951 when Queen went 7–9 with an impressive 168⅓/149 IP/H ratio for a nice .233 OBA. He ended his career in 1952 finishing his time in the show with a 27–40 mark and 5.09 ERA.

Jake Wade— Most of "Whistling Jake's" career came in his first three seasons in the majors with the Tigers between 1936 and 1938. He went 14–17 with his best year coming in '37 with a 7–10 mark and .257 OBA. After that, he would spend his last five seasons in the bigs between the Red Sox, Browns, White Sox, Yankees and Senators, the best year coming in 1943 with Chicago, as he had a very impressive 83⅔/66 IP/H ratio with a great .222 OBA and finishing in 1946 with a lifetime 27–40 mark and 5.00 ERA.

Butch Wensloff— The majority of Charles "Butch" Wensloff's major league career came in his rookie season of 1943, when the number two man in the rotation finished 13–11 and a miniscule 2.54 ERA.

He didn't return to the majors until 1947, finishing at 3–1 with a

51⅔/41 IP/H ratio and 2.61 ERA with a .217 OBA. His career would last only one more season, with the World Champion Indians in 1948, lasting all of one game.

1945 Cleveland Indians
73–72–11 GB

1941	1942	1943	1944	1945
1B-Hal Trosky	Les Fleming	Mickey Rocco	Rocco	Rocco
2B-Ray Mack	Mack	Mack	Mack	Dutch Meyer
SS-Lou Boudreau	Boudreau	Boudreau	Boudreau	Boudreau
3B-Ken Keltner	Keltner	Keltner	Keltner	Don Ross
OF-Jeff Heath	Oris Hockett	Roy Cullenbine	Cullenbine	Seerey
OF-Roy Weatherly	Weatherly	Hockett	Hockett	Felix Mackiewicz
OF-Gee Walker	Heath	Heath	Pat Seerey	Jeff Heath
CA-Rollie Hemsley	Otto Denning	Buddy Rosar	Rosar	Frankie Hayes
PI-Bob Feller	Bagby	Bagby	Harder	Gromek
PI-Al Milner	Mel Harder	Smith	Smith	Reynolds
PI-Al Smith	Smith	Allie Reynolds	Steve Gromek	Bagby
PI-Jim Bagby	Chubby Dean	Harder	Reynolds	Smith

The Cleveland Indians would endure a few losses in 1945. Two members of their starting infield, Ray Mack and Ken Keltner, went into the service, while Hall of Fame shortstop Lou Boudreau suffered a broken ankle and outfielder Jeff Heath would miss time due to a knee injury. Despite it all, the Tribe would finish on the plus side of .500 after a disappointing season the year before.

When Boudreau and Heath went down, they were leading what was an anemic offense, with Boudreau hitting .306 and Heath leading the squad with 15 homers and a .305 average. The team as a whole was down significantly offensively from the year before, scoring only 557 runs, next to last in the AL, compared to 643 the year before. Despite all the poor performances, Dutch Meyer had a good campaign at second, replacing Mack after his stint in the military, when the Indians brought him and Don Ross over from Detroit in April. Meyer would hit .292 in 524 at-bats after the two-year layoff.

The pitching staff was much improved and the key to the Indians' overall development. Their combined team ERA dropped from 3.66 to 3.32, led by Steve Gromek, 19–9–2.55, and Allie Reynolds, 18–12–3.20.

In what would prove to be a sign of good things to come, Hall of Fame hurler Bob Feller finally returned from the Navy after a four-year layoff on August 24th. The war hero would toss 6⅔ hitless innings, striking out 12 en route to a 4–2 victory over Detroit.[65] Feller finished the year 5–3 with a 2.50 ERA, but more importantly, his return would not only signal the end of the war years for Cleveland, but a return to the top of the baseball world that would come a mere three years later.

Who Left for the War	Who Replaced Them
2B-Ray Mack	Dutch Meyer
2B-Rusty Peters	
3B-Ken Keltner	Don Ross

Ray Mack — Ray Mack was a decent fielding, light hitting second baseman who started for the Cleveland Indians throughout most of the war years. Mack broke into the starting lineup in his third major league campaign in 1940 and would have by far his best season in the show. He was selected to his one and only All-Star game, hitting lifetime highs in homers, 12 out of a career 34, RBIs, 69, batting average, .283 (his career total was only .232), on base percentage, .346 and slugging at .409, against a lifetime mark of .330. Ray would also make the great defensive play that saved Bob Feller's no-hitter.[66]

Even though Mack would start the next four seasons between 1941 and 1944, he never hit above .232, coming in at a combined .225 for the time period.

Ray entered the armed service after 1944 and would return in 1946, hitting .205 in 171 at-bats with the Indians. He would finish up his time in the big leagues after 1947 when he played with the Yankees and Cubs.

Dutch Meyer, who had been out of the majors since 1942 when he entered the military, took over for Mack in 1945. Dutch was truly his offensive superior, hitting .292 with 29 doubles and a .418 slugging percentage, although he had -32 fielding runs, far below the worst season Mack ever had.

Rusty Peters — Peters was a very versatile light hitting infielder that played almost as much at short as he did at second in his career.

Rusty basically was reserve most of the time he was in the majors, which began in 1936 with the A's. His best year by far was in 1937, hitting .260 with 43 of his lifetime 117 RBIs, in 339 at-bats.

He ended up in Cleveland in 1940 and towards the end of the war years was Mack's main backup. He hit only .222 for the Tribe between 1940 and 1944, so he really wasn't a capable alternative to Mack who hit .225 in a comparable time period.

Peters would mirror Mack in average and by going into the service after the '44 season. Ironically, he returned in 1946 and ended his major league career the following season, again just like Ray Mack. He finished things up after only 68 at-bats for the Indians and Browns his final two seasons.

Ken Keltner— Ken "Butch" Keltner was one of the best Indians third basemen in the history of the franchise, if not the best. Although he should have been most noted for that, Keltner's most memorable moment in the majors was on July 17th, 1941, when he stopped two line drives off the bat of Joe DiMaggio to end his fabled 56 game hitting streak.[67]

Ken started off dramatically in his official rookie season of 1938, smacking 26 homers with 113 RBIs before hitting a career high .325 the following season.

Keltner would begin his streak of six consecutive All-Star game appearances in 1940 by not only hitting well, but also showing what a good fielder he was. Butch would lead all AL third baseman in fielding percentage on three occasions, including back-to-back years in 1941 and 1942. He would also accumulate 39 fielding runs in those two campaigns.

After slumping badly in 1943, knocking in only 39 runs, the Milwaukee native came back strong the following year hitting .295 with 91 RBIs. He would head into the service after the season, playing for the Great Lakes Naval team.[68]

When Keltner returned in 1946, he would be selected to play in another All-Star game, although hitting only .241. Ken would enjoy one more moment in the sun, saving the best for last as he had a marquee year with the 1948 world championship Cleveland squad. Butch achieved career highs in homers, 31, RBIs, 119, on base percentage, .395, slugging, .522 while hitting .297.

It was the beginning of the end as he slumped to .232 in 1949, before retiring after 28 at-bats with the Red Sox in 1950. Keltner would have a fine career, hitting .276 with 1,570 hits, 163 homers and 852 RBIs, missing probably no major statistical plateaus while in the service.

Don Ross, who the Indians picked up with Dutch Meyer from the Tigers for Roy Cullenbine in April of 1945, replaced Keltner in 1945 and was neither adept in the field with -13 fielding runs, or at the plate, 2 homers for a .270 average, when compared to Keltner.

The unusual thing about the Chicago White Sox during the war years was their consistency. While most other teams would move up and down depending on the draft, the Sox, except for a brief rise to 4th in 1943, would be very consistent between 1942 and 1945, consistently bad, finishing either 6th or 7th led by a punchless offense that would accumulate only 45 homers in 1944 and 1945.

A couple of 30+ year old players would be the only positive thing Chicago fans would see in '45 when the Pale Hose would come up to bat. The 37-year-old Tony Cuccinello would lead the team at .308, while

1945 Chicago White Sox
71–78–15 GB

1941	1942	1943	1944	1945
1B-Joe Kuhel	Kuhel	Kuhel	Hal Trosky	Kerby Farrell
2B-Bill Knickerbocker	Don Kolloway	Kolloway	Roy Schalk	Schalk
SS-Luke Appling	Appling	Appling	Skeeter Webb	Cass Michaels
3B-Dario Lodigiani	Bob Kennedy	Ralph Hodgin	Hodgin	Tony Cuccinello
OF-Taffy Wright	Wally Moses	Moses	Moses	Moses
OF-Mike Kreevich	Hoag	Thurman Tucker	Tucker	Oris Hockett
OF-Myril Hoag	Wright	Guy Curtright	Eddie Carnett	Johnny Dickshot
CA-Mike Tresh	Tresh	Tresh	Tresh	Tresh
PI-Thornton Lee	John Humphries	Humphries	Dietrich	Grove
PI-Eddie Smith	Smith	Dietrich	Grove	Lee
PI-Johnny Rigney	Bill Dietrich	Orval Grove	Ed Lopat	Lopat
PI-Ted Lyons	Lyons	Smith	Humphries	Humphries

Thirty-five-year-old Johnny Dickshot would "lead" the club with 4 homers while chipping in with a .302 average. First baseman Hal Trosky would again be forced to sit out as he missed the 1945 season with severe migraines.[69]

One thing the White Sox usually would come up with was a decent mound force; this would not be one such season as the team ERA of 3.70 was 7th highest in the league. The only bright spot was Thornton Lee, as he came in at 15–12 with a 2.44 ERA. Orval Grove was 14–12, but had a substandard 217/233 IP/H ratio.

As the war years ended, White Sox fans would have something to look forward to — more consistency, as they would hit an AL low 37 team homers and a 5th place finish in 1946. In Chicago's case consistency was not a welcome guest.

Who Left for the War	Who Replaced Them
CA-Ed Fernandes	
2B-Bill Metzig	
OF-Ralph Hodgin	Tony Cuccinello
OF-Thurman Tucker	Oris Hockett
PI-Don Hanski	
PI-Gordon Maltzberger	

Ed Fernandes— Ed Fernandes played two seasons in the majors six years apart. The first one was in 1940 for the Pirates, hitting .121 in 33 at-bats, the second for the White Sox in 1946 with a .250 average in 32 at-bats.

Bill Metzig— The Iowa native was 2 for 16 in his major league career, all with Chicago in 1944.

Ralph Hodgin— After playing briefly for the Braves in 1939, Hodgin would reappear in the majors in 1943 for the White Sox, as he hit .314 in 407 at-bats his official rookie season, splitting time between third base and left field. The third baseman would have another fine campaign in 1944, hitting .295 before heading into the service.

Ralph returned in 1946 and was in the midst of a fine season in 1947 (he finished at .294) when he was beaned by Hal Newhouser and suffered a concussion.[70] He would not be the same, as the .285 career hitter would be done in the majors after a .266 performance the following year.

Probably the two levels that Hodgin certainly would have achieved had he not been in the service was 500 hits, he was 19 short, and 200 RBIs, needing only 12 more.

Tony Cuccinello took over at third in 1945 as the 15-year veteran hit .308 and was selected to the All-Star game in what would turn out to be his final major league season.

Thurman Tucker— Tucker was a baseball player whose star truly shined during the war years. Tucker came up in 1942 and became the White Sox' starting center fielder the next season. He would make his only All-Star game appearance in 1944, as he hit .287 and showed what a good fielder he was, leading the circuit in fielding percentage at .991 while garnering 18 fielding runs.

Tucker was lost to the service in 1945 and reemerged in the majors the following season. "Joe E.," as he was called, had his only decent post-war season in '46, hitting a career high .288.

The Texas native was shipped to Cleveland before the 1948 campaign and hit .260 in their world championship run. He would single and walk in 4 plate appearances in his only Fall Classic appearance.

Thurman played for three more seasons in Cleveland as a reserve outfielder, ending his major league career after 1 hitless at-bat in 1951.

In 1945 Oris Hockett came over from the Indians after an All-Star season in 1944. He would have a fine campaign in 1945, replacing Tucker in center, hitting .293 with a .340 on base percentage. It proved to be Hockett's swan song, as it was his last major league season.

Don Hanski— Hanski pitched for the White Sox in 1943 and 1944, giving up 8 runs, 4 earned, in 4 innings of work for his major league career.

Gordon Maltzberger— Gordon "Maltzy" Maltzberger would be a very effective reliever for the White Sox during the war years.

He would lead the circuit in saves his first two seasons in 1943 and 1944 with 14 and 12 respectively while going a combined 17–9 with ERAs of 2.46 and 2.96.

After a stint in the service in 1945, Maltzberger returned in '46 to go 2–0 with a 1.59 ERA and .205 OBA in 39⅔ innings. Gordon would finish his major league career after the 1947 campaign with a 2.70 lifetime ERA and a .236 OBA in 135 games, all in relief.

1945 Boston Red Sox
71–83–17.5 GB

1941	1942	1943	1944	1945
1B-Jimmie Foxx	Tony Lupien	Lupien	Lou Finney	Metkovich
2B-Bobby Doerr	Doerr	Doerr	Doerr	Newsome
SS-Joe Cronin	Johnny Pesky	Skeeter Newsome	Newsome	Eddie Lake
3B-Jim Tabor	Tabor	Tabor	Tabor	Johnny Tobin
OF-Lou Finney	Finney	Pete Fox	Fox	Johnny Lazor
OF-Dom DiMaggio	DiMaggio	Catfish Metkovich	Metkovich	Culberson
OF-Ted Williams	Williams	Leon Culberson	Bob Johnson	Johnson
CA-Frankie Pytlak	Bill Conroy	Roy Partee	Partee	Bob Garbark
PI-Dick Newsome	Tex Hughson	Hughson	Joe Bowman	Boo Ferriss
PI-Charlie Wagner	Wagner	Yank Terry	Hughson	O'Neill
PI-Mickey Harris	Joe Dobson	Newsome	Emmett O'Neill	Jim Wilson
PI-Lefty Grove	Newsome	Dobson	Pinky Woods	Randy Heflin

In 1944, Boston struggled back up the latter into the pennant race in September, before Uncle Sam would pluck Bobby Doerr, Jim Tabor, Tex Hughson and Hal Wagner from its roster, plummeting the Sox back down to .500. Things would not improve for Boston as they ended the 1945 season in 7th place 17½ games out.

Despite the fall to mediocrity, the real story of the 1945 campaign was the tremendous rise of rookie pitcher David "Boo" Ferriss, who was released early from the Army due to asthma and burst onto the major league scene in a way that few pitchers have.[71] He won his first 10 starts, held opponents to a record 22 consecutive scoreless innings to start his career, defeated every American League team and was on pace to win 30 games, which he was curtailed from doing because of his asthmatic condition.[72] Ferriss would finish the season 21–10 with a 2.96 ERA.

No other Boston pitcher would win more than 8 games, as Ferriss was definitely the high mark on a team that had the highest ERA in the league at 3.80 and walked the most batters with 656.

Offensively, Johnny Lazor and Bob Johnson led the way with 5–45–.310, 12–74–.280 seasons respectively. Thirty-eight-year-old superstar first baseman Dolph Camilli attempted a comeback with the Red Sox, but could only muster a .212 average with 2 homers.

The year 1945 would prove to be a short bump in the road for Boston as Uncle Sam, who took away in 1944, would give it all back in 1946 as Ted

Williams, Johnny Pesky, Dom DiMaggio, Doerr, Hughson and Wagner would reappear, giving the Red Sox the American League crown.

Who Left for the War	Who Replaced Them
CA-Bill Conroy	
CA-Roy Partee	Bob Garbark
CA-Hal Wagner	
2B-Bobby Doerr	Skeeter Newsome/Eddie Lake
3B-Jim Tabor	Johnny Tobin
PI-Tex Hughson	Emmett O'Neill/Jim Wilson

Bill Conroy— The first three years of Bill Conroy's career occurred between 1935 and 1937, when he had 66 at-bats and hit .212 for the Philadelphia A's, before leaving the show.

Conroy would get a second chance during the war years when he was picked up by the Red Sox, hitting .200 in 250 of his career 452 bats. He would spend two more years in the big leagues before going into the service after the 1944 campaign. He would not return to the majors after he came home, finishing his career one point under the Mendoza line at .199.

Roy Partee— Roy Partee came up during the war years in 1942, taking over the starting reins in 1943 when he hit for a fine .281 average in his rookie campaign. Roy would follow that up with a .243 average, smacking his only 2 career homers, before answering his call to arms.

Partee returned to the Red Sox in 1946, hitting a lifetime best .315, slumping to .231 the next season before finishing his time in the show in 1948 with the Browns, a .250 career hitter.

Bob Garbark replaced Partee in 1945, as the career backup would come up for 199 out of his lifetime 327 at-bats while hitting .261. He was gone from the majors the next season.

Hal Wagner— The first five years of Hal Wagner's professional baseball career were spent as a little used catcher for the A's between 1937 and 1941. As baseball entered the war years, Wagner would take full advantage of the situation, taking over the starting spot behind the plate in Philadelphia and was selected to play in the All-Star game in 1942.

Hal hit .237 in his two years as the Philadelphia catcher before being traded to the Red Sox in 1944 for Fred Garrison. He would hit a sizzling .332 to help lead the Sox to within 3½ games of the AL lead before being included in the mass exodus of players who left to serve their country late in the campaign, causing Boston to fall down to a mere .500 by season's end.

There was a short time during the war years that Wagner worked in a war important factory. He would play only on weekends for Philadelphia just when they were in traveling distance.[73]

Wagner came back to Boston in 1946, being selected to play in the midsummer classic once again as he would finish the season with a .230 average. The New Jersey native would play in his only World Series that year, going hitless in 13 at-bats.

He was shipped off to the Tigers midway in the 1947 season, hitting .288 for Detroit after the trade to finish at .273. It would be his last decent season as he could only muster up a .188 average in 117 at-bats for Detroit and the Phillies over the next two seasons, ending his stay in the majors in 1949.

Wagner, a .248 lifetime hitter, would come within 42 hits of 500 in his career, which he probably would have easily achieved had he not missed the 1945 season.

Bobby Doerr— Doerr was a wonderful all around second baseman for Boston in the 1940s who not only was the best player the Red Sox had after Ted Williams went into the service, but received the ultimate honor a player could hope to achieve by being selected to Cooperstown in 1986.

After coming up in 1937, Doerr broke into the starting lineup the following year, hitting .289. He would hit .318 in 1939, showing what a great fielder he was by leading the AL in fielding runs with 27.

Bobby had his first true breakout season in 1940, smacking 22 homers, knocking in 105 while hitting .291 and accumulating 18 fielding runs. Doerr was selected to play in the All-Star game in 1941, which would be the first of seven consecutive seasons selected in the years that he played.

The Los Angeles native would lead the league in fielding percentage in 1942 and 1943, before hitting .325, with the best slugging percentage in the AL at .528 in 1944, leaving the team late in the season for the service. He returned in 1946 with another overall monster season, with 116 RBIs and league highs in both fielding percentage and fielding runs at .986 and 27. Doerr would play in his only Fall Classic that season, hitting .409 with a double, homer and 3 RBIs for the American League champions.

After a sub par 1947 where he checked in with a .258 average (although he knocked in 95 and once again was the kingpin of fielding runs in the junior circuit with 24), Bobby went on the best streak of his major league career, going 27–111–.285, 18–109–.309 in 1948 and 1949 before his marquee offensive season of 1950 where he hit 27 homers with a career best 120 RBIs while leading the circuit in triples at 11 and fielding with a .988 percentage.

Doerr would retire following the next campaign while he was still at his peak, due to a back injury.[74]

Bobby, who was a nine time All-Star game participant, finished his career with 2,042 hits, 1,247 RBIs, 223 homers and a .288 average. On the defensive side he would end up 20th on the all time fielding runs list with 180 (sixth all time best for a second baseman). He was 5th best in double plays for a second baseman with 1,507 and 8th in putouts at 4,928. Add it all up and Doerr would have the 48th best TPR of all time at 40.5.

Replacing Doerr at second in 1945 was Skeeter Newsome, who moved over from short. Newsome would hit .290, but did not have Doerr's power, hitting only 1 homer. Eddie Lake moved into Newsome's spot at short, hitting .279 with a league high .412 on base percentage.

Jim Tabor—"Rawhide," as he was known, was a tough, hard drinking third baseman who was a very effective for the Red Sox during the war years. He came into the majors in 1938, taking over third base the following season. Jim would hit 4 of his 15 1939 homers in a doubleheader on July 4th, 2 being grand slams, as he knocked in 11.[75]

Tabor would hit .285 in 1940 before breaking the century mark in RBIs for the one and only time in 1941 with 101 while he hit 16 homers. He would average 13 homers and 77 RBIs over the next three years between 1942 and 1944, hitting a combined .258, prior to leaving for the Army before the end of the 1944 season.[76]

Rawhide returned in 1946 with the Phillies and hit .268 with only 50 RBIs, finishing his time in the majors following the next season in Philadelphia.

Johnny Tobin replaced Tabor, a .270 lifetime hitter, at third in 1945. Tobin was a 24-year-old rookie who hit .252 with no homers and only 21 RBIs in his only major league season.

Tex Hughson—Cecil "Tex" Hughson will go down as one of the best pitchers that were produced during the war years. After a 5–3 rookie campaign in 1941, Hughson burst onto the scene in a big way in '42, leading the AL in wins with 22 and strikeouts at 113, finishing with a 22–6 mark and 2.59 ERA, making the first of three consecutive All-Star games.

Despite a sub par 12–15 mark in 1943, Hughson would have a fine season with a 2.64 ERA and .247 OBA. Tex saved his best war years performance for last as he was 18–5 with a league high .783 winning percentage and career low 2.26 ERA and .225 OBA before leaving the Red Sox prior to the end of the 1944 season for the Navy, eventually transferring over to the Army Air Force.[77]

He returned to help lead the Red Sox to the American League pennant in 1946, proving his war years performance was no fluke, finishing at 20–11 with a 2.75 ERA. Hughson hurt his arm in 1947 and would retire after the 1949 season, finishing only 7–3 his last two years.

In his short 8 year career, Tex compiled an impressive 96–54 record with a .640 winning percentage and 2.94 ERA. The one stat he obviously did not achieve because of his time in the service was the 100 win plateau which, pretty much barring major injury, would have been a certainty had Hughson not gone to war.

Emmett O'Neill would slide into Hughson's spot in 1945, finishing 8–11 with a 5.15 ERA. Jimmy Wilson took over O'Neill's spot, in essence taking over for Hughson. Wilson finished a mediocre 6–8 although he had a miniscule .228 OBA.

1944 Philadelphia Athletics
52–98–34.5 GB

1941	1942	1943	1944	1945
1B-Dick Siebert	Siebert	Siebert	Bill McGhee	Siebert
2B-Bennie McCoy	Bill Knickerbocker	Suder	Hall	Hall
SS-Al Brancato	Suder	Irv Hall	Ed Busch	Busch
3B-Pete Suder	Buddy Blair	Eddie Mayo	George Kell	Kell
OF-Wally Moses	Elmer Valo	Johnny Welaj	White	Hal Peck
OF-Sam Chapman	Mike Kreevich	Jo Jo White	Estalella	Estalella
OF-Bob Johnson	Johnson	Bobby Estallella	Ford Garrison	Mayo Smith
CA-Frankie Hayes	Hal Wagner	Wagner	Wagner	Buddy Rosar
PI-Phil Marchildon	Marchildon	Jesse Flores	Bobo Newsom	Newsome
PI-Jack Knott	Roger Wolff	Harris	Black	Christopher
PI-Les McCrabb	Lum Harris	Wolff	Flores	Flores
PI-Bill Beckman	Dick Fowler	Don Black	Russ Christopher	Black

The Athletics returned back down to earth, finishing in the cellar for the fifth time in six years. The Athletics would be almost as far away from 7th place (17 games back), as the 7th place team, Boston, would be from the American League pennant (17½ games back). Despite the embarrassing performance, the highlight of the season would be the gutsy and inspiring comeback of former prisoner of war Phil Marchildon.

After his troublesome time spent in Stalag Luft III as a prisoner of the Nazi armed forces, Marchildon, who would contract dysentery and a bad case of shattered nerves in his ordeal, would valiantly come back to pitch in 1945. Although his season was somewhat short, giving up 4 earned runs and 5 hits in 9 innings, while walking 11, he would eventually return to his form as the Athletics' ace by going 19–9 in 1947.

Russ Christopher would lead the mound corps winning 13 of the team's 58 games while colorful war years star Bobo Newsom would lose 20 games in an 8–20 season. Joe Berry was the star out of the pen and maybe the club's best pitcher with an 8–7 mark in 52 relief appearances for a team low 2.35 ERA.

Offensively their were no stars as outfielder Bobby Estallela was the cream of the crop, leading the team in hitting at .299 and homers with 8. The team would finish at the bottom of the heap in runs scored with 494, the lowest American League total during the war years of 1942 to 1945.

Overall it was business as usual for the A's except for Marchildon's inspiring march back to the majors. It would put a final positive spin on what was otherwise one of the most troubling times in the franchise's history.

Who Left for the War	*Who Replaced Them*
OF-Hal Epps	
PI-Lum Harris	

Hal Epps— After 2-year stints in St. Louis with the Cardinals (1938 and 1940) and the Browns (1943 and 1944), Hal Epps went to the A's early in 1944 where he had 229 of his lifetime 391 at-bats, hitting .262. He would go into the service after the season, never returning to the show.

Lum Harris— Harris, who was better known for his 8-year managerial career with Baltimore, Houston and Atlanta in the '60s and '70s, was a decent pitcher who had the misfortune of playing on some extremely poor teams in his 6-year major league career.

After coming up in 1941 with the A's, he would break into the starting rotation in 1942, finishing with an 11–15 mark and 3.74 ERA. He would follow that up with a disastrous 7–21 campaign in '43 before righting the ship with his best season ever in 1944. Harris would have his only winning season with a 10–9 record and 3.30 ERA before answering his call to arms.

When Harris reemerged in 1946, he suffered with his poorest year ever, going 3–14 with a career high 5.24 ERA. He would end his time in the show the following year after 3 games with the Senators.

Starting Lineups and Who Went to War

NATIONAL LEAGUE

After years of second division finishes with manager Jimmy Wilson, Charlie Grimm took over the reins of the Chicago Cubs early in 1944 and led them to the National League pennant in 1945.

Phil Cavarretta, who easily captured the MVP over Boston's Tommy Holmes, with a league leading .355 average and 97 RBIs, led them. Stan Hack and Don Johnson also chipped in, hitting over .300 with .323 and

1945 Chicago Cubs
98–56–0 GB

1941	1942	1943	1944	1945
1B-Babe Dahlgren	Cavarretta	Cavarretta	Cavarretta	Cavarretta
2B-Lou Stringer	Stringer	Eddie Stanky	Don Johnson	Johnson
SS-Bobby Sturgeon	Lennie Merullo	Merullo	Merullo	Merullo
3B-Stan Hack	Hack	Hack	Hack	Hack
OF-Bill Nicholson	Nicholson	Nicholson	Nicholson	Nicholson
OF-Phil Cavarretta	Dallessandro	Peanuts Lowrey	Andy Pafko	Pafko
OF-Dom Dallessandro	Lou Novikoff	Ival Goodman	Dallessandro	Lowrey
CA-Clyde McCullough	McCullough	McCullough	Dewey Williams	Mickey Livingston
PI-Claude Passeau	Passeau	Passeau	Hank Wyse	Wyse
PI-Vern Olson	Lee	Bithorn	Passeau	Derringer
PI-Bill Lee	Olson	Paul Derringer	Bob Chipman	Passeau
PI-Larry French	Hi Bithorn	Ed Hanyzewski	Bill Fleming	Ray Prim

.302 averages respectively. Outfielder Andy Pafko would add the pop, knocking in 110, as the offense would lead the majors in hitting with a team .277 average, 16 points over their 1944 output.

As impressive as the offense was, it was the pitching that truly turned this club around. They took off over ½ run from their 1944 team ERA as they dropped from 3.59 to 2.98, which was the National League low. Hank Wyse was the number one man with a 22–10 mark and 2.68. Three over 35-year-old pitchers rounded out the rotation as 36-year-old Claude Passeau and 38-year-old Paul Derringer and Ray Prim chipped in with 17–9–2.46, 16–11–3.45 and 13–8–2.40 seasons.

The pitching staff also got a shot in the arm as it picked up Hank Borowy from the Yanks for $97,000 in late July. He would truly be a steal as Hank went 11–2 with a league best 2.13 ERA the rest of the way.

Even though they blew a 2–1 lead in the series, losing to eventual champion Detroit in seven games, it was truly a masterful performance, as they would improve 23 games with basically the same cast of characters as the previous season. It was a proud moment in the Windy City, one that would have to last for 56 years, as it was the last time the Cubs have played in the World Series.

Who Left for the War	Who Replaced Them
CA-Joe Stephenson	
OF-Dom Dallessandro	Peanuts Lowrey
OF-Lou Novikoff	
PI-Dale Alderson	
PI-Bill Fleming	Ray Prim
PI-Red Lynn	

Joe Stephenson— Stephenson was a little used catcher for the Giants and Cubs who hit .179 in 67 at-bats during his 3-year major league career.

Dom Dallessandro—"Dim Dom" short for "Diminutive Dominick" because he was only 5'6",[78] broke in with the Braves in 1937 before reappearing with the Cubs in 1940.

Dom split time between left and center in 1941, hitting .272 while driving in a career high 85 runs. After slumping to .222 in 1943, Dallessandro would have his finest major league season the following year with a lifetime best .304 in 381 at-bats during the 1944 campaign. He would head into the service after the season, returning in 1946 to hit .260 in 204 at-bats his final two years in the show, leaving after the 1947 season.

Replacing Dallessandro in 1945 was 13-year vet Peanuts Lowrey. Lowrey was more than an ample replacement, with a .283 batting average and 89 RBIs, while hitting .310 in his only World Series appearance.

Lou Novikoff—"The Mad Russian," who was named *The Sporting News* minor league player of the year in 1939,[79] broke in with the Cubs in 1941, before becoming their starting left fielder the following season. Nineteen forty-two would prove to be Novikoff's banner year as he hit .300 with 64 of his lifetime 134 RBIs.

After becoming a reserve with Chicago in '43 and '44, Lou would go into the service, coming back with the Phillies in 1946, where he went 7 for 23 to end his major league career with a .282 career average.

Dale Alderson— Dale Alderson would finish his two-year major league career between 1943 and 1944 with a 0–1 mark, a 6.56 ERA and a .349 OBA. Not surprisingly, he didn't return to the big leagues after his time in the service.

Bill Fleming— The California native started his major league career in 1940 with the Red Sox before spending his time in the war years with the Cubs.

Probably Fleming's most successful season came in 1942 when he was 5–6 for the Cubs primarily out of their bullpen. He had career lows in both ERA, 3.01, and OBA, .230, while maintaining a nice IP/H ratio of 134⅓/117.

Bill would slump in '43 before getting a spot in the Chicago rotation in 1944 as the Cubs' number four man, although still appearing 21 times in relief. It was a decent if unspectacular season, going 9–10 with a 3.13 ERA.

Fleming returned to the majors in 1946 after a 1-year hiatus in the military, where he ended his major league career with a 0–1 record in 14 games.

Replacing Fleming in 1945 was Ray "Pop" Prim who had a wonderful season with a 13–8 record and 2.40 ERA for the National League champs. Prim led the NL with a .228 OBA while maintaining a nice 88/23 K/BB ratio.

Red Lynn— Japhet "Red" Lynn had a short 3 year major league career for the Tigers, Giants and Cubs, going 10–8 in 85 games, mostly in relief.

After being out of the game for 4 years, he reemerged with the Cubs in 1944 and finished with a 5–4 record and a 4.06 ERA. Uncle Sam would come calling after the 1944 season, which would be his last in a major league uniform.

1945 St. Louis Cardinals
95–59–3 GB

1941	1942	1943	1944	1945
1B-Johnny Mize	Hopp	Ray Sanders	Sanders	Sanders
2B-Creepy Crespi	Crespi	Lou Klien	Emil Verban	Verban
SS-Marty Marion	Marion	Marion	Marion	Marion
3B-Jimmy Brown	Whitey Kurowski	Kurowski	Kurowski	Kurowski
OF-Enos Slaughter	Slaughter	Musial	Musial	Hopp
OF-Terry Moore	Moore	Harry Walker	Hopp	Buster Adams
OF-Johnny Hopp	Stan Musial	Danny Litwhiler	Litwhiler	Red Schoendienst
CA-Gus Mancuso	Walker Cooper	W. Cooper	W.Cooper	Ken O'Dea
PI-Lon Warneke	M. Cooper	M. Cooper	M.Cooper	Red Barrett
PI-Ernie White	Johnny Beazley	Lanier	Lanier	Blix Donnelly
PI-Mort Cooper	Lanier	Harry Gumbert	Harry Brecheen	Ken Burkhart
PI-Max Lanier	Harry Gumbert	Howie Krist	Ted Wilks	Brecheen

The Cardinals, who truly were the most dominant team during the war years, finally felt the bite of Uncle Sam as they lost all time great Stan Musial all season, and war stars pitcher Max Lanier and catcher Walker Cooper to the military in midseason. Couple that with the losses of starting pitchers Ted Wilks to a sore arm and star Mort Cooper to an elbow injury and then a trade to the Braves, and one would figure that the floor would fall out and the Cards would tumble down the National League standings. Like the Yankees, good teams find a way to win and even though this would be the only war season that the Cardinals did not spend in the World Series, they still won 95 games, finishing only 3 out.

Whitey Kurowski picked up some of the slack for the departed Musial as he had his best season to date, hitting 21 homers with 102 RBIs while leading the team in hitting at .323. Buster Adams, who was picked up in May for John Antonelli and Glenn Crawford, also came up big with a 20–101–.292 campaign after he came to St. Louis.

The mound corps, which figured to be much poorer after the losses of Lanier, Wilks and Cooper, got a boost from pitcher Red Barrett, whom the Cardinals got in exchange from Boston for Cooper. Red won a league high 23 games, 21 for St. Louis after coming over, finishing with a 23–12 mark and 3.01 ERA. Ken Burkhart, 18–9–2.90, and Harry Brecheen, 15–4–2.52, also had solid seasons as the team. Instead of falling down, the Cards finished second in the league in team ERA at 3.24.

Despite the positives, a second place finish would not be good enough as they would celebrate the return of their star players from the military with another world championship the following season.

Who Left for the War	*Who Replaced Them*
OF–Danny Litwhiler	Red Schoendienst
OF–Stan Musial	Johnny Hopp/Buster Adams
PI–George Munger	
PI–Freddy Schmidt	

Players Who Missed Part of the 1945 Season in the Military

Max Lanier, Walker Cooper

Danny Litwhiler — Danny Litwhiler saved the best for first in his major league career, as his 3½ year stint with Philadelphia between 1940 and 1943 to start his time in the show would prove to be the best seasons he ever enjoyed.

After a .345 rookie campaign in 1940, Litwhiler would hit .305 with a career best 18 homers and 17 fielding runs in 1941, taking over the starting reins in left. He followed that up with his first and only selection to the All-Star game in '42, hitting .271 with a league leading 1.000 fielding percentage.

Danny would slump to start the 1943 season for the Phils and was sent to the Cardinals with Earl Naylor for Buster Adams, Cooker Triplett and Dain Clay and would go from the cellar to the penthouse, winning two NL championships and a world championship in 1944 with St. Louis. He would enjoy a fine offensive season in '44, hitting 15 homers with a lifetime best 82 RBIs and a pivotal homer in Game 5 of the Fall Classic.

Litwhiler, who was bothered by chronic knee problems his whole career, was reclassified from 4-F and sent into the Army after failing his physical six times. It was during a time when the draft boards were pinpointing ballplayers to be drafted.[80] He would spend his time playing baseball at Fort Lewis.[81]

When he returned in 1946, Danny would not be the same player. He was sold to the Braves in 1946 before heading over to the Reds two years later. He enjoyed one final decent season, hitting .291 and 11 homers in 292 at-bats during the 1949 season before leaving the game in 1951.

Litwhiler missed two career marks due to his time in the Army. The career .281 hitter had 982 hits, only 18 shy of 1,000 and 451 RBIs, 49 away from 500. He most certainly would have made the hit plateau, but the 49 RBIs, although achievable, were not a cinch as he went over 49 just once in his last 6 years between 1946 and 1951 (he did get 82 RBIs in 1944, though).

Replacing Danny during his stay in the service was Hall of Famer Red Schoendienst, who was a rookie in 1945 and played his only season in the outfield. He hit .278 with a homer and a league high 26 stolen bases in his freshman campaign.

Stan Musial—"Stan the Man" was bottom line one of the top three, if not the best player ever turned out in the National League. He was a 20 time All-Star, a 7-time batting champ who between 1941 and 1958 never hit below .310, a 3 time MVP, 4th all time in hits, 3,630, and RBIs 1,951, while maintaining a lofty .331 career average. All the while he was one of the classiest men the game ever produced.

Stan Musial of the St. Louis Cardinals meets with an excited fan. Musial would win the MVP award three times, 1943, 1946 and 1948, on his way to 3,630 hits and a .331 average and a place in Cooperstown. Courtesy of the St. Louis Cardinals.

Musial had a fine rookie season in 1942 before claiming his first MVP award the following season when he lead the NL in hits, 220, doubles and triples, 48 and 20, on base percentage, .425, slugging .562 and capturing his first batting title with a .357 mark.

Stan went into the service, repairing ships for the Navy at Pearl Harbor in 1945 before heading back to St. Louis.[82] He returned to the Cardinals in a big way winning two more MVPs in his first three postwar seasons, leading the NL in runs, 124, hits, 228, doubles, 50, triples, 20, average, .365, and slugging, .587, in 1946 before perhaps his best ever offensive season in 1948 when he again led in runs, 135, hits, 230, doubles, 46, triples, 18, average, .376, and slugging, .702. He would also add the RBI crown with 131, on base percentage with a .450 mark and TPR at 6.6. It would be career highs for Musial in every category but doubles and triples. He would also add a lifetime best 39 homers in '48.

After "slumping" to .338 and 123 RBIs in 1949, Musial would go on a streak where he would win three consecutive batting titles between 1950 and 1952 hitting .346, .355 and .336 respectively. Stan led the league in RBIs with 109 in 1956 before winning his last batting title the following season at .351 with an NL high .428 on base percentage at 36 years old.

The Man would hit over .300 only 2 more times, .337 in 1958 and .330 at the age of 41 in 1962 when he came in at .330 with 19 homers and 82 RBIs. Musial retired after the following year and ended up in Cooperstown in 1969.

He missed practically no major marks in his career stats due to his year in the Navy, but let's look at where he might have ended up on the all time lists had he played. He averaged 208 hits the two years prior to his induction, which had he added to his total, would have given him 3,838 hits, moving into 3rd place all time ahead of Hank Aaron. Perhaps if he gets that close or even closer with a bigger 1945 season, he hangs around to try and get to 4,000. Musial averaged about 87 RBIs a year at that point, which would have put him over 2,000, again into 3rd place all time, ahead of Lou Gehrig. He was not quite the power hitter yet and never came close to the 25 homers he would have needed to eclipse 500 at that point in time in his career. The 50 doubles a year he was averaging would have vaulted him into 2nd all time with 775, only 17 away from Tris Speaker.

Johnny Hopp moved over from center to right in 1945, taking over for Musial although his 3–44–.289, which was good, was very un–Musial like. Buster Adams took over for Hopp in center after coming over from the Phils in May and did have by far his best season ever, hitting .292 with 20 homers and 101 RBIs with the Cards and 22–109–.287 overall.

George Munger—"Red" Munger was 11–3 with a 1.34 ERA and a .212

OBA in 1944 when he was called into the service the morning of the All-Star game in 1944, the first one he was selected to in his sophomore season, costing him perhaps one of the greatest seasons a pitcher ever enjoyed.[83]

He returned briefly in 1946, going 2–2, winning Game 4 of the World Series, before finishing with career high 16 victories in 1947 and a 16–5 mark with 123 strikeouts.

Munger made his third All-Star game in 1949 with a 15–8 record before falling to a combined 11–14 his next two years for the Cardinals. He headed to Pittsburgh in 1952 where he ended his career very ineffectively in 1956 with a 3–7 record and ERA's of 7.92 and 4.04 his last two seasons in a Pirate uniform.

Red would finish his time in the show at 77–56 for a lifetime .579 winning percentage.

Freddy Schmidt— Schmidt would have a nice rookie campaign in 1944 going 7–3 with a .222 OBA, tossing 3⅓ one hit scoreless innings in the World Series before going into the service.

Freddy pitched only two seasons following his return in 1946 for the Cardinals, Phillies and Cubs, with a combined 6–8 record before ending his stay in the show after 1947.

1945 Brooklyn Dodgers
87–67–11 GB

1941	*1942*	*1943*	*1944*	*1945*
1B-Dolph Camilli	Camilli	Camilli	Howie Schultz	Galan
2B-Billy Herman	Herman	Herman	Eddie Stanky	Stanky
SS-Pee Wee Reese	Reese	Vaughan	Bobby Bragan	Eddie Basinski
3B-Cookie Lavagetto	Arky Vaughan	Frenchy Bordagaray	Bordagaray	Bordagaray
OF-Dixie Walker	Walker	Walker	Walker	Walker
OF-Pete Reiser	Reiser	Augie Galan	Goody Rosen	Rosen
OF-Joe Medwick	Medwick	Luis Olmo	Galan	Olmo
CA-Mickey Owen	Owen	Owen	Owen	Mike Sandlock
PI-Kirby Higbe	Higbe	Higbe	Hal Gregg	Gregg
PI-Whit Wyatt	Wyatt	Wyatt	Davis	Vic Lombardi
PI-Luke Hamlin	Curt Davis	Davis	Rube Melton	Davis
PI-Hugh Casey	Ed Head	Head	McLish	Tom Seats

The year 1945 would see the Dodgers rise from the second division all the way back to third place. They would be led by a devastating offense that scored 105 more runs than it did in 1944, giving them a NL best 795.

Dixie Walker had a phenomenal season, knocking in a league high 124 runs while hitting .300. He would be helped by Goody Rosen and Luis Olmo, each of whom turned around poor 1943 performances with

12–75–.325 and 10–110–.313 seasons respectively. Augie Galan, who had a fine '44 campaign, chipped in with a 9–92–.307 year.

The pitching staff, which went from last in the NL in ERA at 4.68, to third in 1945 with a 3.71 mark, was led by 23-year-old second year pro Hal Gregg, who was 18–13 with a 3.47 ERA despite leading the league in walks with 120. Southpaws Tom Seats and Vic Lombardi would help round out the rotation with 41-year-old Curt Davis, finishing with 10–7, 10–11 and 10–10 marks correspondingly.

Even with all the success they would enjoy during the season, it was an off season move by Branch Rickey that would not only change the course of the franchise, but professional sports as whole. He would sign Jackie Robinson, eventually making him the first African-American to play in the majors since Fleet Walker in 1884.

The social ramifications of the move were obvious, but in baseball terms it would open the door for Rickey to sign several more Negro League stars such as Don Newcombe and Roy Campanella, the cornerstones of the National League dynasty that would go on for the next 11 seasons.

Who Left for the War	Who Replaced Them
1B-Jack Bolling	
2B-Lou Rochelli	
SS-Bobby Bragan	Eddie Basinski
SS-Gene Mauch	
3B-Eddie Miksis	
PI-Ed Head	
PI-Cal McLish	Tom Seats
PI-Rube Melton	Curt Davis/Vic Lombardi

Players Who Missed Part of the 1945 Season in the Military

Mickey Owen

Jack Bolling— The Mobile, Alabama, native was a decent hitting infielder who played two seasons in the majors, five years apart.

He came up with the Phillies in 1939, hitting .289 in 211 at-bats. Bolling would be out of the show until he got another chance during the war years in 1944, when he came in with a .351 average, 14 doubles and 25 RBIs in only 131 at-bats, before he answered his call to arms in the middle of the 1944 campaign. Jack would not return to the big leagues after his time in the service.

Lou Rochelli— Rochelli was 3–17 with a triple in his only major league season in 1944 for the Dodgers.

Bobby Bragan— A colorful manager who was more known for an episode with the Pirates where he was kicked out of a game, then proceeded to enter the field with an orange drink and a straw, offering the umpires a drink, than he was for his seven year playing career.[84]

Bragan entered the majors in 1940 with the Phillies and immediately took over the starting spot at short. He hit .222 with 7 of his lifetime 15 homers. He followed that up hitting .251 and .218 before being shipped to the Dodgers for Tex Kraus and cash in May of 1943.

Bobby would move behind the plate in '43 before taking over the starting spot at short in 1944, splitting time with Tommy Brown and a host of others (at least nine players would see time at short for Brooklyn in '44). He would hit a career best .267 that year although knocking in only 17 in 266 at-bats, leaving for the service after the season was completed.

The Birmingham, Alabama, native returned in 1947 but his career would be all but over after a meeting with GM Branch Rickey. When asked by Rickey if he would play with Jackie Robinson, Bragan claimed he would rather be traded.[85] Bobby wasn't traded but only came up 36 times in '47 before ending his career in 1948 with 12 at-bats.

The .240 lifetime hitter was only 44 hits short of 500, which he most certainly would have attained had he not missed 1945 and 1946 in the military.

Replacing Bragan in 1945 was Eddie "Bazooka" Basinski who took advantage of his only season as a starter as he hit .262 in 336 at-bats.

Gene Mauch— Gene "Skip" Mauch was an 18-year-old rookie in 1944 with the Dodgers, going 2 for 15, before he went into the service. When he returned in 1947, he would go on to be a much-traveled reserve for the next eight seasons.

Mauch would end up with the Pirates, Dodgers, Cubs, Braves, Cardinals and Red Sox before ending his major league career after the 1957 season, a season that would see Gene have his most successful year. He hit .270 in a career high 222 at-bats (he would only come up 737 times in nine years) with 28 of his lifetime 62 RBIs.

After an unsuccessful career as a player, Mauch would begin his new calling in 1960, managing 26 years in the show, finishing with 1,901 wins.

Eddie Miksis— Miksis was part of the youth brigade in the majors in 1944 when he came up as a 17-year-old player, hitting .220 in 91 at-bats before heading into the service.

Like Gene Mauch, Miksis would spend the better part of his career as a reserve except for three seasons with the Cubs.

The first was in 1951 after Eddie came over from the Dodgers in June as part of an 8-man deal that included Rube Walker and Andy Pafko. After coming up only 10 times with Brooklyn, Miksis would receive 421 at-bats with the Cubs, hitting .266 the rest of the way and taking over the reins at second.

The second big season came in 1953 when he came up 577 times, with a .251 average splitting time between second and shortstop. His final year as a regular was two years later in 1955 when Miksis moved into the outfield, playing most of his time in center, leading NL outfielders with a .989 fielding percentage, but hitting only .235.

Eddie played three more seasons, finishing his career in 1958 with the Orioles and Reds.

Ed Head— After coming up in 1940 with the Dodgers, Ed Head would move into the starting rotation with Brooklyn in 1942.

He went 10–6 that season with an impressive 136⅔/118 IP/H ratio with a fine .232 OBA. Head slumped a little the following year at 9–10, before heading into the service in the middle of what would be shaping up to be his finest season. Ed was 4–3 with a career low 2.70 ERA and a .232 OBA before being taken by Uncle Sam.

Head returned in fine fashion in 1946, throwing a no-hitter on April 23rd, before hurting his arm, which ended his career.[86]

Cal McLish— Named by his father, who had not been allowed to pick out the name for any other of his children (for good reasons obviously), Cal's official name is, Calvin Coolidge Julius Caesar Tuskahoma McLish, or "Buster" for short.[87]

McLish was 18 when he came up to the Dodgers for a disastrous rookie season in 1944, going 3–10 with a 7.82 ERA and .321 OBA. After coming back from the service, he was a little used reliever/starter marching back and forth from the minors until he was sent to Cleveland in 1956.

Cal would finally establish himself as a fine major league pitcher in 1957, going 9–7, mostly out of the pen, with a 2.74 ERA and .220 OBA. He would get his opportunity to finally break into the starting rotation in 1958 when Early Wynn was sent to Chicago and Mike Garcia was down with a sore arm.[88] McLish took advantage with a 16–8 mark and 2.99 ERA before having his finest moment in 1959. The Oklahoma native would be selected to play in his one and only All-Star game in '59, going 19–8 for the Tribe.

Cal was sent to the Reds in 1960 with Gordy Coleman and Billy Martin for Johnny Temple and came nowhere near repeating his fabulous 1959 performance, ending the year at 4–14. McLish was sent off to the White Sox the following career before ending up with the Phillies in 1962.

He had a fine 11–5 1962 campaign (despite a horrendous .293 OBA) before going 13–11 in '63 with a 3.26 ERA. Cal ended his career with a 92–92 record the following year due to an arm injury.[89]

Tom Seats would replace McLish in 1945 as the number four man in the rotation, responding with a 10–7 record and a 4.36 ERA in his last major league season.

Rube Melton — Melton was a pitcher who would see most of his action in the war years with the Phillies and Dodgers.

He would start out in 1941, moving into the rotation in Philadelphia the following year, ending up with a 9–20 mark. The season wasn't as bad as it appeared, as his OBA was only .234 with a 3.70 ERA.

Rube was sent packing to Brooklyn after the season for Johnny Allen and $30,000 and moved into the rotation in 1944, going 9–13 before entering the armed forces.

The righty returned in 1946 and had his best season ever with a 6–3 mark, 1.99 ERA and a .206 OBA. It would prove to be the beginning of the end, as Melton pitched in only 4 more major league games before ending his career in 1947.

Curt Davis would move into Rube's slot as the number 3 man in 1945, going 10–10 with a 3.25 ERA. Vic Lombardi took over Davis' spot, finishing 10–11 with a 3.31 mark.

1945 Pittsburgh Pirates
82–72–16 GB

1941	1942	1943	1944	1945
1B-Elbie Fletcher	Fletcher	Fletcher	Babe Dahlgren	Dahlgren
2B-Frank Gustine	Gustine	Coscarart	Coscarart	Coscarart
SS-ArkyVaughan	Pete Coscarart	Gustine	Gustine	Gustine
3B-Lee Handley	Elliott	Elliott	Elliott	Elliott
OF-Bob Elliott	Johnny Barrett	Barrett	Barrett	Barrett
OF-Vince DiMaggio	DiMaggio	DiMaggio	DiMaggio	Al Gionfriddo
OF-Maurice Van Robays	Jimmy Wasdell	Jim Russell	Russell	Russell
CA-Al Lopez	Lopez	Lopez	Lopez	Lopez
PI-Rip Sewell	Sewell	Sewell	Sewell	Roe
PI-Max Butcher	Bob Klinger	Klinger	Butcher	Strincevich
PI-Ken Heintzelman	Heintzelman	Wally Hebert	Nick Strincevich	Sewell
PI-Johnny Lanning	Butcher	Butcher	Preacher Roe	Butcher

Bob Elliott and Preacher Roe came to the forefront, as the Pirates would finish in the first division for the third consecutive year.

Elliott proved to be one of the best players in the NL, knocking in 108 runs the third season in a row he would accomplish that feat, while hitting .290. Al Gionfriddo and Jim Russell would both chip in with .284 averages while catcher Bill Salkeld, who split time with veteran Al Lopez, led the club in batting average at .311 and homers with 15 in 267 at-bats.

Roe stepped up and led the league in strikeouts with 148 while going 14–13 with a 2.87 ERA. Nick Strincevich and Max Butcher also came in strong with 16–10–3.31 and 10–8–3.03 seasons respectively. Forty-year-old Boom-Boom Beck came over from the Reds and pitched very well, coming in with a 6–1 mark and 2.14 ERA in 14 games.

Yes, the war years were very good to Pittsburgh. When the players would come back from the service in 1946, their fortunes would turn around as they would fall to the second division, but for the time being, it was a nice three-year stretch.

Who Left for the War   *Who Replaced Them*
CA-Roy Jarvis

Players Who Missed Part of the 1945 Season in the Military
Bill Rogers, Fritz Ostermueller

Roy Jarvis— Roy Jarvis would have a very brief major league career, going 8 for 50 in 3 major league seasons with the Dodgers and Pirates between 1944 and 1947. He finished with a .160 average and a homer.

1945 New York Giants
78–74–19 GB

1941	1942	1943	1944	1945
1B-Babe Young	Johnny Mize	Joe Orengo	Phil Weintraub	Weintraub
2B-Burgess Whitehead	Mike Witek	Witek	George Hausmann	Hausmann
SS-Billy Jurges	Jurges	Jurges	Buddy Kerr	Kerr
3B-Dick Bartell	Bill Werber	Bartell	Hugh Luby	Nap Reyes
OF-Mel Ott	Ott	Ott	Ott	Ott
OF-Johnny Rucker	Willard Marshall	Rucker	Rucker	Rucker
OF-Jo-Jo Moore	Babe Barna	Joe Medwick	Medwick	Danny Gardella
CA-Harry Danning	Danning	Gus Mancuso	Ernie Lombardi	Lombardi
PI-Hal Schumacher	Schumacher	Melton	Bill Voiselle	Voiselle
PI-Cliff Melton	Bob Carpenter	Johnnie Wittig	Harold Feldman	Feldman
PI-Carl Hubbell	Hubbell	Ken Chase	Ewald Pyle	Van Lingle Mungo
PI-Bill Lohrman	Lohrman	Rube Fischer	Fischer	Jack Brewer

The war times were not the best of times for the New York Giants, but things would improve a little during the 1945 season as they would finish on the plus side of .500 for the first time since 1942.

Player-manager Mel Ott led an offense that was at the top of the NL in homers with 114. Ott smacked a team high 21 while hitting .308. After a poor 1943, Hall of Fame catcher Ernie Lombardi enjoyed a resurgence that would see him come in with a 19–70–.307 performance. The bench would be a strong suit for New York as Billy Jurges hit .324 and 18-year-old Whitey Lockman came in at .341 before being called into the service.

The mound squad, led by 14-year pro Van Lingle Mungo, who had an All-Star season of 14–7–3.20, was improved slightly over the 1943 version. Ace Adams would again prove to be the king of the pen as he led the league in saves at 15 with an 11–9 record in 65 appearances.

Unfortunately, unlike their fellow National League brethren in Brooklyn, 1945 would not signal the beginning of a new winning tradition, as the club from Manhattan would fall into the cellar in1946.

Who Left for the War	Who Replaced Them
3B-Hugh Luby	Nap Reyes

Players Who Missed Part of the 1945 Season in the Military
Whitey Lockman, Andy Hansen

Hugh Luby— Luby played two seasons in the majors, the first in 1936 with the A's and the second in 1944 when the Idaho native would get another shot during the war as the starting third baseman with the Giants. He would split time with Nap Reyes and Billy Jurges, hitting .254 with a .364 on base percentage in 323 at-bats.

Replacing Luby at third in 1945 was Nap Reyes, who was an improvement at the plate hitting .288.

1945 Boston Braves
67–85–30 GB

1941	1942	1943	1944	1945
1B-Buddy Hassett	West	Johnny McCarthy	Buck Etchison	Vince Shupe
2B-Bama Rowell	Sisti	Connie Ryan	Ryan	Wietelmann
SS-Eddie Miller	Miller	Whitey Wietelmann	Wietelmann	Dick Culler
3B-Sibby Sisti	Nanny Fernandez	Eddie Joost	Damon Phillips	Workman
OF-Gene Moore	Paul Waner	Chuck Workman	Workman	Holmes
OF-John Cooney	Tommy Holmes	Holmes	Holmes	Carden Gillenwater
OF-Max West	Chet Ross	Butch Nieman	Nieman	Nieman
CA-Ray Berres	Ernie Lombardi	Phil Masi	Masi	Masi
PI-Manny Salvo	Javery	Javery	Tobin	Tobin
PI-Jim Tobin	Tobin	Tobin	Andrews	Bob Logan
PI-Al Javery	Lou Tost	Nate Andrews	Javery	Andrews
PI-Art Johnson	Tom Earley	Red Barrett	Barrett	Javery

Thirty players came and went into the military for Boston during the war years. They had three different managers and a ton of different players. Despite it all, the Braves were the model of consistency, finishing in 6th place for the third consecutive season.

War years star Tommy Holmes was the exception to the rule, as he led Boston with an absolutely monster season, hitting NL highs in slugging percentage, .577, hits, 224, doubles, 47 and homers with 28. Holmes would also knock in 117 with a .352 average. Chuck Workman also had a solid season with 25 homers and 87 RBIs.

Probably the Braves' best pitcher in the war years was Jim Tobin, who not only threw two no-hitters in 1944, but also hit 3 homers in a game in 1942, a record for a pitcher. Tobin would be sold to the Tigers midway in the season, after a 9–14 start. The man who helped lead the Cardinals to three consecutive National League championships, Mort Cooper, would replace him. The Braves picked up Cooper from St. Louis for Red Barrett and $60,000 in May. Mort went 7–4 with a 3.35 ERA. Twenty-six-year-old Ed Wright also had a fine season with an 8–3 record and 2.51 ERA.

Del Bissonette replaced Bob Coleman at the helm 91 games into the season, but could not really put the spark into the team. That shouldn't come as a surprise as Hall of Fame manager Casey Stengel couldn't do much better earlier in the decade. With the way the team had been set up, the master himself, Joe McCarthy, probably couldn't have moved this team up.

Who Left for the War	Who Replaced Them
CA-Hugh Poland	
INF-Gene Patton	
SS-Tony York	
SS-Connie Ryan	Whitey Wietelmann/Dick Culler
3B-Damon Phillips	Chuck Workman/Carden Gillenwater
OF-Chet Clemens	
OF-Chet Ross	
PI/1B-Max Macon	
PI-Woody Rich	

Hugh Poland— The bulk of Hugh Poland's major league career occurred in his rookie season of 1943 when he hit .183 for the Giants and Braves in 153 at-bats.

The .185 lifetime hitter would only have 58 at-bats in the remaining four seasons he spent in the majors, which ended in 1948 with Cincinnati.

Gene Patton— Gene Tunney Patton was in the same league with the great Moonlight Graham when it came to his major league career, as he played in one game as a pinch runner, never coming to bat, in 1944.

Tony York— York would never actually play for the Braves as he hit .235 in 85 at-bats for the Cubs in 1944, his only season in the show.

Connie Ryan— After breaking in with the Giants in 1942, Ryan came over with Hugh Poland to the Braves for Hall of Fame catcher Ernie

Lombardi. He would immediately take over the starting spot at second, hitting .212 with a -20 fielding runs.

Connie was off to his best season ever in 1944, with a career best .295 average, 13 fielding runs and a selection to play in his only All-Star game, when Uncle Sam came calling and Ryan went into the Army.[90]

When he returned in 1946, he had two decent seasons, before being reduced to a reserve role in 1948 and 1949. Ryan was sent to the Reds in May of 1950 for Walker Cooper and it was there he found a power stroke. He hit a lifetime high 16 homers in 1951 before smacking 12 the next season for the Phillies (he would only have a total of 56 in entire 12 year career).

Ryan lasted only two more seasons with the Phils, White Sox and Reds, ending his stay in the show after 1 walk in his only plate appearance in 1954.

Connie ended his time in the majors with a .248 average and was only 12 hits away from 1,000, which he certainly would have reached if not for his year and a half in the service.

Whitey Wietelmann took over at second for Ryan in 1945, moving over from short, hitting .271 with 4 homers. Dick Culler would cover Wietelmann at short with a .262 average.

Damon Phillips— All but 86 of Damon Phillips' career at-bats would come in 1944 when he held down the third base spot for the Braves. He hit .258 with 53 RBIs and his only major league homer in 489 at-bats. He went 1 for 2 in his only major league season after the war in 1946.

Chuck Workman moved from the outfield to third base full time, replacing Phillips in 1945, hitting .274 with 25 homers and 87 RBIs, fielding poorly with -17 fielding runs and a meager .910 fielding percentage. Carden Gillenwater took over Workman's spot in the outfield, hitting a career best .288 with 7 homers, 72 RBIs and a .379 on base percentage.

Chet Clemens— After coming up in 1939 with the Braves, Clemens would have to wait 5 years to play in his second and last year in the show. He only had 40 at-bats in his career, hitting .200.

Chet Ross— His sophomore season with the Braves in 1940 would prove to be by far the marquee year in the 6-year career of the Buffalo native. He hit 17 homers and knocked in 89 while hitting .281 with a .460 slugging percentage.

Chet would only hit .211 in his remaining 740 at-bats of his 6-year career. He hit merely 17 more homers with 80 RBIs, finishing with a lifetime .241 average. Ross was truly a one-year wonder.

Max Macon— Like Hugh Poland, the bulk of Max Macon's career would come in one season, 1944, with the Braves at first base.

Macon hit .273 with 36 RBIs in 366 of his career 502 at-bats in '44. He would come up only one more time in his major league career after he returned from the service in 1947.

Macon also pitched as he went 17–19 in 81 career games, the majority coming in 1937 with a 4–11 record and 4.11 ERA in 38 games with the Cardinals.

Woody Rich— Woody Rich pitched in parts of four seasons for the Braves between 1939 and 1944 (he was out of the majors in 1942 and 1943), going a combined 6–4 in 117⅓ innings with a 5.06 ERA and .280 OBA.

1945 Cincinnati Reds
61–93–37 GB

1941	*1942*	*1943*	*1944*	*1945*
1B-Frank McCormick	McCormick	McCormick	McCormick	McCormick
2B-Lonny Frey	Frey	Frey	Woody Williams	Williams
SS-Eddie Joost	Joost	Eddie Miller	Miller	Miller
3B-Bill Werber	Bert Haas	Steve Mesner	Mesner	Mesner
OF-Jim Gleeson	Max Marshall	Marshall	Walker	Al Libke
OF-Harry Craft	Gee Walker	Walker	Dain Clay	Clay
OF-Mike McCormick	Eric Tipton	Tipton	Tipton	Tipton
CA-Ernie Lombardi	Ray Lamanno	Ray Mueller	Mueller	Al Lakeman
PI-Bucky Walters	Vander Meer	Vander Meer	Walters	Heusser
PI-Johnny Vander Meer	Ray Starr	Walters	Ed Heusser	Joe Bowman
PI-Paul Derringer	Walters	Riddle	Clyde Shoun	Walters
PI-Elmer Riddle	Derringer	Starr	Tommy de la Cruz	Vern Kennedy

A mixture of injuries and losses due to the draft combined to send the Cincinnati Reds from the penthouse of the first division, in which they resided since a last place finish in 1937, all the way down to 7th place in the standings, winning 28 games less than they did the year before.

Their pitching staff, which had been the mainstay for the team over the decade, had ballooned from a 2.98 ERA in 1944 all the way up to 4.01 in 1945. The key losses were that of Clyde Shoun, who had gone off into the service and 36-year-old starting pitcher Bucky Walters, who injured his arm during the season. Former starter Elmer Riddle had also been lost as the team suspended him. Ed Heusser, Joe Bowman and Vern Kennedy, the latter two coming from the Red Sox and Phillies during the season respectively, tried to replace what was once a proud rotation of Walters, Riddle, Johnny Vander Meer, Ray Starr and Paul Derringer, but were unable to.

Offensively they were as ineffective as they were the year before. They lost starting shortstop Eddie Miller during the season to a broken knee. Despite that, he would still lead the team in homers with 13. There were some credible performances though, as first baseman Frank McCormick would contribute with a 10–81–.276 campaign while Dain Clay hit .280 with a team high 19 stolen bases.

Two returning vets came back from the military to play with the Reds this season. Hank Sauer hit a team high .293 in 116 at-bats while Eddie Lukon would return for a short time, going 1 for 8.

Unfortunately for the Reds, 1945 would mark the end of a successful run that saw them win two consecutive National League pennants in 1939 and 1940, the second of which they took the Series. They would spend a few years in the second division before rising back up in 1956.

Who Left for the War	Who Replaced Them
CA-Ray Mueller	Al Lakeman
1B-Lonnie Goldstein	
OF-Max Marshall	
PI-Joe Beggs	
PI-Harry Gumbert	
PI-Jim Konstanty	
PI-Bob Malloy	
PI-Kent Peterson	
PI-Clyde Shoun	Buck Walters/Joe Bowman

Ray Mueller— Mueller was a reserve catcher with the Braves and Pirates between 1935 and 1940, hitting .235 in 812 at-bats when he was sent back to the minors. The war years would give Mueller a second chance to show what he could do, and he was a man that took full advantage of the situation.

Mueller resurfaced with Cincinnati in 1943 and took over the starting reins behind the plate. He responded both at the plate, hitting .260, and in the field where he accumulated a career high 20 fielding runs.

As good a season as 1943 was, it was his year in 1944 that Ray would be most remembered for. He acquired the name "Iron Man" as he set a major league record for most games caught, 155.[91] Mueller also set career highs in homers, 10, RBIs, 73, and batting average at .286. The Pittsburg, Kansas, native also was selected to play in his one and only All-Star game.

It was at this point that the service derailed Mueller's baseball career. After being turned down several times for duty because of a stomach ulcer, the draft board, which was targeting 4-F ball players, suddenly found him fit to serve.[92]

After missing the 1945 season, Mueller returned in 1946, hitting .254 with 8 homers for the Reds with a NL high .994 fielding percentage for catchers. It would be the last time the Iron Man would play over 100 games as he toiled as a backup for the Reds, Giants, Pirates and Braves, until he left the majors in 1951.

Although he missed no key statistical plateaus during his time in the service, the .252 career hitter had his career saved by the lack of manpower during the war and ended up extending what was a short 6 year stay into a long 14 year one.

Replacing Mueller in 1945 was Al Lakeman. Lakeman would not match Mueller's 1944 performance, as he hit .256 with 8 homers and 31 RBIs with a poor -11 fielding runs.

Lonnie Goldstein— Goldstein was 1 for 10 in two seasons with the Reds, 1943 and 1946.

Max Marshall— Max Marshall's entire career in the majors was spent during the war years as a starting right fielder for the Reds until he was drafted midway in the 1944 campaign.

He broke in with the Reds in 1942, hitting .255 and .236 his first two seasons in the show before the .245 year he was enjoying when he was taken into the service.

Joe Beggs— Beggs would spend the first six years of his career, between 1938 and 1944, mostly as a reliever. His best season during that time period was probably his best one overall. In 1940 he went 12–3–2.00 with a league high 7 saves in helping pitch the Reds to the world championship that year.

Beggs had two other nice seasons out of the pen during that stretch, one in 1942 when he was 6–5–2.13 with a .206 OBA, and the next season when Joe came in with a 7–6–2.34 performance.

He left for the service early in the 1944 season and when he returned, Beggs would finally be given a shot in the rotation. He had a fine year with a 12–10 mark and a 2.32 ERA with a nice .247 OBA. It would be the last good season he had as after a 0–3–5.29 start in 1947, he was sent to the Giants where his career ended in 1948 after only ⅓ of an inning.

Harry Gumbert—"Gunboat" Gumbert had a long and successful 15 year run in the majors that saw him go 143–113 with 48 saves, as he would become an effective reliever late in his career.

Gumbert started out with the Giants in 1935, finishing an impressive 11–3 in his official rookie season the following year. His first big season came in 1939 when he went 18–11, replacing an aging Carl Hubbell in the rotation.[93]

After slumping to 12–14 in 1940, he was sent to the Cardinals early in 1941 with Paul Dean and cash for Bill McGee. The trade would prove to be very fortuitous for St. Louis, as Gumbert would roll off consecutive 11–5–2.74, 9–5–3.26 and 10–5–2.84 campaigns between 1941 and 1943.

Gunboat was sold to the Reds in June of 1944 and responded with a 10–8 record after arriving in Cincinnati (14–10 for the entire season). He headed into the service following the season and when he returned in 1946, he was primarily sent to the bullpen for the remainder of his career, which included a phenomenal year for the Reds in 1948. Harry would have a 10–8 record that season with NL highs in appearances, 61, and saves, 17.

He ended up with the Pirates the following year where he finished his time in the majors in 1950 after only 1 game.

The one mark that Gumbert would have probably achieved if not for his time in the service was 150 wins, of which he was 7 short.

Jim Konstanty— Casmir James Konstanty went from a little used reliever/starter with the Reds and Braves to a man who not only won the MVP in 1950, but helped create the role of the closer which is arguably the most sought after position in the majors today.

He began with the Reds in 1944 as a 27-year-old rookie, going 6–4 in 12 starts with a 2.80 ERA before joining the service. Jim was sent to the Braves when he came back in 1946 with cash for Max West where he pitched in only 10 games. He went to the Phillies in 1948 and became a valuable member of the their relief corps in 1949, going 9–5 with 7 saves.

It was 1950 when Konstanty etched his name in the record books as he had a wonderful 16–7 mark while leading the senior circuit in both appearances with 74 and saves at 22. Jim also came in with a magnificent 2.60 ERA and a minuscule .205 OBA. His IP/H ratio was 152/108. He won the MVP award easily over Stan Musial, becoming the first reliever ever to be given such a prestigious honor. Konstanty was a pivotal part of the Phillies' inspired run to the National League crown and when down on starters, was named the surprise starter in Game 1 of the World Series where he gave up only a run on 4 hits, unfortunately losing the game 1–0.[94]

Jim would slump a little in '51 and '52 before splitting time as a starter and reliever in 1952. He went 14–10 that year with 5 saves in 19 starts (48 games overall). He was sent to the Yanks in 1954, helping down the stretch in 9 games, saving 2 with a 0.98 ERA and .183 OBA. He returned to save 11 with a 7–2 mark in 1955 before retiring in 1956 after being sent to the Cardinals. He ended his time in the majors with a 66–48 record and 74 saves, not only having one of the great relief years of all time, but helped usher in the game we know today.

Bob Malloy— Bob Malloy was a little used reliever with Cincinnati and the Browns for most of his 5 year career in the majors, going 4–7 in 48 appearances, most of which came in 1946 when he was 2–5 with a 2.75 ERA in 27 games with the Reds.

Kent Peterson— The bulk of Kent "Pete" Peterson's 8 year major league career would come between 1947 and 1949 as a starter/reliever with the Reds.

He was 18 years old when he arrived on the scene, pitching 1 scoreless inning for the Reds in 1944. He would return from the service in 1947 and went 6–13–4.25 and 2–15–4.60 in '47 and '48. After a 4–5 mark with a 6.24 ERA in 1949, Peterson would be reduced to a little used relief role the next four seasons with the Phillies and Reds, tossing only 36 games during that time period which ended in 1953, finishing with a career 13–38 mark for a .255 winning percentage.

Clyde Shoun— After spending most of his 14 year major league career coming out of the pen, Clyde Shoun would take advantage of his opportunity during the war years to have probably his two most successful seasons.

"Hardrock" came up with Cubs in 1935 and was involved in a trade with St. Louis in 1938 where he, Curt Davis, Tuck Stainback and $185,000 went to the Cubs for the great one himself, Dizzy Dean. Shoun would have a couple of nice years with the Cards, leading the NL in appearances in both 1939 and 1940 while posting a league high 9 saves in '39 and coming in at 13–11 the following year.

Clyde was sold to the Reds in 1942 and came out of the pen to post an impressive 74⅓/56 IP/H ratio with a 2.18 ERA and .215 OBA. He followed that up with a 14–5–3.06 performance in 1943 before getting a career high 21 starts in 1944 and a 13–10 mark. He would throw his best game ever in '44, tossing a 1–0 no-hitter at the Braves on May 15th against Jim Tobin, a man who had thrown a no-hitter just a couple of weeks earlier.

Shoun would go into the service after the 1944 campaign, returning in 1946. He pitched in four more seasons, mostly as a reliever for the Reds, Braves and White Sox, ending his major league career in 1949 with a 73–59 career mark, 28–18 in the war years.

Bucky Walters would slide down to the number 3 spot in 1945, replacing Shoun, as Bucky would suffer an arm injury. He ended up at 10–10 with a 2.68 ERA. Joe Bowman would come over from the Red Sox and take Walters' place, in essence taking Shoun's place in the rotation. He ended up 11–13 after the trade with a 3.59 ERA.

In a series of embarrassing seasons, the Phillies/Blue Jays would turn in the worst during the war years when they would fall 52 games off the pace with a miserable 46–108 mark.

In a sea of poor moves, they would make probably their best as they got Vince DiMaggio from the Pirates for Al Gerheauser. DiMaggio would lead them with 19 of the team's 56 homers and 84 RBIs, although he would lead the circuit in strikeouts with 91. Jimmy Wasdell would crack the .300 plateau, becoming the only regular to do so on a team that hit a league low .246.

1945 Philadelphia Phillies
46–108–52 GB

1941	1942	1943	1944	1945
1B-Nick Etten	Etten	Jimmy Wasdell	Tony Lupien	Wasdell
2B-Danny Murtaugh	Al Glossup	Murtaugh	Moon Mullen	Fred Daniels
SS-Bobby Bragan	Bragan	Glen Stewart	Roy Hamrick	Bitsy Mott
3B-Pinky May	May	May	Stewart	John Antonelli
OF-Stan Benjamin	Ron Northey	Northey	Northey	Vance Dinges
OF-Joe Marty	Lloyd Waner	Buster Adams	Adams	Vince DiMaggio
OF-Danny Litwhiler	Litwhiler	Coaker Triplett	Wasdell	Triplett
CA-Bennie Warren	Warren	Mickey Livingston	Bob Finley	Andy Seminick
PI-Cy Blanton	Hughes	Schoolboy Rowe	Ken Raffensberger	Barrett
PI-Johnny Podgajny	Rube Melton	Al Gerheauser	Charley Schanz	Schanz
PI-Tommy Hughes	Johnson	Tex Kraus	Gerheauser	Charlie Sproull
PI-Si Johnson	Podgajny	Dick Barrett	Bill Lee	Dick Mauney

Except for Andy Karl, who was 8–8 out of the bullpen with an NL high 15 saves and a respectable 2.99 ERA, there was no redeeming value from the pitching staff, which at 4.64 was .58 higher than the next worst team ERA of the Giants at 4.06. Dick Barrett would not enjoy the distinction of being the only 20 game loser in the league, finishing at 8–20.

It wasn't all bad things that happened to Philadelphia during the season. Hugh Mulcahy, the first major leaguer drafted, returned home and despite fighting a case of dysentery in the Philippines, which did in fact help to curtail his career, he came back valiantly, going 1–3 with a 3.86 ERA.

Things were tough yet colorful for the franchise during this time. They lost an National League high 35 players to the military; they had an embarrassing owner in William Cox for a season (strangely enough their most successful season during the war) and they changed their name in the hopes of changing their luck. Inevitably they would decide that superior front office maneuvers would be the thing that can always change bad luck and they went go on to win the pennant five years later in 1950.

Who Left for the War	Who Replaced Them
CA-Benny Culp	
2B-Moon Mullen	Fred Daniels
2B-Charlie Letchas	
SS-Ray Hamrick	Bitsy Mott
OF-Ron Northey	Vance Dinges
PI-Rogers McKee	

Players Who Missed Part of the 1945 Season in the Military
Tony Lupien, Granny Hamner, Ken Raffensberger

Benny Culp—Benny Culp was a little used catcher for the Phillies between 1942 and 1944, coming up only 26 times for a .192 average.

Moon Mullen—Mullen played one major league season in 1944 and immediately became the starter in Philadelphia at second base. He hit .267 in 464 at-bats before heading into the service, never to return to the show.

Fred Daniels replaced Mullen at second, hitting only .200 in his one season in the big leagues.

Charlie Letchas—He would play in 4 major league seasons between 1939 and 1946 with the Phillies and Senators, yet all but 65 of his career at-bats would come in 1944.

Letchas hit .237 with 33 of his lifetime 37 RBIs in 396 at-bats. He split time that season at three infield positions, playing almost each equally (47 games at second, 32 at third and 29 at short). After entering the service he would return in 1946 to go 3 for 13, ending his major league career.

Ray Hamrick—The Nashville native played two seasons in the majors for the Phillies in 1943 and 1944, starting at short the second season where he was weak at the plate, hitting .205 in 292 at-bats, yet had a nice season with the glove, accumulating 20 fielding runs.

Bitsy Mott, one of the great names in the war years, who hit .221 with 13 fielding runs in his only major league season, replaced him in 1945.

Ron Northey—The best years in Ron Northey's career would occur right at the beginning, during the war years with the Phillies.

After hitting .251 his rookie campaign of 1942 where he took over the starting spot in right field, Northey came into his own, hitting 16 homers in 1943 before his marquee season in 1944 where he smacked career bests in both homers, 22, and RBIs with 104 while maintaining a .288 average.

It was at that point when Northey's career would take a controversial twist. In the selective service's desire to put 4-F ballplayers into the service, they three times gave Northey physicals, only to have him flunk each time due to the fact he was hard of hearing in one of his ears. Without any notice his classification was changed from 4-F to acceptable for induction and he was ordered to report to the Army where he was sent to Fort Lewis in Washington. He played for their baseball team for the duration of the war.[95]

He returned to Philadelphia in 1946 and was sent to St. Louis for Harry Walker and Freddy Schmidt. Ron broke .300 for the only time in his career for the Cardinals in 1948. Northey hit .321 with 13 homers and 64 RBIs in only 265 at-bats.

It would be his last good season as he spent the last years of his major league career as a reserve outfielder for the Reds, Cubs, White Sox and Phillies, where he ended his time in the show in 1957.

The one statistical plateau that Northey had an opportunity to break had he not spent a year in the Army was the 1,000 hit barrier. He was 126 short which with the 164 he averaged in the prior two seasons would have given him a decent shot at the mark.

Vance Dinges replaced Northey in 1945 and hit .287 with a homer his rookie season in the majors.

Rogers McKee— McKee went 1–0 in 5 appearances for Philadelphia between 1943 and 1944. He went into the service and would not return to the majors afterwards.

The Aftermath

In his classic book, *The Bill James Historical Baseball Abstract*, statistical guru Bill James makes the statement that when concerning the turnover in baseball in the National League between 1945 and 1946, the first postwar season, out of 64 starters in the senior circuit in 1945, only 22 would play 100 or more games the next season.[1]

That statement was the inspiration for this chapter. What will be included are the following two things:

• Starting lineups for each team during the following four seasons: 1941, the last season of peace time ball; 1942, the first war ball season; 1945, the last war ball season and 1946, the first postwar season. The teams will be listed in the order of their 1946 finish.

• A list of each player bumped from the starting lineup or the starting rotation and a short synopsis of how long their major league careers lasted afterwards in the postwar era.

1946—American League

1946 Boston Red Sox
104–50–0 GB

1941	1942	1945	1946
1B-Jimmie Foxx	Tony Lupien	Metkovich	Rudy York
2B-Bobby Doerr	Doerr	Skeeter Newsome	Doerr
SS-Joe Cronin	Johnny Pesky	Eddie Lake	Pesky
3B-Jim Tabor	Tabor	Johnny Tobin	Rip Russell
OF-Lou Finney	Finney	Johnny Lazor	Metkovich
OF-Dom DiMaggio	DiMaggio	Leon Culberson	DiMaggio
OF-Ted Williams	Williams	Bob Johnson	Williams
CA-Frankie Pytlak	Bill Conroy	Bob Garbark	Hal Wagner

1941	1942	1945	1946
PI-Dick Newsome	Tex Hughson	Boo Ferriss	Hughson
PI-Charlie Wagner	Wagner	Emmett O'Neill	Ferriss
PI-Mickey Harris	Joe Dobson	Jim Wilson	Harris
PI-Lefty Grove	Newsome	Randy Heflin	Dobson

Players Who Lost Their Starting Positions

2B-Skeeter Newsome— Spent 1946 and 1947 as the starting shortstop of the Philadelphia Phillies, hitting .232 and .229 before leaving the majors.

SS-Eddie Lake— Played until 1950 with the Tigers. Was their starting shortstop in 1946 and 1947.

3B-Johnny Tobin— Played only one season in 1945, was out of the majors afterwards.

OF-Johnny Lazor— Played one more year in Boston in 1946, came up 29 times for a .138 average.

OF-Leon Culberson— Played in Boston until 1948 as a reserve outfielder where he hit .277 in 292 at-bats during his last three years.

OF-Bob Johnson— Left the game after 1945, although he was a legitimate star before the war with a .296 lifetime average, 288 homers and 2,051 hits for his career.

CA-Bob Garbark— After being out of the majors since 1939, Garbark resurfaced in 1944 and would be gone from the show for good after 1945.

PI-Jim Wilson— Was a rookie in 1945 and would go on to pitch with seven teams, finishing his major league career in 1958 with an 86–89 mark.

PI-Randy Heflin— Was 0–1 in 5 games with Boston in 1946, his last major league season.

1946 Detroit Tigers
92–62–12 GB

1941	1942	1945	1946
1B-Rudy York	York	York	Hank Greenberg
2B-Charlie Gehringer	Jimmy Bloodworth	Eddie Mayo	Bloodworth
SS-Frank Croucher	Billy Hitchcock	Skeeter Webb	Eddie Lake
3B-Pinky Higgins	Higgins	Bob Maier	George Kell
OF-Bruce Campbell	Ned Harris	Roy Cullenbine	Cullenbine
OF-Barney McCosky	Doc Cramer	Cramer	Hoot Evers
OF-Rip Radcliff	McCoskey	Jimmy Outlaw	Dick Wakefield
CA-Birdie Tebbetts	Tebbetts	Bob Swift	Tebbetts
PI-Bobo Newsome	Al Benton	Newhouser	Newhouser
PI-Hal Newhouser	Dizzy Trout	Trout	Trout
PI-Tommy Bridges	Hal White	Al Benton	Virgil Trucks
PI-Johnny Gorsica	Newhouser	Stubby Overmire	Fred Hutrchinson

Players Who Lost Their Starting Positions

1B-Rudy York— A great power hitter for Detroit in the 30s and 40s, York was sent off to Boston in 1946 to make room for the great Hank Greenberg, when Greenberg returned from the war. He hit .276 with 17 homers for the AL champs, before ending his career in 1948 with the A's.

SS-Skeeter Webb— Was a utility infielder for the Tigers and A's the remainder of his career, which ended in 1948.

3B-Bob Maier— Played one season in the majors with Detroit in 1945 and was gone afterwards.

OF-Doc Cramer— The 20 year vet went on to play 3 more seasons as a reserve outfielder for the Tigers, ending his career after 1948.

OF-Jimmy Outlaw— Played until 1949 with the Tigers and was a reserve outfielder/third baseman in the post war era of his career.

CA-Bob Swift— Played until 1953 with the Tigers. Reclaimed his starting post in 1947 and 1948, hitting .251 and .223 respectively, before becoming a backup the remainder of his career.

PI-Al Benton— Was 11–7 with Detroit in 1946. Went on to pitch until 1952 with the Tigers, Indians and Red Sox until 1952, mostly out of the bullpen. He finished with 98 wins, two short of the magical 100 plateau.

PI-Stubby Overmire— Also pitched until 1952, with the Tigers, Yankees and Browns. Except for 1950, where he started 19 games for St. Louis and went 9–12, Overmire mainly threw out of the bullpen the remainder of his time in the show.

1946 New York Yankees
87–67–17 GB

1941	1942	1945	1946
1B-Johnny Sturm	Buddy Hassett	Nick Etten	Etten
2B-Joe Gordon	Gordon	Snuffy Stirnweiss	Gordon
SS-Phil Rizzuto	Rizzuto	Frank Crosetti	Rizzuto
3B-Red Rolfe	Frank Crosetti	Oscar Grimes	Stirnweiss
OF-Tommy Henrich	Henrich	Bud Metheny	Henrich
OF-Joe DiMaggio	DiMaggio	Tuck Stainback	DiMaggio
OF-Charlie Keller	Keller	Hersh Martin	Keller
CA-Bill Dickey	Dickey	Mike Garbark	Aaron Robinson
PI-Marius Russo	Tiny Bonham	Bill Bevens	Chandler
PI-Red Ruffing	Chandler	Bonham	Bevens
PI-Lefty Gomez	Ruffing	Monk Dubiel	Joe Page
PI-Spud Chandler	Hank Borowy	Borowy	Bonham

Players Who Lost Their Starting Positions

SS-Frank Crosetti— Only had 74 at-bats in three years as a reserve after the war, ending his 17-year career in 1948.

3B-Oscar Grimes— Played 73 games in 1946 for the Yankees and A's, his last year in the majors.

OF-Bud Metheny— Went 0 for 3 with the Yanks in 1946, ending his 4-year career.

OF-Tuck Stainback— Was a 13-year vet who played 91 games for the A's in 1946, his last year in the majors.

OF-Hersh Martin— Came to the Yankees in 1944 after a 4-year absence from the majors. 1945 would be his last major league season.

CA-Mike Garbark— Played 2 major league seasons, his last in 1945.

PI-Monk Dubiel— Pitched with the Cubs and Phils after the war until 1952, finishing at 45–53.

PI-Hank Borowy— Was traded to the Cubs midway in 1945 and went 11–2 the rest of the way, helping them to the NL pennant. Even though Borowy pitched until 1951 with the Cubs, Phillies, Tigers and Pirates, he could never match the success he had in the war years where he was one of the best pitchers during the time period. During the war years he was 67–32 for a .677 winning percentage. In the other years Hank pitched he was only 41–50, a .451 percentage.

1B-Nick Etten— Even though he kept his starting position at first in 1946, war years star Nick Etten would not last much longer in the majors. 1946 would show that Etten could not reach the lofty standards he had achieved during 1942–45 as he slumped to .232 with only 9 homers and 49 RBIs a season after he led the AL in that category with 111. He played one more season in Philadelphia for the Phils in 1947, going only 5 for 41, before heading to the minors.

1946 Washington Senators
76–78–28 GB

1941	*1942*	*1945*	*1946*
1B-Mickey Vernon	Vernon	Joe Kuhel	Vernon
2B-Jimmy Bloodworth	Ellis Clary	George Myatt	Jerry Priddy
SS-Cecil Travis	John Sullivan	Gil Torres	Travis
3B-George Archie	Bobby Estalella	Harlond Clift	Billy Hitchcock
OF-Buddy Lewis	Bruce Campbell	Lewis	Lewis
OF-Doc Cramer	Stan Spence	George Binks	Spence
OF-George Case	Case	Case	Joe Grace
CA-Jake Earley	Early	Rick Ferrell	Al Evans
PI-Dutch Leonard	Bobo Newsom	Roger Wolff	Haefner
PI-Sid Hudson	Hudson	Dutch Leonard	Leonard
PI-Ken Chase	Early Wynn	Mickey Haefner	Newsom
PI-Steve Sundra	Alex Carrasquel	Marino Pieretti	Ray Scarborough

Players Who Lost Their Starting Positions

1B-Joe Kuhel—Was at the end of an 18-year career when 1946 came around. He would end up playing only two more seasons until 1948 with the White Sox.

2B-George Myatt—Myatt was out of the majors since 1939 when the Senators resurrected his career in 1943. Would only accumulate 41 at-bats the two seasons after the war, ending his career in 1947.

SS-Gil Torres—Hit .254 in 63 games with Washington in 1946, his last major league season.

3B-Harlond Clift—1945 would be the last season of Clift's 12-year career.

OF-George Binks—Binks would last until 1948 with the Senators, A's and Browns. Except for his .258 average in 333 at-bats for the A's in '47, was basically a poor hitting, little used outfielder after the war.

OF-George Case—Case, a good hitter who had a career .282 average in 11 seasons, started in left field for Indians in 1946 hitting only .225. He would end his career the next season with Washington.

CA-Rick Ferrell—Ferrell was at the end of an 18-year career when the war came. Did not play in 1946, but would hit .303 in 99 at-bats with the Senators in 1947.

PI-Roger Wolff—After winning 20 games for Washington in 1945, Wolff would last only 2 more seasons with the Senators, Pirates and Indians, going a combined 6–12.

PI-Marino Pieretti—Pitched with the Senators, White Sox and Indians until 1950. Was a combined 16–25 between 1946 and 1950 after a 14–13 rookie year in 1945.

1946 Chicago White Sox
74–80–30 GB

1941	1942	1945	1946
1B-Joe Kuhel	Kuhel	Kerby Farrell	Hal Trosky
2B-Bill Knickerbocker	Don Kolloway	Roy Schalk	Kolloway
SS-Luke Appling	Appling	Cass Michaels	Appling
3B-Dario Lodigiani	Bob Kennedy	Tony Cuccinello	Lodigiani
OF-Taffy Wright	Wally Moses	Moses	Wright
OF-Mike Kreevich	Hoag	Oris Hockett	Thurman Tucker
OF-Myril Hoag	Wright	Johnny Dickshot	Kennedy
CA-Mike Tresh	Tresh	Tresh	Tresh
PI-Thornton Lee	John Humphries	Orval Grove	Lopat
PI-Eddie Smith	Smith	Lee	Grove
PI-Johnny Rigney	Bill Dietrich	Ed Lopat	Joe Haynes
PI-Ted Lyons	Lyons	Humphries	Smith

Players Who Lost Their Starting Positions

1B-Kerby Farrell— Was gone from the majors in 1946.

2B-Roy Schalk— After spending one year in the majors in 1932 with the Yankees, Schalk would not reappear in the show until the White Sox came calling in 1944. He would not return to the majors in 1946.

SS-Cass Michaels— Played with the White Sox, Senators, Browns and A's until 1954. His best postwar season was in 1949 with Chicago when he hit .308 with 83 RBIs.

3B-Tony Cuccinello— After a 15 year major league career would not return to the majors in 1946.

OF-Wally Moses— Played mainly as a reserve until 1953 with the White Sox, Red Sox and A's.

OF-Oris Hockett— After 4 years of starting with the Indians and White Sox during the war years was out of the majors in 1946.

OF-Johnny Dickshot— Had been out of the majors since 1939 when Chicago picked him up in 1944. He would not come back in 1946.

PI-Thornton Lee— After a 15–12 season with the White Sox in 1945, the 16 year veteran would pitch only 3 more seasons after the war with Chicago and the Yankees, going a combined 6–14.

PI-John Humphries— Would go 0–0 in 10 games with the Phillies in 1946, his last major league season.

1946 Cleveland Indians
68–86–36 GB

1941	1942	1945	1946
1B-Hal Trosky	Les Fleming	Mickey Rocco	Les Fleming
2B-Ray Mack	Mack	Dutch Meyer	Meyer
SS-Lou Boudreau	Boudreau	Boudreau	Boudreau
3B-Ken Keltner	Keltner	Don Ross	Keltner
OF-Jeff Heath	Oris Hockett	Pat Seerey	Hank Edwards
OF-Roy Weatherly	Weatherly	Felix Mackiewicz	Seerey
OF-Gee Walker	Heath	Heath	George Case
CA-Rollie Hemsley	Otto Denning	Frankie Hayes	Jim Hegan
PI-Bob Feller	Bagby	Steve Gromek	Feller
PI-Al Milner	Mel Harder	Allie Reynolds	Reynolds
PI-Al Smith	Smith	Bagby	Red Embree
PI-Jim Bagby	Chubby Dean	Smith	Gromek

Players Who Lost Their Starting Positions

1B-Mickey Rocco— Came up 98 times for Cleveland in 1946, hitting .245 to end his career.

2B-Don Ross— Hit .268 in 55 games for the Indians in 1946, his last major league season.

OF-Felix Mackiewicz— Hit .260 in 258 at-bats for the Indians in 1946 before closing out his career the following season with a combined 1 for 11 performance with Cleveland and Washington.

OF-Jeff Heath— Played with Washington, the Browns and the Braves after the war until 1949. The best season during that time period for the 14-year vet was in 1948 when he hit .319 with 20 homers and 76 RBIs for the National League champion Boston Braves.

CA-Frankie Hayes— Hayes hit .233 in 335 at-bats for Cleveland and the White Sox in 1946 before ending his 14 year career, which included a record 155 games caught in 1944 for the A's, with a 2 for 13 performance in 1947 with the Red Sox.

PI-Jim Bagby— Went 12–10 for the Red Sox and Pirates in 1946 and 1947, mostly as a reliever, his last two seasons in the show.

PI-Al Smith—1945 would be the last of Smith's 12 big league seasons that saw him come 1 win short of 100 with a 99–101 record.

<h3 align="center">1946 St. Louis Browns
66–88–38 GB</h3>

1941	1942	1945	1946
1B-George McQuinn	McQuinn	McQuinn	Chuck Stevens
2B-Don Heffner	Don Gutteridge	Gutteridge	Berardino
SS-Johnny Berardino	Vern Stephens	Stephens	Stephens
3B-Harland Clift	Clift	Mark Christman	Christman
OF-Chet Laabs	Laabs	Gene Moore	Al Zarilla
OF-Walt Judnich	Judnich	Mike Kreevich	Judnich
OF-Roy Cullenbine	Glenn McQuillen	Milt Byrnes	Jeff Heath
CA-Rick Ferrell	Ferrell	Frank Mancuso	Mancuso
PI-Elden Auker	Auker	Nels Potter	Kramer
PI-Bob Muncrief	Johnny Niggeling	Jack Kramer	Galehouse
PI-Bob Harris	Galehouse	Sig Jakucki	Sam Zoldak
PI-Denny Galehouse	Al Hollingsworth	Tex Shirley	Potter

Players Who Lost Their Starting Positions

1B-George McQuinn— Started at first with the A's and Yankees between 1946 and 1948, his last three major league seasons. His best year was 1947 when he hit .304 with 13 homers and 80 RBIs.

2B-Don Gutteridge— Hit .183 with the Red Sox and Pirates between 1946 and 1948 in 180 at-bats, his last three major league seasons.

OF-Gene Moore—1945 was the last of a 14-year career for the .270 lifetime hitter.

OF-Mike Kreevich— Kreevich would not return after the 1945 season.

OF-Milt Byrnes— Byrnes' three-year career during the war, in which he hit .274, was over after 1945.

PI-Sig Jakucki— The ex-marine, who had not played since his rookie season of 1936 when the Browns came calling in '44, ended his fairy tale story after the 1945 season when he went 25–19 between the two seasons.

PI-Tex Shirley— Shirley was 6–12 with a 4.96 ERA in his last major league season of 1946.

1946 Philadelphia Athletics
49–105–55 GB

1941	1942	1945	1946
1B-Dick Siebert	Siebert	Siebert	George McQuinn
2B-Bennie McCoy	Bill Knickerbocker	Irv Hall	Gene Handley
SS-Al Brancato	Suder	Ed Busch	Suder
3B-Pete Suder	Buddy Blair	George Kell	Hank Majeski
OF-Wally Moses	Elmer Valo	Hal Peck	Valo
OF-Sam Chapman	Mike Kreevich	Bobby Estalella	Barney McCosky
OF-Bob Johnson	Johnson	Mayo Smith	Chapman
CA-Frankie Hayes	Hal Wagner	Buddy Rosar	Rosar
PI-Phil Marchildon	Marchildon	Bobo Newsom	Marchildon
PI-Jack Knott	Roger Wolff	Russ Christopher	Fowler
PI-Les McCrabb	Lum Harris	Jesse Flores	Lou Knerr
PI-Bill Beckman	Dick Fowler	Don Black	Bob Savage

Players Who Lost Their Starting Positions

1B-Dick Siebert— His career ended after the 1945 season with a career .282 average.

2B-Irv Hall— Hall hit .249 in 63 games for the A's in his last major league season of 1946.

SS-Ed Busch— His 3-season war year career was over after 1945.

3B-George Kell— In a classic Philadelphia A's move, they traded Kell to the Tigers for Barney McCosky in 1946, where Kell went on to hit .306 in his 15 year career that ended in 1957, and was selected to Cooperstown in 1983. McCosky had three nice seasons starting for the A's, hitting .318, .328 and .326, before a back injury reduced him to a part time role in 1949, ending his effectiveness for the rest of his career.

OF-Hal Peck— Peck as basically a backup outfielder for the remainder of his career between 1946 and 1949 for the A's and Indians. The lone exception was 1947 when he hit .293 in 392 at-bats for Cleveland.

OF-Bobby Estalella— Estalella, who had his most effective seasons by far during the war years, was basically done after 1945, except for a 5 for 20 performance in 1949 with the A's.

OF-Mayo Smith— Smith's career would last only one season in 1945. He would be more successful as a manager, winning a World Series with the Tigers in 1968. He would accumulate a 662–612 record in 9 seasons at the helm of the Phillies, Reds and Tigers.

PI-Bobo Newsom— The much traveled 20 season veteran who was traded 10 times in his career, playing with 8 teams, hung around until 1948 going 25–28 with the A's, Senators, Yankees and Giants. He would try a comeback in 1952, hanging them up for good the following year after a 6–5 combined record. Newsom finished his career at 211–222.

PI-Russ Christopher— Christopher would pitch 3 more seasons between 1946 and 1948 for Philadelphia and Cleveland after the war, going 18–16 mostly out of the bullpen.

PI-Jesse Flores— After a decent run during the war years, Flores would pitch for the A's in 1946 and 1947, going 9–7 and 4–13 respectively. He would be out of the majors until 1950 when he went 3–3 for the Indians in 28 appearances.

PI-Don Black— Black would pitch 3 years for the Indians between 1946 and 1948. His best season would be 1947, when he went 10–12 with a 3.92 ERA.

1946—National League

1946 St. Louis Cardinals
98–58–0 GB

1941	1942	1945	1946
1B-Johnny Mize	Hopp	Ray Sanders	Musial
2B-Creepy Crespi	Crespi	Emil Verban	Schoendienst
SS-Marty Marion	Marion	Marion	Marion
3B-Jimmy Brown	Whitey Kurowski	Kurowski	Kurowski
OF-Enos Slaughter	Slaughter	Hopp	Slaughter
OF-Terry Moore	Moore	Buster Adams	Moore
OF-Johnny Hopp	Stan Musial	Red Schoendienst	Harry Walker
CA-Gus Mancuso	Walker Cooper	Ken O'Dea	Joe Garagiola
PI-Lon Warneke	M. Cooper	Red Barrett	Howie Pollet
PI-Ernie White	Johnny Beazley	Blix Donnelly	Brecheen
PI-Mort Cooper	Lanier	Ken Burkhart	Murry Dickson
PI-Max Lanier	Harry Gumbert	Harry Brecheen	Beazley

Players Who Lost Their Starting Positions

1B-Ray Sanders— After a fabulous run through the war years, Sanders was sent to the Braves to make space for the return of Stan Musial. He hit

.243 with 6 homers in 80 games for the Braves, before he broke his arm, an injury that reduced his major league career to just 25 more at-bats, ending in 1949.

2B-Emil Verban—Verban bounced around between the Cardinals, Phillies, Cubs and Braves after the war ended until he ended his stay in the majors in 1950. The best postwar season he enjoyed was 1947 with the Phillies when he hit .285 in 540 at-bats.

OF-Johnny Hopp— Hopp would play with some success, at least early in the postwar period, until he ended his stay in the majors in 1952. He was much traveled after leaving the Cardinals in 1946, going from the Braves to the Pirates, Dodgers, Yankees and Tigers. His top post war campaigns were 1946 when he hit .333 with the Braves and 1950 in Pittsburgh where Hopp came in with a .340 mark.

OF-Buster Adams— Adams would hit .185 and .247 his only two postwar seasons with the Cardinals and Phillies.

CA-Ken O'Dea— He hit .157 in 89 at-bats his last major league season of 1946 with St. Louis and the Boston Braves.

PI-Red Barrett— Although unable to achieve the success of 23 wins in 1945, Barrett pitched with the Cardinals and Braves until 1949. His best year was 1947 when Red went 11–12 with a 3.55 ERA.

PI-Blix Donnelly— Donnelly's career lasted until 1951 with the Cards, Phillies and Braves. He was basically used as a spot starter and reliever, going a combined 17–25 in the seasons after the war.

PI-Ken Burkhart— After a fabulous 18–8 mark his rookie campaign in 1945, Burkhart would pitch successfully as a spot starter for the Cards in 1946 with a 6–3 record and 2.88 ERA before going into the pen fulltime with St. Louis and Cincinnati until 1949.

1946 Brooklyn Dodgers
96–60–2 GB

1941	*1942*	*1945*	*1946*
1B-Dolph Camilli	Camilli	Augie Galan	Ed Stevens
2B-Billy Herman	Herman	Eddie Stanky	Stanky
SS-Pee Wee Reese	Reese	Eddie Basinski	Reese
3B-Cookie Lavagetto	Arky Vaughan	Frenchy Bordageray	Lavagetto
OF-Dixie Walker	Walker	Walker	Walker
OF-Pete Reiser	Reiser	Goody Rosen	Carl Furillo
OF-Joe Medwick	Medwick	Luis Olmo	Reiser
CA-Mickey Owen	Owen	Mike Sandlock	Bruce Edwards
PI-Kirby Higbe	Higbe	Hal Gregg	Joe Hatten
PI-Whit Wyatt	Wyatt	Vic Lombardi	Higbe
PI-Luke Hamlin	Curt Davis	Davis	Lombardi
PI-Hugh Casey	Ed Head	Tom Seats	Gregg

Players Who Lost Their Starting Positions

1B-Augie Galan— Hit .310 in 1946 sharing time at first with Ed Stevens, before coming in at .314, starting in the outfield with the Reds in 1947. He was reduced to a backup role after that until leaving the majors in 1949, splitting the season with the Giants and A's.

SS-Eddie Basinski— Played in only one postwar season, 1947 with the Pirates, hitting .199 in 161 at-bats.

3B-Frenchy Bordagaray— Frenchy's career ended after 1945.

OF-Goody Rosen— Played in one postwar season and hit .281 in 313 at-bats with the Dodgers and Giants

OF-Luis Olmo— Played in parts of three seasons after the war between 1949 and 1951 for the Dodgers and Braves, his best being in '49 when he hit .305 in 105 at-bats.

CA-Mike Sandlock— Sandlock hit .147 in 34 at-bats, not reappearing in the majors until 1953, with Pittsburgh, hitting .231 in 64 games.

PI-Curt Davis— The 13-year vet would pitch in only 1 game in 1946 before ending his stay in the show.

PI-Tom Seats— After being out of the majors since his rookie campaign in 1940, the Dodgers picked Seats up in 1945, which would prove to be his only other major league season.

1946 Chicago Cubs
82–71–14.5 GB

1941	*1942*	*1945*	*1946*
1B-Babe Dahlgren	Cavarretta	Cavarretta	Eddie Waitkus
2B-Lou Stringer	Stringer	Don Johnson	Johnson
SS-Bobby Sturgeon	Lennie Merullo	Merullo	Billy Jurges
3B-Stan Hack	Hack	Hack	Hack
OF-Bill Nicholson	Nicholson	Nicholson	Cavarretta
OF-Phil Cavarretta	Dallessandro	Andy Pafko	Lowery
OF-Dom Dallessandro	Lou Novikoff	Peanuts Lowrey	Marv Rickert
CA-Clyde McCullough	McCullough	Mickey Livingston	McCullough
PI-Claude Passeau	Passeau	Hank Wyse	Johnny Schmitz
PI-Vern Olson	Lee	Paul Derringer	Hank Borowy
PI-Bill Lee	Olson	Passeau	Wyse
PI-Larry French	Hi Bithorn	Ray Prim	Passeau

Players Who Lost Their Starting Positions

SS-Lennie Merullo— Hit .218 in 499 at-bats his last two major league seasons in 1946 and 1947.

OF-Bill Nicholson— Slumped to .220 the year after his great war years run in 1946 and was never quite able to recapture the magic he had between

1942 and 1945. Played with the Cubs and Phils until 1953, his best season being in 1947 with Chicago when he hit 26 homers.

OF-Andy Pafko— Had a nice long career after the war until 1959 with the Cubs, Dodgers and Braves. His best season was 1950 hitting 36 homers, 92 RBIs and a .304 average for Chicago. Did not start in 1946 as he broke both his arm and his ankle.

CA-Mickey Livingston— Spent his career after the war until 1951 with the Cubs, Giants, Braves and Dodgers as a backup catcher.

PI-Paul Derringer— Had a great 15-year career in which he was 223–212 that ended after his 16–11 campaign with the Cubs in 1945.

PI-Ray Prim— Prim was out of the majors since 1935 when the Cubs came calling in 1943. He would pitch in one postwar campaign of 1946, going 2–3 with the Cubs.

1946 Boston Braves
81–72–15.5 GB

1941	1942	1945	1946
1B-Buddy Hassett	West	Vince Shupe	Ray Sanders
2B-Bama Rowell	Sisti	Whitey Wietelmann	Connie Ryan
SS-Eddie Miller	Miller	Dick Culler	Culler
3B-Sibby Sisti	Nanny Fernandez	Chuck Workman	Fernandez
OF-Gene Moore	Paul Waner	Holmes	Holmes
OF-John Cooney	Tommy Holmes	Carden Gillenwater	Gillenwater
OF-Max West	Chet Ross	Butch Nieman	Bama Rowell
CA-Ray Berres	Ernie Lombardi	Phil Masi	Masi
PI-Manny Salvo	Javery	Tobin	Johnny Sain
PI-Jim Tobin	Tobin	Bob Logan	Mort Cooper
PI-Al Javery	Lou Tost	Nate Andrews	Ed Wright
PI-Art Johnson	Tom Earley	Javery	Bill Lee

Players Who Lost Their Starting Positions

1B-Vince Shupe— Would play in only one major league campaign in 1945.

2B-Whitey Wietelmann— Hit .223 in 206 at-bats for the Braves and Pirates in 1946 and 1947.

3B-Chuck Workman— Played with the Braves and Pirates in his only postwar season of 1946, hitting .207 in 193 at-bats.

OF-Butch Nieman— After a three-year war season career did not play following the 1945 campaign.

PI-Jim Tobin— A star for the Braves who not only hit 3 homers in a game in 1942, but threw two no-hitters in 1944. Was done in the majors after the 1945 season as he was traded to Detroit in midseason. Finished with a career 105–112 record, the majority, 57–73, coming during the war years with poor Boston Brave teams.

PI-Bob Logan—Had been out of the majors since 1941, when the Braves picked him up for the 1945 season, his last one in the show.

PI-Nate Andrews—Andrews won 37 of his lifetime 41 games during the war years. He would pitch in one postwar season, 1946, going 3–4 for the Giants and Reds.

PI-Al Javery—Winning 41 of his career 51 wins during the war years, Javery went 0–1 for the Braves in 1946, ending his stay in the big leagues.

1946 Philadelphia Phillies
69–85–28 GB

1941	1942	1945	1946
1B-Nick Etten	Etten	Jimmy Wasdell	Frank McCormick
2B-Danny Murtaugh	Al Glossup	Fred Daniels	Emil Verban
SS-Bobby Bragan	Bragan	Bitsy Mott	Skeeter Newsome
3B-Pinky May	May	John Antonelli	Jim Tabor
OF-Stan Benjamin	Ron Northey	Vance Dinges	Northey
OF-Joe Marty	Lloyd Waner	Vince DiMaggio	Johnny Wyrostek
OF-Danny Litwhiler	Litwhiler	Coaker Triplett	Del Ennis
CA-Bennie Warren	Warren	Andy Seminick	Seminick
PI-Cy Blanton	Hughes	Dick Barrett	Oscar Judd
PI-Johnny Podgajny	Rube Melton	Charley Schanz	Ken Raffensberger
PI-Tommy Hughes	Johnson	Charlie Sproull	Schoolboy Rowe
PI-Si Johnson	Podgajny	Dick Mauney	Schanz

Players Who Lost Their Starting Positions

1B-Jimmy Wasdell—The 11-year vet spent 1946 with the Phillies and Indians, hitting .261 in 92 at-bats. 1947 would be his last season, accumulating 1 hitless at-bat with Cleveland.

2B-Fred Daniels—Played in only one major league season in 1945.

SS-Bitsy Mott—Like Daniels, Mott played only in 1945.

3B-John Antonelli—Antonelli would not return to the majors after 1945.

OF-Vance Dinges—Although Dinges would hit a nice .308 in 104 at-bats, they would be his last 108 major league at-bats.

OF-Vince DiMaggio—The war years star would hit only .091 in 44 at-bats for the Phils and Giants in 1946, his last big league season.

OF-Coaker Triplett—Did not play in the show after 1945.

PI-Dick Barrett—He had been out of the majors since 1934, when he came on with the Cubs in 1943. He did not play again after losing 20 for the Phils in 1945.

PI-Charlie Sproull— Pitched in only one major league season in 1945.

PI-Dick Mauney— Was 6–4 with a nice 2.70 ERA before pitching in his last season in 1947.

1946 Cincinatti Reds
67–87–30 GB

1941	1942	1945	1946
1B-Frank McCormick	McCormick	McCormick	Haas
2B-Lonny Frey	Frey	Woody Williams	Bobby Adams
SS-Eddie Joost	Joost	Eddie Miller	Miller
3B-Bill Werber	Bert Haas	Steve Mesner	Grady Hatton
OF-Jim Gleeson	Max Marshall	Al Libke	Libke
OF-Harry Craft	Gee Walker	Dain Clay	Clay
OF-Mike McCormick	Eric Tipton	Tipton	Eddie Lukon
CA-Ernie Lombardi	Ray Lamanno	Al Lakeman	Ray Mueller
PI-Bucky Walters	Vander Meer	Ed Heusser	Vander Meer
PI-Johnny Vander Meer	Ray Starr	Joe Bowman	Ewell Blackwell
PI-Paul Derringer	Walters	Walters	Walters
PI-Elmer Riddle	Derringer	Vern Kennedy	Ed Beggs

Players Who Lost Their Starting Positions

1B-Frank McCormick— McCormick was sold to the Phils for $30,000 in 1946 and started in Philadelphia, hitting .284 with 11 homers. He played only two more seasons in a part time role with the Phillies and Braves.

2B-Woody Williams— Came up with the Dodgers in 1938 and did not play in the majors again until the Reds picked him up in 1943. Did not play after the 1945 season.

3B-Steve Mesner— His career, which was mainly during the war years, ended after 1945.

OF-Eric Tipton— Was a three-year starter for the Reds in the war years and did not return to play in the postwar era.

CA-Al Lakeman— Played in three abbreviated seasons for the Reds, Phillies and Braves between 1946 and 1949 hitting .156 in 288 at-bats. He came back in 1954 going hitless in 6 at-bats for the Tigers.

PI-Ed Heusser— Pitched in two postwar seasons. Went 7–14 with the Reds in 1946 with a 3.22 ERA before a 3–2 mark with the Phillies in 1948.

PI-Joe Bowman— Had been out of the majors since 1941 when he signed with the Braves in '44. Did not return after 1945.

PI-Vern Kennedy— His 12-year career ended after 1945 with a 104–132 record.

1946 Pittsburgh Pirates
63–91–34 GB

1941	*1942*	*1945*	*1946*
1B-Elbie Fletcher	Fletcher	Babe Dahlgren	Fletcher
2B-Frank Gustine	Gustine	Coscarart	Gustine
SS-Arky Vaughan	Pete Coscarart	Gustine	Billy Cox
3B-Lee Handley	Elliott	Elliott	Handley
OF-Bob Elliott	Johnny Barrett	Barrett	Elliott
OF-Vince DiMaggio	DiMaggio	Al Gionfriddo	Russell
OF-Maurice Van Robays	Jimmy Wasdell	Jim Russell	Ralph Kiner
CA-Al Lopez	Lopez	Lopez	Lopez
PI-Rip Sewell	Sewell	Preacher Roe	Fritz Ostermueller
PI-Max Butcher	Bob Klinger	Nick Strincevich	Heintzelman
PI-Ken Heintzelman	Heintzelman	Sewell	Strincevich
PI-Johnny Lanning	Butcher	Butcher	Sewell

Players Who Lost Their Starting Positions

1B Babe Dahlgren— Hit .175 in 80 at-bats for the Browns in 1946 to end his 12-year career.

2B-Pete Coscarart— The Bucs' last remaining piece of the Arky Vaughan trade in 1942. Would be hitless in 2 at-bats for the Bucs in 1946, his last major league season.

OF-Johnny Barrett— Hit .193 in 114 at-bats for the Pirates and Braves in his last season in the show in 1946.

OF-Al Gionfriddo— Although he only batted .224 in 165 postwar at-bats in 1946 and 1947, he saved his most enduring moment for last as he made a magnificent catch costing Joe DiMaggio a homer and the Yankees the game in the 1947 Fall Classic prompting DiMaggio to show his rare yet classic moment of disgust.[2]

PI-Preacher Roe— Roe was one of the few war years players that actually had much more success after the war than during. After a 4–15 debacle for the 1947 Bucs, Roe went to Brooklyn with Billy Cox and Gene Mauch for Dixie Walker, Hal Gregg and Vic Lombardi. He would become a central cog in the National League dynasty of the Dodgers including a 22–3 season in 1951. Unfortunately he left the majors in 1954, a year before the Bums finally won their long awaited title.

PI-Max Butcher— Butcher's 10-year career ended after the war years in 1945.

1946 New York Giants
61–93–36 GB

1941	*1942*	*1945*	*1946*
1B-Babe Young	Johnny Mize	Phil Weintraub	Mize
2B-Burgess Whitehead	Mike Witek	George Hausmann	Buddy Blattner
SS-Billy Jurges	Jurges	Buddy Kerr	Kerr
3B-Dick Bartell	Bill Werber	Nap Reyes	Bill Rigney
OF-Mel Ott	Ott	Ott	Goody Rosen
OF-Johnny Rucker	Willard Marshall	Rucker	Marshall
OF-Jo-Jo Moore	Babe Barna	Danny Gardella	Sid Gordon
CA-Harry Danning	Danning	Ernie Lombardi	Walker Cooper
PI-Hal Schumacher	Schumacher	Bill Voiselle	Dave Koslo
PI-Cliff Melton	Bob Carpenter	Harold Feldman	Monte Kennedy
PI-Carl Hubbell	Hubbell	Van Lingle Mungo	Voiselle
PI-Bill Lohrman	Lohrman	Jack Brewer	Ken Trinkle

Players Who Lost Their Starting Positions

1B-Phil Weintraub— Had been out of the majors since 1938 when the Giants signed for the 1944 and 1945 seasons, his last two in the show.

2B-George Hausmann— Played in only one postwar season in 1945, hitting .128 in 47 at-bats for the Giants in 1949.

3B-Nap Reyes— Went hitless in his one post war at-bat in 1950.

OF-Mel Ott— After hanging on through the war years to help out the team, the Giants player-manager reduced his time after the war going only 5 for 72 (.069 average) ending his 22 year Hall of Fame career in 1947.

OF-Johnny Rucker— Rucker hit .264 in 95 games for the Giants in his only season in the postwar era of 1946.

OF-Danny Gardella— Gardella's post war career mirrored teammate Nap Reyes as he also went hitless in one at-bat in 1950, his only postwar season.

CA-Ernie Lombardi— The Hall of Fame catcher would end his 16-year major league career in 1947, hitting .287 in 348 at-bats and 16 homers in his two postwar seasons of 1946 and 1947.

PI-Harold Feldman— After spending all but 3 games of his career in the war years, Feldman went 0–2 in 1946, ending his stay in the big leagues.

PI-Van Lingle Mungo— His 14-season career in the majors ended with the culmination of the war years in 1945 with a 120–115 mark.

PI-Jack Brewer— Brewer would pitch only one game in the majors in 1946 ending his time in the show.

Negro League Players
Who Served in World War II

This section is comprised of players taken from a list found on Gary Bedingfield's Baseball in Wartime Bibliography web site: *http://baseballinwartime.freeservers.com/bibliography.htm.*

The list is broken down by team, which are listed in alphabetical order in the National and American Leagues with the players put on the team they were part of when they were called into service. Included with the players are the teams they played for in their career, taken from the book *The Biographical Encyclopedia of the Negro Baseball Leagues* by James A. Riley, and pertinent career stats if they played in the majors. If career stats in the Negro Leagues are mentioned, the information comes from *The Complete Book of Baseball's Negro Leagues* by John Holway. If a player made the major leagues, his minor league teams will not be mentioned.

The Negro American League

BIRMINGHAM BLACK BARONS

CA-Paul Hardy— Played for the Montgomery Grey Sox, 1931-32, the Detroit Stars, 1933, the Nashville Elite Giants, 1934, the Columbus Elite Giants, 1935, the Washington Elite Giants, 1936, the Chicago American Giants, 1937-38, 1951-52, the Kansas City Monarchs, 1939, 1942, the Birmingham Black Barons, 1940-43, the Memphis Red Sox, 1947. Played for the Harlem Globetrotters in 1947. Served in the Army.

1B-Lyman Bostock— Played for the Brooklyn Royal Giants, 1938-39, the Birmingham Black Barons, 1940–46, the Chicago American Giants,

1947, 1949, the New York Cubans, 1948, Guaymas in the Mexican League, 1948, Winnipeg and Carman in the minor leagues, 1950–54. Father of Lyman Bostock Jr., who played in the major leagues in the 70's and was shot to death by his wife in 1978. Hit .341 for his Negro League career. Served in the Army.

1B-Joe Scott— Played for the Detroit Senators, 1946, the Birmingham Black Barons, 1947–49, the Chicago American Giants, 1950. Served in the Army's 350th Field Artillery that fought in France. Arrived six days after the D-Day invasion.

PI-Dan Bankhead— Played for the Chicago American Giants, 1940, the Birmingham Black Barons, 1940-42, the Memphis Red Sox, 1946-47, the Brooklyn Dodgers, 1947, 1950-51, the Mexican Leagues, 1954–65. Was 9–5 with a 6.52 ERA in three major league seasons, all but one loss occurring in 1950. Served in the Marines.

PI-Nat Pollard— Played for the Birmingham Black Barons, 1943, 1946–50. Served in the Navy.

CHICAGO AMERICAN GIANTS

CA-Lonnie Summers— Played for the Baltimore Elite Giants, 1938, Tampico and the Mexico City Reds of the Mexican League, 1946-47, 1949, the Chicago American Giants, 1948-49, 1951, Caracus in the Venezuelan League, 1950, San Diego, Boise and Yakima in the minor leagues, 1952–56. Best year in minors was 1954 where he hit .312 at Yakima. Served in the Army.

OF-Jimmy Crutchfield— Played for the Birmingham Black Barons, 1930, the Indianapolis ABC's, 1931, the Pittsburgh Crawfords, 1931–36, the Philadelphia Stars, 1933, the Newark Eagles, 1937-38, the Toledo Crawfords, 1939, the Indianapolis Crawfords, 1940, the Chicago American Giants, 1941–45, the Cleveland Buckeyes, 1944. Was sometimes referred to as the Black Lloyd Waner. Served in the Army.

CLEVELAND BUCKEYES

2B-Billy Horne— Played for the American Giants, 1938–41, the Cincinnati Buckeyes, 1942, the Harrisburg-St. Louis Stars, 1943, the Cleveland Buckeyes, 1943–46, the minor Leagues, 1951. Served in the Army.

3B-Andy "Big Six" Watts— Played for the Cleveland Buckeyes, 1946, the Birmingham Black Barons, 1950, the Indianapolis Clowns, 1952. Served in the Navy where he played for the Great Lakes Naval team in 1944.

PI-Sam Barber— Played for the Birmingham Black Barons, 1940-1941, the Cleveland Clippers, 1946, the Cleveland Buckeyes, 1942, 1946–1950. Served in the Army.

PI-Jim Bolden— Played for the Cleveland Buckeyes, 1946, the Birmingham Black Barons, 1947, 1952, the Chattanooga Choo Choos, 1948, The New Orleans Creoles, 1949, the Brooklyn Cuban Giants, 1950, the Elmwood Giants of the Mandak League in the minor leagues. Served in the Army.

PI-Herb Bracken— Played for the St. Louis Stars, 1940, the Cleveland Buckeyes, 1946-47. Served in the Navy where he pitched for the Great Lakes Naval Base in 1944 and was 13–1.

PI-Willie Jefferson— Played for the Claybrook Tigers, 1936, the Cincinnati Tigers, 1937, the Memphis Red Sox, 1938-39, Monterrey of the Mexican League, 1940, the Cincinnati Buckeyes, 1942, the Cleveland Buckeyes, 1943–46, the minor leagues, 1951. Served in the Army.

INDIANAPOLIS CLOWNS

CA-Leonard "Fatty" Pigg— Played for the Indianapolis Clowns, 1947–49, 1951, the Cleveland Buckeyes, 1950, Brandon of the Canadian League, 1950, the Canadian League, 1952–54. The Chicago White Sox tried to sign him in 1951 and wanted to send him to the minors, but Pigg opted to go back to Indianapolis. Served in the Army in the Philippines.

OF-Fred Wilson— Played for Miami, 1934–37, the Ethiopian Clowns, 1938–42, the New York Black Yankees, 1938, the Newark Eagles, 1939-40, the Cincinnati Clowns, 1943, the Cincinnati-Indianapolis Clowns, 1945. Served in the Army.

PI-Jim Cohen— Played for the Indianapolis Clowns, 1946–52. Served in the Army.

PI-Leo "Preacher" Henry— Played for the Jacksonville Red Caps, 1938, 1941-42, the Cleveland Bears, 1939-40, the Cincinnati Clowns, 1940, the Indianapolis Clowns, 1946-47, 1951. Served in the Army.

KANSAS CITY MONARCHS

CA-Joe Greene— Played with the Atlanta Black Crackers, 1932–38, the Homestead Grays, 1939, The Kansas City Monarchs 1939–47, the Cleveland Buckeyes, 1948, Elmwood in the minor leagues, 1951, where he hit .301. Served with the Army's 92nd division in Algiers and Italy, being decorated for his time in combat. His company was responsible for tearing down the dead body of Mussolini in Italy.

1B-Hank Thompson— Played in the Negro Leagues with the Kansas City Monarchs, 1943–48, Tampico of the Mexican League, 1945, the St. Louis Browns and the New York Giants in the major leagues between 1947–56 where he hit .267 in 3,003 at-bats. Served in the Army.

1B-Buck O'Neill— Played with the Miami Giants, 1934, the New York Tigers, 1935, the Shreveport Acme Giants, 1936, the Memphis Red Sox, 1937, the Zulu Cannibal Giants, 1937 and the Kansas City Monarchs, 1938–55. Was a manager with the Monarchs also as well as becoming the first black coach in major league history in 1962 with the Cubs. Served in the Navy.

SS-Jackie Robinson— Played with the Kansas City Monarchs in 1945 and the Brooklyn Dodgers 1947–56. Became the first Negro League player to be signed by the major leagues. Hit .311 in 10 major league seasons with

Buck O'Neill was not only a great first baseman for the Kansas City Monarchs, he also was a successful manager for them. Buck would become the first African American coach in the majors with the Cubs in 1962.

1,518 hits. Was elected to the Hall of Fame in 1962, the first African-American to be so honored. Had the ultimate honor of having his number retired by every major league team in 1997. Served in the Army where he was attempted to be court marshaled after refusing to go to the back of the bus.

SS-Alan "Lefty" Bryant— Played for the All-Nations team, 1937–38, the Memphis Red Sox, 1937 and 1940, the Kansas City Monarchs 1939–41, 1943, 1945–47, the Edmonton Eskimos of the Canadian League, 1948–49. Served in the Army where he achieved the rank of sergeant.

SS-Jesse Williams— Played for the Kansas City Monarchs, 1939–47, 1951, St. Louis of the Mexican League, 1946, the Indianapolis Clowns, 1948–50, Vancouver and Beaumont in the minor leagues, 1952–54. Was the player who moved to second, allowing Jackie Robinson to play short in 1945. Served in the Army.

OF-Willard "Home Run" Brown— Played for the Monroe Monarchs, 1934, the Kansas City Monarchs 1935–1943 and 1946–1951, the Mexican League in 1940, the St. Louis Browns in 1947 where he hit .179 in 67 at-bats, Ottawa, Topeka and Dallas in the minor leagues, 1950, 1953–1956. One of the Negro League greats who never quite lived up to his potential. A career .347 hitter in the Negro Leagues. Served in the Army.

OF-Ted Strong— Played for the Indianapolis A's, 1937, the Indianapolis ABCs, 1938, Nuevo Laredo of the Mexican League, 1940, the Kansas City Monarchs 1937–47, the Indianapolis Clowns, 1948, Minot of the Mandak League in the minors where he hit .236 in 1950, the Chicago American Giants, 1951. Hit .351 in his Negro League career. An original member of the Harlem Globetrotters. Served in the Army.

PI-John Ford Smith— Played for the Chicago American Giants, 1939, the Indianapolis Crawfords, 1940, the Kansas City Monarchs, 1941–48, Jersey City, Drummondville, Phoenix and El Paso in the minor leagues, 1949–54. Served in the Army Air Corps and became a lieutenant.

PI-Connie Johnson— Played for the Indianapolis Crawfords, 1940, the Kansas City Monarchs, 1941–1950, St. Hyacinthe in the Canadian League, 1951, the Chicago White Sox and the Baltimore Orioles, 1953, 1955–58 where he had a career record of 40–39 with a 3.44 ERA. His best major league season was in 1957 with Baltimore when he was 14–11 with a 3.20 ERA in 30 starts. Also played with Puebla in the Mexican League, 1961. Served in the Army.

MEMPHIS RED SOX

1B-Olan "Jelly" Taylor— Played for the Birmingham Black Barons, 1934, the Pittsburgh Crawfords, 1935, the Cincinnati Tigers, 1936-37, the Memphis Red Sox, 1938–46. Served in Army, one of the first to be drafted from the Negro Leagues.

PI-Robert Sharpe— Played for the Chicago American Giants, 1941, Chicago Brown Bombers, 1943, the Memphis Red Sox 1944–48. Served in the Army.

The Negro National League

BALTIMORE ELITE GIANTS

CA-Henry Frazier Robinson— Played for the Kansas City Monarchs, 1942-43, the New York Black Yankees, 1943, the Baltimore Greys, 1942, the Baltimore Elite Giants, 1943–50. Served in the Navy.

INF-Frank Russell— Played for the Baltimore Elite Giants, 1943–49. Served in the Army.

1B-Lamb "Bud" Barbee— Played for the Baltimore Elite Giants, 1943, the Louisville Buckeyes, 1949, the Kansas City Monarchs, 1949, St. Jean and Granby of the Canadian League, 1949–51, 1954, Minot, Pampa and Texas City of the minor leagues, 1952–55. Served in the Army.

1B-Clint "Butch" McCord— Played for the Nashville Cubs, 1946, the Nashville Black Vols, 1947, the Baltimore Elite Giants, 1948–50, the Chicago American Giants, 1950, Paris, Denver, Richmond, Columbus, Louisville, Macon, Victoria and St. Paul in the minor leagues, 1951–61. Won two batting titles in the minors and two silver gloves. Served in the Army.

1B-James "Red" Moore— Played for the Chattanooga Choo Choos, 1935, the Mohawk Giants, 1936, the Atlanta Black Crackers, 1935, 1938, the Newark Eagles, 1936-37, 1940,Indianapolis ABCs, 1939, the Baltimore Elite Giants, 1939–40. Served in the Army in the European Theater with the combat engineers that were part of General Patton's Third Army.

1B-Johnny Washington— Played for the Montgomery Grey Sox, 1933, the Birmingham Black Barons, 1934, the Pittsburgh Crawfords, 1936–38, the New York Black Yankees, 1938–40, the Baltimore Elite Giants, 1941–48, the Houston Eagles, 1949-50, the New Orleans Eagles, 1951. Served in the Army.

2B-Sammy T Hughes— Played for the Louisville White Sox, 1929–31, the Washington Pilots, 1932, the Nashville Elite Giants, 1936-37, the Baltimore Elite Giants, 1938–40, 1942–46, Torreon of the Mexican League, 1941. Served in the Army with the 196th Support Battalion, which was part of the invasion of New Guinea.

OF-Jimmy Zapp— Played for the Baltimore Elite Giants, 1945-46, 1950-51, 1954, the Nashville Cubs, 1946, the Atlanta Black Crackers, 1947, the Birmingham Black Barons, 1948, 1950, Paris, Danville, Lincoln, Big Springs and Port Arthur in the minor leagues, 1952–55. His best minor league season was 1954 with Big Springs when he hit .311 with 29 homers. Served in the Navy.

PI-Bill Barnes— Played for the Baltimore Elite Giants, 1941-42, 1946, the Memphis Red Sox, 1943, the Indianapolis Clowns, 1947. Served in the Army.

PI-Joe Black— Played for the Baltimore Elite Giants 1943–50, the Brooklyn Dodgers, 1952–55, the Cincinnati Reds, 1955-56, the Washington Senators, 1957. Was 30–12 in his major league career, a .714 winning percentage. His best season was his rookie year in 1952 when he was 15–4 with 15 saves and a 2.15 ERA. He was third in winning percentage that season at .789 and third in the MVP race. Won Rookie of the Year in 1952 and became the first Negro League pitcher to win a World Series game in the majors. Served in the Army.

PI-Jonas Gaines— Played with the Newark Eagles, 1937, the Washington Elite Giants, 1937, the Baltimore Elite Giants, 1932–48, Vera Cruz in the Mexican League, 1940, the Philadelphia Stars, 1949-50, Minot, Pampa, Bismarck and Carlsbad in the minor leagues, 1951-52, 1954–57, the Japanese League, 1953. Served in the Army.

PI-Bill Harvey— Played for the Memphis Red Sox, 1931–33, the Cleveland Giants, 1933, the Pittsburgh Crawfords, 1933–38, the Cleveland Red Sox, 1934, the Toledo Crawfords, 1939, the Indianapolis Crawfords, 1939, Monterrey and Tampico of the Mexican League, 1940-41, the Baltimore Elite Giants, 1942–47, Youngstown of the Mid-Atlantic League, in 1950 where he was 5–10 in his only minor league season. Was in Mexico when the FBI went searching for him to bring him back to the Army. Joined the Giants after he was escorted home.

PI-Robert Romby— Played for the Baltimore Elite Giants, 1946–50. Served in the Army.

HOMESTEAD GRAYS

2B-Matthew "Lick" Carlisle— Played for the Birmingham Black Barons, 1931, the Montgomery Grey Sox, 1932, the Memphis Red Sox, 1933, the

New Orleans Crescent Star 1934, the Homestead Grays, 1935–46. Served in the Navy.

3B-Howard Easterling— Played for the Cincinnati Tigers, 1936-37, the Chicago American Giants, 1938, the Homestead Grays, 1940–47, the New York Cubans, 1949, Monterrey of the Mexican League, 1951, 1953. An important part of the championship Gray teams during the time period. Hit .311 in his Negro League career. Served in the Army.

3B-Clarence "Pint" Israel— Played for the Newark Eagles, 1940–42, 1946, the Homestead Grays, 1943–45, 1947. Served in the Army.

OF-Bob Thurman— Played for the Homestead Grays, 1946–48, the Kansas City Monarchs, 1949, the Cincinnati Reds, 1955–59, where he hit .246 in 663 major league at-bats. His best season was 1956 when he hit .295 with 8 homers in 139 at-bats.

OF-David "Speed" Whatley— Played for the Birmingham Black Barons, 1936–38, the Memphis Red Sox, 1938, the Jacksonville Red Caps, 1939, the Cleveland Bears, 1939, the Homestead Grays, 1939–44, the New York Black Yankees, 1944–45, the Pittsburgh Crawfords, 1946. Served in the Army.

Wilmer Fields was a fine player with the Homestead Grays for 11 years before winning 3 MVP awards with Brantford of the Canadian League.

OF-Frank Williams— Played for the Homestead Grays, 1942–46, Served in the Army.

PI-Garnett Blair— Played for the Homestead Grays, 1942–48, the Richmond Giants, 1949–52, Richmond in the Piedmont League, 1953, where he did not have a decision in his only minor league season.

PI-Wilmer "Red" Fields— Played for the Homestead Grays, 1940–50, Brantford of the Canadian League, 1951, 1953–55, Toronto and Fort Wayne in the minor leagues, the Mexico City Reds of the Mexican League, 1958. Also played every other position on the field but first. Was a 3-time MVP while playing at Brantford. Hit .299 at Toronto. Served in the Army.

PI-Jerry Gibson— Played with the Homestead Grays, 1934, the

Cincinnati Tigers, 1936, 1940, 1943. Also played in the outfield. Served in the Army.

PI-Roy Welmaker— Played for the Atlanta Black Crackers, 1930, 1933–1935, the Macon Black Peaches, 1931-32, the Homestead Grays, 1936–39, 1942–45, The Toledo Crawfords, 1939, the Philadelphia Stars, 1939-40, Torreon in the Mexican League, 1940-41, Vargas and Maracaibo, the Venzuelan League, 1946–48, Wilkes-Barre, San Diego, Hollywood and Portland in the minor leagues 1949–53. Served in the Army.

PI-Johnny Wright— Played for the Newark Eagles, 1937-38, the Atlanta Black Crackers, 1938, the Pittsburgh Crawfords, 1938, the Toledo Crawfords, 1939, the Indianapolis Crawfords, 1940, the Homestead Grays, 1941–45, 1947-48, Montreal and Three Rivers in the minor leagues, 1946. He played with Jackie Robinson in Montreal, only lasting 2 games before he was sent to Three Rivers where he was 12–8. Served in the Navy where he pitched for the Great Lakes Naval team.

NEWARK EAGLES

CA-Charlie Parks— Played for the New York Black Yankees, 1939, the Newark Eagles, 1941–47. Served as a sergeant in the Army where he won three Bronze Stars.

CA-Leon Ruffin— Played for the Brooklyn Eagles, 1935, the Newark Eagles, 1936, 1939, 1942–46, the Pittsburgh Crawfords, 1937-38, the Toledo Crawfords, 1939, Philadelphia Stars, 1939-40, Torreon of the Mexican League, 1940-41, Mexican League 1947-48, the Houston Eagles 1949-50. Served in the Navy.

INF-Larry Doby— Played for the Newark Eagles, 1942–47, the Cleveland Indians, 1947–55, 1958, the Chicago White Sox 1956-57, 1959, the Detroit Tigers 1959, Japanese League 1962. The first player from the Negro League to play in the American League. Was one of four players to participate in the World Series in both the Negro Leagues and major leagues. Hit .283 in his career with 1,515 hits and 253 homers. Best year was in 1954 when he finished second in the MVP vote leading the AL in both homers, 32, and RBIs at 126. Was a career .384 hitter in the Negro Leagues. Managed the White Sox in 1978. Elected to the Hall of Fame in 1998. Served in the Navy.

SS-Earl Richardson— Played for the Newark Eagles in 1943. Served in the Navy.

OF-Russell Awkard— Played for the New York Cubans, 1940, the Newark Eagles, 1940-41. Served in the Army's Quartermaster Corps.

OF-*Monte Irvin*— Played for the Newark Eagles, 1937–48, Vera Cruz of the Mexican League, 1942, the New York Giants, 1949–55, the Chicago Cubs, 1956. Hit .293 with 99 homers in 2,499 at-bats in the majors. Finished third in the 1951 MVP race, leading the league in RBIs with 121 while hitting .312 and smacking a career best 24 homers. One of four players to play in the World Series in both the Negro Leagues and major leagues. Was a lifetime .345 hitter in the Negro Leagues. Elected to the Hall of Fame in 1973. Served in the Army Engineers.

OF-*Wilmore Williams*— Played for the Newark Eagles, 1943. Served in the Navy.

PI-*James Brown*— Played for the Newark Eagles, 1939, 1941–43, 1948, the Indianapolis Clowns, 1947. Served in the Army.

Monte Irvin, who hit .345 in his Negro League career with the Newark Eagles and .293 in his major league career, primarily with the Giants, was elected to the Hall of Fame in 1973.

PI-*Leon Day*— Played for the Baltimore Black Sox, 1934, the Brooklyn Eagles, 1935, the Newark Eagles, 1936–39, 1941–46, Vargas in the Venezuelan League, 1940, Vera Cruz in the Mexican League, 1940, Mexico City Reds in the Mexican League, 1947-48, the Baltimore Elite Giants, 1949-50, the Toronto Maple Leafs, the Scranton Miners, the Edmonton Eskimos, and Brandon in the minor leagues, 1950–54. Had a 68–30 career Negro League mark. Served in the Army where he landed on Utah Beach during D-Day. Elected to the Hall of Fame in 1995.

PI-*Jim Elam*— Played for the Newark Eagles, 1943. Served in the Army.

PI-*Rufus Lewis*— Played for the Pittsburgh Crawfords, 1936-37, the Newark Eagles, 1946–48, the Houston Eagles, 1949-50, Mexico City of the Mexican Leagues, 1950–52, Chihuahua of the Arizona-Texas League, 1952. Served in the Army Air Corps.

PI-Max Manning— Played for the Newark Eagles, 1938–48, the Houston Eagles, 1949, Torreon in the Mexican League, 1951, Sherbrooke and Branford of the Canadian League, 1951. Was 70–32 in his Negro League career. Served in the Army 101st Airborne Division.

NEW YORK CUBANS

PI-Tom Parker— Played for the Memphis Red Sox, 1929, the Indianapolis ABCs, 1931, the Monroe Monarchs, 1934, the Nashville Elite Giants, 1934, the Homestead Grays, 1935–39, 1948, the Indianapolis Athletics, 1937, the Toledo Crawfords, 1939, the New Orleans-St. Louis Stars, 1943, the New York Cubans, 1945, the Birmingham Black Barons, 1945, the Boston Blues, 1946, the Detroit Senators, 1947, the Mandak League of the minor leagues, 1951–53. Best minor league season was in 1951 when he was 5–2. Served in the Army.

PI-Johnny "Schoolboy" Taylor— Played for the New York Cubans, 1935–38, 1940, 1942, 1945, the Pittsburgh Crawfords, 1938, the Toledo Crawfords, 1939, Cordoba and Vera Cruz of the Mexican League, 1939–41, 1945-46, Hartford in the minor leagues, 1949. Was 6–7 in his only minor league season with a 3.39 ERA. Threw a no-hitter in 1937 for the National League All-Stars against Satchel Paige and his team of stars. Served in the Army.

NEW YORK BLACK YANKEES

CA-Johnny Hayes— Played for the Newark Dodgers, 1934-35, the Newark Eagles, 1936–39, the New York Black Yankees, 1940–48, the Pittsburgh Crawfords, 1946, the Boston Blues, 1946, the Baltimore Elite Giants, 1949–51, Hartford in the minor leagues, 1952. Hit .357 at Hartford. Served in the Army.

CA-Josh Johnson— Played for the Homestead Grays, 1934-35, 1938–42, the New York Black Yankees, 1938, 1942, the Cincinnati Tigers, 1935–37, the Brooklyn Royal Giants, 1939. Served in the Army becoming a second lieutenant. Later became a major while serving in the Army Reserves.

2B-Dickie Seay— Played for the Philadelphia Giants, 1924, the Pennsylvania Red Caps of New York, 1925, the Brooklyn Royal Giants, 1925, 1927–31, the Newark Stars, 1926, the Baltimore Black Sox, 1926, 1932-33, the Newark Browns, 1931, the Philadelphia Stars, 1934–36, the Pittsburgh Crawfords, 1935-36, the New York Black Yankees, 1936, 1941–47, the Newark Eagles, 1937–40. Considered the Bill Mazeroski of his day when it came to defensive second baseman, one of the best of all time. Was a valuable member of the 1935 world championship Pittsburgh Crawfords team, considered one of the greatest Negro League teams of all time if not one of the greatest in all of baseball. Served in the Army.

SS-Curtis Henderson— Played for the Homestead Grays, 1936, the New York Black Yankees, 1937, 1942, the Washington Black Senators, 1938, the Toledo Crawfords, 1939, the Indianapolis Crawfords, 1940, the Philadelphia Stars, 1941, the American Giants, 1941. Served in the Army.

3B-Spencer Davis— Played for the Jacksonville Red Caps, 1937, the Atlanta Black Crackers, 1938, the Indianapolis ABCs, 1939, the New York Black Yankees, 1940–42. Served in the Army.

PI-Bob Griffith— Played for the Nashville Elite Giants, 1933-34, the Columbus Elite Giants, 1935, the Washington Elite Giants, 1936-37, the Baltimore Elite Giants, 1938, 1941, Nuevo Laredo of the Mexican League, 1940, the New York Black Yankees, 1942–48, the Kansas City Monarchs, 1946, the Philadelphia Stars, 1949–51, the Indianapolis Clowns, 1952, Granby and Brandon of the Canadian League, 1951, 1953. Best minor league season was with Brandon when he was 8–5 in 1953. Served in the Army in the European theater where he became a corporal.

PI-Gene Smith— Played for the Atlanta Black Crackers, 1938, Monterrey of the Mexican League, 1939, the Ethiopian Clowns, 1939, the St. Louis Stars, 1939, the New Orleans-St. Louis Stars, 1940-41, the Kansas City Monarchs, 1941, the New York Black Yankees, 1942, the Pittsburgh Crawfords, 1946, the Homestead Grays, 1946-47, the Cleveland Buckeyes, 1947-48, 1950, the Louisville Buckeyes, 1949, the Chicago American Giants, 1949–51. Served in the Army.

PHILADELPHIA STARS

CA-Bill Cooper— Played for the Atlanta Black Crackers, 1938, the Philadelphia Stars, 1939–42, the New York Black Yankees, 1946. Served in the Army.

CA-Bill Perkins— Played for the Birmingham Black Barons, 1928–30, the Cleveland Cubs, 1931, the Pittsburgh Crawfords, 1931–36, the Cleveland Stars, 1932, the Philadelphia Stars, 1938-39, 1946-47, the Baltimore Elite Giants, 1940, 1947-48, the New York Black Yankees, 1945-46. Served in the Army.

INF-Mahlon Duckett— Played for the Philadelphia Stars, 1940–49, the Homestead Grays, 1949-50. Served in the Army.

SS-James "Bus" Clarkson— Played for the Pittsburgh Crawfords, 1937-38, the Toledo Crawfords, 1939, the Indianapolis Crawfords, 1940, the Newark Eagles, 1940, 1942, Tampico and Vera Cruz of the Mexican League,

1941, 1946-47, the Philadelphia Stars, 1942, 1946, 1949-50, St. Jean, the Canadian League, 1948, the Boston Braves, 1952. Played in the minors for six years, his best season was with Dallas of the Texas League in 1954 where he hit .324, with 42 homers and 135 RBIs. He was 5 for 25 for a .200 average and one RBI in his short major league career. Served in the Army.

SS-Jake Dunn— Played for the Detroit Stars, 1930, the Washington Pilots, 1932, the Nashville Elite Giants, 1933, the Baltimore Black Sox, 1933, the Philadelphia Stars, 1933–40. One of the first Negro League players to go into the service after Pearl Harbor. Served in the Army.

3B-Andrew "Pat" Patterson— Played for the Cleveland Red Sox, 1934, the Homestead Grays, 1934, the Pittsburgh Crawfords, 1935, 1937, the Kansas City Monarchs, 1936, 1941, the Philadelphia Stars, 1938-39, 1941-42, Mexico City of the Mexican League, 1940, the Newark Eagles, 1946-47, the Houston Eagles, 1949. Served in the Army.

OF-Al "Apples" Wilmore— Played for the Philadelphia Stars, 1946-47, the Baltimore Elite Giants, 1948–50, Winnipeg and Lincoln in the minor leagues, 1951-52. Was a part of the Philadelphia A's organization. Served in the 93rd Division in the Army stationed in the South Pacific (although he pitched for the 369th Infantry).

PI-Chester Buchanan— Played for the Philadelphia Bacharach Giants, 1931–36, the Philadelphia Stars, 1940-44. Served in the Navy.

PI-Barney Brown— Played for the Cuban Stars, 1931-32, the New York Black Yankees, 1936–39, the Philadelphia Stars, 1937, 1942–49, Vera Cruz, Mexico City and Torreon of the Mexican League, 1939–41, 1945, 1950–52, the Mandak League in the minor leagues, 1952-53. Best minor league season was 1953 when he was 9–4. Was able to play in the Negro Leagues while serving in the Army.

PI-Joe Filmore— Played for the Philadelphia Stars, 1940–52, the Baltimore Grays, 1946. Served in the Army.

PI-Ralph Johnson— Played for the Philadelphia Stars, 1940–45. Served in the Army.

PI-Larry Kimbrough— Played for the Philadelphia Stars, 1941–48, the Homestead Grays, 1949-50. Pitched and batted both as a lefty and righty. Served in the Army.

PI-Raymond Smith— Played for the Philadelphia Stars, 1945-46. Served in the Army.

Minor League Players Who Perished During World War II

More than 5,000 men from professional baseball served in the Armed Forces during World War II and several gave up their lives defending their country. The following list honors many of the minor league players who made the ultimate sacrifice. In developing this list, my two most important sources were Gary Bedingfield's Baseball in Wartime Bibliography web site *http://baseballinwartime.freeservers.com/bibliography.htm* which offers a wealth of information on many of these players, and *The Sporting News*, always a starting point for baseball researchers. If I have omitted any men, I also honor their courage and their sacrifice.

The players are listed in alphabetical order with the team and league they played for when they were inducted, what branch of the service they were in, where and when they died and pertinent information on their career. The classes for the various teams are taken from the *Encyclopedia of Minor League Baseball* by Lloyd Johnson and Miles Wolff. The various classes of minor league baseball played in 1941 were as follows in order of importance: class AA, class A1, class A, class B, class C and class D.

3B-Forest Brewer— Played for Charlotte in the class B Piedmont League. Won 25 games in 1938. Served with the 82nd Airborne Division where he died in France on 6/6/1944.

PI-Ordway Cisgen— Played for Utica in the class C Canadian-American League. Served in the Army where he was killed in France on 6/11/1944.

PI-Howard DeMartini— Played for Jersey City in the class AA International League. Was 17–7 in 1940 with Salisbury in the North Carolina State League. Served with the 262nd Infantry where he was killed in the English Channel on 12/25/1944.

2B-Billy Herbert— Played for Oakland in the class AA Pacific Coast

League. Served in the U.S. Navy where he was killed at Guadalcanal on 10/31/1942. The Oaks first dedicated a flagpole and bronze plaque to him at Oak Park Field before renaming the stadium, Billy Herbert Field in 1951.

OF-Manuel Hernandez— Played for San Diego of the class AA Pacific Coast League. Served with the 376th Infantry where he was killed in Germany on 3/22/1945.

OF-Gordon Houston— Played for Texarkana of the class C Cotton States League. Was killed in 1942.

CA-Ardys Keller— Played for Toledo in the class AA American Association. Also played with the House of David. Served in the 36th Infantry where he was killed in France on 9/29/1944.

PI-Lester Kirkkala— Played for Fremont of the class D Ohio State League. Was killed in France on 9/6/1944.

CA-Walter Lake— Played for Cedar Rapids of the class B Three-I League. Served with the 9th Infantry where he was killed in France on 7/26/1944.

PI-Walter Navie— Played for Shreveport in the class A1 Texas League. Was killed on 10/9/1945.

PI-Harry Nowak— Played for New Orleans in the class A1 Southern Association. Was a 20 game winner with the Albany Cardinals in the Georgia-Florida League. Served in the Army where he was killed in Belgium on 1/1/1945. Camp Lee's athletic field, where Nowak pitched and trained, was named in his honor.

PI-Joe Pinder— Played for Greenville in the class D Alabama State League. Served with the 1st Infantry where he was killed on the beaches of Normandy in D-Day, 7/6/1944. Was responsible for the vital radio equipment when his boat was stranded 100 yards from shore. Pinder was shot three times refusing treatment so he could bring the equipment ashore to communicate information. Was killed after being shot for the third time. Awarded the Congressional Medal of Honor posthumously.

OF William Sarver— Played with Augusta of the class B South Atlantic League. Served with the 3rd Armored Division where he was killed in Aachen, Germany on 4/6/1945.

PI-Franklin Schulz— Played for Wilkes-Barre of the class A Eastern League. Served as a second lieutenant in the Air Force where he was killed in the Philippines on 6/17/1945.

OF-Marshall Sneed— Played for Topeka of the class C Western Association. Served as a captain in the Air Force where he was killed in North Africa on 2/22/1943.

PI-Rod Sooter— Played for Seattle in the class AA Pacific Coast League. Served in the Air Force with the 1st BADA where he died in

Germany on 2/1/1946 as his plane went down while delivering recreational supplies.

OF-William Southworth Jr. — Played for Toronto of the class AA International League. Served with the 303rd Bomb Group where he flew 25 successful bombing missions in Europe. Was killed while flying in Long Island, New York, on 2/12/1945. Son of the great St. Louis manager Billy Sr.

PI-James Trimble — Played at Duke University. Is included because the Washington Senators right out of high school signed him. Was a member of the 3rd Marine Division where he was killed on Iwo Jima on 3/1/1945. A baseball field is named after him in Guam.

PI-Arthur Vivian — Played for Newark in the class AA International League. Served in the Army where he was killed in France on 8/20/1944.

PI-Joseph Yeske — Played for Hartford of the class A Eastern League. Was killed in Italy on 12/21/1944.

SS-John Zulberti — Played for Miami Beach in the class D Florida East Coast League. Was killed in North Africa in 1944.

Note: Eugene Stack was also listed as a minor leaguer who was killed while with the Army on 6/26/1942. There was no team listed for him.

8

The War's Effect on
Hall of Fame Careers

There were many Hall of Fame players who played throughout the war years. Some like Early Wynn, Stan Musial and Bobby Doerr played three of the four seasons, while others like Joe DiMaggio, Ted Williams, Bob Feller, Ted Lyons and Johnny Mize would either play one season or none at all. Bob Lemon and Warren Spahn were in the very early stages of their careers and really were not affected whatsoever statistically. Wynn, Musial and Doerr would have significant stats during the time, Doerr hitting a career high .325 when he was taken in 1944, but the more significant parts of their careers would come during the post war era. When you also consider the fact they lost one full season, it more than made up for the fact that playing three seasons of substandard baseball might have enhanced their career statistics.

Throughout it all, there were basically six Hall of Fame players that lasted the course of the time period: Joe Cronin, Ernie Lombardi, Mel Ott, Joe Medwick, Lou Boudreau and Hal Newhouser. This chapter will look at these six players and judge whether or not playing in the inferior war years padded their career statistics to the point that they should not have been included in Cooperstown.

Cronin was basically at the end of his career and hit only .273, far under his .301 lifetime mark, in 355 at-bats in four years, so it's safe to say playing in the war years had no effect on his career and he belongs in the Hall of Fame.

The slow-footed catcher, Ernie Lombardi, did play significant time between 1942 and 1945, hitting .297, including a league high .330 in 1942, for the Braves and Giants in 1,345 at-bats while being selected to the All-Star game twice in '42 and '43. As good an average as it was, especially in the poor hitting time period, it was still nine points under his .306 career mark.

The question here is not if the war years vaulted Lombardi into the Hall of Fame; since his true peak was 1935–40, I would guess not. But does he in fact deserve to be in the Hall? Although he only had 1,792 hits, he rates 6th among the 12 catchers inducted, while his .306 average is only behind Mickey Cochrane and Bill Dickey. Ernie had only 990 RBIs, but again when it comes to catchers enshrined, it puts him in the middle of the pack at 6th. It's safe to say that he was one of the better offensive players inducted at Cooperstown.

Defensively was another question. He was known to have a good arm, but his play behind the plate would be spotty at best as he accumulated a -113 fielding runs throughout his 17-year career. Bill James put it best about players who were elected far after their playing days ended, as Lombardi was when the Veterans Committee chose him in 1986. James said that as more time goes on, the defensive play is more forgotten as the offensive statistics become more and more important.[1] Regardless, he was one of the top offensive catchers to play the game in the first half of the century and despite the fact he might not be one of the best ever to grace the steps of Cooperstown, it probably is correct that he is included.

Only Bill Nicholson's 96 homers would top the 95 that Ott hit during the war. While it's probable that the war inflated his career home run stats as evidenced by the fact that when it ended, Mel would play only two more seasons, hitting a paltry .069 in 72 at-bats, Ott still had some of the best statistics for his career at the time the war began and was a certain choice to be included in the Hall. His best seasons were between 1929 and 1939 and his wartime average of .284 was 20 points below his .304 lifetime mark.

Despite the fact he is a worthy Hall of Fame selection and one of the all time greats, the war most likely put Ott over the 500 home run plateau. As quick a decline as he experienced after the war, it's doubtful he would have made it into that select club.

Ducky Medwick was another player like Ott, whose career would fall once the war ended, but also like the former Giant, he would see his peak in the prewar seasons. Joe would eclipse the 100 RBI plateau six consecutive times between 1934 and 1939, leading the league three times between '36 and '38. His best year was in 1937 when he hit a career highs in homers, 31, RBIs, 154 and average at .374, leading the league in all three categories for the rare triple crown. He would also lead the circuit in runs, 111, hits, 237, doubles, 56, slugging, .641 and fielding, .988.

The war years were good to Medwick, but by far were not his peak years. He hit a fine .302, 6th best during the war, but it was 22 points under his .324 career average. Ducky would not hit with much power as he hit only 16 of his lifetime 205 homers. With a .324 average, which is the 40th best mark all time, Medwick is no question a Hall of Famer.

That leaves us with two more players in Boudreau and Newhouser. These are the two players we will look at closely as they were the only two who had their peak seasons right smack in between the war years and it can be argued that their statistics during the substandard war seasons could have erroneously vaulted them into the Hall of Fame.

While it was very difficult to figure out a proper way to analyze what kind of effect the war years had on each player's career, I settled on rating Boudreau against the rest of the starting shortstops in the American League during the war years and during his non war-years peak of 1940-41 and 1946–49. Newhouser is rated against the league averages at five stages in his career:

- During the war years.
- During his three incredible seasons between 1944 and 1946.
- During his significant career outside the war years.
- During his significant career outside 1944 and 1946.
- During his significant career.

Newhouser's significant career would include the seasons between 1940 and 1952 when he started at least 10 games per season, he was a mere 7–4 in six starts in 1939 and 1953–55, his career outside his significant seasons.

The following are charts of Boudreau seasons by year versus the other starting shortstops during the seasons outlined above. The starting short-stops are taken from the Neft and Cohen encyclopedia and are listed with Boudreau first and the remaining starters listed in order of how their teams finished in the standings that particular season:

Boudreau During the War Years

1942	Runs	2B	3B	HR	RBI	Ave	Slug	Field %	Fielding Runs
Boudreau-Cleve	57	18	10	2	58	.283	.370	.965	0
Rizzuto-NY	79	24	7	4	68	.284	.374	.962	25
Pesky-Bost	105	29	9	2	51	.331	.416	.955	18
Stephens-StL	84	26	6	14	92	.292	.433	.944	-10
Hitchcock-Det	27	8	1	0	29	.211	.246	.944	-3
Appling-Chic	78	26	4	3	53	.262	.341	.948	-7
Sullivan-Wash	38	16	1	0	42	.235	.286	.936	-11
Suder-Phil	46	20	4	4	54	.256	.340	.954	3
League Average	64.3	20.9	5.3	3.6	55.9	.276	.363	.952	1.9

1943	Runs	2B	3B	HR	RBI	Ave	Slug	Field %	Fielding Runs
Boudreau-Cleve	69	32	7	3	67	.286	.388	.970	28
Crosetti-NY	36	8	1	2	20	.233	.279	.946	3
Sullivan-Wash	49	12	2	1	55	.208	.250	.946	11
Appling-Chic	63	33	2	3	80	.328	.407	.957	7
Hoover-Det	78	15	8	4	38	.243	.318	.944	-6
Stephens-Stl	75	27	3	22	91	.289	.482	.943	-25
Newsome-Bost	48	21	2	1	22	.265	.327	.962	14
Hall-Phil	37	15	4	0	54	.256	.298	.948	-11
League Average	56.8	20.3	3.6	4.5	53.4	.266	.348	.952	2.6

1944	Runs	2B	3B	HR	RBI	Ave	Slug	Field %	Fielding Runs
Boudreau-Cleve	91	45	5	3	67	.327	.437	.978	26
Stephens-Stl	91	32	1	20	109	.293	.462	.954	-4
Hoover-Det	67	20	2	0	29	.236	.290	.932	15
Milosevich-NY	27	11	4	0	32	.247	.308	.954	7
Newsome-Bost	41	26	3	0	41	.242	.309	.963	11
Busch-Phil	41	11	3	0	40	.271	.306	.940	-30
Webb-Chic	44	19	6	0	30	.211	.271	.944	-5
Sullivan-Wash	49	12	1	0	30	.251	.280	.934	-14
League Average	56.3	22	3.1	2.9	47.3	.262	.339	.950	0.8

1945	Runs	2B	3B	HR	RBI	Ave	Slug	Field %	Fielding Runs
Boudreau-Cleve	50	24	1	3	48	.306	.408	.983	1
Webb-Det	43	12	2	0	21	.199	.238	.957	23
Torres-Wash	39	12	5	0	48	.237	.276	.953	-21
Stephens-Stl	90	27	3	24	89	.289	.473	.961	-17
Crosetti-NY	57	12	0	4	48	.238	.293	.946	-8
Michaels-Chic	47	8	5	2	54	.245	.299	.936	10
Lake-Bost	81	27	1	11	51	.279	.410	.948	19
Busch-Phil	37	10	3	0	35	.250	.288	.952	1
League Average	55.5	16.5	2.5	5.5	49.3	.255	.338	.953	1

Boudreau During His Peak Outside the War

1940	Runs	2B	3B	HR	RBI	Ave	Slug	Field %	Fielding Runs
Boudreau-Cleve	97	46	10	9	101	.295	.443	.968	12
Bartell-Det	76	24	3	7	53	.233	.330	.953	12
Crosetti-Ny	84	23	4	4	31	.194	.273	.954	14
Cronin-Bost	104	35	6	24	111	.285	.502	.948	2
Appling-Chic	96	27	13	0	79	.348	.442	.953	-2
Berardino-Stl	71	31	4	16	85	.258	.424	.939	-13
Pofahl-Wash	34	23	5	2	36	.234	.330	.952	-5
Brancato-Phil	42	11	2	1	23	.191	.252	.949	0
League Average	75.5	27.5	5.9	7.9	64.9	.261	.385	.952	2.5

1941	Runs	2B	3B	HR	RBI	Ave	Slug	Field %	Fielding Runs
Boudreau-Cleve	95	45	8	10	56	.257	.415	.966	13
Rizzuto-Ny	65	20	9	3	46	.307	.398	.957	16
Cronin-Bost	98	38	8	16	95	.311	.508	.958	-8
Appling-Chic	93	26	8	1	57	.314	.390	.948	0
Croucher-Det	51	21	4	2	39	.254	.325	.935	-3
Berardino-Stl	48	30	4	5	89	.271	.384	.954	-14
Travis-Wash	106	39	19	7	101	.359	.520	.964	2
Brancato-Phil	60	20	9	2	49	.234	.317	.915	-19
League Average	77	29.9	8.6	5.8	66.5	.290	.410	.949	-1.6

1946	Runs	2B	3B	HR	RBI	Ave	Slug	Field %	Fielding Runs
Boudreau-Cleve	51	30	6	6	62	.293	.410	.970	16
Pesky-Bost	115	43	4	2	55	.335	.427	.955	18
Lake-Det	105	24	1	8	31	.254	.339	.947	-21
Rizzuto-Ny	53	17	1	2	38	.257	.310	.961	13
Travis-Wash	45	22	3	1	56	.252	.318	.959	-19
Appling-Chic	59	27	5	1	55	.309	.378	.951	7
Stephens-Stl	67	19	4	14	64	.307	.460	.950	0
Suder-Phil	38	20	3	2	50	.281	.352	.959	1
League Average	66.6	25.3	3.4	4.5	51.4	.288	.375	.956	1.9

1947	Runs	2B	3B	HR	RBI	Ave	Slug	Field %	Fielding Runs
Boudreau-Cleve	79	45	3	4	67	.307	.424	.982	17
Rizzuto-Ny	78	26	9	2	60	.273	.364	.969	16
Lake-Det	96	19	6	12	46	.211	.322	.943	-29
Pesky-Bost	106	27	8	0	39	.324	.392	.976	-1
Joost-Phil	76	22	3	13	64	.206	.330	.956	-3
Appling-Chic	67	29	0	8	49	.306	.412	.949	-7
Christman-Wash	27	15	2	1	33	.222	.281	.969	-32
Stephens-Stl	74	18	4	15	83	.279	.406	.970	12
League Average	75.3	25.1	4.4	6.9	55.1	.268	.369	.964	-4.6

1948	Runs	2B	3B	HR	RBI	Ave	Slug	Field %	Fielding Runs
Boudreau-Cleve	116	34	6	18	106	.355	.534	.975	8
Stephens-Bost	114	25	8	29	137	.269	.471	.971	10
Rizzuto-NY	65	13	2	6	50	.252	.328	.973	-11
Joost-Phil	99	22	2	16	55	.250	.395	.973	5
Lipon-Det	65	18	8	5	52	.290	.397	.970	-12
Pellagrini-Stl	31	8	3	2	27	.238	.307	.964	24
Christman-Wash	38	17	2	1	40	.259	.318	.967	3
Michaels-Chic	47	12	6	5	56	.248	.329	.957	13
League Average	71.9	18.6	4.6	10.3	65.4	.273	.397	.969	5

1949	Runs	2B	3B	HR	RBI	Ave	Slug	Field %	Fielding Runs
Boudreau-Cleve	53	20	3	4	60	.284	.364	.982	5
Rizzuto-Ny	110	22	7	5	65	.275	.358	.971	3
Stephens-Bost	113	31	2	39	159	.290	.539	.966	4
Lipon-Det	57	14	6	3	59	.251	.330	.965	4
Joost-Phil	128	25	3	23	81	.263	.453	.969	8
Appling-Chic	82	21	5	5	58	.301	.394	.964	-1
Pellagrini-Stl	26	8	1	2	15	.238	.306	.961	7
Dente-Wash	48	24	4	1	53	.273	.332	.957	-9
League Average	77.1	20.6	3.9	10.3	68.9	.274	.385	.967	2.6

The Boudreau Totals

During the War Years	Runs	2B	3B	HR	RBI	Ave	Slug	Field %	Fielding Runs
Boudreau-Cleve	66.8	29.8	5.8	2.8	60	.301	.401	.973	13.8
Average Totals for Starting Shortstops in the War Years	58.2	19.9	3.6	4.1	51.4	.264	.347	.952	1.6
% + or − of Boudreau's Stats versus the Average Totals	+14.8%	+49.7%	+61.1%	-31.7%	+16.7%	+14.0%	+15.6%	+2.3%	+762.5

During Boudreau's Peak Outisde of the War	Runs	2B	3B	HR	RBI	Ave	Slug	Field %	Fielding Runs
Boudreau-Cleve	81.8	36.7	6	8.5	75.3	.298	.434	.973	8.9
Average Totals for Starting Shortstops in 1940-1941, 1946–1949	73.9	24.5	5.1	7.6	62.0	.275	.386	.959	1.5
% + or − of Boudreau's Stats versus the Average Totals	+10.6%	+49.8%	+17.6%	+11.8%	+21.4%	+8.4%	+12.4%	+1.5%	+513.7%

THE BOUDREAU FINAL ANALYSIS

When I began to look at Boudreau's career, I fully expected to find his dominance over the average shortstop in the war years to be much more significant than that over his contemporaries in his peak seasons outside of the war years, causing him to be considered a Hall of Fame mistake.

Lou Boudreau would not only be one of the greatest shortstops of the war years, but also the entire 1940s. He went on to manage the Indians in 1948 to the world championship while also being named the MVP.

What I surprisingly found was a player who was consistently better than his peers in both time periods.

While he was 4 percent better versus the average in runs, wartime versus non-war, he scored on average 15 more runs per season in the non-war campaigns. A lot of that could be explained by the better offensive seasons the game experienced after the war, or his marquee 1948 campaign, but it still is a significant number.

He remained the same in doubles, being the most significant doubles hitter of his time, while dropping off in triples, average and slugging although he still remained as one of the best during his non war time in the latter two categories.

Boudreau's power numbers actually improved over his same output during the war years as he was below the average in homers between 1942 and 1945 and over afterwards. His RBI output improved significantly after the war as his non-war total of 75.3 was much more impressive and 46.5 percent higher than his 51.4 war years average.

Defensively he was dominant in both eras as he had the top fielding percentage by far. Boudreau most likely would have won 8 gold gloves, 1940, 1941, 1943, 1944, 1945, 1946, 1947 and 1949, while having a decent shot in 1948.

The negative on Boudreau is he only had 10 significant seasons, but he has to be considered the best defensive shortstop of the 1940s. Despite the brevity of his career, his 134 fielding runs place him 62nd all time. Offensively his .295 average is 7th out of the 19 shortstops in the Hall of Fame. Arguably, after Vern Stephens, Lou might have been the second best shortstop offensively in his time. Add to the mix that his 42.5 career total player rating in *Total Baseball* is the 37th best figure of all time, his non-war year 1948 most valuable player award and his 16 year managerial career, which included a world championship in 1948, and one comes to the conclusion the Boudreau does in fact belong in Cooperstown despite having the meat of his career during the war.

THE NEWHOUSER REPORT

I looked at Newhouser's career in the five categories listed on page 314. I took the three seasons 1944–46 because Hal tossed three of the best seasons a modern day pitcher ever achieved, winning 80 games and taking the American League MVP awards in back to back campaigns of 1944 and 1945, while finishing a close second to Ted Williams in 1946. The year 1946 had always been noted by some as a poor offensive season because of the war, even though it technically wasn't a war season, with the claim that because the returning vets had been out of the majors for various years, their timing was not quite there yet. When I looked at the production in 1946, only 9,953 runs were scored compared to 10,830 in 1947, an 8.9% gain over '46. In 1946, the ERAs were 3.42 and 3.51 in the NL and AL respectively while in '47 they rose to 4.07 and 3.71, a 19.0% and 5.7% increase.

The chart below will show Newhouser's significant seasons with a comparison in ERA by year versus the league, opponents' batting average versus the league and Newhouser's winning percentage versus Detroit's winning percentage. The second chart will show Hal's total percentage + or – versus the league average by each of the five classifications. Plus percentages in ERA and OBA mean they are above the league average which is not where you want to be, whereas a plus percentage in winning percentage versus your teams winning percentage is very advantageous.

Year	Hal's Era	League Era	% + or – vs the League in ERA	Hal's OBA	League OBA	% + or – vs the League in ERA	Hal's Winning %	Detroit's Winning %	% + or – vs Winning %
1940	4.82	4.39	9.7%	.282	.272	3.6%	.500	.584	-14.3%
1941	4.79	4.15	15.4%	.249	.267	-6.7%	.450	.487	-7.6%
1942	2.45	3.66	-33.0%	.207	.258	-19.8%	.364	.474	-23.2%
1943	3.04	3.30	-7.9%	.224	.250	-10.4%	.320	.506	-36.8%
1944	2.22	3.44	-35.5%	.230	.260	-11.5%	.763	.571	33.3%
1945	1.81	3.37	-46.2%	.211	.256	-17.6%	.735	.575	27.8%
1946	1.94	3.51	-44.7%	.201	.256	-21.5%	.743	.597	24.5%
1947	2.87	3.71	-22.6%	.249	.256	-2.7%	.500	.552	-9.4%
1948	3.01	4.29	-29.8%	.242	.266	-9.0%	.636	.506	25.7%
1949	3.36	4.20	-20.0%	.251	.264	-4.9%	.621	.565	9.9%
1950	4.34	4.58	-5.2%	.279	.271	3.0%	.536	.617	-13.1%
1951	3.92	4.13	-5.1%	.268	.263	2.0%	.500	.474	5.5%
1952	3.74	3.68	1.6%	.254	.253	0.4%	.500	.325	53.8%

The Newhouser Totals

Categories	Hal's Average % + or - ERA vs the League	Hal's Average % + or - OBA vs the League	Hal's Record and Winning Percentage	Detroit's Winning Percentage	The % + or - of Hal's Winning % vs Detroit's
War Years	-30.7%	-42.1%	70–49–.588	.532	10.5%
1944–1946	-42.1%	-16.9%	80–27–.748	.581	28.7%
Career in Non War Years	-11.1%	-4.0%	130–97–.572	.523	9.3%
Career Outside of 1944–1946	-9.7%	-4.5%	120–119–.502	.509	-1.4%
Career in Significant Seasons	-17.2%	-4.0%	200–146–.578	.525	10.0%

The Newhouser Final Analysis

Unlike the Boudreau analysis, there are questions about Newhouser's qualifications for the Hall of Fame. In looking at the categories we compared, I felt it was proper to include Hal's phenomenal 1946 campaign in somewhat of a war years situation for the reasons stated above. Where it is true that his 29–9, 25–9 and 26–9 campaigns in those three seasons were among the best in the modern era and his back-to-back MVP's in the last two years during the war, 1944 and 1945, were very impressive, it still must be considered that the war enhanced his career totals.

When we look at his significant seasons outside those three marvelous seasons, we find that Newhouser is basically a .500 pitcher. Although he rates very well in any category when his ERA and OBAs are compared to the league average, they are not enough to make up for his 120–119 mark outside of 1944–46.

Bottom line, while Newhouser is a very good pitcher and certainly had a career to be proud of, the war years probably were the reason for putting him in the Hall of Fame, and in retrospect, makes him the only one of the six Hall of Fame members to play the entire war years that probably really doesn't belong there.

9

A Sabermetric Look
at the War Years

When Franklin Roosevelt made the decision to continue the national pastime through the duration of World War II, in the interest of country morale, it began a time period in baseball that certainly was very unsure.

Most of the game's great stars would eventually be sent abroad. Ted Williams and Bob Feller, among others, would make headlines more as war heroes rather than baseball heroes. The game would be left to the likes of Ray Sanders and Nick Etten. Sanders and Etten were certainly of major league caliber before the war, but the opportunity that would be provided to them between 1942 and 1945, made them stars. Whereas their stars burned out once the war was over, Sanders would be traded from the Cardinals to the Red Sox after 1945 to make way for a returning Stan Musial at first and only have 274 at-bats in the 3 years that followed, compared to the 1,908 during the war. Etten would have only one year and 14 games after '45, then he was out of the majors. The role they played during the war cannot be understated. Roosevelt was correct, the country needed baseball to provide a much needed lift during times when it was unsure whether or not the country would even be able exist in the democratic life it had been accustomed to for some 166 years.

This report in general is meant to give a long overdue celebration of the careers of players such as Etten and Sanders and their long forgotten efforts to help pick up the nation in a time when it so desperately needed something to pick it up.

Part I: The Hitters

The basis of the report is twofold:

A) Through a formula based on the top 25 hitters in each of 10 hitting categories and the percentage of those figures attained during the seasons of 1942–45 as compared to their careers as a whole, I was able to figure out which players most took advantage of their opportunities and turned what in most cases were average to below average careers, into ones that during that time period could be considered among the best in the game. The highest point total in the report is named the George Bailey Award Winner after the fictional character in the movie *It's a Wonderful Life*. Bailey of course stayed at home during the war and provided many beneficial jobs in the war effort at home.

B) Through a point system that rewards the top 25 leaders of HR, hits, ave., slugging, total bases, runs and RBIs specific points in reverse order of their various positions in the specific categories (for example the tops in hits would receive 25 points and the 25th position would receive 1 point), the top 10 positions in doubles and triples and the top 5 positions in stolen bases, we want to find out who is the Most Valuable Player of this time period.

The Formula

The formula is basically as follows: The total figure in HR, hits, doubles, triples, stolen bases, total bases, runs and RBIs accumulated during the war years for the player, multiplied by the percentage of those stats attained during 1942 through 1945. We then divided HR, doubles, triples and RBIs by 3, hits and stolen bases by 5, and total bases by 6. The reason is to try and give each category their appropriate total weight in the final numbers. For batting average and slugging percentage, we took the total numbers achieved during '42–'45 and divided it by their numbers over the course of their careers. We then took that number and multiplied the batting average by 300 and slugging by 200, again to give these numbers the appropriate weight in the final total. We only rated the top 25 in each category, making sure we were getting players that actually succeeded during that time.

Introducing the George Bailey Award Winner: *Ray Sanders*

The George Bailey Award Report

Position	Name	Points	Position	Name	Points
1	R. Sanders	563.65	33	Adams	98.85
2	Etten	511.7	34	Barrett	94.91
3	Holmes	476.74	35	Heath	29.84
4	Nicholson	471.07	36	Stirnweiss	23.28
5	Kurowski	443.38	37	Kuhel	21.16
6	Cullenbine	417.31	38	E. Miller	16.39
7	V. Stephens	377.07	39	Lupien	14.37
8	Cavarretta	368.67	40	Workman	14.11
9	Elliott	361.95	41	Marion	13.78
10	D. Walker	360.64	42	Neiman	12.33
11	McCormick	352.43	43	Olmo	11.2
12	Spence	349.83	44	Keller	10.59
13	Galan	332.22	45	Hopp	10.13
14	Boudreau	311.22	46	Myatt	9.66
15	B. Johnson	308.7	47	Laabs	7.12
16	Musial	292.91	48	Northey	5.7
17	York	284.84	49	Merullo	5.05
18	Estalella	236.78	50	Lindell	4.71
19	Ott	233.59	51	Taber	4.62
20	J. Russell	222.5	52	Tucker	4.58
21	V. DiMaggio	219.49	53	Rucker	4.52
22	Gutteridge	208.26	54	Lombardi	4.38
23	Doerr	202.17	55	Clay	4.32
24	Medwick	200.87	56	Litweller	4.03
25	Case	197.54	57	Gustine	3.63
26	Hack	197.35	58	Metkovich	3.57
27	Siebert	195.82	59	Vernon	3.51
28	Keltner	175.44	60	Appling	2.26
29	Cramer	163.82	61	Fox	2.23
30	Hockett	151.30	62	A. Vaughan	1.33
31	Moses	125.43	63	G. Walker	0.92
32	McQuinn	117.58	64	T. Williams	0.83

Leaders by Category

Totals by Category for years 1942–45

Points accumulated by formula per category

Homers

Position	Name	Total HRs	Position	Name	HR points
1	Nicholson	96	1	Etten	14.4
2	Ott	95	2	Workman	14.11
3	York	91	3	Nicholson	13.89
4	Stephens	80	4	Kurowski	12.47
5	Keller	67	5	Neiman	12.33

Homer pts with formula

Leaders by Category (cont.)

Totals by Category for years 1942–45			*Points accumulated by formula per category*		

Hits

Hit pts with formula

Position	Name	Total hits	Position	Name	Hit points
1	Holmes	744	1	Hockett	108.64
2	Cramer	666	2	R Sanders	93.28
2	Elliott	666	3	Etten	80.26
4	Nicholson	664	4	Holmes	73.51
5	Cavarretta	658	5	Kurowski	67.29

Batting average

Batting Average pts with formula

Position	Name	Average	Position	Name	Batting average points
1	Musial	.341	1	Musial	105.37
2	D. Walker	.313	2	Cavarretta	98.39
3	Cavarretta	.310	3	Spence	97.63
4	Holmes	.303	4	D. Walker	96.06
4	Spence	.303	5	Galan	94.05

Slugging pct.

Slugging pts with formula

Position	Name	Slugging percentage	Position	Name	Slugging percentage points
1	Musial	.538	1	Musial	103.51
2	Ott	.491	2	Nicholson	100.77
3	Nicholson	.484	3	Stephens	92.77
4	Stephens	.462	4	D. Walker	92.7
5	Doerr	.460	5	Doerr	91.82

Doubles

Double pts with formula

Position	Name	Doubles	Position	Name	Double points
1	Holmes	146	1	Hockett	34.06
2	D. Walker	139	2	R. Sanders	29.83
3	Musial	131	3	Holmes	24.33
4	Cavarretta	124	4	Etten	22.02
4	B. Johnson	124	5	Cullenbine	21.81

Triples

Triple pts with formula

Position	Name	Triples	Position	Name	Triple points
1	Musial	44	1	Barrett	10.67
2	Stirnweiss	42	2	Stirnweiss	8.65
3	Elliott	41	3	J. Russell	7.12
4	Moses	40	4	Lupien	6.94
5	Cavarretta	38	5	Olmo	6.45

Total bases			Total base pts with formula		
Position	Name	Total bases	Position	Name	TB points
1	Nicholson	1131	1	R. Sanders	115
2	Holmes	1092	2	Etten	102.88
3	York	1050	3	Holmes	92.09
4	Stephens	1024	4	Kurowski	88.2
5	Elliott	970	5	Nicholson	82.56

Runs			Run pts with formula		
Position	Name	Runs	Position	Name	Run points
1	Nicholson	376	1	Barrett	70.83
2	Caverretta	352	2	R. Sanders	60.19
3	Holmes	349	3	Etten	45.99
4	Ott	347	4	Gutteridge	45.92
5	Hack	344	5	Holmes	43.63

RBIs			RBI pts with formula		
Position	Name	RBIs	Position	Name	RBI points
1	Nicholson	416	1	R. Sanders	86.43
2	Elliott	406	2	Etten	77.58
3	York	393	3	Estalella	62.32
4	Stephens	381	4	Nicholson	60.87
5	Etten	350	5	Kurowski	57.09

Stolen bases			Stolen base pts with formula		
Position	Name	Stolen bases	Position	Name	Stolen Base points
1	Case	184	1	Case	19.39
2	Moses	104	2	Stirnweiss	14.63
3	Stirnweiss	99	3	Barrett	13.41
4	Barrett	68	4	Moses	12.44
5	Myatt	59	5	Myatt	9.66

Introducing the MVP Award Winner: *Bill Nicholson*

Most Valuable Player Points of the Best Players from the War Years

Position	Name	Points	Position	Name	Points
1	Nicholson	157	8	B. Johnson	116
2	Holmes	143	9	Ott	107
3	Stephens	141	10	Musial	102
4	B.Elliott	127	11	McCormick	97
4	Cavarretta	127	12	Kurowski	92
6	D. Walker	125	13	Etten	91
7	York	120	14	Cullenbine	69

Position	Name	Points	Position	Name	Points
15	Galan	67	32	Heath	17
16	Hack	65	33	Laabs	16
17	Spence	57	33	Lombardi	16
18	Doerr	52	33	Adams	16
19	Case	50	36	Barrett	13
19	Moses	50	37	Stirnweiss	12
21	Cramer	45	38	Workman	10
22	Boudreau	42	38	Keltner	10
23	Medwick	38	40	Hockett	8
24	V. DiMaggio	37	40	Northey	8
25	Gutteridge	32	42	Taber	5
26	R Sanders	30	43	Kuhel	4
27	McQuinn	27	43	Neiman	4
28	J. Russell	23	45	T. Williams	3
29	Siebert	22	45	Litweller	3
30	Keller	21	47	Lindell	1
31	Estalella	19	47	Myatt	1

Part II: The Pitchers

The basis of the pitching report is also twofold:

A) Through a formula based on the top 25 pitchers in each of six pitching categories during the seasons between 1942 and 1945. I then took those stats achieved during the war and used it as a percentage to their total stats throughout their major league careers. The idea was to see which pitchers most took advantage of their opportunities and turned what in most cases were average to below average careers into ones that, during that time period, could be considered among the best in the game. As with the hitters, the highest point total in the report is named the George Bailey Award Winner after the fictional character in the movie *It's a Wonderful Life.*

B) Through a point system that rewards the top 25 leaders of wins, winning percentage, strikeouts, ERA, K/BB ratio and H/IP ratio specific points in reverse order of their various positions in the specific categories (for example the tops in wins would receive 25 points and the 25th position would receive 1 point), we want to find out who is the Cy Young Award Winner of this time period.

THE FORMULA

The formula for pitching is a little more complicated than the ones for hitters. It was constructed a little different, again to give the appropriate weights to the specific categories.

The formula is basically as follows:

• WINS: Wins achieved during 1942–45 times the percentage of those wins versus their individual totals. We took that total and multiplied it by 4. (Wins achieved during the war years × percent of those wins to their career wins) × 4.

• STRIKEOUTS: The formula for strikeouts was the same as wins except instead of multiplying the total by 4 we divided it by 10. (Strikeouts achieved during the war years × percent of those strikeouts to their career totals)/10.

• WINNING PERCENTAGE: We took the winning percentage achieved between '42–'45, multiplied it by the percent over or below their career winning percentage and took that total and multiplied it by 150. (<Winning percent during the war years × percent over or below their career winning percentage> × 150).

• ERA: ERA was a little difficult. We took the career ERA and the ERA between '42–'45 and took the decimal out (a 2.33 ERA became 233). Then we took the difference between the two, then figured out the percentage + or – of the war ERA versus the career ERA (<Career ERA-war ERA>/Career ERA) and put that number after 1 (if a player's war time ERA was 33 percent over his career ERA it would read 1.33). We then took the difference between career versus war ERA and multiplied it by the percentage + or – of the war ERA versus the career ERA (again the percentage + or – was placed after the number 1 which in our previous example was 1.33).

• K/BB RATIO: The K/BB ratio category was basically the war years figure multiplied by the percent + or – the career K/BB ratio. We took that number and divided it by 2 (<K/BB ratio in the war years × the percent + or – versus their career ratio>/2).

• H/IP RATIO: Like ERA we took the decimal out of the figure (.868 became 868). We then subtracted the difference between the war years H/IP and their total career H/IP. We then took that figure and multiplied it by the percentage + or – versus the total career H/IP and divided it by 2 (<the difference between career H/IP and war years H/IP × the percentage +career H/IP>/2).

Add up all categories and it gives you the pitching war points. As with hitting we only rated the top 25 in each category, making sure we were getting players that actually succeeded during that time.

Introducing the George Bailey Award Winner for Pitchers: *Nels Potter*

The George Bailey Award Report

Position	Name	Points	Position	Name	Points
1	Potter	576.49	29	Javery	156.61
2	M.Cooper	557.86	30	J. Tobin	137.17
3	Borowy	466.50	31	Newsom	125.43
4	Newhouser	431.61	32	C. Davis	115.00
5	Lanier	406.03	33	R. Barrett	112.29
6	Wyse	402.06	34	Derringer	109.24
7	Hughson	388.75	35	Gumbert	103.73
8	Passeau	368.12	36	Ostermueller	99.71
9	Shoun	363.63	37	Butcher	98.82
10	Bonham	354.95	38	Higbe	91.98
11	Chandler	348.87	39	Galehouse	89.42
12	Trout	333.22	40	Donald	88.30
13	Gromek	307.78	41	Bagby	87.22
14	Muncrief	302.43	42	Haefner	86.07
15	Breechen	290.16	43	Ryba	83.52
16	J. Kramer	285.39	44	Lopat	63.21
17	Wolff	270.31	45	Dietrich	63.32
18	Walters	261.03	46	Zuber	33.17
19	Sewell	242.64	47	Judd	29.68
20	Haynes	240.97	48	Reynolds	28.50
21	Niggeling	240.75	49	A. Adams	23.63
22	Vander Meer	226.12	50	Feldman	23.06
23	Strincevich	220.85	51	Christopher	22.95
24	Wyatt	195.67	52	Voiselle	13.95
25	Benton	191.46	53	Bithorn	12.48
26	Leonard	184.18	54	R. Melton	12.33
27	Roe	183.60	55	Flores	4.04
28	O. Grove	157.76			

Leaders By Category

Totals by Category for years 1942–45			Points accumulated by formula per category		
Wins			Win pts with formula		
Position	Name	Total Wins	Position	Name	Win points
1	Trout	77	1	M. Cooper	171.09
2	M. Cooper	74	2	Borowy	167.77
3	Sewell	70	3	Wolff	162.84
4	Newhouser	70	4	O. Grove	140.25
5	Borowy	67	5	Trout	139.52

Strikeouts			Strikeout pts with formula		
Position	Name	Total K's	Position	Name	K points
1	Newhouser	646	1	Wolff	31.15
2	Newsom	526	2	Javery	29.77

Strikeouts			Strikeout pts with formula		
Position	Name	Total K's	Position	Name	K points
2	M.Cooper	449	3	Niggeling	27.76
4	Trout	443	4	Newhouser	23.26
5	Niggeling	415	5	Feldman	23.06

Win % average			Win % pts with formula		
Position	Name	Win %	Position	Name	Win % points
1	Chandler	.792	1	Breechen	134.13
2	M. Cooper	.740	2	Potter	131.86
3	Breechen	.727	3	Chandler	130.68
4	Borowy	.677	4	M. Cooper	129.87
4	Hughson	.667	5	Strincevich	126.32

ERA			ERA pts with formula		
Position	Name	ERA	Position	Name	ERA points
1	Chandler	2.16	1	Potter	174.23
2	M. Cooper	2.25	2	Kramer	166.40
3	Newhouser	2.29	3	Benton	153.12
4	Lanier	2.43	4	Haynes	143.36
5	Benton	2.50	5	Shoun	128.52

K/BB ratio			K/BB ratio pts with formula		
Position	Name	K/BB ratio	Position	Name	K/BB ratio points
1	Roe	2.25	1	Roe	132.75
2	M. Cooper	1.86	2	Kramer	118.99
3	Leonard	1.82	3	Lanier	113.11
4	Hughson	1.79	4	M. Cooper	108.81
4	Lanier	1.74	5	Leonard	103.74

H/IP ratio			H/IP ratio pts with formula		
Position	Name	H/IP ratio	Position	Name	H/IP ratio points
1	Vander Meer	.780	1	Potter	79.06
2	Newhouser	.799	2	Shoun	61.53
3	Niggeling	.819	3	Newhouser	52.64
4	Chandler	.833	4	Borowy	52.17
5	M. Cooper	.837	5	VanderMeer	41.25

Introducing the Cy Young Award Winner: *Mort Cooper*

Cy Young Award Points
the Best Players from the War Years

Position	Name	Points	Position	Name	Points
1	M. Cooper	140	29	J. Tobin	21
2	Newhouser	116	29	Javery	21
3	Lanier	105	31	R. Melton	17
3	Hughson	105	32	O. Grove	16
5	Borowy	98	32	Donald	16
6	Chandler	89	34	Higbe	15
7	Potter	86	34	Gumbert	15
8	Breechen	80	36	Haynes	14
9	Passeau	75	36	J. Kramer	14
10	Bonham	70	38	Haefner	13
11	Niggeling	65	39	Galehouse	12
12	Trout	63	40	C. Davis	11
13	Vander Meer	61	40	R. Christopher	11
14	Gromek	59	40	Voiselle	11
15	Walters	51	40	Bagby	11
16	Wyse	42	44	Judd	9
17	Sewell	41	45	Zuber	7
17	Newsom	41	45	R. Barrett	7
19	Shoun	39	47	Butcher	5
20	Leonard	38	47	Ryba	5
21	Muncrief	37	49	Flores	4
22	Wolff	36	50	Ostermueller	3
23	Reynolds	34	51	Dietrich	2
24	Derringer	31	52	Feldman	1
25	Roe	28	52	A. Adams	1
26	Strincevich	26	52	Bithorn	1
26	Benton	26	52	Lopat	1
28	Wyatt	24			

10

Great Military Teams
of World War II

While the major leagues were losing men at an alarming rate during the Second World War, the military would be the great beneficiary, producing wonderful teams with the big league players they would receive in the draft.

The first such team was put together on July 8th, 1942, to play the American League All-Stars, winners of the 1942 midsummer classic, in a matchup at Cleveland. There were 62,094 fans in Cleveland Stadium that night to witness a service All-Star team made up of Bob Feller, Johnny Rigney, Cecil Travis and Benny McCoy, among others, lose to a junior circuit squad with Joe DiMaggio, Ted Williams, Phil Rizzuto and Tex Hughson 5–0.[1] DiMaggio, Williams, Rizzuto and Hughson, of course, would all soon join the ranks of their baseball military brethren.

With so many players soon to be inducted, military All-Star teams would give way to teams formed in the various armed forces training facilities. Most squads would go on to win the vast majority of their games, some against major league and minor league competition.

There were several solid clubs that played during the war: New Cumberland, Pennsylvania; Waco, Texas; and Curtis Bay, Maryland, to name just a few, but there were six teams that stood out far above the others.

The first one was in Fort Riley, Kansas, and included among its ranks Harry Walker, Joe Garagiola, Murry Dickson, Ken Heintzelman, Rex Barney, Creepi Crespi and Pete Reiser.[2]

There would be some special amenities offered the players of Fort Riley, some advantageous and some not. Dickson would be allowed to play in the 1943 World Series for the Cardinals while on furlough, an opportunity not afforded to other ballplayers, especially Larry French who desperately wanted to win three more games to get to the 200 win plateau. On the other side, Reiser would come down with a severe case of pneumonia, and was close to being discharged when it was decided he would stay on because of his ability playing baseball.[3]

North Carolina produced an outstanding club at the University of North Carolina Pre-flight Naval School. It included such greats as Ted Williams, Harry Craft, Johnny Pesky, Johnny Sain, Buddy Gremp and Buddy Hassett[4] while at the Sampson Naval Station in New York, with Johnny Vander Meer, Hal White and Tom Carey, they would severely beat such major league teams as the Red Sox, 20–7, and the Indians, 15–2, in 1944.[5]

Probably the most exciting win for Samson in '44 came against the Cincinnati Reds in an 8–7 win in front of 10,000 fans. Vander Meer would meet his former and soon to be club, tossing 7 innings before giving up 4 runs in his last frame. White would come in and shut the door the rest of the way, pitching 2 one hit frames.[6]

Bainbridge, Maryland, was the home of a naval squad that would boast itself as one of the best in the country. It was comprised of such major league players as Dick Bartell, Buddy Blattner, Fred Chapman, Ray Hamrick and Elbie Fletcher.[7]

The Commodores went 5–3 against the major leagues in 1944 that included a season-ending 5–0 victory against the Philadelphia A's, in a game where Chapman got a broken nose and two black eyes when a grounder hit him in the face. Bainbridge would also beat the Phillies, Braves, Reds and Red Sox to cap off a 56–15 campaign that included a split in 10 games with the fabled Norfolk Training Station squad.[8]

Fletcher would lead the way for the team, hitting a team high .344 with 15 doubles, 9 triples, 6 homers and 49 RBIs.

Like most armed service squads, the great Bainbridge club of 1944 broke up at the end of the season when their training was over, as Fletcher, Chapman and Blattner were all sent overseas.[9]

They would be replaced in 1945 by a team that went 72–27, including a sparkling 6–2–1 mark against teams from the big leagues. Stan "The Man" Musial, Dick Wakefield, Stan Spence and Ken Raffensberger would make this club a more powerful squad than their 1944 counterparts.[10]

As good as Bainbridge was, the squad at the Norfolk Naval Training Center in Norfolk, Virginia, might have been that much better. They opened up for play in 1942 and were led that first year by Bob Feller, Fred Hutchinson, Pirate Vinnie Smith and Sam Chapman. The team went 92–8 in '42 with Feller winning 19 and Hutchinson coming away with 23 in the victory column.[11]

The Norfolk squad in 1943 would be bolstered with an influx of major league talent that sent them to a 75–25 record, which included a thrilling 4–3 win over the Washington Senators at a soldout Griffith Stadium. The roster included Phil Rizzuto, who led the way with a .347 average, Dom

DiMaggio, Pee Wee Reese, Tom Earley, Charlie Wagner, Don Padgett and Walter Masterson.[12]

An all–Navy World Series was in the works between Norfolk and the powerful Great Lakes club. It would unfortunately never materialize as a matchup with the Norfolk Air Station was set up instead. The Naval Station prevailed in a close seven game series.[13]

After most of the '43 squad left for assignment overseas, a team that included Howie Schenz, who led Norfolk with a .369 average, Red McQuillen, 98 RBIs, and Eddie Robinson, a .282 mark with a club high 99 RBIs, was put together and finished 83–22–2 in 1944 that including 9–4 and 6–3 victories versus the Browns and Senators respectively. The pitching staff was the key to Norfolk's success, as Johnny Rigney, Russ Meers and Tommy Byrne would finish with corresponding 22–4, 17–5 and 16–2 marks.[14]

When it came to military teams during the war years, the one squad that rose above all the others came from the Great Lakes Naval Station in Illinois. A mighty athletic program, set up by Captain Robert Emmet, not only boasted one of the great baseball programs, but also had a football team that was ranked 7th in 1943 and 17th in 1944 (military teams were included in the NCAA football polls during 1943 through 1945).[15]

Hall of Fame catcher Mickey Cochrane, who managed the team to a 166–26 record between 1942 and 1944, and Gene Tunney, the former Heavyweight Champion, who was the physical training advisor and recruiter, led the Bluejackets.[16]

During Cochrane's tenure, he always had a full stable of major league stars. The following is a list from *The Sporting News* on August 13th, 1944, that showed what players performed for Great Lakes between 1942 and 1944:

1942	*1943*	*1944*
1B-Chester Hajduk	Johnny Mize	Johnny McCarthy
2B-Benny McCoy	Chester Hajduk	Billy Herman
SS-Ernie Andres	Carl Fiore	Merrill "Pinky" May
3B-John Lucadello	Eddie Pellagrini	Al Glossop
LF-Don Padgett	Glenn McQuillen	Mizell Platt
RF-Joe Grace	Joe Grace	Dick West
CF-Earl Bolyard	Barney McCosky	Gene Woodling
CA-Frank Pytlak	George Dickey	Walt Millies
CA-Sam Harshany	Warren Robinson	Bill Baker
CA-_____	Marv Felderman	Clyde McCullough
PI-Russ Meers	Vern Olson	Virgil Trucks
PI-Johnny Rigney	Bob Harris	Jim Trexler
PI-Jim Reninger	Johnny Schmitz	Bob Klinger
PI-Frank Marino	Tom Ferrick	Schoolboy Rowe
PI-Cliff Clay	Jack Hallett	Si Johnson
PI-Don Dunker	_____	Ed Weiland
PI-_____	_____	Bill Brandt

The club started out in 1942 with a 63–14 mark before going 58–10–1 in '43. It would be 1944 that would separate Great Lakes from the rest of the pack, going 48–2, defeating 11 out of 12 major league teams, losing only to the Dodgers. The other Bluejacket loss would be one of the great upsets of the war years, as they were downed 2–1 by a group of players from the Ford Motor Company. With the score tied at 1–1 in the 9th inning, Rowe decided to toss a pitch that Pirate hurler Rip Sewell made famous, the eephus pitch. A Ford Motor player smacked the ball over 400 feet, scoring on an inside the park homer and the victory. Rowe would spend time in Cochrane's doghouse after the ill-fated toss.[17]

Other than that very low point, it was a season of nothing but successes. Against major league competition there would be several great and exciting moments, most headed up by the phenomenal pitching of Trucks.

In a much brighter moment for Rowe, he got a chance to play in right field and responded with a 2 run shot on the way to a 3–1 victory versus the Phillies in May.[18] Great Lakes would follow that up with a Trucks 2 hit, 12 strikeout performance in a 3–1 win over the Red Sox.[19]

Virgil also got the chance to dominate lesser competition as he showed when he struck out 19 in a 14–1 win over the MUNY All-Stars and mowed down 11 in an 8–2 victory against Notre Dame.

As good as he was in those games, it was against major league competition that brought the best out of Trucks, as evidenced by his 9 strikeouts in a 3 hit 5–1 win against the Giants before his 1–0, 2 hit performance against the White Sox.

The day after the White Sox win would bring with it the infamous loss to the Dodgers as Brooklyn came back down 3–2 in the 6th inning to win 7–4. It would be the last loss of 1944 for Great Lakes as they would close out the season with majestic 17–4 crunching of the Cleveland Indians. Trucks finished off the last piece of his 10–0 season by striking out 13, giving him 161 in only 113 innings. Rowe would shine as he once again was in right; hitting 2 homers to lead a 21 hit attack.[20]

Indians hurler Bob Feller took over the reins of the Bluejackets in 1945 as Cochrane was transferred to the Pacific. He was 13–2, striking out 130 in 95 innings before giving way to Pinky Higgins when Feller was discharged in August and went back to Cleveland.[21] The club would include such major leaguers as Ken Keltner, Dick Wakefield, Clyde Shoun, Max Marshall and Walker Cooper.[22]

The war years provided us with a time period where the best baseball

Hall of Famer Bob Feller is seen here cheering on his team at the Great Lakes Naval Center in Illinois. Feller took over the reins of the club in 1945 as manager when Mickey Cochrane was reassigned to the Pacific. Feller would leave Great Lakes midway during the season and return to the Indians. Courtesy of Transcendental Graphics.

in the world may not have been played in the major leagues. Each military team deserves to be honored as they provided the country with every bit as much of a morale lift as their counterparts in the big leagues did. It also gave us a team in the 1944 Great Lakes squad that certainly goes down as a club that not only many felt would easily win the pennant if they played in the National or American Leagues, but one that could be considered as one of the best ever to play, regardless of league, during the war years.

Appendix

This section encompasses a look at who were the best and worst during the war years. The lists are the following:

- The All-Star teams between 1942 and 1945, both based on the war years saber-metric report on what players were most influenced in their careers by the war years and the MVP report on which were the best players during the time period.
- The top 10 players whose careers were improved by the war years and the top 10 players whose careers were hurt by the war years (included in this list is the 1944 Boston Red Sox team).
- The top 10 greatest names during the time period.
- The top 10 best war teams from all leagues in baseball and the worst 10 teams.

All-Star Teams of the War Years

A List of the Players Who Were the Best by Position During 1942–45 According to the Sabermetric MVP Report

FIRST TEAM		SECOND TEAM	
Position	*Player*	*Position*	*Name*
1B	Phil Cavarretta	1B	Rudy York
2B	Bobby Doerr	2B	Don Gutteridge
SS	Vern Stephens	SS	Lou Boudreau
3B	Bob Elliott	3B	Whitey Kurowski
OF	Tommy Holmes	OF	Bob Johnson
OF	Bill Nicholson	OF	Stan Musial
OF	Dixie Walker	OF	Ray Cullenbine
CA	Ernie Lombardi	CA	Al Lopez*
RHP	Mort Cooper	RHP	Tex Hughson
LHP	Hal Newhouser	LHP	Max Lanier

Lopez scored no MVP points, but since Lombardi was the only catcher to amass MVP points, it was judged that since Lopez was a decent hitter and arguably the best defensive catcher during the war years, as he led the league in fielding 3 times during that span, he got the nod as the number 2 man.

The War Points All-Star Team: A List of the Players Who Most Benefited from Playing During 1942–45 or the George Bailey All American Team According to the Sabermetric War Points Report

FIRST TEAM		SECOND TEAM	
Position	*Player*	*Position*	*Name*
1B	Ray Sanders	1B	Nick Etten
2B	Don Gutteridge	2B	Bobby Doerr
SS	Vern Stephens	SS	Lou Boudreau
3B	Whitey Kurowski	3B	Bob Elliott
OF	Tommy Holmes	OF	Dixie Walker
OF	Bill Nicholson	OF	Stan Spence
OF	Ray Cullenbine	OF	Augie Galan
CA	Ernie Lombardi	CA	Al Lopez*
RHP	Nels Potter	RHP	Mort Cooper
LHP	Hal Newhouser	LHP	Max Lanier

Lopez scored no war points, but since Lombardi was the only catcher to amass war points, it was judged that since Lopez was a decent hitter and arguably the best defensive catcher during the war years, as he led the league in fielding 3 times during that span, he got the nod as the number 2 man.

Top 10 Players Whose Careers Were Helped by the War

1. *Bob Lemon*—Was a little used third baseman when he went into the service. He learned to pitch while in the Armed Forces and became a Hall of Fame pitcher.
2. *Hal Newhouser*—Went 54–18 in 1944 and 1945, twice winning the AL MVP.
3. *Mort Cooper*—Won 20 games 3 times in the war years. Was the 1942 MVP.
4. *Bill Nicholson*—According to the report, the MVP of the war years. 3rd and 2nd in the MVP race in 1943 and 1944.
5. *Nels Potter*—Although he was the first man thrown out of a game for tossing a spitball, he was the pitcher whose career was most improved by the war according to the report.
6. *Nick Etten*—Went from obscurity in Philadelphia to one of the best first basemen in the American League with the Yankees.
7. *Ray Sanders*—Was the everyday player most affected by the war years according to the report. Was done after 1946.
8. *Lou Boudreau*—His Hall of Fame career was enhanced by having his prime during the war years.
9. *Ray Mueller*—Had been a reserve catcher who had not played in the majors since 1940 when the Reds came calling. Set the record for most games caught in 1944 and ended up playing until 1951 after his second chance.
10. *Joe McCarthy*—The great manager of the Yankees who proved just how good he was, winning an AL title and world championship despite the fact he probably had the worst losses due to the draft in the war years. Never finished below .500 during the time period.

Top 10 Players Whose Careers Were Hurt by the War

1. *Cecil Travis*—Hit over .300 eight times before the war. Suffered frostbite in the Battle of the Bulge, which some say limited his mobility and ended his career after three sub par post war seasons where he didn't break .252 (although Travis denies the frostbite was the reason for his decline). Might have cost him a trip to Cooperstown.

2. *Johnny Beazley*—Went 21–6 his rookie year in 1942 before going into the service. Hurt his arm pitching in the armed service and was only 9–6 in four post war seasons.

3. *Hugh Mulcahy*—Was the ace of the Phils before becoming the first player drafted. A case of dysentery hurt his strength and his fastball. He went only 3–7 after the war.

4. *Taffy Wright*—Wright hit .324 in his first five major league seasons between 1938 and 1942, with consecutive .300 campaigns of .350, .309, .337, .322 and .333. When he came back, he was not the same player, as he hit only .292, a mark that was bolstered by a .324 1947 season, in his last four years which ended in 1949. Had there been no war, the .311 hitter might have just continued on the pace he was on and ended up in Cooperstown.

5. *Bruce Campbell*—A .290 hitter before the war who did not play in the majors afterwards. Bruce took baseball to court to try a regain his major league salary.

6. *Creepy Crespi*—The starting second baseman for St. Louis in 1941 before heading to war. After breaking his leg playing in the service, got involved in a wheelchair race while recuperating and crashed, breaking his leg in a different place, ending his baseball career.

7. *Benny McCoy*—Was the starting second baseman for the A's in 1940 and 1941. Did not get a shot to return to the majors after the war.

8. *Hank Greenberg and the Detroit Tigers*—Led the Tigers to the AL championship in 1940, before leaving for the service in 1941. His time out cost Greenberg the 500 HR plateau and sent the Tigers to the second division from 1941 to 1943. When Greenberg returned, he led the Tigers to the world championship in 1945.

9. *Ted Williams and Bob Feller*—Two Hall of Famers who probably lost the most statistically out of every player who went into the service. As great as they were, had they not lost time in the service their career numbers would have gone down as some of the greatest the game has ever seen.

10. *The 1944 Boston Red Sox*—Were 3½ games out of first place in September when Uncle Sam took Hal Wagner, Bobby Doerr, Jim Tabor and Tex Hughson, their four best players. The team fell to 77–77 before tumbling all the way down to 7th place the following season.

Top 10 Greatest Names in the War Years

1. *Leonard "Fatty" Pigg*—Catcher with the Indianapolis Clowns during the 40s and 50s.

2. *Creepy Crespi*—Shortstop for the Cardinals in the early 40s who ended his career by breaking his leg in a wheelchair race while in the hospital during his time in the service.

3. *Snuffy Stirnweiss*—Infielder with the Yankees who saved his best for the war years, winning the batting title in 1945 while finishing 4th and 3rd in the MVP vote in 1944 and 1945.

4. *Sig Jakucki*—A hard drinking ex-marine who won 25 games with the Browns in 1944 and 1945.

5. *Spoony Palm*—A catcher with the Philadelphia Stars.

6. *Catfish Metkovich*—Best years were during the war with the Red Sox.

7. *Buster Brown*—Good hitting catcher with the Cleveland Buckeyes, not as famous as his shoe namesake.

8. *Henry "Prince" Oana*—Hawaiian born pitcher who had a brief stay with the Tigers during the war.

9. *Bitsy Mott*—Elisha "Bitsy" Mott started for the Phillies in 1945 at short, his only major league season.

10. *Crash Davis*—Spent a little longer in the majors than the character by the same name in the classic film *Bull Durham*. Was the inspiration for the name of the lead character.

Top 10 War Years Teams

1. *1942 St. Louis Cardinals*—106–48, won the world championship. The beginning of one of the great dynasties.

2. *1942 New York Yankees*—103–61, won the American League championship.

3. *1944 St. Louis Cardinals*—105–49, won the world championship.

4. *1944 Great Lakes Naval Base Team*—Went 48–2 with a collection of some fine major league players. Defeated 11 out of 12 big league teams, losing only to the Dodgers. Some believed would have easily won the pennant in either league.

5. *1943 St. Louis Cardinals*—105–49, won the pennant by 18 games. Lost in the World Series.

6. *1943 Homestead Grays*— 44–15, won the Negro League world championship.

7. *1942 Brooklyn Dodgers*—104–50, finished second to the Cardinals after blowing a big August lead.

8. *1943 New York Yankees*— 98–56, won the world championship despite losing most of their stars to the service.

9. *1942 Kansas City Monarchs*— 28–10, won the Negro League world championship in the classic Satchel Paige–Josh Gibson World Series.

10. *1945 Chicago Cubs*— 98–56, National League champions. Led the league in both hitting with a .277 average and ERA at 2.98. Was the last Cub team to play in the Fall Classic.

Bottom 10 Worst Teams in the War Years

1. *1942 Philadelphia Phillies*— 42–109, in the NL cellar 62.5 games behind.

2. *1945 Memphis Red Sox*—17–61, in the cellar of the Negro American League.

3. *1943 Philadelphia A's*— 49–105, last place in the AL.

4. *1945 Philadelphia Phillies*— 46–108, last place in the NL, 52 games behind.

5. *1943 New York Giants*— 55–98, last in the NL, 49.5 games behind.

6. *1944 New York Black Yankees*— 4–24, last in the Negro National League.

7. *1942 Boston Braves*— 59–89, in 7th place in the NL, saved only by the worst team from the war years.

8. *1942 Philadelphia A's*— 55–99, at the bottom of the AL, 48 games behind.

9. *1944 Brooklyn Dodgers*— 63–91, in 7th place in the National League with the circuit's worst pitching staff. Only the lack of wanting to add another Philadelphia team to this list got the Dodgers here, who finished 1.5 ahead of the Phillies.

10. *1942 Hickory Rebels*—18–80, last in the class D North Carolina State League. At a .184 winning percentage (which was the worst winning percentage between 1942–45, except for the Wichita Fall/Big Spring club in the short season class D West Texas–New Mexico League that was 8–47 for a .145 percentage), was the worst team in the minors during the war years, which possibly might make them the worst minor league team of all time.

Notes

Introduction

    1. Pg. 2501 *Total Baseball* edited by John Thorn, Pete Palmer and Michael Gershman, 7th edition.
    2. Pg. 2501 *Total Baseball* edited by John Thorn, Pete Palmer and Michael Gershman, 7th edition.
    3. Pg. 2494 *Total Baseball* edited by John Thorn, Pete Palmer and Michael Gershman, 7th edition.

Chapter 1

    1. Pg. 19 *Spartan Seasons* by Richard Goldstein.
    2. Pg. 8 *Spartan Seasons* by Richard Goldstein.
    3. Pg. 397 *Baseball Timeline* by Burt Solomon.
    4. 1/24/42 *Pittsburgh Press*, UP story.
    5. 2/27/42 *Pittsburgh Press*, UP story.
    6. 3/3/42 *Pittsburgh Press*, UP story.
    7. 3/6/42 *Pittsburgh Press*, UP story.
    8. 3/6/42 *Pittsburgh Press*, UP story.
    9. 3/24/42 *Pittsburgh Press*, UP story.
10. 1/24/42 *Pittsburgh Press*, UP story.
11. 1/25/42 *Pittsburgh Press*, UP story.
12. 1/25/42 *Pittsburgh Press*, UP story.
13. 2/1/42 *Pittsburgh Press*, UP story.
14. 2/1/42 *Pittsburgh Press*, UP story.
15. 2/2/42 *Pittsburgh Press*, UP story.
16. 1/25/42 *Pittsburgh Press*, UP story.
17. 2/2/42 *Pittsburgh Press*, UP story.
18. 2/3/42 *Pittsburgh Press*, UP story.
19. 2/3/42 *Pittsburgh Press*, UP story.
20. 1/30/42 *Pittsburgh Press*, UP story.
21. 2/3/42 *Pittsburgh Press*, UP story.
22. 2/8/42 *Pittsburgh Press*, UP story.

23. 1/25/42 *Pittsburgh Press*, UP story.
24. 2/25/42 *Pittsburgh Press*, UP story.
25. 3/12/42 *Pittsburgh Press*, UP story.
26. 3/19/42 *Pittsburgh Press*, UP story.
27. 4/10/42 *Pittsburgh Press*, UP story.
28. 4/4/42 *Pittsburgh Press*, UP story.
29. 4/15/42 *Pittsburgh Press*, UP story.
30. 5/9/42 *Pittsburgh Press*, UP story.
31. 7/9/42 *Pittsburgh Press*, UP story.
32. 4/1/42 *Pittsburgh Press*, UP story.
33. 4/10/42 *Pittsburgh Press*, UP story.
34. 5/14/42 *Pittsburgh Press*, UP story.
35. 7/8/42 *Pittsburgh Press*, UP story.
36. 7/9/42 *Pittsburgh Press*, Joe Williams column.
37. Pgs. 398–399 *The Complete Book of Baseball's Negro Leagues* by John Holway.
38. Pg. 398 *Baseball Timeline* by Burt Solomon.
39. 12/4/42 *Pittsburgh Press*, UP story.
40. 12/3/42 *Pittsburgh Press*, UP story.
41. 10/29/42 *Pittsburgh Press*, UP story.
42. Pg. 397 *Baseball Timeline* by Burt Solomon.
43. Pg. 347 *The Biographical Encyclopedia of Baseball* by the editors of *Total Baseball*.
44. 3/17/42 *Pittsburgh Press*, UP story.
45. 3/17/42 *Pittsburgh Press*, UP story.
46. Pg. 541 *The Biographical Encyclopedia of Baseball* by the editors of *Total Baseball*.
47. *Baseball and the Armed Services* by Harrington E. Crissey: http://enelpunto.net/beisbol/history/leagues/military/armedintro.html.
48. Pg. 250 *Spartan Seasons* by Richard Goldstein.
49. Pg. 1030 *The Biographical Encyclopedia of Baseball* by the editors of *Total Baseball*.
50. Pg. 233 *Spartan Seasons* by Richard Goldstein.
51. A letter from Benny McCoy.
52. Pgs. 225–226 *Spartan Seasons* by Richard Goldstein.
53. Pg. 229 *Spartan Seasons* by Richard Goldstein.
54. Pg. 233 *Spartan Seasons* by Richard Goldstein.
55. 4/1/42 *Pittsburgh Press*, UP story.
56. Pg. 1221 *The Biographical Encyclopedia of Baseball* by the editors of *Total Baseball*.
57. 2/7/42 *Pittsburgh Press* a story by Jack Guenther UPI.
58. 2/18/42 *Pittsburgh Press* a story by Chester Smith.
59. Pg. 1162 *The Biographical Encyclopedia of Baseball* by the editors of *Total Baseball*.
60. 2/2/42 *Pittsburgh Press*.
61. *Baseball and the Armed Services* by Harrington E. Crissey found on http://enelpunto.net/beisbol/history/leagues/military/armedintro.html.

62. 4/6/42 *Pittsburgh Press.*
63. Pg. 1182 *The Biographical Encyclopedia of Baseball* by the editors of *Total Baseball.*
64. *The Biographical History of Baseball* by Donald Dewey and Nicholas Acocella.
65. The quote is from a letter sent by Hugh Mulcahy.
66. Pg. 326 of *The Biographical History of Baseball* by Donald Dewey and Nicholas Acocella.
67. The quote is from a letter sent by Hugh Mulcahy.
68. The quote is from a letter sent by Hugh Mulcahy.

Chapter 2

1. 2/8/43 *Pittsburgh Press*, United Press (UP) story.
2. 2/8/43 *Pittsburgh Press*, UP story.
3. 2/4/43 *Pittsburgh Press*, story by Oscar Fraley, UPI.
4. 1/15/43 *Pittsburgh Press*, UP story.
5. 1/6/43 *Pittsburgh Press*, story by Tommy Devine UPI.
6. 3/13/43 *Pittsburgh Press*, UP story.
7. 2/11/43 *Pittsburgh Press*, a column by Chester Smith.
8. 2/16/43 *Pittsburgh Press*, UP story.
9. Pg. 404 *Baseball Timeline* by Burt Soloman.
10. 2/19/43 *Pittsburgh Press*, UP story.
11. 7/15/43 *Pittsburgh Press*, UP story.
12. 7/28/43 *Pittsburgh Press*, a story by Chester Smith.
13. 7/29/43 *Pittsburgh Press*, UP story.
14. 8/2/43 *Pittsburgh Press*, UP story.
15. 7/30/43 *Pittsburgh Press*, UP story.
16. 11/23/43 *Pittsburgh Press*, a story by Robert Meyer.
17. 2/4/43 *Pittsburgh Press*, UP story.
18. 2/25/43 *Pittsburgh Press*, UP story.
19. Pg. 331 *The Encyclopedia of Minor League Baseball* edited by Lloyd Johnson and Mike Wolff.
20. 3/15/43 *Pittsburgh Press*, UP story.
21. 4/10/43 *Pittsburgh Press*, UP story.
22. 3/17/43 *Pittsburgh Press*, a story by Chester Smith.
23. *CBS Sportsline Baseball Online Library* http://cbs.sportsline.com/u/baseball/bol/chronology/1943MAY.html.
24. *CBS Sportsline Baseball Online Library* http://cbs.sportsline.com/u/baseball/bol/chronology/1943APRIL.html.
25. 4/23/43 *Pittsburgh Press*, UP story.
26. 4/24/43 *Pittsburgh Press*, UP story.
27. 5/10/43 *Pittsburgh Press*, UP story.
28. 8/6/43 *Pittsburgh Press*, a story by Paul Scheffels, UPI.
29. 7/24/43 *Pittsburgh Press.*

30. 10/19/43 *Pittsburgh Press*, UP story.

31. 10/29/43 *Pittsburgh Press*, UP story.

32. The events of the season were researched through the *Baseball Timeline* by Burt Soloman and the *CBS Sportsline Baseball Online Library* http://cbs.sportsline.com/u/baseball/bol/.

33. 11/15/43 *Pittsburgh Press*, UP story.

34. 12/3/43 *Pittsburgh Press*, UP story.

35. Pg. 404 *The Complete Book of Baseball's Negro Leagues* by Jon Holway.

36. *CBS Sportsline Baseball Online Library* http://cbs.sportsline.com/u/baseball/bol/chronology/1943JANUARY.html.

37. Pg. 411 *The Complete Book of Baseball's Negro Leagues* by Jon Holway.

38. Pgs. 129–144 *The 1945 Major League Baseball Guide* published by Whitman Publishing.

39. Pg. 235 *Spartan Seasons* by Richard Goldstein.

40. 3/7/42 *Pittsburgh Press*, UP story.

41. Pg. 291 *The Biographical Encyclopedia of Baseball* by the editors of *Total Baseball*.

42. Pg. 980 *The Biographical Encyclopedia of Baseball* by the editors of *Total Baseball*.

43. Pg. 236–237 *Spartan Seasons* by Richard Goldstein.

44. Pg. 272 *Spartan Seasons* by Richard Goldstein.

45. Pg. 658 *The Biographical Encyclopedia of Baseball* by the editors of *Total Baseball*.

46. Pg. 658 *The Biographical Encyclopedia of Baseball* by the editors of *Total Baseball*.

47. Pg. 688 *The Biographical Encyclopedia of Baseball* by the editors of *Total Baseball*.

48. Pg. 689 *The Biographical Encyclopedia of Baseball* by the editors of *Total Baseball*.

49. Pg. 235 *Spartan Seasons* by Richard Goldstein.

50. Pg. 405 *The Biographical Encyclopedia of Baseball* by the editors of *Total Baseball*.

51. Pg. 338 *The Biographical Encyclopedia of Baseball* by the editors of *Total Baseball*.

52. Pg. 742 *The Biographical Encyclopedia of Baseball* by the editors of *Total Baseball*.

53. Pg. 2522 *The Baseball Encyclopedia*, 10th Edition, published by Macmillan.

54. Pg. 235 *Spartan Seasons* by Richard Goldstein.

55. Pg. 883 *The Biographical Encyclopedia of Baseball* by the editors of *Total Baseball*.

56. Pg. 233 *Spartan Seasons* by Richard Goldstein.

57. Pg. 289 *The Biographical Encyclopedia of Baseball* by the editors of *Total Baseball*.

58. Pg. 1237 *The Biographical Encyclopedia of Baseball* by the editors of *Total Baseball*.

59. Pg. 233 *Spartan Seasons* by Richard Goldstein.

60. Pg. 371 *The Encyclopedia of Minor League Baseball* edited by Lloyd Johnson and Mike Wolff.

61. Pg. 165 *Total Baseball*, 7th edition, published by Total Sports.

62. Pg. 232 *Spartan Seasons* by Richard Goldstein.

63. Pg. 273 *Spartan Seasons* by Richard Goldstein.

64. Pg. 253 *Spartan Seasons* by Richard Goldstein.

65. Pg. 709 *The Biographical Encyclopedia of Baseball* by the editors of *Total Baseball*.

66. Pg. 709 *The Biographical Encyclopedia of Baseball* by the editors of *Total Baseball*.

67. Pg. 709 *The Biographical Encyclopedia of Baseball* by the editors of *Total Baseball*.

68. Pg. 405 *Baseball Timeline* by Burt Soloman.

69. Pg. 255 *Spartan Seasons* by Richard Goldstein.

70. Pg. 797 *The Biographical Encyclopedia of Baseball* by the editors of *Total Baseball*.

71. Pg. 173 *Baseball Dynasties* by Rob Neyer and Eddie Epstein.

72. Pg. 799 *The Biographical Encyclopedia of Baseball* by the editors of *Total Baseball*.

73. Pg. 236 *Spartan Seasons* by Richard Goldstein.

74. Pg. 405 *Baseball Timeline* by Burt Soloman.

75. Pg. 5 *1944 Major League Baseball Guide* published by Whitman Publishing.

76. Pg. 92 *The Biographical Encyclopedia of Baseball* by the editors of *Total Baseball*.

77. Pg. 91 *The Biographical Encyclopedia of Baseball* by the editors of *Total Baseball*.

78. Pg. 2658 *The Baseball Encyclopedia*, 10th edition Macmillan Publishers.

79. Pg. 406 *Baseball Timeline* by Burt Soloman.

80. Pg. 924–925 *The Biographical Encyclopedia of Baseball* by the editors of *Total Baseball*.

81. Pg. 183 *The Biographical Encyclopedia of Baseball* by the editors of *Total Baseball*.

82. Pg. 231 *Spartan Seasons* by Richard Goldstein.

83. Pg. 255 *Spartan Seasons* by Richard Goldstein.

84. Pg. 383 *The Biographical Encyclopedia of Baseball* by the editors of *Total Baseball*.

85. Pg. 291 *The Encyclopedia of Minor League Baseball* edited by Lloyd Johnson and Mike Wolff.

86. Pg. 283 *The Biographical Encyclopedia of Baseball* by the editors of *Total Baseball*.

87. Pg. 275 *Spartan Seasons* by Richard Goldstein.

88. Pg. 994 *The Biographical Encyclopedia of Baseball* by the editors of *Total Baseball*.

89. Pg. 1062 *The Biographical Encyclopedia of Baseball* by the editors of *Total Baseball*.

90. Pg. 1063 *The Biographical Encyclopedia of Baseball* by the editors of *Total Baseball*.

91. http://cbs.sportsline.com/u/baseball/bol/ballplayers/V/Veeck_Bill.html.

92. Pg. 790 *The Biographical Encyclopedia of Baseball* by the editors of *Total Baseball*.

93. 4/1/42 *Pittsburgh Press* a UP story.

94. Pg. 239 *Spartan Seasons* by Richard Goldstein.

95. Pg. 240 *Spartan Seasons* by Richard Goldstein.

96. Pg. 1011 *The Biographical Encyclopedia of Baseball* by the editors of *Total Baseball*.

Chapter 3

1. Pg. 15 *The Sporting News* 1/13/1944.

2. Pg. 5 *The Sporting News* 1/20/1944.

3. Pg. 2 *The Sporting News* 1/27/1944.

4. Pg. 1 *The Sporting News* 2/17/1944.

5. Pg. 2 *The Sporting News* 3/24/1944.

6. Pg. 1 *The Sporting News* 2/17/1944.

7. Pg. 3 *The Sporting News* 2/10/1944.

8. Pg. 1 *The Sporting News* 3/16/1944.

9. Pg. 7 *The Sporting News* 4/6/1944.

10. Pg. 7 *The Sporting News* 4/6/1944.

11. Pg. 8 *The Sporting News* 2/17/1944.

12. Pg. 8 *The Sporting News* 2/17/1944.

13. Pg. 837 *The Biographical Encyclopedia of Baseball* by the editors of *Total Baseball*.

14. Pg. 415 *Baseball Timeline* by Burt Solomon.

15. Pg. 342 *The Encyclopedia of Minor League Baseball* edited by Lloyd Johnson and Miles Wolff.

16. Pg. 10 *The Sporting News* 5/4/1944.

17. Pg. 413 *Baseball Timeline* by Burt Solomon.

18. Pg. 4 *The Sporting News* 9/14/1944.

19. Pg. 12 *The Sporting News* 7/20/1944.

20. Pg. 12 *The Sporting News* 7/20/1944.

21. Pg. 3 *The Sporting News* 11/2/1944.

22. Pg. 16 *The Sporting News* 1/6/1944.

23. Pg. 9–10 *The Sporting News* 3/19/1944.

24. Pg. 415 *Baseball Timeline* by Burt Solomon.

25. Pg. 3 *The Sporting News* 6/22/1944.

26. Pg. 10 *The Sporting News* 9/14/1944.

27. Pg. 20 *1945 Major League Baseball Guide* by Whitman Publishing.

28. Pg. 20 *1945 Major League Baseball Guide* by Whitman Publishing.

29. Pg. 151 *Pennant Races* by Dave Anderson.

30. Pg. 413 *The Complete Book of Baseball's Negro Leagues* by John Holway.

31. Pg. 416 *The Complete Book of Baseball's Negro Leagues* by John Holway.

32. Pg. 412 *Baseball Timeline* by Burt Solomon.

33. Pg. 131 *1945 Major League Baseball Guide* by Whitman Publishing.

34. All statistical information on the AAGPBL was derived from the *1945 Major League Baseball Guide* by Whitman Publishing Pgs. 129–144.

35. Pg. 415 *Baseball Timeline* by Burt Solomon.

36. Pg. 4 *The Sporting News* 11/30/1944.

37. Pg. 6 *The Sporting News* 11/30/1944.

38. Pg. 1 *The Sporting News* 11/30/1944.

39. Pg. 14 *The Sporting News* 7/6/1944.

40. Pg. 14 *The Sporting News* 1/11/1945.

41. Pg. 137 *Ace* by Phil Marchildon.

42. Pg. 152 *Ace* by Phil Marchildon.

43. Information for Phil Marchildon was taken from the book *Ace* by Phil Marchildon, pgs. 125–163.

44. Gary Bedingfield's web site http://baseballinwartime.freeservers.com/bibliography.htm.

45. Pg. 11 *The Sporting News* 3/2/1944.

46. http://cbs.sportsline.com/u/baseball/bol/chronology/1944JULY.html#day13.

47. Pg. 20 *1945 Major League Baseball Guide* published by Whitman.

48. http://cbs.sportsline.com/u/baseball/bol/ballplayers/W/Wakefield_Dick.html.

49. Pg. 38 *Spartan Seasons* by Richard Goldstein.

50. http://cbs.sportsline.com/u/baseball/bol/ballplayers/B/Bloodworth_Jimmy.html.

51. An interview with Virgil Trucks.

52. An interview with Virgil Trucks.

53. Pg. 1146 *The Biographical Encyclopedia of Baseball* by the editors of *Total Baseball*.

54. An interview with Virgil Trucks.

55. An interview with Virgil Trucks.

56. Pg. 286 *The Biographical Encyclopedia of Baseball* by the editors of *Total Baseball*.

57. Pg. 737 *The Biographical Encyclopedia of Baseball* by the editors of *Total Baseball*.

58. http://cbs.sportsline.com/u/baseball/bol/ballplayers/R/Robinson_Aaron.html.

59. Pg. 422 *The Biographical Encyclopedia of Baseball* by the editors of *Total Baseball*.

60. Pg. 237 *Spartan Seasons* by Richard Goldstein.

61. Pg. 234 *Spartan Seasons* by Richard Goldstein.

62. http://cbs.sportsline.com/u/baseball/bol/ballplayers/B/Byrne_Tommy.html.

63. Pg. 194 *The World Series* by David Neft and Richard Cohen.

64. Pg. 134 *The Biographical Encyclopedia of Baseball* by the editors of *Total Baseball*.

65. Pg. 134 *The Biographical Encyclopedia of Baseball* by the editors of *Total Baseball*.

66. Pg. 240 *Spartan Seasons* by Richard Goldstein.

67. Pg. 210 and 212 *The World Series* by David Neft and Richard Cohen.

68. Pg. 1252 *The Biographical Encyclopedia of Baseball* by the editors of *Total Baseball.*

69. Pg. 232 *Spartan Seasons* by Richard Goldstein.

70. http://cbs.sportsline.com/u/baseball/bol/ballplayers/S/Suder_Pete.html.

71. 6/18/1943 *Pittsburgh Press*, UP story.

72. 6/18/1943 *Pittsburgh Press*, UP story.

73. http://cbs.sportsline.com/u/baseball/bol/ballplayers/K/Kolloway_ Don.html.

74. http://cbs.sportsline.com/u/baseball/bol/ballplayers/A/Appling_Luke. html.

75. http://cbs.sportsline.com/u/baseball/bol/ballplayers/A/Appling_Luke. html.

76. Pg. 236 *Spartan Seasons* by Richard Goldstein.

77. http://cbs.sportsline.com/u/baseball/bol/ballplayers/E/Early_Jake.html.

78. http://cbs.sportsline.com/u/baseball/bol/ballplayers/E/Early_Jake.html.

79. http://cbs.sportsline.com/u/baseball/bol/ballplayers/V/Vernon_Mickey. html.

80. Pg. 1168 *The Biographical Encyclopedia of Baseball* by the editors of *Total Baseball.*

81. http://cbs.sportsline.com/u/baseball/bol/ballplayers/V/Vernon_Mickey. html.

82. Pg. 1168 *The Biographical Encyclopedia of Baseball* by the editors of *Total Baseball.*

83. Pg. 1168 *The Biographical Encyclopedia of Baseball* by the editors of *Total Baseball.*

84. Pg. 904 *The Biographical Encyclopedia of Baseball* by the editors of *Total Baseball.*

85. Pg. 903 *The Biographical Encyclopedia of Baseball* by the editors of *Total Baseball.*

86. Pg. 904 *The Biographical Encyclopedia of Baseball* by the editors of *Total Baseball.*

87. http://cbs.sportsline.com/u/baseball/bol/ballplayers/R/Robertson_Sherry. html.

88. Pg. 236 *Spartan Seasons* by Richard Goldstein.

89. http://cbs.sportsline.com/u/baseball/bol/ballplayers/K/Klein_Lou.html.

90. http://cbs.sportsline.com/u/baseball/bol/ballplayers/K/Klein_Lou.html.

91. http://cbs.sportsline.com/u/baseball/bol/ballplayers/W/Walker_Harry.html.

92. Pg. 228 & 244 *Spartan Seasons* by Richard Goldstein.

93. Pg. 252 *Spartan Seasons* by Richard Goldstein.

94. http://cbs.sportsline.com/u/baseball/bol/ballplayers/W/Walker_Harry. html.

95. http://cbs.sportsline.com/u/baseball/bol/ballplayers/B/Brazle_Al.html.

96. Pg. 244 *Spartan Seasons* by Richard Goldstein.

97. Pg. 287 *The Biographical Encyclopedia of Baseball* by the editors of *Total Baseball.*

98. Pg. 231 *Spartan Seasons* by Richard Goldstein.

99. Pg. 896 *The Biographical Encyclopedia of Baseball* by the editors of *Total Baseball.*

100. http://cbs.sportsline.com/u/baseball/bol/ballplayers/S/Sullivan_Billy. html.

101. Pg. 146 *The Biographical History of Baseball* by Donald Dewey and Nicholas Acocella.

102. Pg. 235 *Spartan Seasons* by Richard Goldstein.

103. http://cbs.sportsline.com/u/baseball/bol/index.html, Baseball Online Library's ask the experts 5/2/2001.

104. http://cbs.sportsline.com/u/baseball/bol/ballplayers/G/Gornicki_Hank. html.

105. http://cbs.sportsline.com/u/baseball/bol/ballplayers/K/Klinger_Bob. html.

106. http://cbs.sportsline.com/u/baseball/bol/ballplayers/H/Haas_Bert.html.

107. Pg. 1001 *The Biographical Encyclopedia of Baseball* by the editors of *Total Baseball.*

108. Pg. 1001 *The Biographical Encyclopedia of Baseball* by the editors of *Total Baseball.*

109. Pg. 1001 *The Biographical Encyclopedia of Baseball* by the editors of *Total Baseball.*

110. Pg. 1001 *The Biographical Encyclopedia of Baseball* by the editors of *Total Baseball.*

111. http://cbs.sportsline.com/u/baseball/bol/ballplayers/M/McCormick_ Mike207.html.

112. http://cbs.sportsline.com/u/baseball/bol/ballplayers/T/Thompson_ Junior.html.

113. Pg. 1159 *The Biographical Encyclopedia of Baseball* by the editors of *Total Baseball.*

114. Pg. 238 *Spartan Seasons* by Richard Goldstein.

115. Pg. 215 *Spartan Seasons* by Richard Goldstein.

116. http://cbs.sportsline.com/u/baseball/bol/ballplayers/M/McCul-lough_Clyde.html.

117. http://cbs.sportsline.com/u/baseball/bol/ballplayers/M/ McCullough_Clyde.html.

118. http://cbs.sportsline.com/u/baseball/bol/ballplayers/B/Bithorn_Hi.html.

119. Pg. 78 *What Happened to the Hall of Fame* by Bill James.

120. Pg. 236 *Spartan Seasons* by Richard Goldstein.

121. Pg. 63 *The Biographical Encyclopedia of Baseball* by the editors of *Total Baseball.*

122. http://cbs.sportsline.com/u/baseball/bol/ballplayers/B/Bartell_ Dick.html.

123. Pg. 235 *Spartan Seasons* by Richard Goldstein.

124. Pg. 174–175 *Whatever Happened to the Hall of Fame* by Bill James.

125. Pg. 174–181 *Whatever Happened to the Hall of Fame* by Bill James.

126. Pg. 423 *The Biographical Encyclopedia of Baseball* by the editors of *Total Baseball.*

127. Pg. 217 *Spartan Seasons* by Richard Goldstein.

128. Pg. 503 *The Biographical Encyclopedia of Baseball* by the editors of *Total Baseball*.

129. Pg. 504 *The Biographical Encyclopedia of Baseball* by the editors of *Total Baseball*.

130. Pg. 491 *The Biographical Encyclopedia of Baseball* by the editors of *Total Baseball*.

131. Pg. 232 *Spartan Seasons* by Richard Goldstein.

132. http://cbs.sportsline.com/u/baseball/bol/ballplayers/H/Hermanski_Gene.html.

133. Pg. 244 *Spartan Seasons* by Richard Goldstein.

134. http://cbs.sportsline.com/u/baseball/bol/ballplayers/B/Barney_Rex.html.

135. Pg. 243 *Spartan Seasons* by Richard Goldstein.

136. Pg. 254 *Spartan Seasons* by Richard Goldstein.

137. http://cbs.sportsline.com/u/baseball/bol/ballplayers/H/Higbe_Kirby.html.

138. Pg. 170 *Spartan Seasons* by Richard Goldstein.

139. Pg. 170 *Spartan Seasons* by Richard Goldstein.

140. http://cbs.sportsline.com/u/baseball/bol/ballplayers/M/May_Pinky.html.

141. Pg. 232 *Spartan Seasons* by Richard Goldstein.

142. http://cbs.sportsline.com/u/baseball/bol/ballplayers/R/Rowe_Schoolboy.html.

143. http://cbs.sportsline.com/u/baseball/bol/ballplayers/R/Rowe_Schoolboy.html.

Chapter 4

1. Pg. 10 *The Sporting News* 2/8/1945.
2. Pg. 1 *The Sporting News* 3/1/1945.
3. Pg. 1 *The Sporting News* 2/15/1945.
4. Pg. 6 *The Sporting News* 4/5/1945.
5. Pg. 6 *The Sporting News* 4/5/1945.
6. Pg. 3 *The Sporting News* 5/3/1945.
7. Pg. 1 *The Sporting News* 2/1/1945.
8. Pg. 203 *Spartan Seasons* by Richard Goldstein.
9. Pg. 204 *Spartan Seasons* by Richard Goldstein.
10. Pg. 1 *The Sporting News* 1/25/1945.
11. Pg. 9 *The Sporting News* 5/17/1945.
12. Pg. 2 *The Sporting News* 5/24/1945.
13. 2/13/1946 "Sports Parade" in the *Post Home News* by Leonard Coleman.
14. An interview with Daniel Price, the son of Fred Price.
15. An interview with Daniel Price, the son of Fred Price.
16. Pg. 8 *The Sporting News* 2/22/1945.

17. Gary Bedingfield's Baseball in Wartime Bibliography web site: http://baseballinwartime.freeservers.com/bibliography.htm.

18. Pg. 420 *Baseball Timeline* by Burt Solomon.

19. Pg. 25 *The Sporting News* 10/4/1945.

20. Pg. 25 *The Sporting News* 10/4/1945.

21. Pg. 420 *Baseball Timeline* by Burt Solomon.

22. Pg. 159 *Ace* by Phil Marchildon.

23. Pg. 422 *Baseball Timeline* by Burt Solomon.

24. Pg. 3 *The Sporting News* 3/22/1945.

25. Pg. 11 *The Sporting News* 4/19/1945.

26. Pg. 11 *The Sporting News* 4/19/1945.

27. Pg. 430 *The Biographical Encyclopedia of Baseball* by the editors of *Total Baseball*.

28. Pg. 430 *The Biographical Encyclopedia of Baseball* by the editors of *Total Baseball*.

29. Pg. 430 *The Biographical Encyclopedia of Baseball* by the editors of *Total Baseball*.

30. Pg. 419 *Baseball Timeline* by Burt Solomon.

31. Pg. 419 *Baseball Timeline* by Burt Solomon.

32. Pg. 8 *The Sporting News* 5/17/1945.

33. Pg. 8 *The Sporting News* 5/17/1945.

34. Pg. 11 *The Sporting News* 6/21/1945.

35. Pg. 11 *The Sporting News* 7/19/1945.

36. Pg. 419–423 *Baseball Timeline* by Burt Solomon for all the above events in the paragraph from 1945.

37. Pg. 11 *The Sporting News* 9/20/1945.

38. Pg. 1 *The Sporting News* 8/23/1945.

39. Pg. 347 *The Encyclopedia of Minor League Baseball* edited by Lloyd Johnson and Miles Wolff. 2nd edition.

40. Pg. 138–157 1946 Major League Baseball Guide published by Whitman Publishing, the resource for all AAGBL info.

41. Pg. 421 *The Complete Book of Baseball's Negro Leagues* by John Holway.

42. Pg. 421 *The Complete Book of Baseball's Negro Leagues* by John Holway.

43. The entire MacPhail text was found on pg. 14, *The Sporting News* 10/4/1945.

44. Pg. 4 *The Sporting News* 11/1/1945.

45. Pg. 4 *The Sporting News* 11/1/1945.

46. Pg. 12 *The Sporting News* 11/1/1945.

47. All the above opinions were found on pages 5–6, *The Sporting News* 11/4/1945.

48. Pg. 434 *The Biographical Encyclopedia of Baseball* by the editors of *Total Baseball*.

49. Pg. 500 *The Biographical Encyclopedia of Baseball* by the editors of *Total Baseball*.

50. Pg. 232 *Spartan Seasons* by Richard Goldstein.

51. Pg. 500 *The Biographical Encyclopedia of Baseball* by the editors of *Total Baseball*.

52. 9/29/1943 *Pittsburgh Press* a UP article.

53. Pg. 20 1945 Major League Baseball Guide by Whitman Publishing.

54. Pg. 232 *Spartan Seasons* by Richard Goldstein.

55. Pg. 1182 *The Biographical Encyclopedia of Baseball* by the editors of *Total Baseball*.

56. http://cbs.sportsline.com/u/baseball/bol/ballplayers/G/Gorsica_Johnny.html.

57. Pg. 422 *Baseball Timeline* by Burt Solomon.

58. Pg. 232 *Spartan Seasons* by Richard Goldstein.

59. Pg. 1260 *The Biographical Encyclopedia of Baseball* by the editors of *Total Baseball*.

60. Pg. 1260 *The Biographical Encyclopedia of Baseball* by the editors of *Total Baseball*.

61. Pg. 5 *The Sporting News* 9/6/1945.

62. Pg. 186 *Spartan Seasons* by Richard Goldstein.

63. Pg. 186 *Spartan Seasons* by Richard Goldstein.

64. http://cbs.sportsline.com/u/baseball/bol/ballplayers/S/Sundra_Steve.html.

65. Pg. 421 *Baseball Timeline* by Burt Solomon.

66. http://cbs.sportsline.com/u/baseball/bol/ballplayers/M/Mack_Ray.html.

67. http://cbs.sportsline.com/u/baseball/bol/ballplayers/K/Keltner_Ken.html.

68. Pg. 232 *Spartan Seasons* by Richard Goldstein.

69. Pg. 1145 *The Biographical Encyclopedia of Baseball* by the editors of *Total Baseball*.

70. http://cbs.sportsline.com/u/baseball/bol/ballplayers/H/Hodgin_Ralph.html.

71. Pg. 353 *The Biographical Encyclopedia of Baseball* by the editors of *Total Baseball*.

72. Pg. 353 *The Biographical Encyclopedia of Baseball* by the editors of *Total Baseball*.

73. http://cbs.sportsline.com/u/baseball/bol/ballplayers/W/Wagner_Hal.html.

74. Pg. 294 *The Biographical Encyclopedia of Baseball* by the editors of *Total Baseball*.

75. Pg. 1109 *The Biographical Encyclopedia of Baseball* by the editors of *Total Baseball*.

76. Pg. 1109 *The Biographical Encyclopedia of Baseball* by the editors of *Total Baseball*.

77. Pg. 228 *Spartan Seasons* by Richard Goldstein.

78. http://cbs.sportsline.com/u/baseball/bol/ballplayers/D/Dallessandro_Dom.html.

79. http://cbs.sportsline.com/u/baseball/bol/ballplayers/N/Noviko›_Lou.html.

80. Pg. 207 *Spartan Seasons* by Richard Goldstein.

81. http://cbs.sportsline.com/u/baseball/bol/ballplayers/L/Litwhiler_Danny.html.

82. Pg. 819 *The Biographical Encyclopedia of Baseball* by the editors of *Total Baseball*.

83. Pg. 811 *The Biographical Encyclopedia of Baseball* by the editors of *Total Baseball.*

84. Pg. 118 *The Biographical Encyclopedia of Baseball* by the editors of *Total Baseball.*

85. Pg. 118 *The Biographical Encyclopedia of Baseball* by the editors of *Total Baseball.*

86. http://cbs.sportsline.com/u/baseball/bol/ballplayers/H/Head_Ed.html.

87. http://cbs.sportsline.com/u/baseball/bol/ballplayers/M/McLish_Cal.html.

88. Pg. 761 *The Biographical Encyclopedia of Baseball,* by the editors of *Total Baseball.*

89. Pg. 761 *The Biographical Encyclopedia of Baseball* by the editors of *Total Baseball.*

90. Pg. 241 *Spartan Seasons* by Richard Goldstein.

91. http://cbs.sportsline.com/u/baseball/bol/ballplayers/M/Mueller_Ray.html.

92. Pg. 204 *Spartan Seasons* by Richard Goldstein.

93. Pg. 451 *The Biographical Encyclopedia of Baseball* by the editors of *Total Baseball.*

94. Pg. 619 *The Biographical Encyclopedia of Baseball* by the editors of *Total Baseball.*

95. Pg. 204 *Spartan Seasons* by Richard Goldstein.

Chapter 5

1. Pg. 185 *The Bill James Historical Baseball Abstract* by Bill James.

2. Pg. 172 *The Biographical History of Baseball* by Donald Dewey and Nicholas Acocella.

Chapter 7

1. Pg. 56 *Whatever Happened to the Hall of Fame* by Bill James.

Chapter 10

1. 7/8/1942 *Pittsburgh Press.*

2. Pg. 229 *Spartan Seasons* by Richard Goldstein.

3. Pgs. 230–231 *Spartan Seasons* by Richard Goldstein.

4. *Baseball and the Armed Services* by Harrington E. Crissey: http://enelpunto.net/beisbol/history/leagues/military/armedintro.html.

5. Pg. 235 *Spartan Seasons* by Richard Goldstein.

6. Pg. 13 *The Sporting News* 8/10/1944.

7. Pg. 8 *The Sporting News* 11/6/1944.
8. Pg. 11 *The Sporting News* 9/7/1944.
9. Pg. 9 *The Sporting News* 10/15/1944.
10. Pg. 3 *The Sporting News* 7/19/1944.
11. Pg. 233 *Spartan Seasons* by Richard Goldstein.
12. The Norfolk Baseball website at http://www.hrnm.navy.mil/baseball.htm.
13. The Norfolk Baseball website at http://www.hrnm.navy.mil/baseball.htm.
14. Pg. 12 *The Sporting News* 9/28/1944.
15. Pg. 65 *The 1994 NCAA Football Records Book* published by Triumph Publishers.
16. Pg. 227 *Spartan Seasons* by Richard Goldstein.
17. Pg. 232 *Spartan Seasons* by Richard Goldstein.
18. Pg. 12 *The Sporting News* 5/18/1944.
19. Pg. 13 *The Sporting News* 6/1/1944.
20. Pg. 13 *The Sporting News* 9/7/1944.
21. Pg. 231 *Spartan Seasons* by Richard Goldstein.
22. Pg. 13 *The Sporting News* 3/29/1944.

Index